# The *Ultimate*
# COFFEE
## RECIPE BOOK

Unlock 180 Creative Coffee Delights for Enthusiasts

# Table of Contents

## Espreso-Based Drinks

# Unique Lattes and Specialties:

# Iced Coffee Creations:

# Hot Chocolate and Hot Beverages:

# Non-Coffee Hot Drinks:

| | | | |
|---|---|---|---|
| Masala Chai | 134 | Almond Vanilla Rooibos Latte | 149 |
| Earl Grey Tea Latte | 135 | Caramel Apple Chai Latte | 150 |
| London Fog Tea Latte | 136 | Rosewater White Hot Chocolate | 151 |
| Matcha Green Tea Latte | 137 | Honey Lavender Chamomile Tea | 152 |
| Spiced Apple Cider | 138 | Cinnamon Almond Milk Steamer | 153 |
| Mulled Wine | 139 | Orange Blossom Herbal Tea Latte | 154 |
| Golden Turmeric Tea | 140 | Toasted Coconut Chai | 155 |
| Minty Hot Cocoa | 141 | Chocolate Mint Rooibos Latte | 156 |
| Spiced Cranberry Cider | 142 | Apricot Vanilla Oolong Latte | 157 |
| Vanilla Rooibos Latte | 143 | Peppermint Stick Tea Latte | 158 |
| Honey Chamomile Tea Latte | 144 | Maple Cinnamon Spice Tea | 159 |
| Coconut Ginger Chai | 145 | Lavender Mint White Hot Cocoa | 160 |
| Cardamom Rose Tea | 146 | Pineapple Ginger Green Tea Latte | 161 |
| Raspberry Hibiscus Tea Latte | 147 | Blueberry Basil White Tea | 162 |
| Ginger Lemongrass Tea | 148 | Cranberry Orange Rooibos Latte | 163 |

# MOCKTAILS AND CREATIVE CONCOCTIONS:

# Espreso-Based Drinks

# Espresso

*Indulge in the bold, robust flavors of a classic Espresso, a simple yet powerful coffee drink cherished by coffee lovers worldwide. With its intense, concentrated taste, espresso forms the foundation of many beloved coffee beverages. Whether enjoyed alone as a quick pick-me-up or used as the base for lattes, cappuccinos, or macchiatos, espresso delivers a punch of flavor that's unmatched in the coffee world.*

## Ingredients:

- 1 shot (1 ounce) of espresso
- [Optional] 1-2 tsp of sugar or sweetener of your choice
- [Optional] A splash of milk or plant-based milk (e.g., oat milk, almond milk) for a softer flavor

## Instructions:

1. Brew a shot of espresso using your preferred espresso machine or stovetop espresso maker.
2. If you like your espresso sweetened, add sugar or sweetener to the cup while the espresso is still hot. Stir until dissolved.
3. [Optional] If you prefer a creamier texture, add a splash of milk or plant-based milk. You can steam the milk for a frothy texture, or simply add it cold for a smoother finish.
4. Enjoy immediately, savoring the full-bodied richness of the espresso.

## Tips and Recommendations:

- For an even more intense espresso flavor, use freshly ground coffee beans and ensure your espresso machine is well-calibrated.
- If you prefer your espresso with a bit of sweetness, try adding a flavored syrup, such as vanilla or caramel.
- For a smoother, creamier taste, consider steaming your milk before adding it to the espresso.

## Variations:

- **Americano:** Add hot water to your espresso to create a milder, more drinkable coffee that retains the rich flavor of espresso but with a less concentrated strength.
- **Espresso Macchiato:** Top your espresso with a dollop of steamed milk for a creamy twist.
- **Iced Espresso:** Pour your freshly brewed espresso over ice and add a splash of milk or a flavored syrup for a refreshing, chilled version.

## Pairing Suggestions:

- Pair with a buttery croissant or biscotti for a perfect breakfast treat.
- Enjoy alongside dark chocolate or a slice of rich cake to balance the coffee's boldness.

## Interesting Fact:

Did you know that espresso is the foundation for many popular coffee drinks? Whether it's the base for a Latte, Macchiato, or Mocha, the rich espresso shot is key to their flavor profile.

## Cultural Connection:

Espresso originated in Italy, where it became a symbol of Italian culture and a daily ritual for many coffee enthusiasts. The name "espresso" itself means "pressed out" in Italian, referring to the method of brewing that forces water through the coffee grounds at high pressure.

# Americano

*The Americano is a simple yet satisfying coffee that delivers all the boldness of espresso, diluted with hot water to create a smoother, milder flavor. It's the perfect choice for those who enjoy the strength of espresso but prefer a more drinkable brew. Legend has it that the Americano was born during World War II when American soldiers in Italy would dilute their espresso with hot water to mimic the coffee they were used to back home. Whether you enjoy it black or with a splash of milk, the Americano is a timeless classic that's easy to prepare and always satisfying.*

## Ingredients:

- 1 shot (1 ounce) of espresso
- 6 ounces of hot water
- [Optional] 1-2 tsp of sugar or sweetener of your choice
- [Optional] A splash of milk or plant-based milk (e.g., oat milk, almond milk) for added creaminess

## Instructions:

1. Brew a shot of espresso using your preferred method (espresso machine, stovetop espresso maker, or manual brewing method).
2. Boil water and pour 6 ounces into a separate cup or directly into your serving cup.
3. Add the brewed espresso shot into the hot water and stir gently to combine.
4. [Optional] If you like your Americano sweetened, stir in sugar or sweetener while the coffee is still hot.
5. [Optional] For a creamier texture, add a splash of milk or plant-based milk and stir to combine.
6. Enjoy immediately, savoring the smooth, bold flavor.

## Tips and Recommendations:

- For a stronger Americano, simply add less water or brew a double shot of espresso.
- If you prefer your Americano black, no need to add any sweeteners or milk. Let the rich espresso flavor shine through.
- You can experiment with different ratios of water to espresso to find the balance that best suits your taste.

## Variations:

- **Iced Americano:** Brew the espresso shot as usual and pour it over a glass of ice for a cool, refreshing version perfect for warmer weather.
- **Flavored Americano:** Add a shot of vanilla or caramel syrup for a sweet, flavored twist.
- **Americano Misto:** Add steamed milk or frothy milk on top of your Americano for a lighter, creamier take.

## Pairing Suggestions:

- Pair with a fresh, flaky croissant or a hearty breakfast sandwich for a satisfying morning.
- Enjoy with a piece of dark chocolate or a slice of almond cake to balance the coffee's bold flavors.

## Interesting Fact:

Did you know that an Americano is often referred to as a "Caffè Americano" in Italy, but is usually just called "Americano" elsewhere in the world? It's one of the simplest yet most satisfying coffee drinks, with a rich history rooted in wartime ingenuity.

## Cultural Connection:

The Americano is believed to have been invented by American soldiers in Italy during World War II. To make espresso more like the drip coffee they were accustomed to, they would dilute it with hot water, creating the milder coffee we now know as an Americano. It's a drink that represents the merging of cultures and the versatility of espresso.

# Latte

*A Latte is the ultimate comforting coffee drink - a harmonious blend of rich espresso and silky steamed milk, crowned with a gentle layer of foam. Known for its smooth and creamy texture, the Latte has become a global favorite, offering a delightful balance of strong coffee and mellow sweetness. Whether enjoyed as a morning pick-me-up or a cozy afternoon indulgence, the Latte is endlessly customizable, making it a perfect canvas for creative variations, from flavored syrups to seasonal spices. Learn how to craft the perfect Latte right in your own kitchen!*

## Ingredients:

- 1 shot (1 ounce) of espresso
- 1 cup of steamed milk (dairy or plant-based milk like oat, almond, or soy)
- [Optional] 1-2 tsp of sugar or sweetener of your choice
- [Optional] A sprinkle of cinnamon or cocoa powder for garnish

## Instructions:

1. Brew a shot of espresso using your preferred method (espresso machine, stovetop espresso maker, or manual brewing method).
2. Steam the milk using a milk frother or steam wand until it reaches about 150°F (65°C). The milk should be frothy with a velvety texture.
3. Pour the brewed espresso into a large mug or cup.
4. Slowly pour the steamed milk into the cup with the espresso, holding back the foam with a spoon. Once most of the milk is in, gently spoon the remaining foam on top.
5. [Optional] Stir in sugar or sweetener to taste, or leave it unsweetened for a more traditional flavor.
6. [Optional] Garnish with a light dusting of cinnamon or cocoa powder for added elegance and flavor.
7. Enjoy your creamy, smooth Latte!

## Tips and Recommendations:

- For a more intense coffee flavor, add a double shot of espresso (also known as a "Doppio").
- If you don't have a milk frother, you can heat the milk in a small saucepan and whisk it vigorously to create froth, or use a French press to froth the milk.
- Experiment with the milk-to-espresso ratio. If you prefer a stronger coffee flavor, use less milk; for a milder taste, use more milk.

## Variations:

- **Vanilla Latte:** Add 1-2 teaspoons of vanilla syrup to your espresso before adding the steamed milk for a fragrant, sweet twist.
- **Iced Latte:** Brew your espresso and allow it to cool. Pour it over ice, then add cold milk or your favorite plant-based alternative for a refreshing, chilled version.
- **Spiced Latte:** Stir in a pinch of ground cinnamon, nutmeg, or cardamom for a warm, spiced version, perfect for fall or winter.

## Pairing Suggestions:

- Pair with a flaky almond croissant or a slice of banana bread for a delicious breakfast or brunch.
- Enjoy alongside a piece of dark chocolate or a cinnamon roll for a sweet, indulgent treat.

## Interesting Fact:

Did you know that the word "Latte" comes from the Italian term "Caffè latte," meaning "milk coffee"? It's said that Lattes were first enjoyed by Italians as a way to mellow the strong taste of espresso with creamy milk.

## Cultural Connection:

The Latte became popular in the United States in the 1980s, largely due to the coffee culture explosion. While Lattes have their roots in Italy, they became a staple in American coffee shops and have since spread across the globe, often customized with various syrups and flavorings. Today, the Latte remains a beloved coffee drink that's often personalized to suit every taste.

# Cappuccino

*The Cappuccino is the epitome of balance in the world of coffee - bold espresso, velvety steamed milk, and a rich foam topping come together to create a truly luxurious experience. This classic Italian coffee drink has charmed coffee lovers for generations, known for its perfect 1:1:1 ratio of espresso, steamed milk, and foam. Whether sipped in a cozy café or made at home, the Cappuccino offers a comforting combination of creamy texture and strong coffee flavor. Learn how to make this iconic drink and discover why it remains a staple in coffee culture worldwide.*

## Ingredients:

- 1 shot (1 ounce) of espresso
- 1/2 cup of steamed milk (dairy or plant-based milk such as oat, almond, or soy)
- 1/2 cup of milk foam (from the steamed milk)
- [Optional] 1 tsp sugar or sweetener of your choice
- [Optional] A sprinkle of cocoa powder or cinnamon for garnish

## Instructions:

1. Brew a shot of espresso using your preferred method (espresso machine, stovetop espresso maker, or manual brewing method).
2. Steam the milk until it reaches about 150°F (65°C), making sure to create a smooth, velvety texture. The key is to froth the milk well so that you get a thick foam that can sit on top of the espresso.
3. Pour the brewed espresso into a cappuccino cup.
4. Using a spoon to hold back the foam, pour the steamed milk into the cup with the espresso. Then, spoon the foam on top, allowing it to form a thick, frothy layer.
5. [Optional] Stir in sugar or sweetener to taste, or leave the Cappuccino unsweetened for a more authentic flavor.
6. [Optional] Garnish with a light dusting of cocoa powder, cinnamon, or a decorative design in the foam.
7. Enjoy your perfectly balanced Cappuccino!

## Tips and Recommendations:

- For a more intense flavor, use a double shot of espresso (Doppio). This will create a stronger coffee base to balance the creamy foam.
- Make sure to steam the milk to the right temperature (around 150°F). If the milk gets too hot (above 160°F), it can lose its creamy texture and sweetness.
- If you don't have a milk frother, you can heat the milk in a small saucepan and use a whisk or French press to create foam.

## Variations:

- **Flavored Cappuccino:** Add a splash of vanilla, caramel, or hazelnut syrup to your espresso before pouring in the steamed milk for a flavored twist.
- **Iced Cappuccino:** Brew your espresso and allow it to cool. Pour it over ice and top with chilled, frothed milk for a refreshing summer version of this classic.
- **Spiced Cappuccino:** Add a dash of cinnamon or nutmeg to your foam for a warm, spiced version, perfect for cozying up on a cold day.

## Pairing Suggestions:

- Pair with a buttery croissant or a warm, flaky pastry for a delightful breakfast treat.
- Enjoy with a slice of chocolate cake or a biscotti for a sweet afternoon indulgence.

## Interesting Fact:

Did you know that the name "Cappuccino" comes from the Capuchin friars of Italy, whose robes were a similar color to the brown foam and coffee mix? The drink was named after them due to its distinctive color and appearance.

## Cultural Connection:

Originating in Italy, the Cappuccino has become an international favorite, particularly in European coffee culture. In Italy, Cappuccinos are traditionally enjoyed only in the morning, often paired with a pastry. Over time, the Cappuccino has evolved, with coffee shops worldwide offering various creative spins on the classic, from iced versions to flavored syrups.

# Mocha

*Indulge in the ultimate combination of rich espresso and decadent chocolate with this Mocha recipe. A perfect harmony of bold coffee and smooth cocoa, the Mocha is a beloved classic that brings together the best of both worlds. Whether you're warming up on a chilly morning or treating yourself to an afternoon pick-me-up, this drink is an irresistible blend of creamy milk, espresso, and a luscious chocolate base. It's the perfect drink for anyone who loves coffee and chocolate equally!*

## Ingredients:

- 1 shot (1 ounce) of espresso
- 2 tbsps (30 grams) of unsweetened cocoa powder or 1 tbsp chocolate syrup (for a sweeter option)
- 1 cup steamed milk (dairy or plant-based milk like oat, almond, or coconut)
- 1 tbsp sugar (or sweetener of your choice)
- [Optional] Whipped cream or frothed milk for topping
- [Optional] A sprinkle of cocoa powder or chocolate shavings for garnish

## Instructions:

1. Brew a shot of espresso using your preferred method (espresso machine, stovetop espresso maker, or manual brewing method).
2. In a small saucepan, heat the milk over medium heat until it's hot but not boiling.
3. If using cocoa powder: In a separate cup, mix the cocoa powder with the sugar and a small amount of hot water to create a smooth chocolate syrup. Add the mixture to the brewed espresso and stir until well combined.
4. If using chocolate syrup: Simply add the syrup to the brewed espresso and stir until smooth.
5. Pour the hot milk into the espresso and chocolate mixture, stirring gently to combine.
6. [Optional] Top with whipped cream or a layer of frothed milk for a creamy finish.
7. [Optional] Garnish with a sprinkle of cocoa powder, chocolate shavings, or even a drizzle of chocolate syrup for extra indulgence.
8. Enjoy your luxurious Mocha!

## Tips and Recommendations:

- For a richer flavor, use a high-quality dark chocolate instead of cocoa powder.
- Adjust the amount of sugar based on your sweetness preference - some chocolate syrups are already sweetened.
- If you prefer a stronger chocolate taste, increase the amount of cocoa powder or chocolate syrup.
- Use a milk frother or steam wand to create a creamy foam for the perfect texture.

## Variations:

- **Iced Mocha:** Brew your espresso and allow it to cool. Pour it over ice and top with chilled milk and whipped cream for a refreshing, cold version.
- **Vegan Mocha:** Use plant-based milk like oat, almond, or coconut, and replace the whipped cream with a dairy-free alternative. You can also use a dairy-free chocolate syrup.
- **Mint Mocha:** Add a few drops of peppermint extract to the chocolate syrup for a festive minty twist.

## Pairing Suggestions:

- Pair with a rich chocolate croissant or a dark chocolate bar to enhance the chocolatey experience.
- Enjoy with a nutty biscotti or a light pastry for a balanced treat.

## Interesting Fact:

Did you know that the Mocha is named after the Yemeni port city of Mocha, which was historically known for its high-quality coffee beans? While the drink itself is a more modern creation, its roots are tied to the rich coffee culture of the Arabian Peninsula.

## Cultural Connection:

The Mocha has a storied history, dating back to the port city of Mocha in Yemen, a historic center for coffee trade. While the chocolate-coffee combination was popularized in the West, the original Mocha flavor was all about the distinctive coffee beans from Yemen, which had a naturally chocolatey profile. Today, the Mocha remains one of the most popular coffee drinks around the world, particularly in coffeehouses and cafes.

# Macchiato

*The Macchiato, meaning "stained" or "spotted" in Italian, is a simple yet elegant coffee drink that showcases the bold, rich flavor of espresso. This classic Italian coffee is made by adding just a splash of milk to your espresso, creating a beautiful contrast between the deep, dark espresso and the creamy, delicate milk. It's perfect for those who enjoy the intensity of espresso but want a touch of creaminess to soften the edge. The Macchiato is a refined, minimalist coffee experience that packs a punch while maintaining balance.*

## Ingredients:

- 1 shot (1 ounce) of espresso
- 1-2 tbsps steamed milk or frothed milk (depending on your preference)
- [Optional] A small amount of caramel or vanilla syrup for sweetness
- [Optional] A sprinkle of cocoa powder or cinnamon for garnish

## Instructions:

1. Brew a shot of espresso using your preferred method (espresso machine, stovetop espresso maker, or manual brewing method).
2. Steam or froth a small amount of milk (1-2 tablespoons). The milk should be hot but not overly frothy. If using a frother, create a soft, velvety foam.
3. Pour the espresso into a small coffee cup.
4. Gently pour or spoon the steamed milk over the espresso, creating a "stain" or spot of milk on top of the dark espresso.
5. [Optional] Add a drizzle of caramel or vanilla syrup if you prefer a touch of sweetness.
6. [Optional] Garnish with a light dusting of cocoa powder or cinnamon for extra flavor.
7. Sip and enjoy the rich, bold, and creamy Macchiato!

## Tips and Recommendations:

- **Adjust milk texture:** If you prefer a softer texture, use steamed milk with a bit of foam. For a more traditional Macchiato, simply add a small amount of milk with no foam.
- **Play with flavors:** If you like sweeter drinks, experiment with flavored syrups like vanilla or hazelnut.
- **Go for strong espresso:** Since the Macchiato is focused on the flavor of espresso, use a dark, bold roast to really highlight the coffee's natural richness.
- **Be mindful of milk-to-espresso ratio:** The beauty of the Macchiato lies in the contrast between the bold espresso and the milk. Don't overdo the milk – just a small "stain" should suffice.

## Variations:

- **Caramel Macchiato:** Add a swirl of caramel syrup to your espresso before adding the milk. For a frothy version, layer frothed milk on top of the espresso and drizzle with caramel sauce.
- **Iced Macchiato:** For a refreshing twist, brew your espresso and allow it to cool. Pour over ice and add cold milk or cream for a chilled, creamy coffee experience.
- **Vegan Macchiato:** Use plant-based milk like oat milk or almond milk. These options froth beautifully and provide a subtle, creamy texture without the dairy.

## Pairing Suggestions:

- Pair with a delicate biscotti or a crisp almond cookie to complement the richness of the espresso.
- Enjoy with a light fruit salad or citrus scones for a fresh contrast to the bold flavor of the Macchiato.

## Interesting Fact:

Did you know that the Macchiato has been a staple in Italian coffee culture for centuries? It was originally created for those who wanted the strength of espresso but with just a bit of milk to round out the flavor.

## Cultural Connection:

The Macchiato is a quintessential Italian coffee, often enjoyed as an afternoon pick-me-up. Unlike other espresso drinks, which are heavily milk-based, the Macchiato remains true to its roots by allowing the espresso to remain the focus. It's a beloved drink in Italy, frequently consumed in coffee bars as a quick, no-fuss option for coffee lovers.

# Flat White

*Indulge in the silky smooth and perfectly balanced Flat White, a beloved coffee drink that originated in Australia and New Zealand. This espresso-based beverage combines the rich, bold flavor of espresso with velvety steamed milk, creating a creamy texture without the overwhelming frothiness of a cappuccino. The key to a great Flat White is the delicate balance between the strong espresso and the microfoam, which forms a smooth, luscious base that allows the coffee's depth to shine through. If you're looking for a coffee that offers the strength of espresso but with a creamy finish, the Flat White is your perfect match.*

## Ingredients:

- 1 shot (1 ounce) of espresso
- 6 ounces steamed milk
- [Optional] 1/2 tsp vanilla syrup or sweetener of choice for sweetness
- [Optional] A dusting of cocoa powder or cinnamon for garnish

## Instructions:

1. Brew a shot of espresso using your preferred method (espresso machine, stovetop espresso maker, or manual brewing method).
2. Steam 6 ounces of milk until it's hot and silky, creating a velvety microfoam. Aim for a smooth texture without large bubbles.
3. Pour the espresso into a medium-sized cup or mug.
4. Slowly add the steamed milk to the espresso, pouring gently to create a smooth, integrated texture. Aim for a 1:3 espresso-to-milk ratio to achieve the signature Flat White balance.
5. [Optional] Add vanilla syrup or your preferred sweetener for a touch of sweetness.
6. [Optional] Garnish with a light dusting of cocoa powder or cinnamon for extra flavor and visual appeal.
7. Sip and enjoy the perfect combination of strong espresso and creamy milk!

## Tips and Recommendations:

- **Steam your milk correctly:** To achieve the perfect Flat White, you need microfoam – smooth and silky with a soft, velvety texture. If you don't have a steam wand, you can use a milk frother or even a French press to create this effect.
- **Adjust milk amount:** While the standard Flat White has 6 ounces of steamed milk, you can adjust this amount based on your personal preference. More milk will make your drink creamier, while less will keep the coffee stronger.
- **Sweeten it lightly:** If you enjoy a sweeter coffee, add just a touch of sweetener. Since the Flat White has less milk foam than a cappuccino, it's a good option if you prefer a less sweet drink.

## Variations:

- **Iced Flat White:** Brew your espresso and let it cool. Serve over ice and add cold, frothed milk for a refreshing twist on the classic.
- **Vegan Flat White:** Use any plant-based milk like oat milk, almond milk, or soy milk. These options froth beautifully and provide a creamy base without dairy.
- **Flavored Flat White:** Add a dash of cinnamon, nutmeg, or vanilla syrup to the milk before steaming to give your Flat White a unique flavor twist.

## Pairing Suggestions:

- Pair with a freshly baked croissant or almond biscotti for a delightful breakfast or mid-afternoon treat.
- A slice of banana bread or a light fruit tart complements the smoothness of the Flat White without overpowering the flavors.

## Interesting Fact:

Did you know that the Flat White has sparked a bit of a debate between Australia and New Zealand over its true origin? Both countries claim to have created the drink, but no matter where it was born, it has become a coffeehouse staple worldwide.

## Cultural Connection:

The Flat White has become a global favorite, originally emerging from the café culture of Australia and New Zealand. It's prized for its smooth texture and balanced flavor, offering coffee lovers a more subtle and less frothy alternative to drinks like lattes and cappuccinos. This beloved coffee has made its mark in coffee shops all over the world, from the streets of Melbourne to the cafes of London and New York.

# Cortado

*For those who enjoy the perfect balance of bold espresso and creamy milk, the Cortado is your ideal coffee companion. A popular choice in Spain and throughout Latin America, this drink is defined by its simple yet refined proportions - a shot of espresso "cut" with an equal amount of steamed milk. The result is a smooth, mellow coffee that retains the strong flavor of espresso while softening its intensity with a velvety texture. The Cortado offers a satisfying, no-fuss coffee experience that's perfect for coffee lovers who appreciate a harmonious balance between milk and espresso.*

## Ingredients:

- 1 shot (1 ounce) of espresso
- 1 ounce steamed milk
- [Optional] Sweetener of choice (sugar, agave, maple syrup)
- [Optional] A pinch of ground cinnamon or cocoa powder for garnish

## Instructions:

1. Brew a shot of espresso using your preferred method (espresso machine, stovetop espresso maker, or manual brewing method).
2. Steam 1 ounce of milk until it's smooth and creamy, but not too frothy. The milk should blend seamlessly with the espresso, creating a rich and balanced texture.
3. Pour the espresso into a small cup (typically 4 ounces).
4. Gently pour the steamed milk into the espresso, using a ratio of 1:1. This creates the signature Cortado balance between the boldness of espresso and the creaminess of milk.
5. [Optional] Add sweetener to taste, if desired.
6. [Optional] Garnish with a light dusting of cinnamon or cocoa powder for an extra layer of flavor.
7. Sip and enjoy the perfect union of strong espresso and smooth milk.

## Tips and Recommendations:

- **Steam your milk carefully:** The milk should be steamed to a silky, creamy consistency, not frothy. The key to a great Cortado is the smooth blend of milk and espresso, which enhances the coffee's depth without overpowering it.
- **Serve in a small cup:** The Cortado is traditionally served in a small glass or a small cup to highlight its balanced proportions. It's designed as a short, satisfying drink, perfect for a quick pick-me-up.
- **Adjust the milk-to-espresso ratio:** If you prefer a slightly stronger coffee flavor, you can reduce the milk amount. Conversely, adding a bit more milk will create a creamier texture while still keeping the boldness of the espresso.

## Variations:

- **Iced Cortado:** Brew a shot of espresso and let it cool. Serve over ice and top with cold steamed milk for a refreshing twist.
- **Vegan Cortado:** Use your favorite plant-based milk such as oat milk, almond milk, or soy milk for a dairy-free version. These milks froth nicely and provide a creamy texture.
- **Flavored Cortado:** Add a touch of flavored syrup (e.g., vanilla, caramel, or hazelnut) for a sweet and aromatic variation of the classic drink.

## Pairing Suggestions:

- Pair with a piece of rich chocolate cake or a buttery almond croissant for a delightful, indulgent treat.
- Enjoy with a light sandwich or a slice of banana bread to complement the drink's bold and smooth flavor.

## Interesting Fact:

Did you know that "Cortado" comes from the Spanish verb "cortar," meaning "to cut"? The name refers to the way the milk cuts through the strong flavor of the espresso, creating a balanced drink.

## Cultural Connection:

The Cortado is a classic drink in Spain and Latin America, where it's enjoyed throughout the day. It's typically served in smaller portions compared to a latte or cappuccino, making it a great option for those who want a strong coffee without too much milk. In Spain, it's often paired with a sweet pastry for a traditional café experience. Over the years, the Cortado has gained popularity worldwide and is now a staple in coffeehouses everywhere.

# Affogato

*Indulge in the decadent simplicity of an Affogato, a dessert-style coffee that combines two beloved pleasures - rich espresso and creamy ice cream. This Italian classic is the ultimate fusion of hot and cold, where a shot of bold espresso is poured over a scoop of ice cream, creating a melting, flavorful blend that's both luxurious and satisfying. The perfect balance of bitter and sweet, the Affogato is ideal for a special treat or after-dinner indulgence. Whether you're a coffee connoisseur or a dessert lover, this drink delivers the best of both worlds in one perfect cup.*

## Ingredients:

- 1 shot (1 ounce) of espresso
- 1 scoop of vanilla ice cream (or a vegan alternative such as coconut or almond milk-based ice cream)
- [Optional] Shaved chocolate or cocoa powder for garnish
- [Optional] A splash of liqueur (e.g., amaretto or Kahlua) for an adult twist

## Instructions:

1. Brew a shot of espresso using your preferred method (espresso machine, stovetop espresso maker, or manual brewing method).
2. While the espresso is brewing, place one scoop of your favorite ice cream into a small glass or cup.
3. Once the espresso is ready, pour it directly over the ice cream. The hot espresso will melt the ice cream, creating a rich, creamy mixture.
4. [Optional] Sprinkle with shaved chocolate or a dusting of cocoa powder for a touch of extra indulgence.
5. [Optional] Add a splash of amaretto or Kahlua for a delightful alcoholic twist.
6. Enjoy immediately as the hot espresso mingles with the cold ice cream, creating a deliciously creamy, bittersweet treat.

## Tips and Recommendations:

- **Ice cream choice:** While vanilla is the classic flavor for Affogato, you can experiment with other flavors such as hazelnut, chocolate, or even coffee ice cream for an extra punch of flavor.
- **Vegan alternatives:** For a dairy-free version, opt for a rich coconut milk-based ice cream or almond milk-based ice cream. These alternatives still provide the creamy texture you want for a satisfying Affogato.
- **Serve immediately:** The beauty of an Affogato lies in the contrast between the hot espresso and the melting ice cream, so be sure to enjoy it right after making it to preserve the texture and flavor balance.

## Variations:

- **Affogato al Caffè:** A traditional variation where the espresso is served over a scoop of vanilla ice cream. To add more depth, consider using a double shot of espresso.
- **Chocolate Affogato:** Add a scoop of chocolate ice cream and top with a drizzle of hot fudge or chocolate syrup. The rich chocolate and espresso create a harmonious pairing.
- **Alcoholic Affogato:** Add a splash of your favorite liqueur, such as Baileys, Kahlua, or Amaretto, for a more adult version of this classic treat.
- **Fruit Infused Affogato:** For a fruity twist, use a scoop of sorbet instead of ice cream and pour over a shot of espresso for a unique, refreshing treat.

## Pairing Suggestions:

- Pair with a buttery biscotti or shortbread cookies for a perfect balance of textures.
- A light fruit salad with berries or citrus can complement the richness of the Affogato, offering a fresh contrast to the dessert-like coffee.

## Interesting Fact:

Did you know that "Affogato" means "drowned" in Italian? It refers to the way the hot espresso is poured over the cold ice cream, "drowning" it in a rich, coffee-infused bath. It's a delightful and decadent experience!

## Cultural Connection:

Affogato is a beloved Italian dessert traditionally served as an after-dinner treat. While it's become a popular coffeehouse offering worldwide, it still retains its Italian roots, where coffee culture and dessert are inseparable. In Italy, it's often enjoyed as a quick indulgence during the afternoon, a perfect pick-me-up on a warm day. The simplicity of the ingredients makes it an elegant yet easy-to-make treat that has stood the test of time.

# Irish Coffee

*Warm up with the iconic Irish Coffee, a delicious fusion of bold espresso, smooth whiskey, and lightly whipped cream. This timeless drink combines the rich depth of coffee with the warmth of Irish whiskey, making it the perfect choice for cozy evenings or a spirited after-dinner treat. Whether you're celebrating St. Patrick's Day or simply enjoying a comforting cup, Irish Coffee brings together both the warmth of alcohol and the invigorating kick of coffee in one satisfying drink. With a dash of sweetness and a creamy finish, it's the ultimate indulgence for coffee lovers and whiskey aficionados alike.*

## Ingredients:

- 1 shot (1 ounce) of espresso
- 1 tbsp brown sugar (or to taste)
- 1 1/2 ounces Irish whiskey (e.g., Jameson or any preferred Irish brand)
- 1/4 cup heavy cream, lightly whipped
- [Optional] A few coffee beans for garnish

## Instructions:

1. Brew a shot of espresso using your preferred method (espresso machine, stovetop, or manual brew method).
2. In a heat-resistant glass or mug, stir the brown sugar into the hot espresso until fully dissolved.
3. Pour in the Irish whiskey and stir gently to combine with the sweetened espresso.
4. Lightly whip the cream until it reaches soft peaks (it should still be pourable but thick enough to float).
5. Carefully pour the whipped cream over the back of a spoon so that it floats on top of the coffee mixture, creating a creamy layer.
6. [Optional] Garnish with a few coffee beans for a decorative touch.
7. Enjoy your rich, creamy Irish Coffee, sipping through the smooth layer of cream to reveal the bold espresso and warming whiskey beneath.

## Tips and Recommendations:

- **Whipping the cream:** For best results, use cold heavy cream and whip just before serving. This ensures a soft, velvety texture that floats nicely on top of the coffee.
- **Whiskey choice:** While Irish whiskey is traditional, feel free to experiment with other whiskies, such as bourbon or Scotch, for different flavor profiles.
- **Adjust sweetness:** Irish Coffee can be made sweeter or less sweet depending on your taste. Add more or less brown sugar to suit your preference.
- **Serving tip:** Use a glass mug to showcase the beautiful layers of the coffee, whiskey, and cream.

## Variations:

- **Vegan Irish Coffee:** For a dairy-free version, use coconut cream or a vegan whipped topping as a substitute for the heavy cream. You can also opt for a plant-based whiskey to make the drink fully vegan.
- **Spiced Irish Coffee:** Add a pinch of cinnamon or nutmeg to the coffee mixture for an extra layer of flavor. This is especially great during the colder months.
- **Bailey's Irish Coffee:** For an indulgent twist, add a splash of Baileys Irish Cream to the coffee along with the whiskey for a creamier, sweeter flavor.

## Pairing Suggestions:

- Pair with a rich slice of chocolate cake or Irish soda bread to complement the smoothness of the whiskey and cream.
- Enjoy with savory appetizers like warm, spiced nuts or a cheese platter to balance the richness of the drink.

## Interesting Fact:

Did you know that Irish Coffee was invented in the 1940s by Joe Sheridan, a chef at a small airport in Ireland? He created the drink to warm up passengers arriving in from a chilly transatlantic flight. The drink became an instant hit and has since become a beloved classic worldwide.

## Cultural Connection:

Irish Coffee is a staple of Irish culture, often served in pubs and cafes as both a pick-me-up and a cozy treat. It has become synonymous with Irish hospitality, offering a delightful mix of coffee and whiskey that has been enjoyed for decades. While its origins are debated, it has become an iconic part of Irish cuisine, especially popular around holidays like St. Patrick's Day and festive gatherings.

# Turkish Coffee

*Step into the world of bold flavors and rich traditions with a cup of Turkish Coffee. This ancient brewing method, beloved across the Middle East and the Balkans, offers a unique coffee experience that's both intense and smooth. Turkish coffee is not just a drink; it's a ritual that brings together finely ground coffee beans, water, and sugar (optional), gently brewed in a special pot called a cezve. With its silky texture and deep, aromatic flavor, this coffee is often enjoyed slowly, shared with friends, or served as part of a meaningful conversation. Whether you're new to this tradition or a seasoned coffee enthusiast, Turkish Coffee promises an unforgettable, sensory experience.*

## Ingredients:

- 1 tbsp finely ground Turkish coffee (or any very finely ground coffee)
- 1/2 cup cold water
- 1-2 tsps sugar (optional, depending on your sweetness preference)
- [Optional] 1/4 tsp ground cardamom or cinnamon for added spice
- [Optional] A small piece of Turkish delight for serving

## Instructions:

1. **Measure the water**: Pour 1/2 cup of cold water into a cezve (or small coffee pot).
2. **Add the coffee**: Stir in 1 tablespoon of finely ground coffee (don't stir yet), ensuring it's evenly distributed in the water. If you like your coffee sweeter, add 1-2 teaspoons of sugar at this point.
3. **Spice it up (optional)**: If desired, add a pinch of ground cardamom or cinnamon to the coffee mixture for an extra aromatic flavor.
4. **Stir gently**: Stir the mixture gently to ensure the coffee grounds and sugar (if using) are well combined with the water.
5. **Heat the coffee**: Place the cezve over low to medium heat. Allow the coffee to warm slowly without stirring. As the coffee heats, a foam will begin to form on top.
6. **Watch the foam rise**: As the foam rises, carefully remove the cezve from the heat just before it overflows. Wait for the foam to settle, then return it to the heat. Repeat this process 2-3 times to create a thick, rich foam on top.
7. **Serve**: Once the foam has formed, pour the coffee into small cups, ensuring each cup gets an even amount of foam. Allow the grounds to settle before drinking.
8. **Enjoy**: Turkish coffee is traditionally served with a glass of water to cleanse the palate, and sometimes with a small piece of Turkish delight on the side.

## Tips and Recommendations:

- **Coffee grind:** The coffee should be ground as finely as possible, almost powdery, to create the thick texture characteristic of Turkish coffee. If using pre-ground coffee, look for "Turkish coffee" grind at specialty stores.
- **Slow brewing:** The key to making perfect Turkish coffee is to heat it slowly and carefully. Do not rush this step, as a steady brew brings out the full depth of flavor.
- **Sugar levels:** The sugar level is up to you. For a traditional Turkish experience, start with 1-2 teaspoons, but feel free to adjust according to your taste preferences.
- **Serving size:** Turkish coffee is served in small cups (about 3 oz), but feel free to adjust the amount based on your preferences.

## Variations:

- **Spiced Turkish Coffee:** Add a pinch of ground cinnamon, cardamom, or cloves for a spiced version of Turkish Coffee.
- **Iced Turkish Coffee:** For a refreshing twist, allow the coffee to cool, then serve over ice with a splash of almond milk or coconut milk.
- **Sweetened Turkish Coffee:** If you prefer a sweeter drink, add more sugar (or even sweeteners like agave or maple syrup) and serve it as a dessert-style coffee.

## Pairing Suggestions:

- **Turkish delight:** Pair your coffee with a piece of Turkish delight, a traditional sweet treat that complements the strong, rich flavors of the coffee.
- **Baklava:** The flaky, honey-soaked layers of baklava make an excellent pairing with the boldness of Turkish coffee.
- **Nuts:** Roasted almonds or pistachios work wonderfully with Turkish coffee, balancing its intense flavors with a bit of crunch.

# Greek Frappé

*Get ready to enjoy the perfect summer coffee with a glass of Greek Frappé! This iconic iced coffee drink, originating from Greece, is beloved for its refreshing, frothy texture and its ability to keep you cool on the hottest days. Made from instant coffee, water, sugar, and ice, the Frappé is a simple yet delicious treat that's all about texture and flavor. Whether you're lounging by the pool or taking a break from your day, a Greek Frappé offers the perfect balance of bold coffee flavor and refreshing coolness, all in one glass.*

## Ingredients:

- 2 tsps instant coffee (preferably Greek-style coffee)
- 1-2 tsps sugar (adjust according to your sweetness preference)
- 1/4 cup cold water
- 1/2 cup ice cubes
- [Optional] 1/4 cup milk or non-dairy milk (for creaminess)
- [Optional] 1 tbsp vanilla syrup or flavored syrup for added sweetness

## Instructions:

1. **Mix the coffee base**: In a tall glass or shaker, combine 2 teaspoons of instant coffee and 1/4 cup of cold water. Add 1-2 teaspoons of sugar (to taste).
2. **Froth the coffee**: Using a hand frother, whisk the coffee mixture vigorously until it becomes frothy and doubles in volume. This step is essential to achieve the signature foam that makes the Frappé so special.
3. **Add ice**: Fill a glass with ice cubes (about 1/2 cup).
4. **Pour and mix**: Pour the frothy coffee mixture over the ice. If you prefer a creamier texture, add 1/4 cup of milk or non-dairy milk at this point and stir gently.
5. **Sweeten and flavor (optional)**: For a sweeter taste, add a splash of vanilla syrup or another flavored syrup, and mix it into the coffee.
6. **Serve**: Enjoy your Greek Frappé immediately with a straw for sipping the foam and a chilled, refreshing coffee experience.

## Tips and Recommendations:

- **Instant coffee**: Choose a high-quality instant coffee for the best flavor, preferably a Greek-style coffee brand like Nescafé.
- **Frothing**: The key to a successful Frappé is the frothy top. Be sure to froth vigorously for 1-2 minutes to get that signature foam.
- **Customize the sweetness**: Adjust the sugar based on your preferences. Greek Frappé is traditionally made with a moderate amount of sugar, but feel free to reduce it or replace it with a natural sweetener.
- **Milk options**: For a dairy-free version, use oat milk, almond milk, or coconut milk for a creamy texture without the dairy.
- **Ice cubes**: Make sure to use plenty of ice to keep the Frappé chilled and refreshing.

## Variations:

- **Mocha Frappé**: Add a tablespoon of cocoa powder or chocolate syrup to your Frappé for a rich, chocolatey twist.
- **Vanilla Frappé**: Add a teaspoon of vanilla extract or a splash of vanilla syrup for a deliciously sweet and aromatic version.
- **Spiced Frappé**: For a spiced kick, sprinkle a pinch of cinnamon or nutmeg on top of the foam or stir it into the coffee before frothing.

## Pairing Suggestions:

- **Baklava**: The sweet, flaky layers of baklava pair perfectly with the cold, bold flavors of Greek Frappé.
- **Pita Chips with Hummus**: A savory snack like pita chips and hummus complements the sweetness of the Frappé and balances the flavors.
- **Fresh Fruit**: Pair with a refreshing bowl of watermelon or berries for a light and fruity side.

## Interesting Fact:

Did you know that the Greek Frappé was accidentally invented in 1957 by a Nescafé salesman in Thessaloniki, Greece? He mixed instant coffee with cold water and ice to create a quick and refreshing drink, and it quickly became a national favorite.

## Cultural Connection:

The Greek Frappé is more than just a coffee drink; it's a part of Greek daily life. Often enjoyed during long, leisurely afternoons or as a refreshing break in the summer heat, the Frappé represents a laid-back, social lifestyle. It's common to see Greeks sipping Frappé at cafés, where the slow pace of the coffee experience encourages conversation and relaxation. Whether you're visiting the Mediterranean or enjoying the comforts of home, a Greek Frappé will transport you to a place where life is meant to be savored.

# Vietnamese Egg Coffee

*Indulge in the creamy, rich experience of Vietnamese Egg Coffee, a unique and decadent drink that has become a beloved specialty in Vietnam. This indulgent coffee features a velvety smooth egg yolk custard layer on top of strong, bold espresso. The combination of the coffee's robust flavor and the sweetness of the egg cream creates a delightful contrast that's sure to impress coffee lovers seeking something special. A true Vietnamese tradition, egg coffee is often enjoyed as a comforting treat during chilly days, but it's a warming delight any time of year.*

## Ingredients:

- 1 shot (1 ounce) of espresso
- 1 large egg yolk (room temperature)
- 2 tbsps sweetened condensed milk
- 1 tbsp sugar (adjust to taste)
- 1/4 tsp vanilla extract (optional for added flavor)
- 1/4 cup hot water
- [Optional] Cocoa powder or cinnamon for garnish

## Instructions:

1. **Brew the espresso**: Prepare a shot of espresso using your preferred method (espresso machine, stovetop Moka pot, or French press).
2. **Prepare the egg mixture**: In a separate bowl, whisk together the egg yolk, sweetened condensed milk, sugar, and vanilla extract (if using) until smooth and frothy.
3. **Add hot water**: Pour in 1/4 cup of hot water into the egg mixture and continue whisking vigorously to create a thick, creamy foam. You can also use a hand mixer or a stand mixer to achieve a smoother texture.
4. **Combine with espresso**: Pour the freshly brewed espresso into a glass or cup, then gently spoon the frothy egg cream on top.
5. **Serve and garnish**: Garnish with a light dusting of cocoa powder or cinnamon, if desired. Serve immediately for a rich and luxurious coffee experience.

## Tips and Recommendations:

- **Egg freshness**: Use fresh, room-temperature eggs to get the best texture for your egg cream.
- **Sweetness**: Adjust the sugar level based on your sweetness preference. The condensed milk already adds some sweetness, so you may want to start with less sugar.
- **Whisking method**: If you don't have an electric whisk, a manual whisk can work too, though it may take a little longer to achieve the desired frothy texture.
- **Vegan alternative**: For a vegan version, try using aquafaba (the liquid from canned chickpeas) instead of egg yolk and a plant-based sweetened condensed milk (such as coconut or almond-based).

## Variations:

- **Coconut Egg Coffee**: Add a teaspoon of coconut cream to the egg mixture for a tropical twist.
- **Iced Egg Coffee**: For a cool variation, brew the espresso ahead of time and chill it in the fridge. Pour over ice and top with the egg cream for an iced version of this creamy delight.
- **Spiced Egg Coffee**: Stir in a pinch of cinnamon, nutmeg, or cardamom into the egg mixture for a warming, spiced twist.

## Pairing Suggestions:

- **Sweet pastries**: Pair this rich and creamy coffee with a buttery croissant, cinnamon roll, or a sweet pastry like baklava for a delicious treat.
- **Fruit**: The richness of the coffee pairs beautifully with fresh fruit like berries or citrus slices to balance out the sweetness.
- **Chocolate**: A small piece of dark chocolate or a chocolate truffle complements the coffee's richness and adds a decadent touch.

## Interesting Fact:

Did you know that Vietnamese Egg Coffee was originally created in the 1940s by a bartender named Nguyen Giang in Hanoi? At a time when milk was scarce, he used egg yolks to create a creamy coffee drink, which soon became a beloved Vietnamese specialty.

## Cultural Connection:

Egg Coffee, or "Cà Phê Trứng," has become a symbol of Vietnam's creative coffee culture. It originated in Hanoi during the French colonial period when fresh milk was hard to come by, leading coffee makers to experiment with egg yolks as a substitute. Today, it's served at many cafes in Vietnam, often in the colder months, where it's enjoyed as a comforting and indulgent treat. The creamy, rich texture of this drink represents the innovative spirit of Vietnamese coffee culture, blending bold flavors with a touch of sweetness and tradition.

# Red Eye

*For those in need of an extra caffeine boost, the Red Eye is a perfect pick-me-up. This simple yet powerful drink combines the strength of a bold shot of espresso with the energy of drip coffee, creating a deeply satisfying and energizing experience. The Red Eye is a no-nonsense coffee drink that's perfect for anyone who wants to start their day with a jolt or power through an afternoon slump. It's the ultimate solution for coffee lovers who crave both strength and speed in their cup.*

## Ingredients:

- 1 shot (1 ounce) of espresso
- 1 cup (8 ounces) of brewed drip coffee
- [Optional] Sugar or sweetener (to taste)
- [Optional] Milk or dairy-free alternative (to taste)

## Instructions:

1. **Brew the drip coffee**: Brew 1 cup of your favorite drip coffee. You can use a drip coffee maker, pour-over method, or French press for best results.
2. **Prepare the espresso**: Brew 1 shot of espresso using your espresso machine, stovetop Moka pot, or another preferred method.
3. **Combine the coffee and espresso**: In a large coffee cup, pour the brewed drip coffee first, followed by the shot of espresso.
4. **Stir and customize**: Stir the mixture to combine. Add sweetener and milk (or a dairy-free alternative) to taste, if desired.
5. **Serve and enjoy**: Serve hot and enjoy the powerful energy boost of your Red Eye.

## Tips and Recommendations:

- **Adjust strength**: If you need an even stronger kick, add another shot of espresso, turning your Red Eye into a Black Eye, or for an extra boost, try a Dead Eye with three shots!
- **Sweeten to taste**: While the Red Eye is typically enjoyed black, a splash of sweetener can balance the bitterness of the coffee. Try brown sugar or maple syrup for a more nuanced flavor.
- **Milk or dairy-free options**: If you prefer a smoother drink, add a little milk, cream, or a dairy-free alternative like oat milk or almond milk. It'll soften the coffee's intensity while still delivering a rich taste.

## Variations:

- **Iced Red Eye**: Brew your drip coffee and espresso, then chill both before combining them over ice for a refreshing iced version.
- **Red Eye Latte**: Add steamed milk to your Red Eye for a creamier version that still packs the caffeine punch.
- **Mocha Red Eye**: For a chocolatey twist, add a teaspoon of cocoa powder and a bit of sugar to the mix for a mocha-inspired Red Eye.

## Pairing Suggestions:

- **Breakfast pastry**: Pair your Red Eye with a light pastry, such as a croissant or muffin, to balance out the intense caffeine hit.
- **Granola or oatmeal**: A hearty breakfast like granola or oatmeal pairs well with the strength of a Red Eye, creating a well-rounded morning meal.
- **Chocolate**: Dark chocolate or a chocolate bar can complement the deep, bold flavors of the Red Eye, making for a delicious and energizing snack.

## Interesting Fact:

Did you know that the Red Eye is often referred to as the "working man's coffee" because it's a fast and effective way to get a strong caffeine hit with minimal fuss? It's the drink of choice for anyone needing to power through a busy day or long night shift.

## Cultural Connection:

The Red Eye is a popular drink in North America, especially among those who need a quick and strong caffeine boost. While it's not tied to any specific coffee culture or region, its straightforwardness and potency make it a favorite among those who want to skip the frills and go straight for the energy. In fact, the Red Eye has become a symbol of efficiency - just like its name suggests, it keeps you awake for those long hours on the road or in the office.

# Black Eye

*If you're looking for a coffee that delivers maximum caffeine in the shortest amount of time, look no further than the Black Eye. This bold drink is a powerhouse, combining the strength of brewed drip coffee with two shots of espresso for a jolt of energy that will keep you awake and alert all day long. The Black Eye is perfect for those who enjoy their coffee strong, simple, and seriously potent. It's a no-frills, no-nonsense coffee that speaks directly to your need for a serious caffeine boost.*

## Ingredients:

- 2 shots (2 ounces) of espresso
- 1 cup (8 ounces) of brewed drip coffee
- [Optional] Sugar or sweetener (to taste)
- [Optional] Milk or dairy-free alternative (to taste)

## Instructions:

1. **Brew the drip coffee**: Brew 1 cup of your favorite drip coffee using your preferred method (drip coffee maker, pour-over, or French press).
2. **Prepare the espresso**: Brew 2 shots of espresso using your espresso machine, stovetop Moka pot, or another espresso method.
3. **Combine the coffee and espresso**: Pour the brewed drip coffee into a large mug, then add the 2 shots of espresso on top.
4. **Stir and customize**: Stir the mixture to combine. If desired, add sweetener and milk (or a dairy-free alternative) to taste.
5. **Serve and enjoy**: Serve hot and savor the bold, energetic boost of your Black Eye.

## Tips and Recommendations:

- **Stronger is better**: The Black Eye is known for its intensity. If you're feeling particularly daring, try adding a third shot of espresso to turn your Black Eye into a Dead Eye, for even more power.
- **Sweeten it up**: This drink is usually enjoyed black, but if you prefer it sweeter, add sugar, honey, or a flavored syrup such as vanilla or caramel.
- **Milk or dairy-free alternatives**: If you want to mellow out the boldness, add a splash of milk or a dairy-free option like oat or almond milk for a creamier taste.

## Variations:

- **Iced Black Eye**: Brew your drip coffee and espresso, then chill both before combining them over ice for a refreshing iced version.
- **Black Eye Latte**: For a smoother, creamier drink, add steamed milk to your Black Eye, making it a latte-style drink without sacrificing the caffeine intensity.
- **Mocha Black Eye**: Add a teaspoon of cocoa powder or a dash of chocolate syrup to your Black Eye for a rich, mocha-flavored twist.

## Pairing Suggestions:

- **Savory pastries**: Pair your Black Eye with a savory breakfast, such as a croissant filled with cheese or a veggie-filled quiche, to balance out the strong coffee flavors.
- **Rich chocolate desserts**: The boldness of the Black Eye pairs beautifully with decadent chocolate desserts like brownies, chocolate cake, or a dark chocolate truffle.
- **Breakfast sandwich**: A hearty breakfast sandwich with eggs, avocado, and cheese works wonderfully alongside the power-packed Black Eye.

## Interesting Fact:

The Black Eye gets its name from its powerful combination of espresso and drip coffee, which can be so strong that it metaphorically "knocks you out" with caffeine! The drink is a favorite among people who need a serious energy boost, whether they're working late or facing a busy day.

## Cultural Connection:

The Black Eye is a popular American coffee drink, known for its simplicity and potency. While not as widely known in traditional coffee cultures like Italy, it has gained popularity among those who appreciate a high-caffeine, no-nonsense coffee experience. The drink is part of a growing trend in the U.S. of creating more potent

# White Eye

*For those who love the intensity of a double shot of espresso but also appreciate a bit of creaminess to balance out the boldness, the White Eye is the perfect choice. Combining the strength of espresso with the smoothness of steamed milk, this drink delivers a full-bodied coffee experience that's rich and velvety. The White Eye is essentially a lighter version of its darker counterpart, the Black Eye, making it an ideal choice for those who want all the caffeine kick but with a creamier, more rounded finish.*

## Ingredients:

- 2 shots (2 ounces) of espresso
- 1 cup (8 ounces) of brewed drip coffee
- 1/2 cup steamed milk or dairy-free alternative (such as oat or almond milk)
- [Optional] Sweetener to taste (sugar, honey, or syrup)

## Instructions:

1. **Brew the drip coffee**: Start by brewing 1 cup of your preferred drip coffee using your favorite method (drip coffee maker, pour-over, or French press).
2. **Prepare the espresso**: Brew 2 shots of espresso using your espresso machine or stovetop Moka pot.
3. **Steam the milk**: Steam 1/2 cup of milk (or a dairy-free alternative) until hot but not boiling. Use a milk frother or steam wand to create a smooth, velvety texture.
4. **Combine the coffee and espresso**: Pour the brewed drip coffee into a large mug, then gently add the 2 shots of espresso.
5. **Add the steamed milk**: Pour the steamed milk into the coffee-espresso mixture, stirring gently to create a smooth, creamy texture.
6. **Sweeten and serve**: Add sweetener to taste if desired, then serve hot. Enjoy the rich and creamy flavor of your White Eye.

## Tips and Recommendations:

- **Frothy milk**: If you prefer a frothier drink, use a milk frother to create a layer of foam on top of your White Eye. This adds an extra creamy texture and enhances the presentation.
- **Milk alternatives**: For a dairy-free version, use oat milk, almond milk, or coconut milk to give your White Eye a unique flavor twist.
- **Strong or mild**: If you want a more intense coffee flavor, use a darker roast for the drip coffee or increase the number of espresso shots. For a milder taste, opt for a lighter roast coffee.

## Variations:

- **Iced White Eye**: Brew the drip coffee and espresso, then chill both before combining them over ice for a refreshing iced version of the White Eye.
- **White Eye Latte**: For a more decadent version, add a bit of flavored syrup like vanilla or hazelnut for a sweet touch, or top with a sprinkle of cinnamon or cocoa powder for extra flavor.
- **Cinnamon White Eye**: Add a dash of ground cinnamon to the steamed milk before combining it with the coffee and espresso for a warming, spiced twist.

## Pairing Suggestions:

- **Flaky pastries**: Pair your White Eye with a buttery croissant or Danish pastry for a delicious and indulgent breakfast or snack.
- **Chocolate desserts**: A slice of rich chocolate cake or a few chocolate truffles complement the creamy richness of the White Eye.
- **Savory options**: For a more savory pairing, try a warm, freshly baked quiche or an avocado toast with a poached egg.

## Interesting Fact:

The White Eye is a popular drink in coffee shops, especially for those who want a stronger coffee flavor than a regular latte but still crave the smoothness of milk. The drink is sometimes referred to as a "Caffe Misto" when brewed with equal parts coffee and steamed milk, but the addition of espresso in the White Eye adds an extra punch.

## Cultural Connection:

The White Eye is part of a growing trend of espresso-based drinks that blend the boldness of espresso with the milder flavors of drip coffee. This hybrid drink has gained popularity in many countries, especially in the U.S., where people enjoy finding new ways to create richer, more flavorful coffee experiences. The White Eye is perfect for those who love the idea of strong coffee but prefer the creaminess of milk to soften the intensity.

# Breve

*Imagine a smooth, creamy coffee that feels like a hug in a cup. The Breve is a luxurious espresso-based drink where bold espresso meets the richness of steamed half-and-half (a mix of milk and cream). This indulgent coffee creation is beloved by those who appreciate a creamy texture and a deep, comforting flavor. It's the perfect treat when you want something more decadent than a traditional latte, without losing that strong espresso kick. Discover the Breve's irresistible, velvety appeal, and let it transform your coffee ritual.*

## Ingredients:

- 1 shot (1 ounce) of espresso
- 1/2 cup steamed half-and-half (or equal parts whole milk and heavy cream)
- [Optional] 1/4 tsp ground cinnamon or nutmeg for garnish

## Instructions:

1. **Brew the espresso**: Start by brewing 1 shot of espresso using your preferred method - whether that's an espresso machine, stovetop Moka pot, or any other technique you prefer.
2. **Steam the half-and-half**: In a milk frother or small pot, steam 1/2 cup of half-and-half until hot but not boiling. The goal is to achieve a smooth, velvety texture.
3. **Pour the espresso**: Once brewed, pour the espresso into a pre-warmed cup.
4. **Add the steamed half-and-half**: Gently pour the steamed half-and-half into the cup, mixing it with the espresso to create a creamy, balanced flavor.
5. **Garnish and serve**: For an extra touch of flavor, sprinkle a pinch of cinnamon or nutmeg on top. Serve immediately and enjoy the indulgent richness of your Breve.

## Tips and Recommendations:

- **For extra creaminess**: If you want a more decadent experience, increase the amount of half-and-half to 3/4 cup for a richer, more luxurious texture.
- **Non-dairy alternatives**: You can use coconut milk, oat milk, or almond milk for a dairy-free option, though the consistency will be slightly different.
- **Perfect froth**: To achieve the best froth, use a steam wand or a handheld milk frother, which will create that velvety microfoam ideal for a Breve.

## Variations:

- **Flavored Breve**: Add a splash of vanilla, caramel, or hazelnut syrup to your Breve for a sweet, flavored twist.
- **Iced Breve**: If you prefer cold coffee drinks, pour your espresso over ice and top it with chilled half-and-half. Stir to combine for an iced Breve that's both refreshing and indulgent.
- **Spiced Breve**: For a warming, spiced version, add a pinch of cinnamon, cardamom, or pumpkin spice to the steamed half-and-half before pouring it into your espresso.

## Pairing Suggestions:

- **Sweet pastries**: Enjoy your Breve with a freshly baked almond croissant or cinnamon roll to balance the richness of the drink.
- **Light breakfast**: Pair with a slice of avocado toast or a fresh fruit salad for a delicious and satisfying breakfast.
- **Chocolatey treats**: A few pieces of dark chocolate or a rich chocolate cake complement the creamy flavor of the Breve beautifully.

## Interesting Fact:

Did you know that "Breve" means "short" in Italian? This refers to the short brewing process used to create the indulgent, creamy nature of this coffee, where the richness of half-and-half takes center stage, creating a coffee that is both strong and luxurious.

## Cultural Connection:

The Breve has become a beloved coffee drink in the U.S., especially in the Pacific Northwest, where espresso-based drinks have a strong cultural presence. The drink's roots are Italian, but its creamy, decadent nature makes it a favorite among those who appreciate indulgent coffee experiences.

# Vienna Coffee

*Transport yourself to the charming coffeehouses of Vienna with this timeless classic, Vienna Coffee. Known for its rich espresso base and indulgent topping of freshly whipped cream, this coffee is both elegant and comforting. A touch of sweetness and a delicate layer of cream make Vienna Coffee an exquisite treat, perfect for an afternoon pick-me-up or a cozy evening indulgence. It's the kind of coffee that invites you to slow down and savor every luxurious sip. Let's dive into the elegance of this historical drink!*

## Ingredients:

- 1 shot (1 ounce) of espresso
- 1 tbsp of sugar (adjust to taste)
- 1/2 cup (120 ml) freshly whipped cream (non-dairy options: coconut cream or whipped oat cream)
- [Optional] 1/4 tsp ground cinnamon or cocoa powder for garnish

## Instructions:

1. **Brew the espresso**: Brew a shot of espresso using your preferred method, whether it's an espresso machine, stovetop Moka pot, or manual espresso maker.
2. **Sweeten the espresso**: Stir 1 tablespoon of sugar into the hot espresso until dissolved. Feel free to adjust the sweetness to suit your taste.
3. **Whip the cream**: Whip 1/2 cup of cream (or coconut/oat cream for a vegan version) until soft peaks form. You can use a hand whisk or an electric mixer to achieve this.
4. **Assemble the coffee**: Pour the sweetened espresso into a warm coffee cup.
5. **Top with whipped cream**: Gently spoon the freshly whipped cream over the espresso, creating a rich, luxurious layer on top.
6. **Garnish and serve**: For a finishing touch, sprinkle a pinch of cinnamon or cocoa powder on top of the whipped cream. Serve immediately and enjoy the smooth, velvety experience of Vienna Coffee.

## Tips and Recommendations:

- **For extra creaminess**: If you like your Vienna Coffee extra indulgent, use a generous dollop of whipped cream and ensure it covers the entire surface of the espresso.
- **Non-dairy whipped cream**: Coconut cream or oat cream are excellent substitutes for traditional dairy cream, providing a rich, vegan-friendly alternative.
- **Adjust the sweetness**: If you prefer a less sweet coffee, reduce the sugar to 1/2 tablespoon, or opt for a natural sweetener like agave or maple syrup.

## Variations:

- **Flavored Vienna Coffee**: Add a dash of vanilla extract or a sprinkle of cinnamon to the whipped cream for an added layer of flavor.
- **Iced Vienna Coffee**: For a refreshing twist, serve this recipe over ice, with chilled whipped cream to top it off.
- **Vienna Mocha**: Stir in a teaspoon of cocoa powder or melted dark chocolate into the espresso for a chocolatey version of Vienna Coffee.

## Pairing Suggestions:

- **Pastries**: Enjoy your Vienna Coffee with a flaky croissant, a buttery Danish pastry, or a rich slice of Sachertorte (a famous Austrian chocolate cake).
- **Light snacks**: Pair with a light snack such as a fruit salad or nuts to balance out the sweetness of the whipped cream.
- **Chocolate**: For a decadent treat, pair this coffee with a few squares of dark chocolate or chocolate truffles.

## Interesting Fact:

Did you know that Vienna Coffee has a rich history that dates back to the 17th century? The drink was popularized after the battle of Vienna in 1683, when coffee was introduced to the city by the invading Ottoman Empire. Today, Vienna Coffee is a symbol of Austrian coffee culture and is still enjoyed in coffeehouses across the country.

## Cultural Connection:

Vienna is known as one of the great coffee capitals of the world, and its coffeehouses have been cultural hubs for centuries. Vienna Coffee, with its origins rooted in the city's rich coffee tradition, is not just a drink - it's a part of the city's soul. Whether in the cozy warmth of a traditional café or served at home, this coffee represents the art of taking a moment to savor life.

# Cuban Coffee

*Welcome to the bold and irresistible world of Cuban Coffee, a drink that embodies the passion and rhythm of Cuban culture. This traditional coffee is brewed with rich, strong espresso and sweetened with demerara sugar, creating a perfect balance of intense flavor and sweetness. Often served as a pick-me-up throughout the day, Cuban Coffee is famous for its deep, smooth taste and creamy texture, with a touch of sweetness that elevates every sip. Get ready to indulge in a Cuban classic that's as vibrant and energetic as the island itself!*

## Ingredients:

- 1 shot (1 ounce) of espresso
- 1 tbsp demerara sugar (or to taste)
- 1/2 tsp of cinnamon (optional)
- [Optional] 1 shot (1 ounce) of hot water (to make a "Café con Leche" variation)

## Instructions:

1. **Brew the espresso**: Brew a strong shot of espresso using your preferred method, such as an espresso machine, stovetop Moka pot, or manual espresso maker.
2. **Sweeten the espresso**: While the espresso is still hot, stir in the demerara sugar until it's fully dissolved. The sugar will create a syrupy texture that enhances the coffee's flavor.
3. **Optional - Add cinnamon**: If you like a spiced touch, add 1/2 teaspoon of cinnamon to the sweetened espresso and stir well.
4. **Serve**: Pour the sweetened espresso into a small espresso cup.
5. **Café con Leche variation**: For a Cuban twist, you can mix the espresso with equal parts steamed milk to create a creamy "Café con Leche." You can also add a shot of hot water for a slightly diluted, yet still flavorful version.
6. **Enjoy**: Take a moment to savor this strong, sweet Cuban delight - perfect for sipping any time of the day.

## Tips and Recommendations:

- **Adjust the sweetness**: Cuban Coffee is traditionally quite sweet, but you can always reduce the amount of sugar if you prefer a less sugary taste.
- **Use a dark roast**: A dark-roast espresso works best for this recipe, as its bold flavor complements the sweetness of the sugar.
- **Serving temperature**: Cuban Coffee is typically served piping hot, but if you're in the mood for something colder, you can pour it over ice for an iced Cuban coffee.
- **Cuban Coffee with milk**: If you want a creamier drink, consider adding steamed milk to your Cuban Coffee for a delicious "Café con Leche" variation.

## Variations:

- **Iced Cuban Coffee**: Brew the espresso as usual and let it cool. Pour it over ice and add a little extra sugar for sweetness.
- **Café con Leche**: Mix your Cuban Coffee with equal parts steamed milk for a creamy, dreamy twist on the classic recipe.
- **Vegan Cuban Coffee**: Replace the milk in the Café con Leche variation with your favorite plant-based milk, such as almond milk or oat milk.

## Pairing Suggestions:

- **Cuban pastries**: Serve with traditional Cuban pastries like pastelitos (sweet pastries filled with guava or cream cheese), or a slice of coconut cake to enhance the sweet, bold flavors of the coffee.
- **Savory snacks**: Pair your Cuban Coffee with a savory snack like a Cuban sandwich, empanadas, or plantain chips for a delightful balance of flavors.
- **Chocolate**: A few squares of dark chocolate or a chocolate croissant make for an indulgent pairing.

## Interesting Fact:

Did you know that Cuban Coffee is also known as cafecito in Cuba? It's a staple of Cuban culture, often shared among friends and family, and it's a symbol of hospitality and togetherness. The sweetened espresso was first popularized in Cuba during the early 19th century, and it remains a cherished tradition today.

## Cultural Connection:

Cuban Coffee is deeply embedded in the country's culture, particularly in the vibrant city of Havana. Known for its intense flavor and sweet, syrupy texture, it is often served in small cups, allowing drinkers to savor its powerful taste in every sip. Coffee culture in Cuba is not just about the drink - it's about connecting with others, taking time to relax, and enjoying life. Whether at a bustling street corner café or in the comfort of your home, Cuban Coffee embodies the spirit of warmth and hospitality.

# Ethiopian Coffee

*Take a journey to the heart of coffee's birthplace with a cup of Ethiopian Coffee. Known for its vibrant, fruity notes and deep, aromatic complexity, Ethiopian coffee is often regarded as one of the best coffees in the world. This recipe is inspired by the traditional Ethiopian preparation, highlighting the natural sweetness and floral undertones of the beans. Paired with a touch of spice and the right brewing technique, Ethiopian Coffee is not just a drink - it's an experience. Get ready to awaken your senses with the bold, aromatic flavors that make Ethiopian coffee unforgettable.*

## Ingredients:

- 1 shot (1 ounce) of espresso (preferably Ethiopian single-origin beans)
- 1/4 tsp ground cardamom
- 1/4 tsp ground cinnamon (optional)
- 1 tbsp honey or maple syrup (optional for sweetness)
- [Optional] 1/2 cup steamed almond milk or oat milk (for a creamy version)
- [Optional] Orange zest or a few coffee beans for garnish

## Instructions:

1. **Brew the espresso**: Brew a shot of espresso using Ethiopian coffee beans for an authentic flavor. You can use an espresso machine, stovetop Moka pot, or manual espresso maker.
2. **Prepare the spices**: While your espresso is brewing, combine the ground cardamom and cinnamon (if using) in a small bowl.
3. **Sweeten the coffee (optional)**: Add honey or maple syrup to the hot espresso if you prefer a touch of sweetness. Stir well to combine.
4. **Add the spices**: Gently stir the spices into the brewed espresso. Cardamom adds a warm, floral kick, while cinnamon enhances the richness of the coffee's flavor.
5. **Optional – Steam the milk**: If you prefer a creamier version, steam almond milk or oat milk to a frothy texture and pour it into the coffee. The plant-based milk complements the coffee's bold flavors without overpowering them.
6. **Serve**: Pour your spiced Ethiopian coffee into your favorite cup.
7. **Garnish (optional)**: Add a pinch of orange zest or a few coffee beans on top to give your coffee a special finishing touch.
8. **Enjoy**: Take a moment to savor the aromatic blend of coffee and spices. Enjoy your cup of Ethiopian Coffee slowly and appreciate its complexity.

## Tips and Recommendations:

- **Adjust the sweetness**: Ethiopian Coffee has a natural fruity sweetness, so you might not need much added sugar. Start with a small amount of honey or syrup, and adjust to your taste.
- **Try whole cardamom pods**: If you want an even fresher flavor, try lightly crushing whole cardamom pods and brewing them with your coffee for an aromatic twist.
- **Stronger coffee flavor**: For a more intense coffee flavor, use a slightly darker roast of Ethiopian beans, which brings out a deeper profile.
- **Experiment with milk alternatives**: Almond milk, oat milk, and coconut milk all pair beautifully with Ethiopian coffee. Each offers its own unique flavor and texture, so feel free to experiment.

## Variations:

- **Iced Ethiopian Coffee**: Brew your espresso and allow it to cool. Pour it over ice and add a splash of almond milk or a drizzle of honey for a refreshing iced coffee treat.
- **Ethiopian Coffee with Spices**: For a spicier twist, try adding a pinch of ground ginger or nutmeg along with the cinnamon and cardamom.
- **Ethiopian Coffee Latte**: Steam your favorite plant-based milk and pour it over the spiced espresso for a smooth, creamy version of this flavorful coffee.

## Pairing Suggestions:

- **Baklava**: The sweet, nutty layers of baklava complement the warm spices in Ethiopian Coffee, creating a perfect pairing.
- **Chocolate**: Dark chocolate or a rich chocolate cake pairs wonderfully with the vibrant flavors of Ethiopian coffee.
- **Nuts**: Roasted almonds or cashews bring out the coffee's subtle nutty undertones and add texture to your coffee break.

## Interesting Fact:

Did you know that Ethiopia is often referred to as the "birthplace of coffee"? According to legend, a goat herder named Kaldi discovered coffee when he noticed his goats becoming energized after eating the red berries from a particular tree - believed to be the first coffee plant.

# Mexican Café de Olla

*Transport your taste buds to the heart of Mexico with a cup of Mexican Café de Olla. This traditional coffee is infused with warm spices and sweetened with piloncillo (unrefined sugar) to create a rich, comforting drink perfect for any occasion. The addition of cinnamon and cloves gives the coffee a unique, aromatic depth, while the espresso base ensures a bold and satisfying flavor. Café de Olla has a long history in Mexican culture, often brewed in clay pots over a fire, making it a drink steeped in tradition and passion. This recipe brings that authentic experience right to your kitchen, with a modern twist using espresso for a quick yet flavorful cup.*

## Ingredients:

- 1 shot (1 ounce) of espresso (preferably dark roast)
- 1/4 cup piloncillo (or dark brown sugar, if unavailable)
- 1 cinnamon stick
- 1-2 cloves (optional)
- 1/4 tsp ground cinnamon
- 1/2 cup steamed oat milk or almond milk (optional, for a creamy version)
- [Optional] 1 tsp vanilla extract (for extra warmth)

## Instructions:

1. **Brew the espresso**: Brew a shot of espresso using your preferred method. For an authentic touch, use a darker roast to match the boldness of the spices.
2. **Infuse the spices**: In a small saucepan, combine the piloncillo, cinnamon stick, and cloves (if using). Add 1/2 cup of water and heat gently over medium heat, stirring occasionally, until the piloncillo dissolves completely.
3. **Simmer the syrup**: Allow the mixture to simmer for about 5-7 minutes, infusing the spices into the syrup. Remove from heat once the syrup has thickened slightly and the flavors have melded together.
4. **Combine the espresso and syrup**: Pour the brewed espresso into your coffee cup. Add 1-2 tablespoons of the spiced piloncillo syrup to the coffee, adjusting to your preferred sweetness.
5. **Optional – Steam the milk**: If you want a creamy version, steam oat or almond milk until it's frothy and pour it over the spiced coffee mixture.
6. **Stir and serve**: Stir the coffee gently to combine the syrup and espresso.
7. **Garnish (optional)**: Add a sprinkle of ground cinnamon on top for a finishing touch, or place a cinnamon stick in the cup for extra flavor and flair.
8. **Enjoy**: Sip slowly and enjoy the warm, comforting flavors of your homemade Mexican Café de Olla.

## Tips and Recommendations:

- **Adjust sweetness**: Piloncillo is naturally very sweet, so start with a small amount of syrup and adjust to taste. If you prefer less sweetness, add less syrup.
- **Experiment with milk alternatives**: Oat milk or almond milk works beautifully in this recipe, providing a creamy texture without overpowering the flavors of the coffee and spices.
- **Spice it up**: For a bolder spice kick, add more cinnamon or a pinch of nutmeg to the syrup.
- **Caffeine levels**: If you prefer a milder coffee, use half a shot of espresso and top it off with more steamed milk.

## Variations:

- **Iced Mexican Café de Olla**: Brew your espresso and allow it to cool. Pour over ice and top with a splash of chilled oat or almond milk for a refreshing iced version of this spicy coffee.
- **Mexican Mocha**: For a chocolatey twist, add a tablespoon of cocoa powder or chocolate syrup to the piloncillo syrup before simmering. This will give the coffee a rich, mocha-like flavor.
- **Spicy Mexican Café de Olla**: If you like heat, add a pinch of cayenne pepper to the syrup for a spicy kick that perfectly balances the sweetness of the piloncillo.

## Pairing Suggestions:

- **Pan de Muerto**: A traditional Mexican sweet bread, perfect for pairing with the aromatic spices in Café de Olla.
- **Churros**: The cinnamon-sugar coating of churros complements the cinnamon in the coffee for a delightful combination.
- **Mexican Chocolate Cake**: Rich, dark chocolate cake pairs wonderfully with the spiced coffee, enhancing its flavors with a sweet contrast.

## Interesting Fact:

Did you know that Café de Olla has been brewed in Mexico for centuries? It was originally made in clay pots, which are said to enhance the flavors of the coffee by imparting a unique, earthy character to the brew. The sweet piloncillo and warm spices became integral to the recipe, symbolizing the warmth of Mexican hospitality.

# Bulletproof Coffee

*Looking for a way to fuel your day with sustained energy and focus? Bulletproof Coffee is a powerhouse drink that combines bold espresso with rich fats to keep you energized for hours. This blend of espresso, grass-fed butter, and MCT oil is designed to give you a clean, smooth energy boost without the crash that often follows sugary drinks. The creamy, frothy texture and rich flavor make Bulletproof Coffee a satisfying way to start your morning or power through a busy afternoon. Whether you're embracing a keto lifestyle or simply looking for a healthier way to enjoy your coffee, this recipe is a game-changer.*

## Ingredients:

- 1 shot (1 ounce) of espresso
- 1 tbsp grass-fed butter (or coconut oil for a dairy-free option)
- 1 tbsp MCT oil (or coconut oil)
- 1/2 tsp vanilla extract (optional, for added flavor)
- [Optional] 1 tsp cinnamon or cocoa powder (for flavor variations)

## Instructions:

1. **Brew the espresso**: Brew one shot of espresso using your preferred method. The bolder the coffee, the more satisfying the Bulletproof effect.
2. **Blend the ingredients**: In a blender, combine the brewed espresso, grass-fed butter, and MCT oil. Blend on high for 20-30 seconds until the mixture becomes frothy and emulsified.
3. **Optional flavor add-ins**: If desired, add vanilla extract, cinnamon, or cocoa powder to the blender for a richer flavor profile.
4. **Serve immediately**: Pour the creamy coffee into your favorite mug and enjoy the rich, buttery texture.
5. **Optional – Add a sweetener**: If you prefer a sweeter cup, add a splash of stevia or monk fruit sweetener to taste.

## Tips and Recommendations:

- **Butter choice**: Grass-fed butter gives the coffee a creamy texture and offers beneficial omega-3s. If you're dairy-free, coconut oil or plant-based butter is a great alternative.
- **Adjust fat levels**: For a lighter version, use 1/2 tablespoon of butter and MCT oil, or increase the amounts for a richer, more satiating drink.
- **Blend thoroughly**: For the best frothy texture, ensure you blend the ingredients thoroughly. If you don't have a blender, an immersion blender works well too.
- **Stay creative**: Experiment with flavors like cinnamon, vanilla, or cocoa to customize your Bulletproof Coffee. A dash of cayenne pepper can add a spicy twist if you like a bit of heat.

## Variations:

- **Vanilla Bulletproof Coffee**: Add 1/2 teaspoon of vanilla extract to the blend for a smoother, aromatic flavor.
- **Chocolate Bulletproof Coffee**: Stir in a teaspoon of cocoa powder for a chocolatey variation.
- **Iced Bulletproof Coffee**: Brew your espresso ahead of time, chill it, and then blend it with the butter and MCT oil over ice for a refreshing, cold version.

## Pairing Suggestions:

- **Almond Flour Muffins**: These low-carb, nutty muffins pair wonderfully with the rich, creamy texture of Bulletproof Coffee.
- **Avocado Toast**: The healthy fats in avocado complement the fats in the coffee, creating a well-rounded, energizing breakfast.
- **Chia Pudding**: For a protein-packed, fiber-rich pairing, enjoy a small bowl of chia pudding alongside your coffee.

## Interesting Fact:

Did you know that Bulletproof Coffee was originally created by entrepreneur Dave Asprey, who wanted to replicate the high-energy effects of traditional Tibetan butter tea? By blending coffee with butter and oil, Asprey developed a drink that provides long-lasting energy and cognitive support without the crash.

## Cultural Connection:

While Bulletproof Coffee is a relatively modern creation, it's inspired by the traditional Tibetan practice of adding yak butter to tea for energy and warmth in the high-altitude regions of the Himalayas. Bulletproof Coffee takes this ancient concept and gives it a modern twist, popularizing it as a staple in the health and wellness community, particularly among those following low-carb or ketogenic diets.

# Dirty Chai Latte

*A Dirty Chai Latte is a cozy fusion of two beloved beverages: spiced chai tea and rich espresso. The result? A spicy, aromatic, and energizing drink with a smooth coffee kick. This indulgent drink features the bold flavors of chai spices - such as cinnamon, cardamom, and cloves - blended with the deep richness of espresso and steamed milk. Whether you're craving something with a little spice or just want a pick-me-up that's both comforting and invigorating, a Dirty Chai Latte is the perfect balance of sweet, spicy, and bold.*

## Ingredients:

- 1 shot (1 ounce) of espresso
- 1 chai tea bag (or 2 tsps loose-leaf chai)
- 1 cup steamed milk (dairy or non-dairy such as oat, almond, or soy milk)
- 1 tbsp maple syrup or sweetener of choice (optional)
- 1/2 tsp ground cinnamon (for sprinkling)
- [Optional] 1/4 tsp ground cardamom or ginger (for added spice)

## Instructions:

1. **Brew the espresso**: Brew one shot of espresso using your preferred method.
2. **Prepare the chai tea**: In a separate pot, bring 1 cup of water to a boil. Add the chai tea bag or loose-leaf chai and steep for 4-5 minutes, depending on how strong you like it.
3. **Steam the milk**: While the chai is steeping, steam your milk (or non-dairy milk) using a milk frother or steam wand until it's hot and frothy.
4. **Combine**: Pour the brewed espresso into a mug, followed by the hot chai tea. Stir to combine.
5. **Add the steamed milk**: Gently pour the steamed milk into the mug, creating a frothy, creamy texture.
6. **Sweeten (optional)**: If desired, stir in your maple syrup or sweetener of choice.
7. **Garnish and serve**: Sprinkle ground cinnamon on top, and if you like, add a pinch of cardamom or ginger for extra warmth. Serve immediately.

## Tips and Recommendations:

- **Spice it up**: If you prefer a stronger chai flavor, add more chai concentrate or a pinch of ground cardamom, cinnamon, or ginger.
- **Make it vegan**: Use a plant-based milk like oat, almond, or soy to make this drink completely vegan.
- **Adjust the sweetness**: If you prefer a sweeter drink, use maple syrup, honey, or a sugar substitute like stevia or monk fruit.
- **Try iced**: If you're in the mood for something cool, try making an iced Dirty Chai Latte. Brew the espresso and chai ahead of time, chill it, then pour over ice and add the steamed (or chilled) milk.

## Variations:

- **Iced Dirty Chai Latte**: Brew espresso and chai, then chill. Pour over ice and top with cold milk for a refreshing iced version.
- **Spiced Dirty Chai Latte**: Add a pinch of cloves, nutmeg, or ginger for a deeper, spicier flavor profile.
- **Caramel Dirty Chai Latte**: For a sweet twist, drizzle caramel syrup over the top of your drink for a rich, indulgent finish.
- **Vanilla Dirty Chai Latte**: Add a drop of vanilla extract or vanilla syrup to bring a smooth, sweet flavor to the drink.

## Pairing Suggestions:

- **Vegan Cinnamon Rolls**: The warm spices in the cinnamon rolls complement the spiciness of the chai perfectly.
- **Spiced Biscotti**: A crunchy, slightly sweet biscotti makes a perfect side to this drink.
- **Almond Croissants**: The nutty sweetness of almond croissants pairs beautifully with the boldness of the chai and espresso.

## Interesting Fact:

Did you know that "Dirty" in Dirty Chai Latte refers to the addition of espresso to the traditional chai tea? It's called "dirty" because it's a bold twist on the classic tea latte, combining two iconic drinks into one satisfying cup.

## Cultural Connection:

Chai tea has deep roots in Indian culture, where it is often enjoyed as a daily ritual, typically served with milk and sugar. The addition of espresso to create a Dirty Chai Latte is a modern twist, originating in coffee shops around the world where chai is paired with coffee to create a fusion of two beloved beverages. This drink bridges cultures, blending the warm spices of traditional chai with the energy-boosting power of espresso.

# London Fog

*Indulge in the soothing comfort of a London Fog, where the bold richness of espresso meets the delicate, fragrant flavors of Earl Grey tea. This elegant beverage is as cozy as a stroll through a misty London morning, blending the floral notes of bergamot with the smooth creaminess of steamed milk. Perfect for those who enjoy a subtle twist on traditional coffee drinks, the London Fog combines the calming qualities of tea with the energizing boost of espresso, creating a drink that's both uplifting and relaxing.*

## Ingredients:

- 1 shot (1 ounce) of espresso
- 1 Earl Grey tea bag (or 2 tsps loose-leaf Earl Grey tea)
- 1 cup steamed milk (dairy or non-dairy such as oat, almond, or soy milk)
- 1 tsp vanilla syrup (or vanilla extract)
- 1 tbsp honey or sweetener of choice (optional)
- [Optional] 1/4 tsp ground cinnamon (for garnish)

## Instructions:

1. **Brew the espresso**: Brew one shot of espresso using your preferred method.
2. **Steep the Earl Grey tea**: In a separate mug, steep the Earl Grey tea in 1 cup of hot water for 4-5 minutes to extract the full flavor.
3. **Steam the milk**: While the tea is steeping, steam your milk (or non-dairy milk) using a milk frother or steam wand until it's hot and frothy.
4. **Combine the espresso and tea**: Pour the brewed espresso into a cup, then add the steeped Earl Grey tea. Stir to combine.
5. **Add the vanilla syrup**: Stir in 1 teaspoon of vanilla syrup or vanilla extract for a sweet, aromatic flavor.
6. **Add sweetness (optional)**: If desired, add honey or your sweetener of choice to taste.
7. **Top with steamed milk**: Gently pour the steamed milk into the mug, allowing the froth to form a creamy layer on top.
8. **Garnish and serve**: Sprinkle ground cinnamon on top for a touch of spice and serve immediately.

## Tips and Recommendations:

- **Adjust sweetness**: Depending on your taste preference, you can use more or less sweetener. Honey pairs wonderfully with Earl Grey's floral notes.
- **Non-dairy option**: Oat milk, almond milk, or coconut milk work particularly well in this recipe for a creamy, smooth texture.
- **Make it extra cozy**: For a richer flavor, add a dash of ground cardamom or nutmeg to the steamed milk for an aromatic touch.
- **Use a quality tea**: The quality of the Earl Grey tea is key. Choose a loose-leaf blend for a more vibrant, aromatic experience.

## Variations:

- **Iced London Fog**: Brew the espresso and tea, then chill. Serve over ice and top with cold milk for a refreshing iced version.
- **Lavender London Fog**: Add a few dried lavender buds to the tea steeping process for a floral twist that enhances the calming qualities of the drink.
- **Cinnamon London Fog**: Stir a pinch of ground cinnamon into the steamed milk for a warm, spiced version of this classic drink.

## Pairing Suggestions:

- **Scones with Clotted Cream**: A traditional British treat, scones with clotted cream are the perfect accompaniment to this fragrant and soothing drink.
- **Vegan Lemon Shortbread Cookies**: The zesty lemon flavor of these cookies pairs beautifully with the floral notes of the Earl Grey tea.
- **Almond Croissants**: The light, buttery sweetness of almond croissants complements the soft, floral flavor of the London Fog perfectly.

## Interesting Fact:

The London Fog is believed to have originated in Vancouver, Canada, not London! It was created by a barista who added a shot of espresso to a traditional Earl Grey latte, and the drink quickly became a popular favorite.

## Cultural Connection:

Though the drink's name evokes the misty mornings of London, the London Fog actually has Canadian roots. Its origins are traced back to Vancouver in the 1990s, where a barista sought to blend the calming qualities of Earl Grey tea with the energizing effects of espresso. Since then, the drink has gained a following in coffee shops around the world, becoming a comforting, sophisticated option for tea and coffee lovers alike.

# Pumpkin Spice Latte

*Fall in love with the comforting flavors of autumn with a Pumpkin Spice Latte, a creamy, spiced masterpiece that captures the essence of the season. This delicious drink combines the bold richness of espresso with the warm, aromatic spices of cinnamon, nutmeg, and cloves, balanced by the smooth sweetness of pumpkin puree and a touch of vanilla. Topped with a frothy layer of steamed milk and a sprinkle of pumpkin spice, this latte is the perfect treat to cozy up with on chilly mornings or to indulge in during a crisp afternoon. It's the ultimate way to bring the cozy fall vibes right into your home.*

## Ingredients:

- 1 shot (1 ounce) of espresso
- 2 tbsps pumpkin puree
- 1 tbsp maple syrup or sweetener of choice
- 1/2 tsp ground cinnamon
- 1/4 tsp ground nutmeg
- 1/4 tsp ground ginger
- 1/4 tsp ground cloves (optional)
- 1 cup steamed milk (dairy or non-dairy such as oat, almond, or soy milk)
- 1/2 tsp vanilla extract
- [Optional] Whipped cream or coconut whipped cream for topping
- [Optional] A sprinkle of pumpkin spice or cinnamon for garnish

## Instructions:

1. **Brew the espresso**: Brew one shot of espresso using your preferred method.
2. **Make the pumpkin spice mixture**: In a small saucepan, combine the pumpkin puree, maple syrup, cinnamon, nutmeg, ginger, and cloves (if using). Heat over low heat for about 2-3 minutes, stirring constantly, until the mixture is well combined and warmed through.
3. **Combine with vanilla**: Stir in the vanilla extract and remove from heat.
4. **Steam the milk**: Steam your milk (or non-dairy milk) using a milk frother or steam wand until it's hot and frothy.
5. **Mix the espresso and pumpkin mixture**: Pour the brewed espresso into a mug, then add the pumpkin spice mixture and stir well to combine.
6. **Add the steamed milk**: Gently pour the steamed milk into the mug, holding back the froth with a spoon, and then spoon the froth on top.
7. **Top and garnish**: For an extra indulgent touch, add a swirl of whipped cream (or coconut whipped cream for a dairy-free option) and sprinkle with pumpkin spice or cinnamon for garnish.

## Tips and Recommendations:

- **Adjust the sweetness**: If you prefer a sweeter drink, feel free to add more maple syrup or your favorite sweetener.
- **Dairy-free option**: Oat milk is a great choice for a creamy, slightly sweet flavor that complements the pumpkin spices. Almond milk is a lighter option with a subtle nuttiness.
- **More spice**: Add an extra pinch of cinnamon or nutmeg for a bolder spice flavor or experiment with a touch of allspice for a different twist.
- **Extra pumpkin flavor**: Increase the amount of pumpkin puree for a more pronounced pumpkin flavor in the latte.

## Variations:

- **Iced Pumpkin Spice Latte**: Brew the espresso and pumpkin mixture, then let it cool. Serve over ice, topping with cold milk and whipped cream for a refreshing fall treat.
- **Vegan Pumpkin Spice Latte**: Use non-dairy milk and coconut whipped cream for a completely dairy-free version of this beloved fall drink.
- **Pumpkin Spice Mocha**: Add 1 tablespoon of cocoa powder or chocolate syrup to the pumpkin spice mixture for a chocolatey twist on this classic latte.

## Pairing Suggestions:

- **Vegan Pumpkin Bread**: A slice of homemade vegan pumpkin bread is the perfect sweet complement to this cozy drink.
- **Cinnamon Roll**: Enjoy your Pumpkin Spice Latte with a warm cinnamon roll for an indulgent, comforting snack.
- **Apple Slices with Almond Butter**: The sweetness of apples and rich flavor of almond butter pair wonderfully with the spices in this latte.

## Interesting Fact:

The Pumpkin Spice Latte, also known as the PSL, was first introduced by Starbucks in 2003 and quickly became a seasonal sensation. It helped popularize the flavor combination of pumpkin and spice in coffee drinks, making it a fall tradition for coffee lovers around the world.

# Hazelnut Latte

*Indulge in the smooth, nutty richness of a Hazelnut Latte - a delicious blend of bold espresso, creamy steamed milk, and the irresistible flavor of toasted hazelnuts. This latte offers a perfect balance between the rich espresso base and the sweet, slightly earthy undertones of hazelnuts, creating a comforting and luxurious coffee experience. Whether you're cozying up at home or treating yourself to a café-style beverage, this Hazelnut Latte is sure to become your go-to drink for any occasion.*

## Ingredients:

- 1 shot (1 ounce) of espresso
- 1 cup steamed milk (dairy or non-dairy such as oat, almond, or soy milk)
- 2 tbsps hazelnut syrup or hazelnut flavoring
- [Optional] 1/4 tsp ground cinnamon or nutmeg
- [Optional] Whipped cream or coconut whipped cream for topping
- [Optional] Crushed toasted hazelnuts for garnish

## Instructions:

1. **Brew the espresso**: Brew one shot of espresso using your preferred method (e.g., espresso machine, Aeropress, or stovetop Moka pot).
2. **Steam the milk**: Steam your milk (or non-dairy milk) using a milk frother or steam wand until it's hot and frothy.
3. **Add the hazelnut syrup**: In a separate cup, combine the freshly brewed espresso with the hazelnut syrup. Stir to mix.
4. **Combine the espresso and milk**: Pour the brewed espresso and hazelnut syrup mixture into a large mug.
5. **Add the steamed milk**: Gently pour the steamed milk into the mug, holding back the froth with a spoon. Spoon the frothy milk on top.
6. **Top and garnish**: If desired, top with whipped cream (or coconut whipped cream for a dairy-free option) and sprinkle with a dash of cinnamon, nutmeg, or crushed toasted hazelnuts for added flavor and texture.

## Tips and Recommendations:

- **Adjust the sweetness**: If you prefer a sweeter drink, add more hazelnut syrup or a touch of maple syrup for an extra layer of flavor.
- **Non-dairy option**: Oat milk is a great choice for a creamy and naturally sweet latte, while almond milk offers a lighter flavor that pairs well with the hazelnut.
- **Hazelnut flavoring**: If you can't find hazelnut syrup, you can use hazelnut extract - just a few drops will add the same nutty richness.
- **More hazelnut flavor**: To enhance the hazelnut taste, try adding a teaspoon of hazelnut butter or a sprinkle of crushed toasted hazelnuts to the drink for extra flavor and texture.

## Variations:

- **Iced Hazelnut Latte**: Brew the espresso and let it cool. Serve over ice and top with cold milk and a drizzle of hazelnut syrup.
- **Hazelnut Mocha**: Add 1 tablespoon of cocoa powder or chocolate syrup to the espresso-hazelnut mixture for a chocolatey, nutty twist on the classic latte.
- **Vegan Hazelnut Latte**: Use your favorite plant-based milk and coconut whipped cream to create a deliciously creamy, dairy-free version of this latte.

## Pairing Suggestions:

- **Almond Croissants**: The buttery richness of almond croissants complements the nutty flavor of the Hazelnut Latte, creating a perfect pairing.
- **Chocolate Biscotti**: A crunchy chocolate biscotti adds a delightful texture and sweetness that enhances the flavor profile of the latte.
- **Apple Slices with Almond Butter**: The sweetness of apples paired with the creamy almond butter is a refreshing contrast to the rich, nutty latte.

## Interesting Fact:

Did you know that hazelnuts are rich in healthy fats, antioxidants, and vitamins? These little nuts not only provide a unique, earthy flavor but also offer numerous health benefits, including improved heart health and skin.

## Cultural Connection:

Hazelnuts have been a cherished ingredient in European and Middle Eastern cuisines for centuries, especially in desserts and sweets. The Hazelnut Latte is a modern twist on this tradition, blending the rich, comforting flavors of hazelnuts with the beloved espresso culture. It's a nod to the timeless pairing of coffee and nuts, enjoyed by coffee lovers around the world.

# Almond Joy Latte

*Craving a decadent treat that combines the rich flavor of espresso with the creamy goodness of chocolate and almond? Look no further than the Almond Joy Latte! Inspired by the classic candy bar, this indulgent drink layers a bold espresso shot with sweet, nutty almond syrup, smooth chocolate, and a frothy milk base. It's the perfect coffee experience for those who love their lattes with a twist of chocolate and a hint of toasted almond flavor. Get ready to savor a latte that's as comforting as it is delicious.*

## Ingredients:

- 1 shot (1 ounce) of espresso
- 1 cup steamed milk (dairy or non-dairy such as oat, almond, or soy milk)
- 2 tbsps almond syrup
- 1 tbsp chocolate syrup or cocoa powder
- [Optional] Whipped cream (or coconut whipped cream for a dairy-free option)
- [Optional] Chopped almonds for garnish
- [Optional] Drizzle of chocolate or caramel syrup for extra sweetness

## Instructions:

1. **Brew the espresso**: Brew one shot of espresso using your preferred method (e.g., espresso machine, Aeropress, or stovetop Moka pot).
2. **Steam the milk**: Steam your milk (or non-dairy milk) using a milk frother or steam wand until it's hot and frothy.
3. **Combine the syrups**: In a separate cup, mix the almond syrup and chocolate syrup (or cocoa powder). Stir to combine.
4. **Combine the espresso and syrups**: Pour the freshly brewed espresso into your cup and add the almond-chocolate syrup mixture. Stir well to combine the flavors.
5. **Add the steamed milk**: Pour the steamed milk into the mug, holding back the froth with a spoon. Spoon the froth on top to create a beautiful, creamy finish.
6. **Top and garnish**: For an indulgent touch, top with whipped cream (or coconut whipped cream) and garnish with chopped almonds or a drizzle of chocolate syrup.

## Tips and Recommendations:

- **Sweetness adjustment**: If you prefer a sweeter latte, feel free to add more almond or chocolate syrup to taste.
- **Non-dairy option**: Oat milk or almond milk are both excellent choices for a smooth, creamy texture that pairs perfectly with the almond and chocolate flavors.

- **Chocolate variation**: If you love an extra chocolatey drink, use a rich dark chocolate syrup or melted dark chocolate for a more intense flavor.
- **Frozen twist**: For a summer treat, serve your Almond Joy Latte over ice for a refreshing iced latte version.

## Variations:

- **Almond Joy Mocha**: Add a little extra cocoa powder or chocolate syrup for a more intense chocolate flavor, creating an indulgent mocha-inspired treat.
- **Vegan Almond Joy Latte**: Use plant-based milk and top with coconut whipped cream for a fully vegan version of this luxurious latte.
- **Iced Almond Joy Latte**: Brew the espresso and allow it to cool, then pour it over ice and top with chilled steamed milk and almond-chocolate syrup.

## Pairing Suggestions:

- **Almond Biscotti**: Crunchy almond biscotti is a perfect match, enhancing the almond flavor and providing a satisfying contrast to the creamy latte.
- **Chocolate Croissants**: For a truly indulgent experience, pair this latte with a warm chocolate croissant to complement the chocolatey richness of the drink.
- **Fruit and Nut Bar**: A fruit and nut bar with almonds and dried fruits will complement the nutty undertones of the latte and add a healthy snack option to your coffee break.

## Interesting Fact:

Did you know that almonds are rich in vitamin E, magnesium, and healthy fats, making them a nutritious addition to your diet? Beyond their health benefits, almonds also provide a wonderful nutty flavor that pairs beautifully with coffee.

# Peppermint Mocha

*Bring a burst of festive cheer to your coffee routine with the Peppermint Mocha! A perfect winter indulgence, this drink combines the bold richness of espresso with the refreshing taste of peppermint and smooth chocolate. It's a delightful mix of minty freshness and velvety sweetness, topped off with whipped cream and a sprinkle of cocoa. Whether you're cozying up by the fire or enjoying a holiday gathering, this Peppermint Mocha will keep you in the spirit all season long.*

## Ingredients:

- 1 shot (1 ounce) of espresso
- 1 cup steamed milk (dairy or non-dairy such as oat, almond, or soy milk)
- 2 tbsps chocolate syrup
- 1/4 tsp peppermint extract
- [Optional] Whipped cream (or coconut whipped cream for a dairy-free option)
- [Optional] Crushed peppermint candy or cocoa powder for garnish

## Instructions:

1. **Brew the espresso**: Brew one shot of espresso using your preferred method (e.g., espresso machine, Aeropress, or stovetop Moka pot).
2. **Steam the milk**: Steam your milk (or non-dairy milk) using a milk frother or steam wand until it's hot and frothy.
3. **Prepare the chocolate mixture**: In a separate cup, combine the chocolate syrup with the peppermint extract. Stir to mix.
4. **Combine espresso and syrup**: Pour the freshly brewed espresso into your cup and add the chocolate-peppermint mixture. Stir well to blend the flavors.
5. **Add steamed milk**: Pour the steamed milk into the cup, holding back the froth with a spoon. Spoon the froth on top for a smooth finish.
6. **Top and garnish**: For extra indulgence, top with whipped cream (or coconut whipped cream) and garnish with crushed peppermint candy or a sprinkle of cocoa powder.

## Tips and Recommendations:

- **Adjust the sweetness**: If you prefer a sweeter drink, increase the amount of chocolate syrup or add a little sugar to taste.
- **Non-dairy option**: Oat milk is an excellent choice for a rich, creamy texture, while almond or soy milk adds a subtle nutty flavor.
- **Peppermint intensity**: If you enjoy a stronger mint flavor, increase the peppermint extract to 1/2 teaspoon.
- **Iced version**: For a refreshing twist, brew the espresso ahead of time, allow it to cool, and serve the drink over ice for an iced Peppermint Mocha.

## Variations:

- **Vegan Peppermint Mocha**: Use non-dairy milk and top with coconut whipped cream for a fully vegan treat.
- **Peppermint White Mocha**: Swap out the chocolate syrup for white chocolate syrup for a sweeter, creamier version of this drink.
- **Peppermint Mocha Frappé**: Blend the espresso, milk, chocolate syrup, peppermint extract, and ice together for a frosty, blended version of this holiday favorite.

## Pairing Suggestions:

- **Peppermint Bark**: The cool, crisp peppermint bark will complement the minty richness of your Peppermint Mocha, creating a perfect pairing.
- **Chocolate Chip Cookies**: The gooey chocolate and mint flavors blend seamlessly with this classic cookie, making it a delicious snack to enjoy with your mocha.
- **Cinnamon Buns**: Warm cinnamon buns pair beautifully with the cool freshness of peppermint, balancing the flavors in this indulgent drink.

## Interesting Fact:

Peppermint has been used for centuries as a natural remedy to soothe digestive issues and headaches. Its cool, refreshing taste is not only delicious but also provides a burst of energy and invigoration!

## Cultural Connection:

While the Peppermint Mocha is often associated with holiday seasons and festive gatherings, it has become a year-round favorite for many coffee lovers. Its origins trace back to the growing popularity of flavored coffee drinks in the 1990s, with peppermint becoming a go-to holiday flavor in coffee shops across the world.

# Raspberry Mocha

*Treat yourself to the irresistible combination of fruity sweetness and rich coffee with a Raspberry Mocha. This decadent espresso drink combines the boldness of freshly brewed espresso with a luscious raspberry syrup and velvety chocolate, creating a flavor profile that's both refreshing and indulgent. It's a perfect drink for anyone who loves a little twist on the classic mocha and desires a fruity burst with every sip. A beautiful balance of sweet and tart, the Raspberry Mocha will quickly become your new favorite espresso-based treat.*

## Ingredients:

- 1 shot (1 ounce) of espresso
- 1 cup steamed milk (dairy or non-dairy, such as oat, almond, or soy milk)
- 2 tbsps chocolate syrup
- 2 tbsps raspberry syrup (or fresh raspberry puree)
- [Optional] Whipped cream (or non-dairy whipped cream for a vegan option)
- [Optional] Fresh raspberries for garnish

## Instructions:

1. **Brew the espresso**: Brew one shot of espresso using your preferred method (e.g., espresso machine, Aeropress, or stovetop Moka pot).
2. **Steam the milk**: Steam your milk (or non-dairy milk) using a milk frother or steam wand until it's hot and frothy.
3. **Mix the syrups**: In a separate cup, combine the chocolate syrup and raspberry syrup (or fresh raspberry puree) together. Stir until well mixed.
4. **Combine espresso and syrup**: Pour the freshly brewed espresso into your cup and add the raspberry-chocolate syrup mixture. Stir to blend the flavors evenly.
5. **Add steamed milk**: Pour the steamed milk into the cup, holding back the froth with a spoon. Spoon the froth on top to finish.
6. **Top and garnish**: For extra indulgence, top with whipped cream (or non-dairy whipped cream) and garnish with fresh raspberries for a vibrant, fresh touch.

## Tips and Recommendations:

- **Adjust the sweetness**: If you prefer a sweeter drink, add a little more chocolate syrup or raspberry syrup to taste.
- **Non-dairy option**: Oat milk is an excellent choice for a creamy texture, while almond or soy milk adds a light, nutty flavor.
- **Fresh raspberry puree**: If you can't find raspberry syrup, use fresh raspberries blended with a little sugar to create a natural raspberry puree.
- **Chilled version**: For a refreshing twist, chill the espresso and serve the drink over ice for an iced Raspberry Mocha.

## Variations:

- **Vegan Raspberry Mocha**: Use non-dairy milk and top with coconut whipped cream for a fully vegan version of this treat.
- **Raspberry White Mocha**: Replace the chocolate syrup with white chocolate syrup for a lighter, sweeter take on this drink.
- **Iced Raspberry Mocha**: Brew the espresso ahead of time and allow it to cool. Combine with the syrups, milk, and ice for a delicious chilled version.

## Pairing Suggestions:

- **Chocolate-Dipped Strawberries**: The sweet and tangy combination of chocolate-dipped strawberries complements the rich and fruity Raspberry Mocha perfectly.
- **Almond Biscotti**: The crunchy texture of almond biscotti adds a satisfying contrast to the smooth, creamy mocha.
- **Vanilla Scones**: A buttery vanilla scone will pair beautifully with the raspberry and chocolate flavors in the drink.

## Interesting Fact:

Did you know that raspberries are rich in antioxidants and vitamin C? Not only do they provide a burst of flavor, but they also pack a healthy punch!

## Cultural Connection:

The mocha is a coffee drink that traces its origins to the city of Mocha, Yemen, historically a major port for the coffee trade. Today, it's known as a combination of espresso and chocolate, enjoyed worldwide. The addition of raspberry adds a modern, fruity twist that's become a popular variation of the classic mocha in cafés everywhere.

# Coconut Mocha

*Indulge in the tropical fusion of rich coffee and creamy coconut with this Coconut Mocha. Combining the bold flavor of espresso, velvety chocolate, and the delicate sweetness of coconut milk, this mocha creates a luxurious and exotic twist on a classic favorite. Perfect for when you're craving something a little more indulgent and tropical, the Coconut Mocha is a decadent drink that brings the best of both worlds - smooth, creamy coconut and deep, bold coffee.*

## Ingredients:

- 1 shot (1 ounce) of espresso
- 1 cup steamed coconut milk (or canned coconut milk for extra creaminess)
- 2 tbsps chocolate syrup
- 1 tbsp coconut syrup (or coconut cream for a richer taste)
- [Optional] Shredded toasted coconut for garnish
- [Optional] Whipped cream (or coconut whipped cream for a vegan version)

## Instructions:

1. **Brew the espresso**: Brew a shot of espresso using your preferred method (e.g., espresso machine, Aeropress, or stovetop Moka pot).
2. **Steam the coconut milk**: In a milk frother or steam wand, steam your coconut milk until it's hot and frothy. For a creamier texture, use canned coconut milk.
3. **Mix the syrups**: In a separate cup, combine the chocolate syrup and coconut syrup (or coconut cream). Stir well until fully blended.
4. **Combine espresso and syrup**: Pour the brewed espresso into a mug or glass, then add the chocolate-coconut syrup mixture. Stir to combine.
5. **Add steamed coconut milk**: Pour the steamed coconut milk into the espresso-syrup mixture, holding back the froth with a spoon. Spoon the froth on top.
6. **Top and garnish**: For an extra touch of coconut flavor, top with whipped cream (or coconut whipped cream) and a sprinkle of toasted shredded coconut.

## Tips and Recommendations:

- **Adjust the sweetness**: If you prefer a sweeter drink, add a bit more chocolate syrup or coconut syrup to taste.
- **Coconut milk varieties**: Canned coconut milk provides a richer, creamier texture, while carton coconut milk (usually found in the refrigerated section) is lighter and more fluid.
- **Coconut flavor boost**: For an even stronger coconut flavor, you can add a dash of coconut extract to the syrup mixture.

- **Iced option**: For a refreshing iced version, brew the espresso ahead of time, cool it, and serve the drink over ice.

## Variations:

- **Vegan Coconut Mocha**: Use coconut whipped cream and make sure to choose non-dairy chocolate syrup to keep the drink fully vegan.
- **White Coconut Mocha**: Substitute the chocolate syrup for white chocolate syrup for a lighter, sweeter version of the coconut mocha.
- **Iced Coconut Mocha**: Make this drink chilled by using iced coconut milk and espresso, and serve it over ice with whipped coconut cream on top.

## Pairing Suggestions:

- **Coconut Macaroons**: The chewy, sweet coconut macaroons pair beautifully with the rich coconut mocha, enhancing its tropical vibe.
- **Almond Croissants**: The buttery, nutty flavor of almond croissants complements the smooth, creamy coconut mocha perfectly.
- **Dark Chocolate Truffles**: The richness of dark chocolate truffles pairs wonderfully with the deep flavors of the espresso and the sweetness of the coconut mocha.

## Interesting Fact:

Did you know that coconut is often used in traditional desserts across Southeast Asia and the Caribbean? Its rich flavor and creamy texture make it a perfect complement to coffee and chocolate in this tropical mocha.

## Cultural Connection:

Coconut is a staple ingredient in many tropical regions around the world, from Southeast Asia to the Caribbean. It's celebrated for its versatility and rich flavor. In this Coconut Mocha, the tropical notes of coconut perfectly balance the deep, roasted flavors of espresso, adding a new twist to the beloved mocha. This drink embodies the spirit of coffee culture - innovative, comforting, and always full of surprises.

# Unique Lattes and Specialties:

# White Chocolate Mocha

*Indulge in the rich, velvety allure of a White Chocolate Mocha, a luxurious blend of smooth espresso and creamy white chocolate. This sweet and satisfying drink perfectly balances bold coffee with the delicate sweetness of white chocolate, creating an irresistible treat that coffee lovers will adore. Cozy up with this delightful mocha and enjoy the warmth of a café experience right in your own home.*

## Ingredients:

- 1 shot (1 ounce) of espresso
- 1 cup steamed milk of choice (whole, oat, or almond milk for a vegan option)
- 2 tbsps white chocolate chips or finely chopped white chocolate
- 1 tbsp whipped cream, for garnish (optional)
- [Optional] 1/2 tsp vanilla extract for added flavor depth

## Instructions:

1. Brew a fresh shot of espresso using your preferred method.
2. In a small pot or milk frother, combine the steamed milk and white chocolate chips.
3. Heat the mixture on low, stirring constantly until the white chocolate melts and fully blends with the milk, creating a creamy base.
4. Pour the espresso into a cup and gently add the white chocolate milk mixture, stirring to combine.
5. Top with a dollop of whipped cream, if desired, and serve immediately.

## Tips and Recommendations:

- For a sweeter mocha, add an extra tablespoon of white chocolate or a splash of vanilla syrup.
- If you prefer a stronger coffee flavor, use a double shot of espresso instead of a single.

## Variations:

- **Mint White Chocolate Mocha**: Add a drop or two of peppermint extract to the milk mixture for a festive twist.
- **Caramel White Chocolate Mocha**: Drizzle caramel sauce over the whipped cream for an added layer of richness.
- **Iced White Chocolate Mocha**: Use cold milk and pour over ice for a refreshing cold version.

## Pairing Suggestions:

- Enjoy with a slice of almond biscotti to enhance the nutty, creamy flavors.
- Pair with buttery shortbread cookies for a perfectly sweet companion.
- For a brunch treat, serve alongside a warm pastry or muffin.

## Interesting Fact:

Did you know that white chocolate contains no cocoa solids? It's made primarily from cocoa butter, giving it a creamy texture and milder flavor compared to traditional chocolate.

## Cultural Connection:

The White Chocolate Mocha has become a modern favorite in cafés across the globe, blending American coffee culture's love for indulgence with the traditional Italian espresso.

# S'mores Latte

*Indulge in the nostalgic flavors of a campfire classic with this S'mores Latte! Imagine the rich essence of espresso, velvety steamed milk, and sweet hints of chocolate and marshmallow, topped with graham cracker crumbs. This cozy, sweet latte combines the beloved flavors of s'mores into a delightful, warming drink perfect for chilly days or whenever you crave a taste of childhood memories by the fire.*

### Ingredients:

- 1 shot (1 ounce) of espresso
- 3/4 cup steamed milk of choice (whole, oat, or almond milk)
- 1 tbsp chocolate syrup
- 1 tbsp marshmallow fluff (or 1-2 marshmallows, toasted)
- 1 tsp crushed graham crackers, for garnish
- [Optional] 1 tbsp whipped cream, for garnish

### Instructions:

1. Brew a shot of espresso using your preferred method.
2. In a small pot or milk frother, steam the milk until it's hot and frothy.
3. Pour the espresso into a mug and stir in the chocolate syrup until fully combined.
4. Gently add the steamed milk to the espresso mixture.
5. Top with a dollop of marshmallow fluff or toasted marshmallows.
6. Sprinkle crushed graham crackers over the marshmallow topping and add whipped cream if desired.
7. Serve immediately and enjoy!

### Tips and Recommendations:

- To add a smoky flavor, lightly toast the marshmallow fluff using a kitchen torch before adding the graham cracker crumbs.
- For an extra rich taste, use chocolate milk instead of regular milk.

### Variations:

- **Mint S'mores Latte**: Add a drop of peppermint extract to the milk for a holiday twist.
- **Salted Caramel S'mores Latte**: Drizzle salted caramel sauce over the whipped cream and graham cracker crumbs for a sweet-salty flavor combination.
- **Iced S'mores Latte**: Make this drink cold by pouring espresso and chocolate syrup over ice, then add cold milk and garnish with marshmallows and graham crackers.

### Pairing Suggestions:

- Try with a slice of chocolate cake for an extra indulgent treat.
- Perfectly complements cinnamon rolls or buttery shortbread cookies.
- Enjoy alongside a toasted marshmallow or brownie for a full s'mores experience.

### Interesting Fact:

Did you know that s'mores are an American camping tradition dating back to the 1920s? The name "s'mores" is short for "some more," referring to the craving for "some more" of this delicious treat.

### Cultural Connection:

S'mores are deeply rooted in American culture, often associated with camping trips and childhood memories around a campfire. Bringing this into a latte combines two beloved pastimes: coffee culture and classic campfire treats.

# Lavender Latte

*Indulge in the soothing, floral notes of a Lavender Latte, where the subtle essence of lavender blends beautifully with rich espresso and creamy milk. This unique latte offers a taste of tranquility with every sip, inspired by the aromatic lavender fields of Provence. Perfect for unwinding, this drink creates a peaceful, café-style experience at home.*

## Ingredients:

- 1 shot (1 ounce) of espresso
- 3/4 cup steamed milk of choice (whole, oat, or almond milk)
- 1 tbsp lavender simple syrup (see note below)
- [Optional] 1/2 tsp vanilla extract for added depth
- [Optional] Dried lavender flowers, for garnishLavender Simple Syrup:1/4 cup water
- 1/4 cup sugar
- 1 tbsp dried culinary lavender

## Instructions:

1. To make the lavender syrup, combine water, sugar, and dried lavender in a small pot over medium heat. Stir until sugar dissolves, then let simmer for 2-3 minutes. Strain and allow to cool.
2. Brew a shot of espresso using your preferred method.
3. In a milk frother or saucepan, steam the milk until hot and frothy.
4. Add the lavender syrup and vanilla extract (if using) to the espresso in a mug.
5. Pour the steamed milk into the mug, stirring gently to blend.
6. Garnish with a sprinkle of dried lavender flowers, if desired, and enjoy immediately.

## Tips and Recommendations:

- Start with a small amount of lavender syrup and adjust to taste, as lavender has a strong, aromatic flavor.
- For a stronger coffee flavor, add an extra shot of espresso.

## Variations:

- **Iced Lavender Latte**: Use cold milk and pour the lavender syrup and espresso over ice for a refreshing, floral latte.
  - **Honey Lavender Latte**: Add a drizzle of honey for extra sweetness and a hint of warmth.
  - **Vanilla Lavender Latte**: Add a splash of vanilla syrup for a delightful combination of floral and creamy notes.

## Pairing Suggestions:

- Complement with a buttery croissant for a light, French-inspired treat.
- Pairs wonderfully with lemon scones or shortbread cookies for an afternoon indulgence.
- Serve alongside a lavender-infused dessert for an elegant twist.

## Interesting Fact:

Did you know lavender has been used in traditional medicine for centuries for its calming properties? It's believed to reduce stress and promote relaxation, making it a perfect addition to a cozy latte.

## Cultural Connection:

Lavender has long been celebrated in French culture, particularly in Provence, where lavender fields stretch for miles. Incorporating this beloved flower into a latte brings a touch of French charm and elegance to your coffee routine.

# Honey Cinnamon Latte

*Warm up with the cozy sweetness of a Honey Cinnamon Latte, where rich espresso meets the comforting flavors of honey and cinnamon. This aromatic blend is perfect for a chilly day, offering a delightful touch of sweetness balanced with spice. Embrace this homemade twist on a café favorite and enjoy the cozy taste of autumn in every sip.*

## Ingredients:

- 1 shot (1 ounce) of espresso
- 3/4 cup steamed milk of choice (whole, oat, or almond milk)
- 1 tbsp honey (or maple syrup for a vegan option)
- 1/4 tsp ground cinnamon
- [Optional] Cinnamon stick, for garnish

## Instructions:

1. Brew a shot of espresso using your preferred method.
2. In a small bowl, mix the honey and ground cinnamon until well combined.
3. In a milk frother or small pot, steam the milk until hot and frothy.
4. Add the honey-cinnamon mixture to the espresso in a mug and stir to blend.
5. Pour the steamed milk over the espresso, stirring gently to incorporate.
6. Garnish with a cinnamon stick or a sprinkle of cinnamon on top if desired.

## Tips and Recommendations:

- Adjust the amount of honey to suit your sweetness preference.
- For a more intense cinnamon flavor, add a small pinch of ground cinnamon directly to the espresso before blending.

## Variations:

- **Iced Honey Cinnamon Latte**: Use cold milk and pour over ice for a refreshing, sweet latte.
- **Vanilla Honey Cinnamon Latte**: Add a splash of vanilla extract for a layered, cozy flavor.
- **Spiced Honey Latte**: Mix a pinch of nutmeg or a dash of cardamom for an exotic twist.

## Pairing Suggestions:

- Enjoy with a warm slice of banana bread for a satisfying morning treat.
- Pairs well with buttery shortbread cookies or ginger snaps.
- Serve alongside an apple pastry for a full seasonal experience.

## Interesting Fact:

Did you know that cinnamon is one of the oldest spices, valued for its warming properties in traditional medicine? Its sweet and spicy profile makes it a popular choice for autumn-inspired drinks worldwide.

## Cultural Connection:

Honey and cinnamon have both been prized for centuries in various cultures for their healing properties, especially in the Middle East and Mediterranean regions. This latte brings these ancient flavors into the modern coffee ritual, adding a touch of tradition to your cup.

# Matcha Latte

*Experience the vibrant, earthy flavors of Japan with this Matcha Latte, a green tea-based drink that brings calm and focus with every sip. This silky latte blends high-quality matcha powder with warm, frothy milk, creating a beautifully rich and comforting drink that's both energizing and soothing. Enjoy the bright, vegetal notes of matcha in a creamy, balanced latte that's as delightful to look at as it is to taste.*

## Ingredients:

- 1 tsp matcha powder
- 1/4 cup hot water (not boiling)
- 3/4 cup steamed milk of choice (oat, almond, or whole milk)
- [Optional] 1-2 tsps honey or agave syrup for sweetness

## Instructions:

1. In a small bowl, sift the matcha powder to remove any lumps.
2. Add the hot water to the matcha and whisk briskly using a bamboo whisk or small handheld frother until the matcha is smooth and frothy.
3. In a milk frother or small pot, steam the milk until hot and foamy.
4. Pour the matcha mixture into a mug, then gently pour the steamed milk over it.
5. Stir in honey or agave if desired, and enjoy immediately.

## Tips and Recommendations:

- Use a high-quality, ceremonial-grade matcha for the best flavor and vibrant color.
- Adjust the sweetness level to your preference; a little honey or agave enhances the natural sweetness of the matcha without overpowering its flavor.

## Variations:

- **Iced Matcha Latte**: Prepare the matcha with cold milk and pour over ice for a refreshing twist.
  - **Vanilla Matcha Latte**: Add a dash of vanilla extract for a sweet, smooth flavor profile.
  - **Coconut Matcha Latte**: Substitute coconut milk for a tropical twist that pairs beautifully with the matcha.

## Pairing Suggestions:

- Pair with light, buttery pastries like shortbread or almond biscotti.
- Enjoy with fresh fruit, particularly berries, to balance the earthy matcha flavor.
- Serve alongside a small matcha-flavored dessert, like a matcha macaron or mochi, for a cohesive treat.

## Interesting Fact:

Did you know that matcha has been a part of Japanese tea ceremonies for over 800 years? Its unique preparation and vibrant color have made it a symbol of mindfulness and focus.

## Cultural Connection:

Matcha's popularity has spread worldwide, but its roots are deeply embedded in Japanese culture, where it has long been appreciated for its calming effects and health benefits. Savoring a Matcha Latte is a simple way to embrace this time-honored tradition in a modern format.

# Golden Milk Latte

*Indulge in the warm, soothing flavors of a Golden Milk Latte, a comforting blend of turmeric, spices, and creamy milk. This vibrant drink is inspired by traditional Ayurvedic practices and is known for its anti-inflammatory benefits. The earthy turmeric pairs beautifully with ginger and cinnamon, creating a latte that's both nourishing and delicious. Perfect for unwinding or as a morning pick-me-up, the Golden Milk Latte is a golden treasure in every cup.*

## Ingredients:

- 1 cup milk of choice (oat, almond, or whole milk)
- 1/2 tsp ground turmeric
- 1/4 tsp ground cinnamon
- 1/4 tsp ground ginger
- 1 tsp honey or maple syrup (optional for sweetness)
- Pinch of black pepper
- [Optional] 1/4 tsp vanilla extract for added flavor

## Instructions:

1. In a small saucepan over medium heat, combine the milk, turmeric, cinnamon, ginger, and black pepper.
2. Whisk continuously until the milk is warm and the spices are fully dissolved.
3. Add honey or maple syrup and vanilla extract, if using, and continue to heat until steaming.
4. Pour the mixture into a mug. For a frothy texture, use a milk frother or whisk vigorously before serving.
5. Garnish with a sprinkle of cinnamon on top and enjoy warm.

## Tips and Recommendations:

- Adjust the turmeric amount to taste if you prefer a milder or stronger flavor.
- For added creaminess, use full-fat coconut milk or mix in a splash of heavy cream.
- Black pepper helps with the absorption of turmeric's active ingredient, curcumin, so don't skip it!

## Variations:

- **Iced Golden Milk Latte**: Prepare as directed, then let cool, pour over ice, and enjoy as a refreshing cold drink.
- **Spiced Vanilla Golden Milk Latte**: Add a dash of vanilla extract and a pinch of cardamom for a fragrant twist.
- **Coconut Golden Milk Latte**: Substitute half the milk with coconut milk for a tropical, richer flavor profile.

## Pairing Suggestions:

- Pair with almond biscotti or ginger cookies for a delightful flavor combination.
- Enjoy with a slice of lemon loaf or a spiced carrot muffin to complement the latte's warm spices.
- Serve alongside dried apricots or figs for a balanced, slightly sweet accompaniment.

## Interesting Fact:

Did you know that turmeric has been used in India for over 4,000 years? It's a key ingredient in both cooking and Ayurvedic medicine, celebrated for its healing properties.

## Cultural Connection:

Golden milk, or "haldi doodh," is a traditional Indian drink that has been cherished for generations. Originally used as a natural remedy, it has now gained global popularity as a wellness beverage.

# Turmeric Latte

*Embrace the warmth and healing power of a Turmeric Latte, a soothing blend known for its golden glow and wellness benefits. This creamy, spiced latte combines turmeric with ginger, cinnamon, and a hint of sweetness for a delicious drink that's both comforting and energizing. With its origins rooted in Ayurvedic tradition, the Turmeric Latte offers a unique and healthful alternative to classic coffee, perfect for chilly mornings or winding down in the evening.*

## Ingredients:

- 1 cup milk of choice (almond, oat, or dairy milk)
- 1/2 tsp ground turmeric
- 1/4 tsp ground ginger
- 1/4 tsp ground cinnamon
- 1 tsp maple syrup or honey (optional for sweetness)
- Pinch of black pepper
- [Optional] 1/4 tsp vanilla extract for extra flavor

## Instructions:

1. In a small saucepan over medium heat, combine the milk, turmeric, ginger, cinnamon, and black pepper.
2. Whisk the ingredients together until the milk is hot but not boiling.
3. Add maple syrup or honey, and vanilla extract, if desired, stirring until well incorporated.
4. Pour the mixture into a mug, frothing the milk with a milk frother or whisk for a creamy texture if desired.
5. Garnish with a light dusting of cinnamon on top. Enjoy your warm, spiced Turmeric Latte!

## Tips and Recommendations:

- For a slightly milder flavor, reduce the turmeric to 1/4 teaspoon.
- Black pepper is essential for enhancing the absorption of turmeric's benefits.
- Substitute coconut milk for a creamier, richer flavor that pairs well with the spices.

## Variations:

- **Iced Turmeric Latte**: Cool the mixture and pour over ice for a refreshing take.
- **Vanilla-Spice Turmeric Latte**: Add a dash of vanilla and a pinch of cardamom for a sweet, aromatic twist.
- **Coconut Turmeric Latte**: Replace half of the milk with coconut milk for a tropical richness.

## Pairing Suggestions:

- Enjoy with almond biscotti or shortbread cookies to balance the spice.
- Try a slice of banana bread or a handful of dried apricots for a complementary flavor.
- Pair with a date or nut-based energy ball for a healthful, energizing snack.

## Interesting Fact:

Did you know turmeric is often called "Indian Saffron" due to its vibrant color and historical roots in Indian cuisine and medicine?

## Cultural Connection:

This drink is inspired by "haldi doodh" (turmeric milk), a traditional Indian remedy that has been enjoyed for centuries for its health benefits and warming qualities. Today, the Turmeric Latte has gained popularity around the world as a delicious wellness drink.

# Rosemary Infused Coffee

*Savor the delicate, earthy aroma of rosemary paired with the bold richness of coffee in this unique and aromatic infusion. Rosemary Infused Coffee offers a sophisticated twist on your daily brew, bringing a touch of herbal freshness to every sip. Perfect for those who love to experiment with flavor, this drink adds an unexpected layer to coffee that's both invigorating and calming - a delightful experience for any time of day.*

## Ingredients:

- 1 cup freshly brewed coffee (French press or pour-over recommended)
- 1 small sprig fresh rosemary
- 1 tsp honey or maple syrup (optional for sweetness)
- 1/4 cup steamed milk of choice (optional for creaminess)

## Instructions:

1. Brew a fresh cup of coffee using your preferred method.
2. Place the rosemary sprig in the coffee and let it steep for 3-5 minutes, depending on your desired intensity.
3. Remove the rosemary and add honey or maple syrup for sweetness, if desired.
4. Stir in the steamed milk, if you prefer a creamier version.
5. Pour into a cup, garnish with a small rosemary sprig for a beautiful presentation, and enjoy.

## Tips and Recommendations:

- Adjust the rosemary steeping time based on your flavor preference; longer steeping will create a stronger rosemary flavor.
- For an even richer taste, try adding a splash of almond or oat milk.
- This coffee pairs beautifully with a pinch of sea salt to enhance the herbal notes.

## Variations:

- **Iced Rosemary Coffee**: Cool the infused coffee and pour over ice for a refreshing cold drink.
- **Rosemary Maple Latte**: Sweeten with maple syrup instead of honey and add steamed milk for a smooth, slightly sweet variation.
- **Cinnamon-Rosemary Coffee**: Add a small cinnamon stick to the coffee while it steeps for a warm, spicy note that complements the rosemary.

## Pairing Suggestions:

- Enjoy with a buttery croissant or almond biscotti to balance the coffee's herbal undertones.
- Pair with a slice of lemon loaf or a piece of dark chocolate for a sophisticated flavor combination.
- Rosemary coffee also complements savory breakfast items like avocado toast or tomato bruschetta.

## Interesting Fact:

Did you know rosemary was traditionally used to enhance memory and concentration? Its herbal aroma is said to have cognitive-boosting properties that pair perfectly with coffee's natural caffeine kick.

## Cultural Connection:

Herbs like rosemary have long been used in Mediterranean cuisine and beverages for their unique flavors and health benefits. This infusion celebrates the age-old practice of combining herbs with daily drinks, bringing a Mediterranean touch to your coffee ritual.

# Cardamom Coffee

*Indulge in the warm, aromatic flavors of Cardamom Coffee, a delightful fusion of robust coffee and the exotic, slightly sweet spice of cardamom. Inspired by Middle Eastern and Indian coffee traditions, this recipe adds an exciting layer of complexity with its bold, fragrant taste. Whether you're a coffee aficionado or someone eager to explore new flavors, this coffee offers a unique and comforting experience that will leave you craving more.*

## Ingredients:

- 1 shot (1 ounce) of espresso or 1/2 cup brewed coffee
- 1/4 tsp ground cardamom
- 1 tsp honey or maple syrup (optional for sweetness)
- 1/4 cup steamed milk of your choice (almond, oat, or coconut milk for dairy-free options)
- [Optional] Pinch of ground cinnamon or nutmeg for garnish

## Instructions:

1. Brew a shot of espresso or prepare your preferred method of brewed coffee.
2. In a small bowl, combine the brewed coffee or espresso with ground cardamom, stirring well to evenly distribute the spice.
3. Add honey or maple syrup for sweetness if desired.
4. Steam your milk of choice until it's frothy and hot (but not boiling).
5. Pour the spiced coffee into a cup, then gently add the steamed milk, allowing it to form a creamy layer.
6. Optionally, garnish with a pinch of cinnamon or nutmeg to add extra warmth and visual appeal.
7. Stir and enjoy the rich, aromatic flavor of your Cardamom Coffee.

## Tips and Recommendations:

- Adjust the amount of cardamom based on your taste preference; add more for a stronger spice flavor.
  - For a creamier version, use coconut milk or a mix of oat and almond milk.
  - If you prefer a sweeter coffee, try adding a dash of vanilla syrup or a sprinkle of brown sugar.

## Variations:

- **Iced Cardamom Coffee**: Let the brewed coffee cool, then pour it over ice and add cold milk for a refreshing twist.
- **Cardamom Mocha**: Add 1 tablespoon of cocoa powder or chocolate syrup for a rich mocha version of this spiced coffee.
- **Cardamom Latte**: Increase the milk to 1/2 cup for a creamier latte-style drink, perfect for those who prefer less coffee intensity.

## Pairing Suggestions:

- Pair with a warm slice of gingerbread cake or a honey-drizzled almond biscotti to enhance the coffee's spicy sweetness.
- Enjoy with a light, fluffy croissant or a piece of dark chocolate for a perfect afternoon treat.
- A savory option: Serve with a buttery avocado toast to balance the spice with richness.

## Interesting Fact:

Did you know that cardamom is often called the "queen of spices"? It's one of the most expensive spices in the world, second only to saffron, and has been used for centuries in culinary traditions from the Middle East to Scandinavia.

## Cultural Connection:

Cardamom coffee has its roots in the rich coffee-drinking cultures of the Middle East and South Asia. In countries like India and Turkey, cardamom is often added to coffee and chai to enhance the drink's complexity and aroma. This spiced coffee is a beloved way to bring warmth and comfort, especially during cold seasons or social gatherings.

# Maple Pecan Latte

*Indulge in the irresistible warmth of a Maple Pecan Latte, a comforting drink that combines the rich flavors of roasted pecans with the sweet, earthy notes of maple syrup. This delightful beverage offers a perfect balance of nuttiness and sweetness, making it a favorite for cozy afternoons or chilly mornings. Whether you're enjoying it at home or sharing it with friends, this latte brings a touch of fall to every sip with its creamy, aromatic finish.*

## Ingredients:

- 1 shot (1 ounce) of espresso or 1/2 cup brewed coffee
- 1/4 cup steamed milk of your choice (almond, oat, or coconut milk for dairy-free options)
- 1 tbsp maple syrup
- 1 tbsp pecan butter or pecan syrup
- [Optional] 1/4 tsp ground cinnamon or nutmeg for garnish
- [Optional] Chopped pecans for topping

## Instructions:

1. Brew a shot of espresso or prepare your preferred method of brewed coffee.
2. In a small bowl or jar, mix together the maple syrup and pecan butter (or pecan syrup) until smooth.
3. Steam your milk of choice until hot and frothy (but not boiling).
4. Pour the espresso or brewed coffee into a cup.
5. Add the maple-pecan mixture to the coffee and stir well.
6. Gently pour the steamed milk over the coffee, allowing a creamy texture to form.
7. Optionally, garnish with a sprinkle of ground cinnamon or nutmeg for an extra touch of spice.
8. Top with a few chopped pecans for a delightful crunch and a beautiful finish.
9. Sip and savor the sweet, nutty indulgence of your Maple Pecan Latte!

## Tips and Recommendations:

- If you prefer a stronger nutty flavor, try adding more pecan butter or using roasted pecans to enhance the taste.
- For a dairy-free version, opt for oat milk, which creates a creamy texture without overpowering the flavors.
- Feel free to add more or less maple syrup based on your desired level of sweetness.
- If you want an extra indulgent touch, drizzle a little extra maple syrup on top of the foam.

## Variations:

- **Maple Pecan Iced Latte**: Brew your coffee, then chill it and pour over ice. Add your maple-pecan syrup and cold milk for a refreshing, cool version.
- **Spiced Maple Pecan Latte**: Add a pinch of ground ginger or cloves to the syrup mixture for a spicier kick.
- **Pecan Praline Latte**: Swap the pecan butter for praline syrup for a caramelized twist on this drink.

## Pairing Suggestions:

- Pair with a buttery cinnamon roll or maple scones to complement the sweetness and nuttiness of the latte.
- Enjoy with a light almond croissant or a slice of pecan pie for a delightful coffee-and-dessert experience.
- A savory option: Serve with a cheese and nut platter for a sophisticated pairing that balances the drink's sweetness.

## Interesting Fact:

Did you know that pecans are native to North America and have been enjoyed for centuries by Indigenous people? They are packed with healthy fats, making them a great addition to your diet, especially when paired with coffee!

## Cultural Connection:

The combination of maple syrup and pecans has roots in North American traditions, where maple trees are tapped for their sweet sap, and pecans are a staple in Southern cuisine. This cozy pairing has become a beloved flavor combination, especially during fall, when the warmth of maple and nuts brings comfort and indulgence to every drink.

# Tiramisu Latte

*Indulge in the rich, decadent flavors of a Tiramisu Latte, inspired by the classic Italian dessert. This delightful drink combines the boldness of espresso with the creamy richness of mascarpone (or a vegan alternative) and a touch of cocoa. Infused with vanilla and a hint of coffee liqueur, it brings the essence of tiramisu into your coffee cup, delivering a velvety, comforting experience that transports you straight to Italy with every sip.*

## Ingredients:

- 1 shot (1 ounce) of espresso
- 1/2 cup steamed milk of your choice (oat milk or almond milk work great for a dairy-free version)
- 2 tbsps vegan mascarpone or cashew cream (as a dairy-free substitute)
- 1 tbsp vanilla syrup
- 1 tbsp coffee liqueur (optional)
- 1/2 tsp cocoa powder, for garnish
- [Optional] 1/4 tsp ground cinnamon or nutmeg for added warmth

## Instructions:

1. Brew a shot of espresso using your preferred method.
2. In a small bowl, mix together the vegan mascarpone (or cashew cream) with the vanilla syrup and coffee liqueur (if using) until smooth.
3. Steam your milk of choice until it is hot and frothy.
4. Pour the shot of espresso into a cup, followed by the mascarpone mixture, and stir well to combine.
5. Gently pour the steamed milk into the cup, mixing everything together until smooth.
6. Using a fine mesh sieve, dust the top of your latte with cocoa powder and a pinch of cinnamon or nutmeg for extra flavor and visual appeal.
7. Sip and enjoy the delightful tiramisu-inspired goodness in every cup!

## Tips and Recommendations:

- If you don't have coffee liqueur on hand, a splash of strong brewed coffee or a dash of rum extract will bring out similar flavors.
- For a lighter version, reduce the amount of vanilla syrup and mascarpone.
- If you like a stronger espresso taste, increase the espresso-to-milk ratio or add an extra shot.
- For a richer flavor, try adding a bit more coffee liqueur or a drizzle of chocolate syrup.

## Variations:

- **Iced Tiramisu Latte**: Brew your espresso, then chill it. Pour over ice and add the mascarpone mixture and cold milk for a refreshing twist on the classic latte.
- **Tiramisu Mocha Latte**: Add a teaspoon of melted dark chocolate or chocolate syrup to the mascarpone mixture for a chocolatey indulgence.
- **Vegan Tiramisu Latte**: Ensure all ingredients are dairy-free by using oat milk, cashew cream, and a plant-based vanilla syrup.

## Pairing Suggestions:

- Pair with a slice of classic tiramisu for a perfect match of flavors.
- Enjoy with a buttery almond biscotti or vegan shortbread cookies for a deliciously sweet contrast.
- A savory option: Try with a light vegetable quiche or toasted croissant to balance the richness of the drink.

## Interesting Fact:

Tiramisu, which means "pick me up" in Italian, was first created in the 1960s in the Veneto region of Italy. The drink version gives you that same uplifting feeling in a cup, with espresso, vanilla, and cocoa combining for a deliciously energizing experience.

## Cultural Connection:

Tiramisu is a beloved Italian dessert known for its rich combination of coffee, cocoa, and cream. By transforming this dessert into a latte, we get a delightful new way to experience these classic flavors - perfect for coffee lovers who enjoy indulging in both the traditional and modern sides of Italian cuisine.

# Churro Latte

*Transport your taste buds to a sweet, cinnamon-sugar heaven with this delightful Churro Latte. Inspired by the beloved Spanish and Mexican churros, this warm and comforting coffee combines the aromatic spices of cinnamon and vanilla with a rich espresso base, creating the perfect balance of sweet and spicy. Topped with a frothy milk blend, this latte is a cozy treat that's sure to become a favorite indulgence for those who love both coffee and dessert.*

## Ingredients:

- 1 shot (1 ounce) of espresso
- 1/2 cup steamed milk of your choice (oat milk or almond milk for a dairy-free option)
- 1 tbsp maple syrup or brown sugar
- 1/2 tsp ground cinnamon
- 1/4 tsp vanilla extract
- 1 tbsp coconut whipped cream (optional, for topping)
- 1 tsp cinnamon-sugar (for garnish)
- [Optional] 1/4 tsp ground nutmeg or allspice for extra warmth

## Instructions:

1. Brew a shot of espresso using your preferred method.
2. In a small bowl, combine the cinnamon, vanilla extract, and maple syrup (or brown sugar). Stir until well mixed.
3. Steam your milk of choice until hot and frothy.
4. Pour the espresso into a cup and add the cinnamon-sugar mixture. Stir until fully incorporated.
5. Pour the steamed milk into the cup, gently mixing it with the espresso and cinnamon syrup.
6. Top with a dollop of coconut whipped cream, if using.
7. Sprinkle cinnamon-sugar on top for a finishing touch, and add a pinch of extra cinnamon or nutmeg for added flavor.
8. Sip and enjoy the sweet, spicy goodness of a churro in liquid form!

## Tips and Recommendations:

- For an even sweeter treat, increase the amount of maple syrup or brown sugar.
- If you prefer a dairy-free option, use oat milk or almond milk for a creamy, nutty base that complements the spices.
- Adjust the cinnamon to your taste: add more for a spicier kick or less for a milder flavor.
- For extra foam, use a milk frother or steam wand to achieve a thicker, creamier texture.
- For a vegan topping, opt for coconut or almond-based whipped cream.

## Variations:

- **Iced Churro Latte**: Brew the espresso, then chill it. Pour over ice and top with the cinnamon syrup and cold milk for a refreshing twist on the classic.
- **Churro Mocha Latte**: Add a teaspoon of cocoa powder or chocolate syrup to the espresso and cinnamon mixture for a chocolatey churro experience.
- **Spicy Churro Latte**: Add a pinch of cayenne pepper to the cinnamon syrup for a kick of heat to balance the sweetness.

## Pairing Suggestions:

- Enjoy with a crispy churro for a perfect pairing that combines the flavors of the drink and the dessert.
- Pair with a rich chocolate croissant or a cinnamon roll to enhance the warm, spiced notes of the latte.
- A savory option: Try with a toasted bagel or vegan scone to balance the sweetness of the drink.

## Interesting Fact:

Did you know that churros originated in Spain and were popularized in Latin America and beyond? In many parts of the world, churros are traditionally served with hot chocolate for dipping, creating a deliciously sweet and comforting treat.

## Cultural Connection:

Churros have a deep cultural significance in Spain and Latin America, often enjoyed as a sweet breakfast or afternoon snack. This Churro Latte brings the flavors of this beloved dessert into a coffee drink, making it a fun and indulgent way to celebrate these cultural traditions in every cup.

# Black Forest Coffee

*Indulge in the rich, decadent flavors of the Black Forest Coffee, where the classic pairing of chocolate and cherries meets the boldness of espresso. Inspired by the famous Black Forest cake, this dessert-inspired drink combines the smooth, velvety texture of whipped cream, a hint of cherry syrup, and the deep richness of dark chocolate. Topped with a generous swirl of whipped cream and a sprinkle of cocoa, this coffee is a luxurious treat for coffee lovers and dessert enthusiasts alike.*

## Ingredients:

- 1 shot (1 ounce) of espresso
- 1/2 cup steamed milk (use oat milk, almond milk, or dairy milk for a creamy base)
- 2 tbsps cherry syrup or cherry jam
- 1 tbsp cocoa powder (unsweetened)
- 1 tbsp dark chocolate shavings (for garnish)
- 1/4 tsp vanilla extract (optional)
- 2 tbsps whipped cream (coconut whipped cream for a dairy-free option)
- [Optional] 1/4 tsp ground cinnamon (for a warming spice note)

## Instructions:

1. Brew a shot of espresso using your preferred method.
2. In a small bowl or cup, mix the cherry syrup (or jam) with the vanilla extract (if using) and cocoa powder until smooth.
3. Steam your milk of choice until hot and frothy.
4. Pour the espresso into a large coffee mug or glass.
5. Add the cherry-chocolate mixture to the espresso and stir until well combined.
6. Gently pour the steamed milk into the mug, mixing it into the espresso-cherry-chocolate base.
7. Top with a generous swirl of whipped cream.
8. Garnish with dark chocolate shavings and a sprinkle of cocoa powder (and cinnamon if desired).
9. Sip and savor the sweet, indulgent flavors of the Black Forest in every sip.

## Tips and Recommendations:

- For extra richness, add a splash of heavy cream or coconut cream to the milk.
- If you prefer a more intense cherry flavor, use a homemade cherry syrup or fresh cherry puree.
- For a stronger chocolate flavor, increase the amount of cocoa powder or dark chocolate shavings.
- To make the drink extra indulgent, drizzle a little extra cherry syrup on top of the whipped cream.
- Use a milk frother or steam wand to achieve a thick, frothy texture for a luxurious finish.

## Variations:

- **Iced Black Forest Coffee**: Brew the espresso, then chill it. Pour over ice and add the cherry syrup and cocoa mixture for a refreshing twist.
- **Black Forest Mocha Latte**: Add an extra tablespoon of cocoa powder for a more pronounced chocolate flavor, creating a rich mocha variation.
- **Black Forest Hazelnut Coffee**: For a nutty variation, add a splash of hazelnut syrup along with the cherry syrup for a unique flavor combination.

## Pairing Suggestions:

- Enjoy with a slice of rich chocolate cake or a small plate of chocolate-covered cherries for a perfect dessert pairing.
- Pair with a warm, buttery croissant or a slice of vegan cheesecake to complement the creamy, sweet flavors.
- Try it with a fruit tart or light cookies, like almond shortbread, to balance the richness of the drink.

## Interesting Fact:

Did you know that the Black Forest cake, or "Schwarzwälder Kirschtorte," is named after the Black Forest region in Germany, where the cake originated? The combination of chocolate, cherries, and whipped cream has been a beloved dessert for centuries, and now you can enjoy it as a delicious coffee treat.

## Cultural Connection:

The Black Forest cake is a classic German dessert known for its decadent layers of chocolate, cherries, and whipped cream. This coffee version brings the flavors of the cake into a comforting, drinkable form, perfect for indulging in the rich, cultural tradition of German desserts with a modern coffee twist.

# Orange Mocha

*Indulge in the perfect balance of citrusy brightness and deep chocolatey richness with the Orange Mocha. This innovative twist on the classic mocha combines smooth espresso with the zesty, refreshing flavor of orange, creating a coffee experience that's both invigorating and decadent. Topped with velvety whipped cream and a touch of orange zest, this luxurious drink will transport you to a place where vibrant citrus and rich chocolate harmonize in every sip.*

## Ingredients:

- 1 shot (1 ounce) of espresso
- 1 tbsp cocoa powder (unsweetened)
- 1 tbsp orange syrup or freshly squeezed orange juice
- 1/2 cup steamed milk (use oat milk, almond milk, or dairy milk for a creamy base)
- 2 tbsps whipped cream (coconut whipped cream for a dairy-free option)
- Zest from 1 orange (for garnish)
- [Optional] 1/4 tsp vanilla extract (for a warm undertone)
- [Optional] 1/2 tsp orange liqueur (like Cointreau or Grand Marnier) for an added depth of flavor

## Instructions:

1. Brew a shot of espresso using your preferred method.
2. In a small bowl, mix the cocoa powder with the orange syrup (or juice) until smooth and combined.
3. Steam your milk until hot and frothy.
4. Pour the espresso into a large coffee mug or glass.
5. Add the orange-chocolate mixture to the espresso and stir until fully blended.
6. Gently pour the steamed milk into the mug, combining it with the espresso and orange-chocolate base.
7. Top with a generous swirl of whipped cream.
8. Garnish with a sprinkle of orange zest and, if desired, a few drops of orange liqueur.
9. Sip and enjoy the perfect blend of coffee, chocolate, and citrus flavors.

## Tips and Recommendations:

- For a creamier texture, consider using a higher-fat milk like coconut milk or a creamy oat milk.
- If you prefer a less sweet version, reduce the amount of orange syrup or juice.
- For a more pronounced chocolate flavor, increase the cocoa powder or add a few dark chocolate shavings to the top of the whipped cream.
- Try adding a pinch of cinnamon for a subtle warming spice to complement the orange flavor.

## Variations:

- **Iced Orange Mocha**: Brew the espresso, then chill it. Pour over ice and mix with the orange-chocolate syrup and steamed milk for a refreshing iced version.
- **Orange Mocha Frappe**: Blend the espresso, cocoa powder, orange syrup, milk, and ice for a cold, blended treat.
- **Vegan Orange Mocha**: Use oat milk and coconut whipped cream for a fully dairy-free version.

## Pairing Suggestions:

- Pair with a dark chocolate muffin or a slice of rich chocolate cake to emphasize the chocolate flavor of the drink.
- Enjoy alongside fresh orange scones or a citrusy fruit salad to highlight the bright orange notes.
- Try it with a buttery croissant or cinnamon roll to balance out the richness of the mocha.

## Interesting Fact:

Did you know that orange and chocolate are a classic pairing that dates back to ancient times? The combination was first popularized in Europe during the 17th century, and now it's a beloved flavor combination in everything from desserts to beverages.

## Cultural Connection:

Orange-flavored coffee drinks like this one are a nod to the rich history of citrus use in European desserts, especially in the Mediterranean region. The addition of chocolate to coffee beverages is a modern innovation, bringing together two of the world's most beloved flavors into one indulgent drink.

# Toasted Marshmallow Latte

*Indulge in the comforting, nostalgic flavor of a Toasted Marshmallow Latte - a perfect blend of rich espresso, sweet toasted marshmallow syrup, and velvety steamed milk. This delightful creation brings the warmth and fun of summer campfires into your coffee cup. The caramelized marshmallow flavor is elevated by a smooth, frothy texture, making this latte a sweet treat that's ideal for cozy mornings or special occasions. Get ready to savor a sweet, smoky, and utterly delicious coffee experience!*

## Ingredients:

- 1 shot (1 ounce) of espresso
- 1 tbsp toasted marshmallow syrup (or marshmallow fluff)
- 1/2 cup steamed milk (use oat milk, almond milk, or dairy milk)
- 1 tbsp whipped cream (optional for topping, use coconut whipped cream for a dairy-free version)
- 1/4 tsp vanilla extract (optional for a deeper flavor)
- [Optional] Pinch of cinnamon or toasted coconut for garnish

## Instructions:

1. Brew a shot of espresso using your preferred method.
2. In a small bowl, mix the toasted marshmallow syrup (or fluff) with the vanilla extract if using.
3. Steam your milk until it's hot and frothy.
4. Pour the brewed espresso into a mug or glass.
5. Add the toasted marshmallow mixture to the espresso and stir until well combined.
6. Slowly pour the steamed milk into the mug, blending it with the espresso and syrup for a creamy texture.
7. Top with a swirl of whipped cream.
8. Garnish with a pinch of cinnamon or toasted coconut for extra flavor and visual appeal.
9. Take a moment to enjoy the sweet and comforting aroma before sipping.

## Tips and Recommendations:

- If you prefer a more intense marshmallow flavor, increase the amount of toasted marshmallow syrup or add a small scoop of marshmallow fluff.
- For a more balanced sweetness, reduce the syrup and add a splash of vanilla extract to enhance the flavor complexity.
- Experiment with different milk options, such as cashew milk, for a slightly nuttier flavor profile.
- For extra indulgence, drizzle a little chocolate syrup over the whipped cream for a mocha-marshmallow twist.

## Variations:

- **Iced Toasted Marshmallow Latte**: Brew the espresso, then let it cool. Pour over ice, and mix with the toasted marshmallow syrup and cold milk for a refreshing iced version.
- **Vegan Toasted Marshmallow Latte**: Use oat milk and coconut whipped cream for a completely dairy-free version, and opt for a vegan marshmallow syrup.
- **Toasted Marshmallow Mocha**: Add a tablespoon of cocoa powder or chocolate syrup for a decadent mocha flavor combined with the sweet marshmallow.

## Pairing Suggestions:

- Pair with warm, gooey cinnamon rolls or s'mores-flavored cookies to complement the marshmallow notes.
- Enjoy alongside a rich, nutty biscotti or a slice of decadent chocolate cake for a true indulgence.
- Pair with a lightly salted pretzel to balance out the sweetness of the latte with a touch of savory contrast.

## Interesting Fact:

Did you know that marshmallows were originally made from the mallow plant, which grows in marshes? They were used by ancient Egyptians as a sweet treat and were later transformed into the fluffy version we enjoy today.

## Cultural Connection:

The concept of toasting marshmallows over an open fire is rooted in campfire culture, especially in the United States. The marshmallow itself has evolved from a medicinal plant extract to a fun and nostalgic treat enjoyed by people of all ages.

# Buttered Rum Coffee

*Imagine the cozy warmth of a rich coffee blend, enhanced by the indulgent flavors of smooth butter and rum, all crowned with a velvety foam. The Buttered Rum Coffee is a drink that brings the comforting flavors of a spiked hot drink right into your coffee cup. Combining the deep notes of freshly brewed coffee with a hint of rum flavor and a buttery richness, this latte is the perfect indulgence on chilly evenings or when you want to savor something special. Get ready to embrace a smooth, luxurious coffee experience that's as satisfying as it is delicious.*

## Ingredients:

- 1 shot (1 ounce) of espresso
- 1 tbsp unsalted vegan butter (or regular butter for non-vegan option)
- 1 tbsp brown sugar (or maple syrup for a lighter option)
- 1/2 tsp dark rum extract (or 1 tbsp dark rum, if you prefer an alcoholic version)
- 1/2 cup steamed milk (use oat milk, almond milk, or dairy milk)
- [Optional] Whipped cream for topping (use coconut whipped cream for a dairy-free option)
- [Optional] Dash of cinnamon or nutmeg for garnish

## Instructions:

1. Brew a shot of espresso using your preferred method.
2. In a small saucepan, melt the vegan butter and brown sugar together over low heat, stirring constantly until the sugar is dissolved and the butter is fully melted.
3. Add the rum extract (or dark rum if using) to the melted butter mixture and stir until combined.
4. Steam your milk until it's hot and frothy.
5. Pour the brewed espresso into a mug, then pour in the butter and rum mixture, stirring well.
6. Gently add the steamed milk to the mug, mixing everything together for a smooth and creamy texture.
7. Top with whipped cream if desired and sprinkle a dash of cinnamon or nutmeg on top for extra flavor and visual appeal.
8. Stir gently and enjoy the rich, buttery goodness of your Buttered Rum Coffee.

## Tips and Recommendations:

- If you want a stronger flavor, add an extra shot of espresso or increase the amount of rum extract for a more pronounced rum taste.
- For a creamier drink, use full-fat coconut milk or add a splash of heavy cream if you're not dairy-free.
- Try making your own homemade rum syrup by simmering rum and brown sugar together for a richer flavor.
- If you prefer a non-alcoholic option, increase the rum extract for a bolder taste or use a rum-flavored syrup.

## Variations:

- **Buttered Rum Mocha**: Add a tablespoon of cocoa powder or chocolate syrup for a delicious mocha twist on this indulgent latte.
- **Iced Buttered Rum Coffee**: Brew the espresso, then let it cool. Pour over ice, mix with the buttered rum syrup, and top with cold milk for a refreshing take on the classic.
- **Dairy-Free Option**: Use a plant-based butter (like coconut or olive oil) and any dairy-free milk of your choice for a fully vegan and dairy-free version of this rich latte.

## Pairing Suggestions:

- Pair with a warm slice of apple cinnamon bread or banana nut muffins for a delightful sweet-and-savory contrast.
- Enjoy with crispy ginger snaps or buttery shortbread cookies to complement the buttery richness of the drink.
- Pair with a light and fluffy croissant for a classic and comforting breakfast combination.

## Interesting Fact:

Did you know that the combination of butter and coffee has been used for centuries in cultures around the world, often as an energizing, warming beverage? The idea of adding butter to coffee is said to have roots in Tibetan butter tea, which is traditionally made with yak butter, salt, and tea. The rich texture created by butter in coffee has been embraced in modern variations like this Buttered Rum Coffee!

## Cultural Connection:

The tradition of buttered drinks has been enjoyed by many cultures around the world. In the United States, the concept of adding butter to coffee has been popularized in recent years, particularly in the form of "bulletproof coffee," which uses butter and coconut oil. This **Buttered Rum Coffee** blends that idea with a cozy, comforting flavor profile that evokes the warmth of a winter evening or holiday celebration.

# Chai Tea Latte

*The Chai Tea Latte is the perfect blend of bold spiced tea and creamy milk, creating a soothing and aromatic drink that warms you from the inside out. Inspired by traditional Indian masala chai, this drink combines the comforting flavors of cinnamon, ginger, cardamom, and cloves, infused into strong tea and topped with frothy milk. Whether you're looking for a cozy afternoon treat or a flavorful pick-me-up, this chai latte will bring a bit of warmth and spice to your day.*

## Ingredients:

- 1 chai tea bag (or 1 tbsp loose-leaf chai blend)
- 1 cup water
- 1 tbsp brown sugar or maple syrup (adjust to taste)
- 1/2 cup steamed milk (use oat milk, almond milk, or dairy milk)
- [Optional] Ground cinnamon or cardamom for garnish

## Instructions:

1. Bring 1 cup of water to a boil in a small saucepan.
2. Add the chai tea bag or loose-leaf chai blend and simmer for 5-7 minutes, depending on how strong you like your tea.
3. Remove the tea bag or strain out the loose-leaf chai.
4. Stir in the brown sugar or maple syrup until dissolved.
5. In a separate saucepan or milk frother, steam the milk until hot and frothy (but not boiling).
6. Pour the chai tea into a mug, then gently add the steamed milk, stirring lightly to combine.
7. Optionally, garnish with a sprinkle of ground cinnamon or cardamom for an extra touch of spice and elegance.

## Tips and Recommendations:

- Adjust the sweetness level by adding more or less sugar or syrup according to your taste.
- If you prefer a spicier chai, add a pinch of black pepper or extra ginger to the steeping tea.
- For a creamier drink, use full-fat coconut milk or heavy cream.
- You can make the chai tea base ahead of time and store it in the fridge for a quick latte on the go.

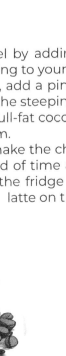

## Variations:

- **Iced Chai Latte**: Brew the chai as directed, let it cool, then pour over ice and add cold milk for a refreshing twist.
- **Vanilla Chai Latte**: Add a splash of vanilla extract or vanilla syrup for a smooth, sweet twist on the classic chai latte.
- **Dirty Chai Latte**: Add a shot of espresso to your chai tea for a coffee-chai fusion that's both bold and comforting.

## Pairing Suggestions:

- Pair with a warm, flaky scone or almond biscotti to enhance the spice and sweetness of the chai.
- Serve with a coconut macaron or a cinnamon roll for an indulgent treat that complements the warming flavors.
- A fresh fruit salad or a yogurt parfait balances the richness of the chai with light and refreshing flavors.

## Interesting Fact:

Did you know that "chai" simply means "tea" in Hindi, and when people refer to "chai tea," they're essentially saying "tea tea"? The spiced version of chai, known as "masala chai," has been a staple in India for centuries, and has become popular around the world for its bold flavors and comforting qualities.

## Cultural Connection:

Masala chai, the basis for this **Chai Tea Latte**, has deep roots in India, where it's traditionally brewed with black tea, spices, and milk. It is often enjoyed as a daily ritual in Indian households and street markets. Over time, this drink has traveled globally, with chai lattes becoming a beloved beverage in coffee shops everywhere, offering a spiced alternative to traditional coffee lattes.

# Almond Milk Iced Coffee

*When the weather heats up, cool down with a refreshing Almond Milk Iced Coffee. This delicious, dairy-free drink combines the smooth richness of almond milk with the bold kick of freshly brewed coffee, served over ice for an invigorating, chilled pick-me-up. Whether you're looking for a healthier alternative to cream or simply want a lighter iced coffee option, this simple yet satisfying beverage is perfect for any time of day. Enjoy it on a warm afternoon or as an energizing start to your day.*

## Ingredients:

- 1 cup brewed coffee, chilled
- 1/2 cup unsweetened almond milk
- 1 tbsp maple syrup or agave syrup (adjust to taste)
- Ice cubes
- [Optional] 1/4 tsp vanilla extract or cinnamon for extra flavor

## Instructions:

1. Brew your coffee using your preferred method (drip, pour-over, or espresso), then let it cool completely.
2. Fill a tall glass with ice cubes.
3. Pour the chilled coffee over the ice.
4. In a separate container, mix the almond milk and maple syrup (or sweetener of choice). Stir until well combined.
5. Pour the almond milk mixture into the glass with coffee.
6. Stir well to combine the flavors.
7. [Optional] Add a splash of vanilla extract or a sprinkle of cinnamon for extra flavor.

## Tips and Recommendations:

- If you prefer a sweeter drink, add more maple syrup or sweetener until it reaches your desired taste.
- For a creamier texture, you can use a barista-style almond milk, which froths up more than regular almond milk.
- If you're looking for an extra caffeine boost, add a shot of espresso to your iced coffee base.
- To make your iced coffee even more flavorful, try infusing the coffee with spices like cinnamon or cardamom while brewing.

## Variations:

- **Iced Coconut Milk Coffee**: Swap almond milk for coconut milk for a tropical twist with a naturally sweeter taste.
- **Almond Milk Mocha**: Add a tablespoon of cocoa powder and a little chocolate syrup to the mix for a rich, chocolatey iced coffee treat.
- **Iced Coffee Float**: Top your iced coffee with a scoop of dairy-free vanilla ice cream for an indulgent, dessert-like twist.

## Pairing Suggestions:

- Pair with a freshly baked almond croissant for a light, crunchy complement to the smooth coffee.
- Enjoy alongside a slice of banana bread or a nut-based snack for a satisfying and wholesome treat.
- A fresh fruit salad with citrus or berries pairs perfectly with the nutty richness of the almond milk.

## Interesting Fact:

Did you know that almond milk has been around for centuries? It was first made in medieval Europe, where it was used as a substitute for dairy during fasting periods. Now, it's become a staple in dairy-free coffee drinks around the world!

## Cultural Connection:

Iced coffee is a beloved drink around the world, particularly in warm climates, where it serves as both a refreshing and energizing beverage. Almond milk has roots in the Middle East and has gained popularity globally as a plant-based milk alternative, especially in coffee culture.

# Thai Iced Coffee

*Transport yourself to the vibrant streets of Thailand with a cup of Thai Iced Coffee. This bold and sweet coffee drink is made with strong brewed coffee, spiced with a touch of cardamom, and sweetened with a luscious mix of condensed coconut milk. Served over ice, it offers the perfect balance of rich, creamy sweetness and bold, aromatic coffee flavor. A true Thai classic, this iced coffee will become your go-to for an exotic and refreshing pick-me-up.*

## Ingredients:

- 1 cup strong brewed coffee (or Thai coffee if available)
- 1 tbsp sugar (adjust to taste)
- 2 tbsps coconut milk or sweetened condensed coconut milk
- Ice cubes
- 1/4 tsp ground cardamom (optional for an authentic flavor)
- [Optional] 1/2 tsp vanilla extract

## Instructions:

1. Brew a cup of strong coffee using your preferred method. Thai coffee can be used for a more authentic flavor, but regular brewed coffee also works great.
2. While the coffee is still warm, stir in the sugar until fully dissolved.
3. Add the ground cardamom to the coffee for that signature Thai flavor. Stir well to combine.
4. Fill a tall glass with ice cubes.
5. Pour the sweetened, spiced coffee over the ice.
6. Add the coconut milk (or condensed coconut milk for extra sweetness) and stir until well combined.
7. [Optional] Add vanilla extract for an added layer of flavor.

## Tips and Recommendations:

- If you prefer a sweeter coffee, feel free to increase the sugar or use sweetened condensed milk instead of coconut milk.
- For a more intense cardamom flavor, adjust the amount of cardamom to your liking, or try adding a few whole cardamom pods to steep with the coffee while brewing.
- If you want to experiment with textures, use a milk frother to create a creamy top before serving.

## Variations:

- **Iced Matcha Thai Coffee**: Add a teaspoon of matcha powder to your brewed coffee for a unique twist on traditional Thai iced coffee.
- **Coconut Iced Coffee**: For a dairy-free version, use full-fat coconut milk instead of condensed coconut milk and add a little extra sugar to taste.
- **Spicy Thai Iced Coffee**: For an added kick, mix in a pinch of ground black pepper or chili powder to complement the sweet and spicy flavors.

## Pairing Suggestions:

- Pair with Thai iced tea-flavored cookies or coconut macaroons for a perfect fusion of Thai-inspired flavors.
- Enjoy alongside a savory Thai snack like vegetable spring rolls or a crispy tofu dish for a balanced coffee break.
- A fresh fruit salad with tropical fruits like mango or pineapple works wonderfully to balance the rich, spiced coffee.

## Interesting Fact:

Did you know that Thai iced coffee is traditionally made using a specific type of coffee bean known for its bold and intense flavor? It's often brewed in large batches, making it ideal for serving during the hot Thai afternoons!

## Cultural Connection:

**Thai Iced Coffee** (or Oliang) is a popular street drink in Thailand, where the combination of strong coffee, spices, and sweetened condensed milk creates a unique blend of flavors. It's enjoyed across the country, offering a cool and energizing escape from the tropical heat. Whether served in markets or local cafes, this beverage is a testament to Thailand's love for bold, sweet, and spiced flavors.

# Cold Brew

*Cold Brew coffee is a smooth, chilled coffee drink that's perfect for warm days or when you're craving a refreshingly strong pick-me-up. Unlike traditional hot brewing methods, cold brew coffee is steeped in cold water over a long period (usually 12–24 hours), creating a less acidic, naturally sweet coffee concentrate. This brew has become a favorite among coffee enthusiasts for its rich flavor and smooth finish. Ready to taste the smooth, mellow vibes of cold brew? Let's dive in!*

## Ingredients:

- 1 cup coarsely ground coffee beans
- 4 cups cold or room temperature water
- [Optional] 1 tbsp sweetener (sugar, agave, or maple syrup)
- [Optional] 1/2 cup almond milk (or your favorite plant-based milk)

## Instructions:

1. Combine the coarsely ground coffee beans and water in a large jar or pitcher. Stir gently to ensure all the coffee grounds are soaked.
2. Cover the jar and let the coffee steep at room temperature for 12 to 24 hours. The longer it steeps, the stronger and more flavorful it will be.
3. After steeping, strain the coffee using a fine mesh strainer or a coffee filter to remove the grounds.
4. Pour the cold brew concentrate into a glass filled with ice cubes.
5. [Optional] Add your preferred sweetener and stir to combine.
6. [Optional] Pour in almond milk (or your favorite milk) to add a creamy texture. Stir gently.

## Tips and Recommendations:

- Cold brew coffee is a concentrate, so it's typically diluted with water or milk before drinking. Adjust the strength by adding more water or milk to suit your taste.
- For a smoother coffee, try using a paper filter or a nut milk bag to strain the coffee grounds.
- Make your cold brew ahead of time and store it in the fridge for up to one week, so you always have a refreshing drink on hand.
- If you like your coffee on the sweeter side, add a dash of cinnamon or a vanilla pod to the steeping jar for an aromatic twist.

## Variations:

- **Iced Vanilla Cold Brew**: Add a few drops of vanilla extract and a splash of sweetened vanilla almond milk for a delightful twist.
- **Cold Brew Tonic**: Mix your cold brew with a splash of tonic water and ice for a fizzy, refreshing version.
- **Cinnamon Cold Brew**: Add a cinnamon stick to your cold brew jar while steeping for a warm, spicy note.

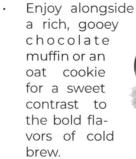

## Pairing Suggestions:

- Pair with a light breakfast like a toasted bagel with avocado or almond butter for a balanced start to your day.
- Enjoy alongside a rich, gooey chocolate muffin or an oat cookie for a sweet contrast to the bold flavors of cold brew.
- A simple fruit salad or smoothie bowl pairs well with cold brew, offering a fresh and healthy counterpoint.

## Interesting Fact:

Did you know that cold brew coffee is less acidic than hot brewed coffee? This makes it a great option for people sensitive to acidity or those who prefer a smoother, richer coffee flavor. Plus, cold brew is naturally sweeter due to the slow brewing process!

## Cultural Connection:

Cold brew coffee, though popular in the US and around the world today, is thought to have originated in Japan in the 1600s, where a similar method called Kyoto-style coffee was used. It's gained a huge following due to its smooth flavor and ability to be enjoyed in various creative ways - from classic black to sweetened and iced variations.

# Nitro Cold Brew

*If you're a coffee enthusiast looking to elevate your cold brew game, Nitro Cold Brew is your ticket to a creamy, frothy experience that's smooth and irresistible. Infused with nitrogen gas, this cold brew takes on a velvety texture and a rich, smooth flavor with a naturally sweet finish. Often served on tap like a draft beer, Nitro Cold Brew creates a stunning cascade effect in your glass as the nitrogen bubbles rise, making it as beautiful to watch as it is to drink. Let's make this café-quality treat right at home!*

## Ingredients:

- 1 cup coarsely ground coffee beans
- 4 cups cold or room temperature water
- 1 nitrogen canister (available in coffee shops or online)
- [Optional] 1 tbsp sweetener (sugar, agave, or maple syrup)
- [Optional] 1/2 cup coconut milk or almond milk

## Instructions:

1. **Brew the Cold Brew**: Combine the coarsely ground coffee beans and water in a large jar or pitcher. Stir to ensure all the coffee grounds are soaked.
2. **Steep the Coffee**: Cover the jar and let it steep at room temperature for 12 to 24 hours. The longer it steeps, the more intense the flavor.
3. **Strain the Coffee**: After steeping, strain the cold brew using a fine mesh strainer or coffee filter to remove the grounds.
4. **Nitrogen Infusion**: Pour the cold brew into a Nitro cold brew keg or any coffee nitro infuser. Attach a nitrogen canister according to the manufacturer's instructions, allowing the gas to infuse into the coffee.
5. **Dispense and Serve**: Serve the Nitro Cold Brew straight from the tap or pour into a glass filled with ice. The coffee should have a thick, creamy foam head similar to a stout beer.
6. **[Optional] Add Sweetener & Milk**: If desired, add a sweetener and a splash of plant-based milk, stirring gently for extra creaminess.

## Tips and Recommendations:

- If you don't have a nitrogen infuser, you can achieve a similar effect by using a whipped cream dispenser with a nitrogen charger.
- For an extra smooth finish, make sure to use coarsely ground coffee beans. Finer grinds can lead to over-extraction and bitterness.
- Nitro Cold Brew is already smooth, but you can further mellow the flavor by using a slightly lighter roast coffee.
- Don't forget the nitrogen! It's what gives this drink its unique frothy texture and creamy mouthfeel.

## Variations:

- **Vanilla Nitro Cold Brew**: Add a drop of vanilla extract to the cold brew before infusing it with nitrogen for a subtle sweet note.
- **Iced Nitro Mocha**: Mix in a tablespoon of chocolate syrup or cocoa powder before adding nitrogen for a delicious mocha twist.
- **Dairy-Free Nitro Cold Brew**: Use oat milk, almond milk, or coconut cream for a rich, creamy texture without dairy.

## Pairing Suggestions:

- Pair with a freshly baked croissant or a flaky almond pastry to complement the smoothness of the Nitro Cold Brew.
- For a more substantial pairing, enjoy your Nitro Cold Brew with a plant-based muffin, like blueberry or banana bread, for a delicious contrast in texture and flavor.
- Serve with a light salad or avocado toast for a refreshing, balanced breakfast.

## Interesting Fact:

Did you know that Nitro Cold Brew was first popularized by cafes serving beer-style coffee on tap? The use of nitrogen gives it a smooth texture and creates a thick, foamy layer, making it one of the most visually impressive coffee drinks around.

## Cultural Connection:

While Nitro Cold Brew originated in the U.S., it draws inspiration from the centuries-old practice of infusing liquids with nitrogen to create creamy textures and a luxurious mouthfeel. Today, it's become a trendy coffee beverage, beloved for its rich taste and smooth, bubbly texture.

# Japanese Iced Coffee

*Japanese Iced Coffee is a refreshing, flavorful twist on the classic iced coffee. Unlike traditional methods of brewing and then cooling coffee, this technique brews the coffee directly onto ice, resulting in a coffee that retains its full flavor without the dilution from melting ice. The key to this method is the use of hot water, which extracts the rich, aromatic oils from the coffee grounds, and the ice, which quickly cools the brew, preserving its bold, intense taste. Perfect for a hot day, this smooth, iced coffee is crisp, clean, and full of character.*

## Ingredients:

- 1/2 cup (about 25g) coarsely ground coffee beans
- 3/4 cup (6 ounces) hot water (around 200°F or 93°C)
- 1/2 cup (4 ounces) ice cubes
- [Optional] 1 tbsp maple syrup, agave, or your preferred sweetener
- [Optional] 1/4 cup plant-based milk (such as oat, almond, or coconut milk)

## Instructions:

1. **Prepare the Ice**: Place the ice cubes in a heat-proof glass or tumbler.
2. **Brew the Coffee**: Using a pour-over method or a French press, brew the hot coffee. Pour the hot water evenly over the coarsely ground coffee beans in a circular motion, allowing the grounds to bloom for a few seconds before continuing to pour.
3. **Pour Over Ice**: Once brewed, immediately pour the hot coffee over the ice. The coffee will cool quickly and form a smooth, flavorful base without losing its strength.
4. **Sweeten (Optional)**: If desired, stir in your sweetener of choice while the coffee is still warm, ensuring it dissolves completely.
5. **Add Milk (Optional)**: For a creamier texture, add a splash of plant-based milk to the iced coffee and stir well.
6. **Serve**: Enjoy your Japanese Iced Coffee straight from the glass, with the ice still in place, or transfer to a chilled cup for an extra cool treat.

## Tips and Recommendations:

- Make sure the water is just below boiling (around 200°F or 93°C) for optimal extraction of the coffee's flavors without bitterness.
- If you prefer a less intense coffee flavor, adjust the coffee-to-water ratio or use ice cubes made from coffee for extra richness.
- For an extra burst of flavor, consider adding a pinch of cinnamon or a couple of crushed cardamom pods to the coffee grounds before brewing.
- If you don't have a pour-over or French press, a strong drip coffee maker will work too - just be sure to brew directly onto the ice.

## Variations:

- **Iced Coffee with Citrus Twist**: Add a slice of lemon or a dash of orange zest to the finished drink for a refreshing citrus note that cuts through the coffee's boldness.
- **Vegan Iced Coffee Float**: Top with a scoop of coconut milk ice cream for a fun, dessert-like treat.
- **Sweetened Iced Coffee**: For a richer flavor, use sweetened condensed coconut milk or add flavored syrups like vanilla or caramel for a café-style twist.

## Pairing Suggestions:

- Pair with a buttery vegan croissant or a chocolate chip cookie for a delightful combination of sweet and bitter.
- Serve alongside a light fruit salad or a piece of dark chocolate for a more sophisticated, bittersweet contrast to the coffee.
- Enjoy with a savory breakfast dish like avocado toast for a balanced start to your day.

## Interesting Fact:

Did you know that Japanese Iced Coffee is often brewed directly onto ice to preserve its full flavor and aroma? This brewing technique was developed to avoid the dilution of traditional iced coffee while maintaining its bold taste.

## Cultural Connection:

The method of brewing directly over ice was developed in Japan, where a high standard of coffee brewing has long been appreciated. This unique approach allows coffee lovers to enjoy an iced coffee without losing the strength or character of the brew, making it popular in Japan and beyond.

# Iced Americano

*The Iced Americano is the perfect balance of bold espresso and crisp, chilled refreshment. With just two simple ingredients - espresso and water - it's a straightforward yet powerful coffee that provides a smooth, rich taste without the heaviness of milk or cream. This classic drink is ideal for those who enjoy the pure flavor of espresso but want a cooler, more refreshing twist. Whether you're cooling off on a hot day or craving a quick, clean caffeine fix, the Iced Americano delivers in every sip.*

## Ingredients:

- 1 shot (1 ounce) of freshly brewed espresso
- 1/2 cup (4 ounces) of cold water
- 1/2 cup (4 ounces) ice cubes
- [Optional] 1 tsp simple syrup or sweetener of choice
- [Optional] 1/4 tsp vanilla extract for a subtle flavor boost

## Instructions:

1. **Brew the Espresso**: Brew one shot of espresso using your preferred method (espresso machine, stovetop Moka pot, or another brewing method).
2. **Prepare the Ice**: Fill a tall glass with ice cubes, ensuring the ice is abundant to chill the coffee without dilution.
3. **Pour the Espresso**: Once the espresso is brewed, immediately pour it over the ice cubes in the glass.
4. **Add Cold Water**: Pour the cold water into the glass over the espresso and ice, allowing it to cool the drink further and balance the strong espresso flavor.
5. **Sweeten (Optional)**: Stir in the simple syrup or any sweetener of choice to taste. If you like a touch of vanilla, add a drop or two of vanilla extract for a unique twist.
6. **Serve**: Enjoy your **Iced Americano** immediately, or let it chill for a few moments longer if you prefer it extra cold.

## Tips and Recommendations:

- If you want to intensify the espresso flavor, use less water, or add another shot of espresso.
- For a slightly sweeter iced coffee, add a flavored syrup like hazelnut, caramel, or cinnamon.
- Try experimenting with different types of ice - coffee ice cubes made from leftover coffee will add extra richness without watering down your drink.
- If you prefer a lighter version, adjust the espresso-to-water ratio by using more water.

## Variations:

- **Iced Americano with Coconut Water**: Swap the cold water for coconut water for a tropical twist with a hint of natural sweetness.
- **Iced Americano with Cinnamon**: Stir in a pinch of ground cinnamon for an aromatic, spicy note that pairs wonderfully with the coffee's bold flavor.
- **Vegan Iced Americano Float**: Add a scoop of coconut milk ice cream for a creamy texture while keeping the coffee's pure flavor.

## Pairing Suggestions:

- Pair with a slice of lemon drizzle cake or a fresh fruit salad to balance the strong, robust flavors of the coffee.
- For a savory snack, try this with a veggie wrap or a lightly salted pretzel.
- Pair with almond biscotti or coconut macaroons for a sweet, crunchy contrast to the smooth coffee.

## Interesting Fact:

Did you know that the **Iced Americano** was created during World War II by American soldiers in Italy? They would dilute espresso with water to mimic the coffee they drank back home, giving birth to this now-iconic coffee style.

## Cultural Connection:

While the **Iced Americano** has become popular worldwide, its roots trace back to Italy and the American military. Its simplicity and boldness have made it a staple in cafes, offering coffee lovers a pure and refreshing way to enjoy espresso, especially in warm weather.

# Iced Latte

*The Iced Latte is the perfect balance of rich espresso and smooth, cold milk, delivering a refreshing yet creamy experience. This chilled coffee delight is ideal for those who crave a cool, energizing treat without sacrificing the deep flavors of espresso. Whether you're relaxing on a sunny day or need an afternoon pick-me-up, the Iced Latte offers a comforting, satisfying drink that combines the best of both worlds. Its versatility allows for endless variations, making it a favorite for coffee lovers everywhere.*

## Ingredients:

- 1 shot (1 ounce) of freshly brewed espresso
- 1 cup (8 ounces) cold milk (dairy or plant-based)
- 1/2 cup (4 ounces) ice cubes
- [Optional] 1 tsp simple syrup or sweetener of choice
- [Optional] 1/4 tsp vanilla extract for a subtle sweetness

## Instructions:

1. **Brew the Espresso**: Brew a shot of espresso using your preferred method (espresso machine, stovetop Moka pot, etc.).
2. **Prepare the Ice**: Fill a tall glass with ice cubes, ensuring the glass is about halfway full.
3. **Add the Espresso**: Pour the freshly brewed espresso over the ice, allowing the coffee to chill quickly.
4. **Pour the Milk**: Add cold milk to the glass, pouring it gently over the coffee for a smooth blend.
5. **Sweeten (Optional)**: Stir in simple syrup or any sweetener of choice to taste. If desired, add a drop or two of vanilla extract for an extra hint of flavor.
6. **Serve**: Stir the drink well to combine the espresso and milk, then enjoy immediately.

## Tips and Recommendations:

- To achieve a stronger coffee flavor, use a double shot of espresso instead of a single shot.
- For a richer texture, opt for whole milk or creamier plant-based alternatives like oat or coconut milk.
- If you prefer a smoother taste, try adding a dash of cinnamon or cocoa powder before mixing.
- Adjust the sweetness to suit your taste - some prefer a more robust coffee flavor, while others enjoy a sweeter version.
- For extra freshness, try a mint sprig garnish to give a refreshing touch.

## Variations:

- **Iced Vanilla Latte**: Add 1 teaspoon of vanilla syrup or extract to enhance the flavor with a subtle sweetness.
- **Iced Matcha Latte**: Replace the espresso with matcha powder to create a green tea version of the iced latte.
- **Iced Caramel Latte**: Add a drizzle of caramel syrup for a rich, sweet twist on the classic iced latte.

## Pairing Suggestions:

- Pair with a chocolate croissant or almond biscotti for a delightful, indulgent treat.
- For a savory option, try a veggie sandwich or avocado toast to balance the sweetness of the drink.
- Enjoy with a slice of lemon cake or fruit scones to complement the refreshing chill of the iced latte.

## Interesting Fact:

Did you know that the **Iced Latte** originated in Italy, but its popularity soared in the United States in the late 20th century? It was initially a way to enjoy espresso in warmer climates but quickly became a global favorite for coffee lovers seeking a cooler, lighter alternative to hot lattes.

## Cultural Connection:

The **Iced Latte** is a modern twist on the traditional Italian espresso-based drinks, offering a cooler, more accessible way to enjoy espresso during the summer months. It has become a staple in cafes worldwide and is known for its versatility and ease of customization. Whether you enjoy it plain or with added flavors, the **Iced Latte** reflects the global love for coffee in a refreshing, everyday form.

# Iced Mocha

*Indulge in the Iced Mocha, a decadent blend of rich espresso, velvety chocolate, and chilled milk, making it the ultimate treat for coffee and chocolate lovers alike. This refreshing iced drink delivers the perfect balance of deep espresso flavor and sweet, creamy chocolate, offering an irresistible combination that's both energizing and satisfying. Ideal for warm days or whenever you're craving something sweet yet caffeinated, the Iced Mocha is a go-to specialty drink that never fails to delight.*

## Ingredients:

- 1 shot (1 ounce) of freshly brewed espresso
- 2 tbsps chocolate syrup or melted dark chocolate
- 1 cup (8 ounces) cold milk (dairy or plant-based)
- 1/2 cup (4 ounces) ice cubes
- [Optional] 1 tsp simple syrup or sweetener of choice
- [Optional] Whipped cream (dairy or plant-based) for garnish
- [Optional] A drizzle of extra chocolate syrup for garnish

## Instructions:

1. **Brew the Espresso**: Brew a shot of espresso using your preferred method (espresso machine, stovetop Moka pot, etc.).
2. **Prepare the Chocolate**: In a small bowl or cup, mix the chocolate syrup or melted dark chocolate with the freshly brewed espresso. Stir well until the chocolate is fully incorporated.
3. **Prepare the Ice**: Fill a tall glass with ice cubes, about halfway full.
4. **Pour the Espresso-Chocolate Mixture**: Pour the espresso and chocolate mixture over the ice, allowing it to chill instantly.
5. **Add the Milk**: Pour cold milk into the glass, mixing gently with the espresso and chocolate.
6. **Sweeten (Optional)**: If you like it sweeter, stir in simple syrup or any sweetener of choice.
7. **Garnish (Optional)**: Top with whipped cream and drizzle extra chocolate syrup on top for an extra indulgent touch.
8. **Serve**: Stir the drink to combine, and enjoy your rich, iced mocha!

## Tips and Recommendations:

- Use high-quality chocolate syrup or melted dark chocolate for a richer, more intense chocolate flavor.
- If you prefer a sweeter drink, feel free to add more sweetener or opt for chocolate syrup that already includes sugar.
- For a creamier texture, try using oat milk or coconut milk, which blends beautifully with the chocolate.
- For a stronger coffee flavor, you can use two shots of espresso or add a splash of cold brew concentrate.
- Try adding a pinch of cinnamon or nutmeg for a hint of spice that pairs beautifully with chocolate.

## Variations:

- **Iced White Mocha**: Swap the regular chocolate syrup with white chocolate syrup for a creamy, sweeter twist.
- **Iced Mocha Frappe**: Blend the ingredients with ice to create a thick, slushy texture for a more dessert-like experience.
- **Iced Mocha with Mint**: Add a few drops of mint extract or a fresh mint sprig to infuse a refreshing minty twist.

## Pairing Suggestions:

- Pair with chocolate chip cookies or a slice of chocolate cake for an ultimate chocolate experience.
- Enjoy with a warm croissant or a buttery scone to balance out the sweetness of the drink.
- A light fruit salad with berries or citrus will offer a fresh contrast to the mocha's richness.

## Interesting Fact:

Did you know that the **Iced Mocha** is a modern variation of the classic mocha? The original mocha, a combination of espresso and chocolate, dates back to the 18th century, but the iced version became popular in the 1990s as coffee culture grew worldwide. It's the perfect fusion of coffee and chocolate, loved by many for its versatility.

## Cultural Connection:

The **Iced Mocha** combines two of the most beloved global flavors - coffee and chocolate - and is often seen as a luxurious, dessert-like drink. Originating from Italy, where the mocha coffee was named after the Yemeni city of Mocha, known for its coffee beans, the iced variation has gained popularity in cafes around the world. Its combination of chocolate and espresso makes it a universal favorite, enjoyed both hot and cold, and often customized to personal tastes.

# Iced Caramel Macchiato

*Indulge in the irresistible allure of the Iced Caramel Macchiato, a cool and creamy coffee treat that effortlessly combines bold espresso with sweet, velvety caramel. This iced version of the classic macchiato delivers the perfect balance of coffee richness and sugary sweetness, all topped with a luscious swirl of caramel for extra indulgence. Perfect for those warm days or whenever you need a sweet coffee pick-me-up, the Iced Caramel Macchiato is a crowd-pleasing drink that's as beautiful as it is delicious.*

## Ingredients:

- 1 shot (1 ounce) of freshly brewed espresso
- 1 cup (8 ounces) cold milk (dairy or plant-based)
- 2 tbsps caramel syrup
- 1/2 cup (4 ounces) ice cubes
- [Optional] 1 tsp simple syrup or sweetener of choice
- [Optional] Caramel drizzle for garnish

## Instructions:

1. **Brew the Espresso**: Brew a shot of espresso using your preferred method (espresso machine, stovetop Moka pot, etc.).
2. **Prepare the Caramel**: In a small bowl or cup, mix 1 tablespoon of caramel syrup with the freshly brewed espresso. Stir well to combine.
3. **Prepare the Ice**: Fill a tall glass with ice cubes, about halfway full.
4. **Pour the Espresso-Caramel Mixture**: Pour the caramel espresso mixture over the ice, allowing it to cool instantly.
5. **Add the Milk**: Gently pour cold milk into the glass, allowing the milk to create beautiful layers with the espresso mixture.
6. **Sweeten (Optional)**: If you prefer a sweeter drink, stir in simple syrup or any sweetener of choice.
7. **Garnish (Optional)**: Drizzle extra caramel syrup over the top for a beautiful finish and added sweetness.
8. **Serve**: Stir the drink gently and enjoy the perfect blend of coffee and caramel!

## Tips and Recommendations:

- Use high-quality caramel syrup for the best flavor, or try making your own homemade caramel sauce for an extra indulgent touch.
- If you prefer a stronger coffee flavor, feel free to add an extra shot of espresso.
- For a dairy-free option, use almond milk, oat milk, or coconut milk - each will bring a unique flavor to the drink.
- Make sure to pour the milk slowly over the back of a spoon to create beautiful layers for a stunning presentation.

## Variations:

- **Salted Caramel Macchiato**: Add a pinch of sea salt to the caramel syrup for a deliciously sweet and salty twist.
- **Iced Mocha Caramel Macchiato**: Add a tablespoon of chocolate syrup to the caramel espresso mixture for a decadent mocha twist.
- **Iced Vanilla Caramel Macchiato**: For an extra layer of flavor, add a splash of vanilla syrup along with the caramel syrup.

## Pairing Suggestions:

- Pair with a buttery croissant or an almond biscotti for a delightful contrast of textures.
- Enjoy with a chocolate chip muffin or a slice of chocolate cake to enhance the caramel's richness.
- A light fruit salad or citrus scones will balance the sweetness of the drink beautifully.

## Interesting Fact:

Did you know that the **Macchiato** is Italian for "stained" or "spotted," referring to the small amount of milk added to the espresso to "stain" it? The **Iced Caramel Macchiato** is a modern, sweetened twist on this classic espresso drink, designed to be served cold for a refreshing experience.

## Cultural Connection:

The **Caramel Macchiato** originated in Italy and was popularized in the US by coffee chains in the 1990s. Over time, this espresso-based drink evolved into various iterations, including the iced version, which is now a favorite worldwide. The caramel element adds a distinctly American twist, bringing together the bitterness of espresso and the sweetness of caramel for a drink loved by coffee enthusiasts everywhere.

# Iced Vanilla Latte

*Indulge in the creamy goodness of an Iced Vanilla Latte, where rich espresso meets smooth, frothy milk and a sweet burst of vanilla. This refreshing drink is perfect for warm afternoons, offering a delightful balance of coffee and sweetness with just a hint of vanilla. Whether you're enjoying it as a midday pick-me-up or a cozy treat, the Iced Vanilla Latte is a simple yet luxurious coffee experience that will transport you to your favorite café with every sip.*

## Ingredients:

- 1 shot (1 ounce) of freshly brewed espresso
- 1 cup (8 ounces) cold milk (dairy or plant-based)
- 2 tbsps vanilla syrup
- 1/2 cup (4 ounces) ice cubes
- [Optional] 1 tsp simple syrup or sweetener of choice
- [Optional] Whipped cream or foam for topping

## Instructions:

1. **Brew the Espresso**: Brew one shot of espresso using your preferred method, whether it's an espresso machine, stovetop Moka pot, or Aeropress.
2. **Prepare the Ice**: Fill a tall glass with ice cubes, about halfway full.
3. **Add the Vanilla Syrup**: Pour 2 tablespoons of vanilla syrup into the glass over the ice.
4. **Pour the Espresso**: Add the freshly brewed espresso over the vanilla syrup, allowing the coffee to combine slightly with the syrup.
5. **Add the Milk**: Slowly pour the cold milk into the glass, gently mixing the drink. For a layered look, pour the milk over the back of a spoon.
6. **Sweeten (Optional)**: If you prefer a sweeter drink, stir in simple syrup or any sweetener of choice.
7. **Garnish (Optional)**: Top with whipped cream or a foam of your choice for an extra indulgent treat.
8. **Serve**: Stir and enjoy your deliciously chilled **Iced Vanilla Latte**!

## Tips and Recommendations:

- For a richer, creamier texture, use full-fat milk or a creamy plant-based option like oat milk.
- You can adjust the sweetness by adding more or less vanilla syrup depending on your taste.
- For a touch of spice, add a pinch of cinnamon or nutmeg to the drink for added warmth and complexity.
- To create beautiful layers, pour the milk slowly over the back of a spoon and let the espresso float on top.

## Variations:

- **Iced Caramel Vanilla Latte**: Add 1 tablespoon of caramel syrup along with the vanilla syrup for a sweet, caramel twist.
- **Iced Almond Vanilla Latte**: Substitute the milk with almond milk for a slightly nutty flavor that complements the vanilla perfectly.
- **Iced Vanilla Latte with a Kick**: Add a splash of Irish cream or hazelnut liqueur for an adult version of this classic.

## Pairing Suggestions:

- Pair with a fresh almond croissant or a slice of lemon pound cake to balance the sweetness of the drink.
- Serve alongside chocolate chip cookies or biscotti for a satisfying, crunchy contrast to the smooth, creamy latte.
- A fruit salad or granola bar pairs nicely with the drink for a light, refreshing snack.

## Interesting Fact:

Did you know that the **Iced Latte** originated as an American adaptation of the traditional Italian espresso? Adding cold milk and ice to espresso became popular as people sought refreshing ways to enjoy coffee during warm weather.

## Cultural Connection:

The **Vanilla Latte** gained popularity in the United States and quickly spread worldwide, with coffee shops offering various syrups and flavorings to customize the drink. Vanilla, a flavor originally from Mexico, has become a coffee staple thanks to its sweet and aromatic qualities, enhancing espresso-based drinks across the globe.

# Horchata Iced Coffee

*Discover the unique fusion of two beloved drinks with Horchata Iced Coffee - a refreshing, creamy, and slightly spiced coffee drink that blends the traditional Mexican horchata with bold, energizing espresso. The result is a perfectly balanced, sweet, and satisfying beverage, ideal for a warm afternoon or as a flavorful alternative to your usual iced coffee. Infused with cinnamon, rice, and almond milk, this iced coffee offers a smooth, aromatic experience with every sip.*

## Ingredients:

- 1 shot (1 ounce) of espresso
- 1 cup (8 ounces) chilled horchata (store-bought or homemade)
- 1/2 cup (4 ounces) ice cubes
- 1 tsp ground cinnamon
- 1 tbsp maple syrup or sweetener of choice (optional)
- [Optional] A splash of vanilla extract
- [Optional] Crushed ice for extra chill

## Instructions:

1. **Brew the Espresso**: Brew one shot of espresso using your preferred method (espresso machine, stovetop Moka pot, or Aeropress).
2. **Prepare the Horchata**: If you're using store-bought horchata, give it a good shake before pouring. If you're making it at home, blend rice, almond milk, cinnamon, and a sweetener of your choice, then strain.
3. **Fill the Glass with Ice**: Fill a tall glass with ice cubes to about halfway. If you prefer an extra chilly drink, you can crush the ice for a frosty texture.
4. **Pour the Horchata**: Pour the chilled horchata into the glass over the ice.
5. **Add the Espresso**: Slowly pour the freshly brewed espresso over the horchata. The rich, dark coffee will swirl beautifully with the creamy, cinnamon-infused milk.
6. **Mix and Sweeten (Optional)**: Stir the drink to combine. If you like it sweeter, add maple syrup or your sweetener of choice and a splash of vanilla extract for extra depth.
7. **Garnish (Optional)**: Sprinkle a pinch of ground cinnamon on top for added flavor and visual appeal.
8. **Serve**: Enjoy your **Horchata Iced Coffee**, a cool and creamy delight!

## Tips and Recommendations:

- If you're looking for a dairy-free option, make sure your horchata is made with almond milk or rice milk instead of dairy.
- To customize the flavor, experiment with adding a hint of nutmeg or a few drops of agave syrup for extra sweetness.
- For a more intense coffee flavor, double the espresso shot or add a shot of cold brew in place of espresso.
- Try garnishing with a cinnamon stick for an extra touch of elegance.

## Variations:

- **Horchata Iced Mocha**: Add 1 tablespoon of cocoa powder or chocolate syrup to the horchata before mixing in the espresso for a chocolatey twist.
- **Spicy Horchata Iced Coffee**: Add a pinch of chili powder or cayenne pepper for a spicy kick that pairs well with the sweetness of the horchata.
- **Horchata Iced Coffee with Coconut**: Use coconut milk instead of almond milk for a tropical flavor boost.

## Pairing Suggestions:

- Pair with cinnamon rolls or churros for a sweet, comforting snack that complements the spiced flavor of the drink.
- A light salad with citrus dressing or a fruit bowl makes a refreshing contrast to the richness of the coffee.
- For a hearty snack, try pairing with a savory avocado toast or grilled vegetable sandwich.

## Interesting Fact:

Did you know that **horchata** dates back to ancient civilizations like the Egyptians, where a similar drink was made with tiger nuts? It became a popular treat in Mexico, where it's made with rice and almonds for a creamy, nutty flavor.

## Cultural Connection:

**Horchata** has its roots in Spain, but in Mexico, it evolved into a deliciously creamy, cinnamon-flavored drink often paired with spicy foods. The combination of horchata with coffee creates a fusion of Mexican tradition with the beloved energy of espresso, offering a unique twist on both cultures.

# Coconut Water Cold Brew

*Experience the invigorating combination of cold brew coffee and hydrating coconut water with this Coconut Water Cold Brew. A refreshing twist on your traditional iced coffee, this recipe offers a naturally sweetened, light, and hydrating drink with a hint of tropical flavor. The coconut water adds a subtle richness, while the cold brew coffee provides a smooth, robust base. Perfect for those hot days when you need a revitalizing, caffeinated pick-me-up.*

## Ingredients:

- 1 cup (8 ounces) cold brew coffee
- 1/2 cup (4 ounces) coconut water
- 1 tbsp maple syrup or sweetener of choice (optional)
- 1/4 tsp vanilla extract (optional)
- Ice cubes (as needed)

## Instructions:

1. **Prepare Cold Brew Coffee**: Brew the cold brew coffee in advance by steeping coarsely ground coffee beans in cold water for 12-24 hours. Strain to remove grounds.
2. **Combine the Ingredients**: In a tall glass, pour the chilled cold brew coffee and coconut water.
3. **Sweeten (Optional)**: Add maple syrup or sweetener to taste, and stir to combine.
4. **Add Ice**: Fill the glass with ice cubes to chill the drink further.
5. **Flavor (Optional)**: For added flavor, add a splash of vanilla extract and stir well.
6. **Serve**: Enjoy your Coconut Water Cold Brew, a revitalizing and smooth coffee drink.

## Tips and Recommendations:

- If you prefer a stronger coffee flavor, use more cold brew or less coconut water.
- For a refreshing twist, try adding a splash of lime juice to bring out the coconut's natural citrusy notes.
- Coconut water can be naturally sweet, so adjust the amount of sweetener based on your preference.

## Variations:

- **Coconut Water Cold Brew with Almond Milk**: Replace coconut water with almond milk for a creamier, richer texture.
- **Spicy Coconut Cold Brew**: Add a pinch of ground cinnamon or nutmeg for a warm, spicy kick that complements the coffee.
- **Iced Coconut Latte**: For a more indulgent version, add a splash of coconut milk and blend with ice for a smooth iced latte.

## Pairing Suggestions:

- Pair with a light coconut macaroon or a fresh fruit salad to balance the coffee's richness with a sweet, tropical treat.
- A grain-based snack, like granola or oat bars, pairs well with this drink, offering a satisfying and energizing combination.

## Interesting Fact:

Did you know that cold brew coffee is less acidic than traditional brewed coffee, making it a gentler option for sensitive stomachs while still delivering a bold flavor?

## Cultural Connection:

Cold brew coffee has gained popularity for its smooth, rich taste and higher caffeine content. The addition of coconut water adds a tropical element, often associated with health and wellness, making this beverage a modern fusion of flavors that's both refreshing and energizing.

# Almond Joy Iced Coffee

*Indulge in the delicious combination of bold coffee, creamy coconut, and nutty almonds with this Almond Joy Iced Coffee. Inspired by the classic candy bar, this decadent iced coffee is the perfect treat for those who love sweet, nutty flavors. The smooth coffee base is complemented by coconut milk, a touch of almond syrup, and a sprinkle of chocolate, making it a refreshing and satisfying drink for any time of day.*

## Ingredients:

- 1 cup (8 ounces) cold brew coffee or strong brewed coffee
- 1/2 cup (4 ounces) coconut milk (or any plant-based milk)
- 2 tbsps almond syrup or hazelnut syrup
- 1 tbsp chocolate syrup (optional)
- Ice cubes (as needed)
- 1/4 cup crushed almonds for garnish
- Chocolate shavings (optional)

## Instructions:

1. **Prepare Coffee**: Brew your cold brew coffee in advance or prepare a strong brewed coffee, and allow it to cool.
2. **Combine the Ingredients**: In a tall glass, pour the chilled coffee and coconut milk.
3. **Add Sweeteners**: Stir in almond syrup (or hazelnut syrup) and chocolate syrup (if using).
4. **Add Ice**: Fill the glass with ice cubes to keep the drink chilled.
5. **Garnish**: Top with crushed almonds and a sprinkle of chocolate shavings for extra flavor and visual appeal.
6. **Serve**: Stir gently before drinking and enjoy your indulgent **Almond Joy Iced Coffee**.

## Tips and Recommendations:

- For an extra creamy texture, use full-fat coconut milk.
- Adjust the amount of almond syrup based on your desired level of sweetness.
- If you prefer a richer chocolate flavor, add more chocolate syrup or drizzle it on top for a gourmet touch.

## Variations:

- **Almond Joy Iced Latte**: Replace coconut milk with steamed almond milk for a creamier version.
- **Decaf Option**: Use decaffeinated coffee to enjoy this treat without the caffeine kick.
- **Sugar-Free Version**: Opt for a sugar-free almond or chocolate syrup for a lighter, low-sugar version.

## Pairing Suggestions:

- Pair with a rich chocolate croissant or almond biscotti for a luxurious treat.
- This drink also pairs beautifully with a light fruit salad, offering a refreshing contrast to the sweet, nutty coffee.

## Interesting Fact:

Did you know that cold brew coffee is made by steeping coffee grounds in cold water for 12 to 24 hours? This slow extraction process creates a smoother, more robust flavor, perfect for blending with sweet syrups and creamy milk.

## Cultural Connection:

The **Almond Joy Iced Coffee** brings together the flavors of the popular candy bar, which has been a favorite in the United States since the 1940s. By merging these nostalgic flavors with cold brew coffee, this recipe offers a delightful fusion of coffee culture and sweet indulgence, ideal for anyone with a sweet tooth.

# Iced Coffee Creations:

# Salted Caramel Cold Brew

*Indulge in the sweet and salty perfection of Salted Caramel Cold Brew, a refreshing iced coffee creation that combines the boldness of cold brew with the rich, buttery flavor of caramel, enhanced by a touch of sea salt. This drink is a perfect balance of sweet and savory, with the cold brew offering a smooth, less acidic base. It's the ultimate treat for anyone craving a cool, creamy coffee indulgence with a twist of saltiness to elevate the flavor.*

## Ingredients:

- 1 cup (8 ounces) cold brew coffee or strong brewed coffee
- 2 tbsps salted caramel sauce
- 1/4 cup (2 ounces) almond milk (or any plant-based milk)
- Ice cubes (as needed)
- 1/4 tsp sea salt (optional, for extra saltiness)
- Whipped cream (optional, for topping)
- Additional salted caramel sauce for drizzling (optional)

## Instructions:

1. **Prepare Coffee**: Brew your cold brew coffee in advance or prepare a strong brewed coffee, and allow it to cool.
2. **Mix the Flavors**: In a glass, pour the cold brew coffee and salted caramel sauce. Stir until the caramel is completely dissolved.
3. **Add Milk**: Pour in the almond milk (or your choice of plant-based milk) and mix until combined.
4. **Ice It**: Fill the glass with ice cubes to chill the coffee and create a refreshing drink.
5. **Garnish**: Optionally, top with whipped cream and a drizzle of salted caramel sauce for an extra indulgent touch.
6. **Finish**: Sprinkle a pinch of sea salt on top for that signature salted caramel flavor. Stir gently before drinking and enjoy!

## Tips and Recommendations:

- For an extra creamy texture, use coconut milk or oat milk.
- Adjust the amount of salted caramel sauce based on how sweet or salty you like your drink.
  - If you prefer a stronger coffee flavor, use a higher ratio of cold brew to milk.

## Variations:

- **Salted Caramel Iced Latte**: Replace the cold brew coffee with espresso for a richer, more robust coffee flavor.
- **Sugar-Free Option**: Use a sugar-free caramel syrup or make your own by combining a sugar substitute and a pinch of sea salt.
- **Vegan Whipped Cream**: For a fully vegan version, use coconut whipped cream as a topping.

## Pairing Suggestions:

- Pair with a decadent chocolate chip cookie or caramelized almond tart to enhance the sweet and salty flavor profile.
- This drink also goes perfectly with a rich, creamy cheesecake or a nut-based granola bar for a snack that complements the coffee's depth.

## Interesting Fact:

Did you know that the combination of sweet and salty in desserts, like salted caramel, is scientifically proven to activate pleasure centers in the brain, making it one of the most irresistible flavor combinations?

## Cultural Connection:

The concept of salted caramel has French origins, where the sweet and savory flavors were first paired in candies and desserts. Over time, it has become a beloved addition to coffee recipes worldwide, providing an indulgent treat that balances rich coffee with decadent caramel.

# Cinnamon Dolce Iced Coffee

*Indulge in the delightful warmth of cinnamon combined with the smooth, refreshing chill of iced coffee. Cinnamon Dolce Iced Coffee is a perfect treat for cinnamon lovers, offering the ideal balance of sweet, spicy, and creamy flavors. With the boldness of cold brew coffee and the rich, aromatic sweetness of cinnamon syrup, this drink provides a cozy yet cool coffee experience. It's an excellent way to beat the heat while savoring a comforting blend of flavors that feels like a luxurious treat on a warm day.*

## Ingredients:

- 1 cup (8 ounces) cold brew coffee or strong brewed coffee, chilled
- 2 tbsps cinnamon dolce syrup (or to taste)
- 1/4 cup (2 ounces) almond milk (or any plant-based milk)
- Ice cubes (as needed)
- Whipped cream (optional, for topping)
- Ground cinnamon (optional, for garnish)

## Instructions:

1. **Brew and Chill Coffee**: Prepare your cold brew coffee in advance or brew a strong coffee and let it cool.
2. **Sweeten with Syrup**: Pour the chilled cold brew coffee into a glass, then stir in the cinnamon dolce syrup until fully combined.
3. **Add Milk**: Pour in the almond milk (or your choice of plant-based milk) and stir to blend the flavors together.
4. **Ice It**: Fill the glass with ice cubes to chill the drink to perfection.
5. **Optional Garnish**: Top with whipped cream for a creamy finish, and sprinkle a pinch of ground cinnamon for an extra touch of spice.
6. **Enjoy**: Stir the drink before sipping to ensure the cinnamon flavor is evenly distributed throughout.

## Tips and Recommendations:

- **Adjust Sweetness**: If you prefer a sweeter drink, increase the amount of cinnamon dolce syrup or use a flavored syrup like vanilla.
- **Dairy-Free Option**: Use oat milk or coconut milk for a creamy, dairy-free version.
- **Extra Spice**: Add a pinch of nutmeg or clove for a deeper, more complex spice flavor.

## Variations:

- **Cinnamon Dolce Iced Latte**: For a more robust coffee flavor, substitute cold brew with espresso or a shot of strong brewed coffee.
- **Iced Cinnamon Dolce Mocha**: Add 1 tablespoon of cocoa powder or chocolate syrup to the mix for a chocolatey twist.
- **Spicy Cinnamon Dolce**: Spice things up with a dash of cayenne pepper or a little ginger for a warming kick.

## Pairing Suggestions:

- Pair with a cinnamon roll or almond croissant for a perfect blend of sweet and spiced flavors.
- Enjoy with a light fruit salad or yogurt parfait to balance the richness of the coffee.

## Interesting Fact:

Did you know that cinnamon has been used for centuries in cooking and medicine? It's thought to have health benefits like reducing inflammation and boosting metabolism, making your Cinnamon Dolce Iced Coffee not only delicious but potentially good for you too!

## Cultural Connection:

Cinnamon is a spice with deep roots in various cultures worldwide, from its use in ancient Egypt to its popularity in Mediterranean and Middle Eastern cuisines. The combination of cinnamon with coffee has been a longstanding tradition in coffee-drinking cultures, offering a fragrant, spiced dimension to the beverage.

# Chocolate Almond Milk Iced Coffee

*If you're craving a refreshing yet indulgent treat, Chocolate Almond Milk Iced Coffee is the perfect choice. The creamy, nutty flavor of almond milk is complemented by the rich depth of chocolate, while the smooth cold brew coffee adds the perfect amount of boldness. This drink is ideal for those who love chocolate and coffee but prefer a dairy-free option without compromising on flavor. It's the perfect way to cool down on a warm day while enjoying a little bit of luxury in your cup.*

## Ingredients:

- 1 cup (8 ounces) cold brew coffee or strong brewed coffee, chilled
- 2 tbsps chocolate syrup (or cocoa powder sweetened with maple syrup)
- 1/2 cup (4 ounces) unsweetened almond milk
- Ice cubes (as needed)
- Whipped coconut cream (optional, for topping)
- Shaved chocolate or cocoa powder (optional, for garnish)

## Instructions:

1. **Prepare the Coffee**: Brew your cold brew coffee or a strong espresso-style coffee. Let it chill for a few hours or overnight.
2. **Mix the Chocolate**: In a small bowl, stir the chocolate syrup into the chilled coffee until fully combined.
3. **Add Almond Milk**: Pour in the almond milk and stir gently to combine.
4. **Serve Over Ice**: Fill a tall glass with ice cubes and pour the chocolate coffee mixture over the ice.
5. **Optional Garnish**: Top with a dollop of whipped coconut cream for extra creaminess, and sprinkle shaved chocolate or a dusting of cocoa powder on top for added elegance.
6. **Enjoy**: Stir before sipping to ensure the chocolate and almond milk are well blended.

## Tips and Recommendations:

- **Adjust Sweetness**: If you like your drink sweeter, add more chocolate syrup or a teaspoon of maple syrup to taste.
- **Dairy-Free & Nut-Free Option**: Swap almond milk for oat milk or coconut milk for a richer, creamier taste.
- **Chocolate Variety**: For a more intense chocolate flavor, use dark chocolate syrup or melt dark chocolate into the coffee instead of using store-bought syrup.

## Variations:

- **Iced Mocha**: Add 1 tablespoon of cocoa powder and 1 teaspoon of sugar to the coffee before mixing with the almond milk for a more intense mocha flavor.
- **Iced Chocolate Almond Latte**: For a richer experience, add 1 shot of espresso to the coffee and almond milk mixture.
- **Mint Chocolate**: Add a few fresh mint leaves or a drop of peppermint extract to give the drink a refreshing mint-chocolate twist.

## Pairing Suggestions:

- Pair with a slice of vegan chocolate cake or brownies for an indulgent treat.
- Enjoy with a light fruit salad or a granola bar to balance the rich flavors of the coffee and chocolate.

## Interesting Fact:

Did you know that the first chocolate-flavored coffee drink was invented in the 17th century by a Spanish monk? It was a blend of coffee, cocoa, and spices, considered an exotic luxury in Europe at the time!

## Cultural Connection:

Chocolate and coffee have a deep-rooted history, especially in Latin American cultures, where both ingredients are native. This fusion of coffee and chocolate has been enjoyed for centuries, creating a rich tradition of indulgence in various forms - from the iconic mocha to chocolate coffee drinks enjoyed across the globe.

# Mint Mojito Iced Coffee

*Get ready for a refreshing twist on your typical iced coffee! Mint Mojito Iced Coffee combines the invigorating flavors of mint and lime with the rich depth of cold brew coffee, creating a vibrant, cooling experience that's perfect for a hot summer day. This delightful fusion of coffee and classic mojito ingredients offers a light, herbal kick, while still delivering that essential caffeine boost. With a burst of citrus and minty freshness, it's the perfect way to wake up and cool down all at once.*

## Ingredients:

- 1 cup (8 ounces) cold brew coffee or strong brewed coffee, chilled
- 6-8 fresh mint leaves (plus extra for garnish)
- 1 tbsp fresh lime juice
- 1 tsp sugar or maple syrup (adjust to taste)
- 1/2 cup (4 ounces) sparkling water or club soda
- Ice cubes (as needed)
- Lime wedge (for garnish)
- Optional: 1-2 tbsps of coconut milk (for extra creaminess)

## Instructions:

1. **Muddle the Mint**: In a glass, lightly muddle the mint leaves with the lime juice and sugar/maple syrup using a muddler or the back of a spoon. This releases the mint oils and infuses the lime juice with refreshing flavor.
2. **Add Cold Brew**: Pour the chilled cold brew coffee into the glass with the muddled mint and lime mixture. Stir well to combine.
3. **Add Ice**: Fill the glass with ice cubes to chill the mixture.
4. **Top with Sparkling Water**: Pour in the sparkling water or club soda and give it a gentle stir to combine.
5. **Optional Creaminess**: For a smoother, creamier texture, add a splash of coconut milk and stir to blend.
6. **Garnish and Serve**: Garnish with extra mint leaves and a wedge of lime. Enjoy your refreshing Mint Mojito Iced Coffee!

## Tips and Recommendations:

- **Sweetness Level**: Adjust the sweetness by adding more or less sugar or maple syrup. You can also try agave syrup for a lower glycemic option.
- **Make it Stronger**: If you prefer a stronger coffee flavor, use a more concentrated cold brew or add an extra shot of espresso.
- **Herbal Twist**: Add a splash of fresh lemon juice for an extra citrusy kick, or use a combination of mint and basil leaves for an herbaceous twist.

## Variations:

- **Mint Mojito Latte**: Add a splash of oat milk or almond milk to turn your Mint Mojito Iced Coffee into a creamy, refreshing latte.
- **Coconut Mojito**: Swap the sparkling water with coconut water for a more tropical flavor.
- **Iced Mocha Mojito**: For a chocolate twist, stir in a teaspoon of cocoa powder or chocolate syrup along with the lime and mint.

## Pairing Suggestions:

- Enjoy with a fresh fruit salad to complement the citrus and mint flavors.
- Pair with a vegan chocolate chip cookie for a sweet and refreshing treat.
- A light quinoa salad with lime and avocado would balance out the fresh, vibrant notes of this drink.

## Interesting Fact:

Did you know that the Mojito originated in Cuba in the 16th century? Originally a medicinal drink made with indigenous herbs, lime, and rum, it was later adapted into the refreshing cocktail we enjoy today. This Mint Mojito Iced Coffee is a non-alcoholic, coffee-infused twist on the classic!

## Cultural Connection:

The Mojito is a beloved Cuban cocktail, known for its refreshing combination of mint, lime, and rum. It has inspired countless variations over the years, and this coffee twist is a fun, innovative take on the classic drink. The addition of cold brew coffee not only adds a modern touch but also taps into the rich Latin American coffee culture.

# Iced Maple Pecan Latte

*Treat yourself to the perfect balance of sweet and nutty with the Iced Maple Pecan Latte. This cold brew masterpiece combines the rich, bold flavor of espresso with the comforting sweetness of maple syrup and the warm, nutty essence of pecans. It's a delightful iced coffee that's perfect for cozy afternoons or a refreshing pick-me-up on a hot day. The smooth, nutty flavor makes it feel like a luxurious fall treat, but it's delicious enough to enjoy any time of year.*

## Ingredients:

- 1 shot (1 ounce) of espresso or 1/2 cup strong brewed coffee, chilled
- 1 tbsp maple syrup
- 1/4 cup pecan milk or other plant-based milk (such as almond or oat milk)
- 1/2 cup ice cubes
- Optional: 1/4 tsp vanilla extract
- Optional: Crushed pecans for garnish

## Instructions:

1. **Brew the Coffee**: Brew a shot of espresso or make a strong cup of coffee and allow it to chill.
2. **Prepare the Milk**: In a small saucepan, warm the pecan milk over low heat, just until it's warm but not boiling. If you prefer a creamy texture, add a splash of vanilla extract to enhance the flavor.
3. **Mix the Drink**: In a tall glass, combine the chilled espresso or coffee with the maple syrup. Stir well to dissolve the syrup completely.
4. **Add Ice**: Fill the glass with ice cubes to chill the drink.
5. **Pour the Milk**: Slowly pour the warm pecan milk over the coffee and maple mixture, allowing it to gently blend.
6. **Garnish and Serve**: Garnish with crushed pecans for added texture and flavor. Enjoy your Iced Maple Pecan Latte!

## Tips and Recommendations:

- **Sweetness Level**: Adjust the sweetness by adding more or less maple syrup, depending on your taste. You can also try agave syrup for a milder sweetness.
- **Creamier Texture**: For a richer texture, increase the amount of pecan milk or add a dash of coconut cream for a velvety finish.
- **Nutty Twist**: Toast the crushed pecans lightly to bring out a deeper flavor before adding them as a garnish.

## Variations:

- **Maple Pecan Mocha**: Add a tablespoon of cocoa powder or chocolate syrup to turn your latte into a mocha.
- **Iced Cinnamon Maple Pecan Latte**: Sprinkle a dash of cinnamon on top for an extra layer of warmth.
- **Vegan Maple Pecan Latte**: For a dairy-free option, stick with pecan or almond milk, and use maple syrup as the sole sweetener.

## Pairing Suggestions:

- Pair with a slice of vegan banana bread or cinnamon rolls for a cozy and satisfying treat.
- Enjoy with a handful of roasted almonds or a small bowl of granola for a crunchy contrast.
- Complement with a light fruit salad to balance the richness of the latte.

## Interesting Fact:

Did you know that maple syrup is made from the sap of sugar maple trees and is a traditional product of North America? It has been used as a sweetener for centuries, making it a perfect match for coffee-based beverages.

## Cultural Connection:

Maple syrup is a quintessential part of Canadian and northeastern U.S. culture, particularly in the colder months. It's often associated with warmth, comfort, and homegrown traditions, making it the perfect complement to a cozy, iced latte like this one. Enjoy the richness of this uniquely North American flavor in your everyday coffee routine!

# Iced Peach Green Tea

*Cool off with a refreshing and aromatic Iced Peach Green Tea, a delightful fusion of delicate green tea and the sweet, juicy essence of ripe peaches. This invigorating drink is perfect for a hot day, combining the antioxidants of green tea with the natural sweetness of peaches. It's light, fruity, and a little floral, making it an ideal thirst-quencher for those who crave a little elegance in their iced beverages. Whether you're lounging on a sunny afternoon or need a break from your usual coffee routine, this iced tea is sure to hit the spot.*

## Ingredients:

- 1 green tea bag
- 1 medium ripe peach, peeled and sliced
- 1 tbsp maple syrup (or to taste)
- 1/2 cup cold water
- 1/2 cup ice cubes
- 1/2 cup sparkling water (optional, for a fizzy twist)
- Optional: A few fresh mint leaves for garnish

## Instructions:

1. **Brew the Green Tea**: In a cup, pour 1/2 cup of boiling water over the green tea bag. Let it steep for 3-4 minutes, then remove the tea bag and allow the tea to cool completely.
2. **Prepare the Peach Purée**: In a blender, blend the peach slices with 1 tablespoon of maple syrup and a small splash of water until smooth.
3. **Combine**: In a tall glass, add the cooled green tea and peach purée. Stir well to combine the flavors.
4. **Add Ice**: Fill the glass with ice cubes, and pour sparkling water on top for a bubbly effect (optional).
5. **Garnish and Serve**: Garnish with a sprig of fresh mint for a refreshing touch. Enjoy your vibrant Iced Peach Green Tea!

## Tips and Recommendations:

- **Peach Sweetness**: Adjust the sweetness by adding more or less maple syrup depending on the ripeness of your peaches.
- **Chill the Tea**: For the best taste, chill the green tea and peach purée before mixing. This prevents the ice from diluting the drink too quickly.
- **Minty Touch**: Muddle a few mint leaves in the bottom of the glass before adding the tea for an extra layer of freshness.

## Variations:

- **Iced Peach Matcha Latte**: Swap the green tea for matcha for a creamy twist on this iced tea.
- **Peach Basil Green Tea**: Add fresh basil leaves to the peach purée for a sweet and herbal flavor combination.
- **Peach Iced Tea Lemonade**: Add a splash of lemon juice for a tangy twist on this fruity iced tea.

## Pairing Suggestions:

- Pair with a light summer salad, such as a spinach and arugula salad with citrus vinaigrette.
- Enjoy with a slice of vegan lemon drizzle cake for a refreshing and sweet combo.
- Complement with light crackers or hummus for a snack that balances the sweetness of the peach.

## Interesting Fact:

Did you know that green tea has been enjoyed for thousands of years, particularly in China and Japan? It's renowned for its numerous health benefits, including boosting metabolism and improving skin health.

## Cultural Connection:

Green tea has long been an integral part of Asian culture, particularly in Japan and China, where it's deeply woven into traditional ceremonies and daily rituals. Combining green tea with fresh fruit, like peach, reflects the creative ways different cultures blend natural flavors to enhance the refreshing properties of tea.

# Watermelon Mint Iced Coffee

*Cool down with a Watermelon Mint Iced Coffee, a refreshing fusion of bold coffee, juicy watermelon, and fresh mint. This inventive iced coffee drink offers the perfect balance between the richness of coffee and the natural sweetness of summer fruits. The watermelon adds a light, hydrating touch, while the mint elevates the drink with a burst of freshness. If you're looking for something different that combines coffee with fruity, refreshing flavors, this is your go-to beverage for those warm afternoons or whenever you crave something new!*

## Ingredients:

- 1 shot (1 ounce) of espresso
- 1/2 cup watermelon, cubed and pureed
- 4-5 fresh mint leaves, plus extra for garnish
- 1 tsp agave syrup (or sweetener of choice)
- 1/2 cup cold water
- 1/2 cup ice cubes
- Optional: A splash of oat milk or almond milk for creaminess

## Instructions:

1. **Brew the Espresso**: Brew a shot of espresso using your preferred method and set aside to cool slightly.
2. **Prepare the Watermelon Mint Purée**: Blend the watermelon cubes and fresh mint leaves together until smooth.
3. **Sweeten**: Add agave syrup (or your preferred sweetener) to the watermelon mint purée and stir to combine.
4. **Mix**: In a tall glass, add the cooled espresso and watermelon mint purée. Stir gently to combine the flavors.
5. **Add Ice**: Fill the glass with ice cubes. If you prefer a creamier texture, you can add a splash of oat or almond milk at this stage.
6. **Garnish and Serve**: Garnish with a few fresh mint leaves and a small wedge of watermelon on the rim of the glass. Serve chilled and enjoy!

## Tips and Recommendations:

- **Minty Freshness**: If you want a stronger mint flavor, gently muddle the mint leaves before blending them with the watermelon.
- **Chilled Espresso**: Let the espresso cool before adding to the drink, or pour it over ice to avoid diluting the flavors.
- **Sweetness Adjustment**: Depending on the sweetness of the watermelon, you may need to adjust the amount of sweetener. Taste and add more as needed.

## Variations:

- **Watermelon Mint Cold Brew**: Use cold brew coffee instead of espresso for a smoother, less acidic flavor.
- **Watermelon Lime Twist**: Add a squeeze of fresh lime juice to the watermelon mint purée for a zesty twist.
- **Coconut Water**: Swap the cold water for coconut water for a hydrating, tropical flavor.

## Pairing Suggestions:

- Pair with a light fruit salad, such as a mix of berries and citrus fruits, to complement the freshness of the watermelon.
- Enjoy with a slice of vegan lemon pound cake or a piece of watermelon sorbet for a cool, sweet treat.
- Pair with crisp, lightly salted crackers or a small serving of guacamole for a savory contrast to the sweetness.

## Interesting Fact:

Did you know that watermelon is 92% water, making it one of the most hydrating fruits you can eat? It's perfect for staying refreshed on hot days, and when blended with coffee, it provides a natural sweetness that pairs wonderfully with the rich, deep flavors of espresso.

## Cultural Connection:

Coffee drinks with fruit infusions, such as the watermelon in this recipe, are gaining popularity as people seek refreshing alternatives to traditional hot coffee. This combination of coffee and fruit is a fusion of two beloved beverage traditions - coffee culture and summer fruit drinks - which offer a new way to enjoy the best of both worlds.

# Cherry Vanilla Iced Coffee

*Indulge in the sweet, tart flavors of Cherry Vanilla Iced Coffee, a delightful and refreshing drink that brings together the rich depth of coffee with the fruity essence of cherries and the comforting warmth of vanilla. This drink balances the natural sweetness of ripe cherries with the smoothness of coffee, creating a perfectly chilled treat for any occasion. Whether you're seeking a summer refresher or a special coffee moment, this iced coffee creation will surely satisfy your cravings with its unique and vibrant twist.*

## Ingredients:

- 1 shot (1 ounce) of espresso
- 1/4 cup fresh cherries, pitted and mashed
- 1 tsp vanilla extract
- 1 tsp agave syrup (or sweetener of choice)
- 1/2 cup cold water
- 1/2 cup ice cubes
- Optional: A splash of oat milk or almond milk for added creaminess

## Instructions:

1. **Brew the Espresso**: Brew a shot of espresso using your preferred method and let it cool slightly.
2. **Prepare the Cherry Puree**: Mash the fresh cherries with a fork or blend them into a smooth puree. If you like your drink sweeter, add a little agave syrup or sweetener of choice to the cherries.
3. **Combine Flavors**: In a tall glass, combine the cooled espresso, cherry puree, and vanilla extract. Stir gently to blend the flavors together.
4. **Add Ice**: Fill the glass with ice cubes to chill the coffee mixture.
5. **Optional Creaminess**: If you prefer a creamier texture, add a splash of oat milk or almond milk. Stir again to combine.
6. **Serve and Enjoy**: Garnish with a few whole cherries or a vanilla bean for an elegant touch. Sip and enjoy this sweet and fruity coffee delight!

## Tips and Recommendations:

- **Sweetness Adjustment**: Taste the cherry puree before adding it to the espresso. If your cherries are particularly tart, you may want to increase the sweetener.
- **Cherry Alternatives**: If fresh cherries are out of season, you can use frozen cherries or even cherry juice concentrate as a substitute.
- **Layering Flavors**: For an extra burst of flavor, try adding a pinch of cinnamon to the cherry puree or a drop of almond extract to the mix.

## Variations:

- **Cherry Almond Iced Coffee**: Add a dash of almond extract for a nutty twist that complements the cherry and vanilla.
- **Cherry Coconut Iced Coffee**: Swap the oat or almond milk for coconut milk for a tropical, creamy variation.
- **Cherry Mocha Iced Coffee**: For a chocolatey upgrade, add a tablespoon of cocoa powder to the espresso before combining it with the cherry puree.

## Pairing Suggestions:

- Pair with a slice of **vegan chocolate cake** or **berry scones** for a delightful afternoon treat.
- Serve with a small bowl of **roasted almonds** or **spiced nuts** to balance the sweetness of the drink with a savory snack.
- Enjoy alongside a fresh **fruit salad** with berries, citrus, and melon for a refreshing and light contrast.

## Interesting Fact:

Did you know that cherries have been enjoyed for over 2,000 years, with records of their cultivation dating back to ancient Rome? Their natural sweetness and refreshing taste make them a perfect addition to many beverages, including this iced coffee.

## Cultural Connection:

Iced coffee drinks with fruity additions, like this **Cherry Vanilla Iced Coffee**, are part of a growing trend to blend the deep, bold flavors of coffee with fresh fruit flavors. This innovative fusion reflects a global move towards refreshing, seasonal beverages that are as delightful as they are energizing.

# Raspberry Lemonade Iced Coffee

*Looking for a bright and tangy twist on your iced coffee? Raspberry Lemonade Iced Coffee is the perfect blend of bold coffee, sweet raspberries, and zesty lemon, creating a refreshing drink that awakens your senses with every sip. This invigorating iced coffee combines the richness of espresso with the fruity freshness of raspberries and a citrusy kick, offering a unique and rejuvenating coffee experience. Perfect for summer afternoons or whenever you need a burst of freshness!*

## Ingredients:

- 1 shot (1 ounce) of espresso
- 1/4 cup fresh raspberries (or frozen raspberries, thawed)
- 1 tbsp lemon juice (freshly squeezed)
- 1 tsp maple syrup or agave syrup (or sweetener of choice)
- 1/2 cup cold water
- 1/2 cup ice cubes
- Optional: A splash of oat milk or coconut milk for added creaminess

## Instructions:

1. **Brew the Espresso**: Brew a shot of espresso and set it aside to cool.
2. **Prepare the Raspberry Puree**: In a small bowl, mash the raspberries with a fork or blend them into a smooth puree. Add the maple syrup (or your preferred sweetener) and lemon juice, and stir to combine.
3. **Mix the Coffee**: In a tall glass, combine the cooled espresso with the raspberry-lemon mixture. Stir gently to blend the flavors.
4. **Add Ice**: Fill the glass with ice cubes to chill the coffee mixture.
5. **Optional Creaminess**: If you want a creamier texture, add a splash of oat or coconut milk. Stir to incorporate.
6. **Serve and Enjoy**: Garnish with extra raspberries or a slice of lemon on the rim of the glass for a vibrant touch. Sip and enjoy your refreshing, fruity iced coffee!

## Tips and Recommendations:

- **Adjust the Sweetness**: If you like your drink sweeter, feel free to add a bit more maple syrup or agave to the raspberry puree.
- **Lemon Zest**: For an extra zing, consider adding a small amount of lemon zest to the drink for an intensified citrus flavor.
- **Berry Variations**: If raspberries aren't available, try using blackberries or strawberries for a different berry twist.

## Variations:

- **Raspberry Lemonade Latte**: Add a splash of steamed oat milk for a creamy version of this iced coffee.
- **Iced Raspberry Lemonade with Espresso Shots**: Skip the espresso and simply mix the raspberry lemonade with cold water for a lighter, non-caffeinated drink.
- **Minty Raspberry Lemonade Iced Coffee**: Add a few fresh mint leaves to the raspberry puree for a refreshing, herbaceous flavor.

## Pairing Suggestions:

- Pair with a light **vegan lemon drizzle cake** or **shortbread cookies** to complement the citrusy notes in the drink.
- Enjoy alongside **vegan yogurt parfaits** with fresh berries and granola for a well-rounded, refreshing breakfast or brunch option.
- Serve with a handful of **roasted almonds** or **spiced cashews** to add a crunchy, savory contrast to the drink's sweet and tart flavors.

## Interesting Fact:

Did you know that raspberries are one of the oldest cultivated fruits in the world, dating back to ancient Greece? Their tart and sweet flavor makes them a perfect pairing for a variety of beverages, including this refreshing iced coffee.

## Cultural Connection:

While lemonade is a classic American summer refreshment, the combination of fruit with coffee is gaining popularity worldwide as a unique twist on traditional iced coffee drinks. **Raspberry Lemonade Iced Coffee** embodies the modern trend of fusing coffee with fresh, seasonal fruits for a vibrant and energizing experience.

# Iced Honey Lavender Latte

*Indulge in the soothing, floral flavors of a Honey Lavender Latte - a delightful fusion of fragrant lavender, sweet honey, and smooth espresso, served over ice for a refreshing, yet cozy treat. This unique iced latte combines the calming essence of lavender with the richness of espresso and a hint of natural sweetness from honey, making it the perfect drink to unwind or savor during a quiet afternoon. Discover how this gentle, aromatic iced coffee creation will transport you to a peaceful moment in every sip.*

## Ingredients:

- 1 shot (1 ounce) of espresso
- 1 tbsp lavender syrup (or homemade lavender simple syrup)
- 1 tsp honey (or maple syrup for a vegan option)
- 1/2 cup ice cubes
- 1/2 cup cold milk of choice (almond milk, oat milk, or dairy milk)
- Optional: A sprinkle of dried lavender buds for garnish

## Instructions:

1. **Brew the Espresso**: Brew a shot of espresso and allow it to cool slightly.
2. **Make the Lavender Syrup**: If you don't have lavender syrup on hand, make it by heating 1/4 cup water, 1/4 cup sugar, and 1 tablespoon dried lavender in a small saucepan. Simmer for 5 minutes, strain out the lavender, and cool.
3. **Sweeten the Coffee**: In a tall glass, combine the cooled espresso with the honey and lavender syrup. Stir gently to combine.
4. **Add Ice**: Fill the glass with ice cubes to chill the coffee mixture.
5. **Pour the Milk**: Slowly pour the cold milk over the coffee and ice, creating a creamy layer on top.
6. **Serve and Enjoy**: Optionally, garnish with a sprinkle of dried lavender buds for an added floral touch and serve immediately.

## Tips and Recommendations:

- **Lavender Intensity**: If you prefer a more pronounced lavender flavor, increase the amount of lavender syrup to taste.
- **Sweetness Levels**: Adjust the honey or maple syrup to your liking. You can also try a few drops of vanilla extract for an added depth of flavor.
- **Cold Foam**: For a frothy texture, try adding a bit of foamed milk on top for extra creaminess.

## Variations:

- **Iced Lavender Honey Mocha**: Add a tablespoon of cocoa powder or chocolate syrup to the drink for a chocolatey twist on this floral latte.
- **Iced Vanilla Lavender Latte**: For an extra layer of flavor, add a teaspoon of vanilla syrup or extract.
- **Iced Honey Lavender Cold Brew**: If you prefer cold brew coffee, substitute cold brew for the espresso shot for a smoother, less acidic coffee flavor.

## Pairing Suggestions:

- Pair with a **vegan scone** or **lemon shortbread cookies** to complement the floral and sweet notes of the latte.
- Enjoy alongside a **fruit salad** or a **vegan almond croissant** to balance the richness of the honey and lavender.
- Perfect with **vegan chocolate truffles** or **chocolate-covered almonds** for a sweet and luxurious snack.

## Interesting Fact:

Did you know that lavender has been used for centuries for its soothing and calming properties? In addition to being a great ingredient in beauty products, it's now making its way into the world of coffee and beverages, adding a unique twist to your daily caffeine routine.

## Cultural Connection:

Lavender is widely used in French cuisine, especially in desserts, and is also a traditional herb in aromatherapy. The combination of lavender with honey has historical significance, as both have been used for centuries to promote relaxation and well-being. This **Iced Honey Lavender Latte** captures the essence of French-inspired flavors, offering a calming yet energizing coffee experience.

# Blueberry Iced Coffee

*Savor the refreshing fusion of rich coffee and vibrant, fruity sweetness with this Blueberry Iced Coffee. This unique creation combines the boldness of freshly brewed coffee with the juicy, tangy flavors of ripe blueberries, resulting in a drink that's both energizing and indulgent. Whether you're looking to cool off on a hot day or enjoy a fresh twist on your classic iced coffee, this recipe delivers a fruity, caffeine-packed experience that's as delightful as it is refreshing.*

## Ingredients:

- 1 shot (1 ounce) of espresso or 1/2 cup brewed coffee (cooled)
- 2 tbsps blueberry syrup (or homemade blueberry simple syrup)
- 1 tsp honey (or maple syrup for a vegan version)
- 1/2 cup ice cubes
- 1/2 cup cold milk of choice (oat milk, almond milk, or dairy milk)
- Optional: Fresh blueberries and mint leaves for garnish

## Instructions:

1. **Brew the Coffee**: Brew your espresso or coffee and allow it to cool to room temperature.
2. **Make the Blueberry Syrup**: For homemade syrup, simmer 1/2 cup fresh blueberries with 1/4 cup water and 1/4 cup sugar for about 10 minutes. Mash the berries, strain the syrup, and cool.
3. **Combine Coffee and Syrup**: In a tall glass, mix the cooled coffee with the blueberry syrup and honey, stirring to combine.
4. **Add Ice**: Fill the glass with ice cubes to chill the drink.
5. **Pour the Milk**: Slowly pour the cold milk over the coffee mixture, creating a creamy, layered effect.
6. **Serve and Enjoy**: Garnish with fresh blueberries and mint leaves, and enjoy immediately!

## Tips and Recommendations:

- **Blueberry Flavor**: Adjust the amount of blueberry syrup based on how sweet and fruity you like your iced coffee. You can also add a few mashed fresh blueberries for extra flavor.
- **Sweetness Level**: If you prefer a less sweet drink, reduce the amount of syrup or honey.
- **Frothy Texture**: For a creamier texture, use a milk frother to froth the milk before adding it to the coffee mixture.

## Variations:

- **Blueberry Coconut Iced Coffee**: Swap the milk for coconut milk for a tropical twist on this fruity iced coffee.
- **Iced Mocha Blueberry Coffee**: Add a tablespoon of cocoa powder or chocolate syrup to the coffee mixture for a delicious chocolate-blueberry combo.
- **Iced Blueberry Latte**: For a more traditional latte version, add more milk and a bit less coffee, creating a smooth, creamy drink.

## Pairing Suggestions:

- Pair with **vegan blueberry muffins** or **lemon shortbread cookies** to complement the sweet and fruity flavors of the iced coffee.
- Enjoy alongside **almond biscotti** or **fruit salad** for a light, refreshing snack.
- Perfect with **cheese croissants** or **vegan pancakes** for a balanced breakfast or brunch.

## Interesting Fact:

Did you know that blueberries are packed with antioxidants and are known for their health benefits, including boosting brain health and improving heart function? Adding them to your coffee not only adds a unique flavor but also a nutritious boost!

## Cultural Connection:

Blueberries have been enjoyed for centuries in North American indigenous cultures, often used in food, medicine, and ceremonial rituals. Today, they remain a popular fruit for both sweet and savory dishes, and their pairing with coffee is a delightful modern twist on this historical favorite.

# Raspberry Rose Iced Latte

*Delicate yet bold, this Raspberry Rose Iced Latte is a refreshing fusion of rich espresso, sweet raspberries, and the floral elegance of rose. Perfect for a warm day or when you're in need of a coffee that's both fruity and floral, this iced latte delivers a dreamy combination of flavors that will captivate your taste buds. Infused with the natural sweetness of raspberries and a hint of rosewater, it's a sophisticated yet refreshing take on the classic iced latte.*

## Ingredients:

- 1 shot (1 ounce) of espresso or 1/2 cup brewed coffee (cooled)
- 2 tbsps raspberry syrup (or homemade raspberry simple syrup)
- 1 tsp rose water
- 1/2 cup ice cubes
- 1/2 cup cold milk of choice (oat milk, almond milk, or dairy milk)
- Optional: Fresh raspberries and edible rose petals for garnish

## Instructions:

1. **Brew the Coffee**: Brew your espresso or coffee and allow it to cool to room temperature.
2. **Make the Raspberry Syrup**: For homemade syrup, simmer 1/2 cup fresh raspberries with 1/4 cup water and 1/4 cup sugar for about 10 minutes. Mash the berries, strain the syrup, and cool.
3. **Combine Coffee and Syrup**: In a tall glass, mix the cooled coffee with the raspberry syrup and rose water, stirring well to combine.
4. **Add Ice**: Fill the glass with ice cubes to chill the drink.
5. **Pour the Milk**: Slowly pour the cold milk over the coffee mixture, creating a creamy, layered effect.
6. **Serve and Enjoy**: Garnish with fresh raspberries and edible rose petals for a visually stunning finish. Serve immediately and enjoy!

## Tips and Recommendations:

- **Floral Note**: Adjust the amount of rose water to your taste, as it can be quite potent. Start with a smaller amount and increase if you want a more pronounced floral flavor.
- **Sweetness Level**: If you prefer a sweeter drink, add a bit more raspberry syrup or sweetener of your choice.
- **Chilled Milk**: For a colder, more refreshing experience, chill the milk before adding it to the iced coffee.

## Variations:

- **Raspberry Lavender Iced Latte**: Replace the rose water with lavender syrup for a relaxing twist.
- **Iced Raspberry Rose Matcha Latte**: Swap the espresso for a shot of matcha for a green, antioxidant-packed version.
- **Iced Raspberry Coconut Latte**: Use coconut milk for a tropical version that complements the fruity notes of raspberry beautifully.

## Pairing Suggestions:

- Pair with **vegan raspberry scones** or **almond biscotti** to bring out the berry flavors and complement the floral notes.
- Enjoy alongside a **lemon loaf cake** or **pistachio cookies** for a sweet and savory contrast.
- Perfect with **avocado toast** or **vegan croissants** for a light and satisfying breakfast or snack.

## Interesting Fact:

Rose water has been used for centuries in Middle Eastern and Mediterranean cultures not only for its floral flavor but also for its calming and therapeutic properties. In this recipe, it adds a touch of luxury and intrigue to a simple iced latte.

## Cultural Connection:

Rose water is a popular ingredient in many Middle Eastern and Indian beverages and desserts, offering a subtle yet aromatic flavor that's been cherished for generations. The combination of rose and raspberry in this iced latte brings together two ingredients often found in traditional sweets, making this drink both modern and timeless.

# Iced Caramel Almond Milk Latte

*Indulge in the smooth, nutty richness of an Iced Caramel Almond Milk Latte - a creamy, decadent coffee drink that perfectly balances the deep, bold flavor of espresso with the sweet, buttery goodness of caramel. Almond milk adds a subtle nutty undertone, while ice brings refreshing chill, making this the ultimate iced coffee treat. Whether you're starting your morning or enjoying an afternoon pick-me-up, this delightful drink is sure to become your new favorite.*

## Ingredients:

- 1 shot (1 ounce) of espresso
- 2 tbsps caramel syrup
- 1/2 cup ice cubes
- 1/2 cup chilled almond milk
- Optional: Whipped cream (dairy-free if desired)
- Optional: A drizzle of caramel syrup for garnish

## Instructions:

1. **Brew the Coffee**: Brew one shot of espresso or make strong coffee and allow it to cool slightly.
2. **Prepare the Glass**: Fill a tall glass with ice cubes.
3. **Mix Espresso and Caramel**: Pour the cooled espresso over the ice and stir in the caramel syrup until well combined.
4. **Add Almond Milk**: Pour chilled almond milk into the glass, mixing with the coffee to create a smooth, creamy texture.
5. **Optional Garnish**: Top with a dollop of whipped cream and drizzle with more caramel syrup for extra sweetness and visual appeal.
6. **Serve and Enjoy**: Stir gently and enjoy your refreshing, sweet iced latte!

## Tips and Recommendations:

- **Sweetness Level**: Adjust the amount of caramel syrup to your taste. Add more for a sweeter treat or less for a more balanced flavor.
- **Chill Your Ingredients**: For an extra cold latte, chill the almond milk in advance or use ice cubes made from almond milk for an even creamier result.
- **Coffee Flavor**: If you prefer a stronger coffee taste, increase the amount of espresso or use a darker roast coffee for a bolder flavor profile.

## Variations:

- **Iced Mocha Caramel Almond Milk Latte**: Add 1 tablespoon of cocoa powder or chocolate syrup to make a mocha version of this iced latte.
- **Salted Caramel Almond Milk Latte**: For a salty-sweet twist, add a pinch of sea salt to your caramel syrup and stir it into the drink.
- **Dairy-Free Version**: Use a plant-based whipped cream (such as coconut whipped cream) to make this recipe fully vegan.

## Pairing Suggestions:

- Pair with **vegan chocolate chip cookies** or **cinnamon rolls** for a sweet, comforting snack.
- Enjoy with a **vegan almond croissant** or **fresh fruit salad** to complement the creamy, nutty flavors of the latte.
- Perfect alongside a **vegan breakfast muffin** or a **vegan chocolate bar** for an indulgent treat.

## Interesting Fact:

Did you know that **caramel** is one of the most popular coffee flavorings worldwide? The caramelization process creates a deep, rich flavor that's perfect for adding sweetness to coffee drinks.

## Cultural Connection:

Caramel coffee drinks have become a beloved part of modern coffee culture, particularly in the U.S. and Europe, where coffee shops often serve caramel lattes as a rich, sweet option. This **Iced Caramel Almond Milk Latte** brings together the indulgent flavors of caramel and the natural sweetness of almond milk, creating a refreshing twist on a classic favorite.

# Strawberry Basil Iced Coffee

*If you're looking for a refreshing twist on your regular iced coffee, the Strawberry Basil Iced Coffee is here to impress! This unique concoction brings together the sweetness of fresh strawberries and the aromatic freshness of basil, creating an intriguing contrast to the bold flavor of coffee. It's a delightful choice for a warm afternoon or an exotic coffee treat. The combination of fruity sweetness and herbaceous notes makes it a perfect iced coffee creation for the adventurous coffee lover.*

## Ingredients:

- 1 shot (1 ounce) of espresso
- 2 fresh strawberries, hulled and sliced
- 4-5 fresh basil leaves
- 1 tbsp maple syrup (or sweetener of choice)
- 1/2 cup ice cubes
- 1/2 cup chilled almond milk (or your preferred plant-based milk)
- Optional: Extra basil leaves and strawberry slices for garnish

## Instructions:

1. **Brew the Coffee**: Brew one shot of espresso or make strong coffee and set aside to cool slightly.
2. **Muddle the Fruit and Herbs**: In a shaker or small jar, combine the sliced strawberries and basil leaves. Use a muddler or spoon to gently mash the ingredients together to release their juices and aromas.
3. **Sweeten the Mixture**: Add maple syrup (or your sweetener of choice) to the muddled strawberries and basil. Stir until the syrup is well incorporated.
4. **Prepare the Glass**: Fill a tall glass with ice cubes.
5. **Mix the Coffee**: Pour the cooled espresso over the ice, then add the muddled strawberry-basil mixture. Stir to combine the flavors.
6. **Add Almond Milk**: Pour the chilled almond milk into the glass, stirring gently to create a creamy, flavorful blend.
7. **Garnish and Serve**: Garnish with extra strawberry slices and a few fresh basil leaves for a beautiful, aromatic touch.
8. **Enjoy**: Stir well and enjoy the refreshing, fruity burst of flavor in every sip!

## Tips and Recommendations:

- **Adjust the Sweetness**: For a sweeter drink, add more maple syrup or a splash of vanilla syrup.
- **Herb Infusion**: If you want a stronger basil flavor, consider letting the basil leaves steep in warm water for a few minutes before adding them to the muddling process.
- **Vegan Creaminess**: For an extra creamy texture, add a bit of coconut cream along with the almond milk.

## Variations:

- **Berry Basil Iced Coffee**: Use a mix of berries, such as raspberries or blackberries, for a more complex berry flavor.
- **Iced Strawberry Lemon Coffee**: Add a squeeze of fresh lemon juice to balance the sweetness of the strawberries with a citrusy tang.
- **Dairy-Free Iced Coffee**: For a non-dairy version, replace almond milk with oat milk or cashew milk for a richer texture.

## Pairing Suggestions:

- Pair with **vegan shortbread cookies** or **coconut macaroons** to complement the herbal sweetness of the iced coffee.
- A **light vegan sandwich** with avocado and fresh veggies would enhance the fresh flavors of the strawberry and basil.
- Enjoy alongside a **fruit salad** to highlight the fruity notes of the coffee.

## Interesting Fact:

Did you know that basil is not only aromatic but also packed with antioxidants and vitamins? It's often used in savory dishes, but it's gaining popularity in beverages for its refreshing, slightly peppery flavor.

## Cultural Connection:

Herbal coffees have a rich history in many cultures, from the Mediterranean's use of herbs in coffee to the growing trend of infusing coffee with fresh, natural flavors. The combination of strawberry and basil in coffee takes inspiration from the art of blending unexpected ingredients, resulting in a truly unique iced coffee experience.

# Iced Brown Sugar Oat Milk Shakerato

*Craving something sweet, refreshing, and oh-so-satisfying? The Iced Brown Sugar Oat Milk Shakerato is here to deliver all that and more. This delicious iced coffee is made by shaking together rich brown sugar syrup, smooth oat milk, and strong espresso, creating a frothy, creamy, and slightly caramelized treat. Perfect for warm afternoons or when you need a pick-me-up, this drink strikes the perfect balance of sweetness and bold coffee flavor. The shaking technique brings air into the mixture, resulting in a velvety texture that's as delightful to drink as it is to look at.*

## Ingredients:

- 1 shot (1 ounce) of espresso
- 1 tbsp brown sugar syrup (see instructions for homemade recipe)
- 1/2 cup chilled oat milk
- 1/2 cup ice cubes
- Optional: Ground cinnamon or cocoa powder for garnish **Brown Sugar Syrup** 1/2 cup brown sugar
- 1/4 cup water

## Instructions:

1. **Prepare the Brown Sugar Syrup**: In a small saucepan, combine the brown sugar and water. Heat over medium heat, stirring constantly, until the sugar has fully dissolved. Let it cool before using.
2. **Brew the Coffee**: Brew a shot of espresso and allow it to cool slightly.
3. **Assemble the Shakerato**: In a cocktail shaker or a jar with a lid, add the brewed espresso, brown sugar syrup, oat milk, and ice cubes.
4. **Shake It Up**: Secure the lid tightly and shake vigorously for 10-15 seconds until the mixture is frothy and well combined.
5. **Serve**: Pour the shakerato into a tall glass filled with ice cubes.
6. **Garnish and Enjoy**: Optionally, dust the top with a sprinkle of ground cinnamon or cocoa powder for an added touch of flavor and visual appeal. Serve immediately and enjoy the smooth, sweet coffee goodness!

## Tips and Recommendations:

- **Customize Your Sweetness**: Adjust the amount of brown sugar syrup to your taste - add more for a sweeter drink or less for a more balanced flavor.
- **Chill Your Glass**: For an extra-cold experience, chill your glass in the freezer for 10 minutes before serving.
- **Make It Frothier**: Use a milk frother to froth the oat milk before adding it to the shaker for an even creamier texture.

## Variations:

- **Iced Brown Sugar Caramel Shakerato**: Add a drizzle of caramel syrup to the shaker for a rich, buttery flavor.
- **Dairy-Free Iced Coffee**: Stick with oat milk for a creamy, dairy-free version, or try other plant-based milks like almond or coconut for different flavors.
- **Iced Brown Sugar Vanilla Shakerato**: For a vanilla twist, add a splash of vanilla extract to the shaker.

## Pairing Suggestions:

- Pair with a **vegan cinnamon roll** or a slice of **vegan banana bread** to complement the warm, caramel notes of the brown sugar syrup.
- A **vegan chocolate chip cookie** or **shortbread** would add a buttery balance to the sweetness of the drink.
- This iced coffee pairs wonderfully with a **fresh fruit salad** for a lighter side to balance the rich flavors.

## Interesting Fact:

Did you know that a **shakerato** is an Italian coffee tradition that involves shaking the coffee with ice to create a frothy, cold coffee drink? It's the perfect way to enjoy coffee in the summer heat while still savoring its full flavor.

## Cultural Connection:

The **shakerato** originates from Italy, where it's a popular method of preparing iced coffee. In its most basic form, it's espresso shaken with ice to create a chilled, frothy coffee experience. Over time, variations like the **Iced Brown Sugar Oat Milk Shakerato** have emerged, adding new flavors and twists to the classic Italian coffee tradition.

# Cold Brew Tonic

*Looking for a refreshing coffee drink that's both invigorating and complex? The Cold Brew Tonic is your new go-to. This vibrant and effervescent drink combines the smooth richness of cold brew coffee with the zesty kick of tonic water. The result is a light, refreshing coffee experience that's perfect for hot days or when you need a pick-me-up with a twist. The slight bitterness from the tonic balances beautifully with the deep, mellow flavor of cold brew, creating a unique and energizing drink.*

## Ingredients:

- 1/2 cup cold brew coffee (store-bought or home-made)
- 1/2 cup tonic water
- Ice cubes
- 1/2 tbsp simple syrup (optional, or to taste)
- 1-2 slices of lemon or orange (optional garnish)

## Instructions:

1. **Prepare the Cold Brew**: Brew your cold brew coffee in advance. If using store-bought cold brew, simply refrigerate it until chilled.
2. **Fill the Glass with Ice**: Add ice cubes to a tall glass, filling it about halfway.
3. **Pour the Cold Brew**: Pour the chilled cold brew coffee into the glass over the ice.
4. **Add the Tonic Water**: Slowly pour the tonic water into the glass with the cold brew. Allow the bubbles to rise and mix gently.
5. **Sweeten (Optional)**: If you prefer a slightly sweeter drink, add 1/2 tablespoon of simple syrup and stir to combine.
6. **Garnish**: Add a slice of lemon or orange for a fresh citrus kick. Serve immediately and enjoy the refreshing, bubbly taste!

## Tips and Recommendations:

- **Adjust the Sweetness**: If you prefer your drink on the sweeter side, experiment with the amount of simple syrup or add a splash of agave syrup for a more subtle sweetness.
- **Chill the Tonic**: Make sure the tonic water is well chilled before pouring it into the drink to maintain the refreshing, effervescent quality.
- **Use High-Quality Cold Brew**: The flavor of the cold brew is key to this drink, so choose a high-quality, smooth cold brew coffee for the best results.

## Variations:

- **Citrus Cold Brew Tonic**: For a zesty twist, use grapefruit tonic water and garnish with fresh lime slices.
- **Herbal Infusion**: Add a sprig of fresh mint or a few basil leaves to infuse the drink with an herbal note.
- **Cold Brew Tonic Mocktail**: For a fun, non-alcoholic version, top the drink with a splash of soda water for extra fizz.

## Pairing Suggestions:

- Pair with **vegan avocado toast** for a savory snack that complements the slightly bitter taste of the cold brew tonic.
- A **fruit salad** or **citrus-based desserts**, like lemon sorbet, would provide a refreshing balance to the richness of the cold brew.
- **Vegan chocolate truffles** or **dark chocolate** are the perfect accompaniment to enhance the bold coffee flavors.

## Interesting Fact:

Did you know that **cold brew coffee** is less acidic than hot coffee due to the long, slow steeping process? This makes it the perfect base for mixing with tonic water, creating a smoother, more balanced drink.

## Cultural Connection:

The **Cold Brew Tonic** is a modern twist on traditional iced coffee, combining two popular drinks: cold brew coffee, which has been gaining popularity worldwide for its smooth and less acidic taste, and tonic water, a classic mixer used in cocktails. This combination reflects the growing trend of pairing coffee with effervescent beverages for a refreshing, unique experience.

# Iced Cinnamon Roll Latte

*Indulge in the sweet, comforting flavors of a freshly baked cinnamon roll with this Iced Cinnamon Roll Latte. Combining bold coffee with creamy milk and a warm, spiced cinnamon flavor, this latte is a perfect treat for anyone who loves the classic taste of cinnamon rolls but prefers it in a refreshing, iced version. The addition of a touch of vanilla and brown sugar creates a balanced sweetness that perfectly complements the rich coffee, making it a cozy yet invigorating drink.*

## Ingredients:

- 1 shot (1 ounce) of espresso or strong brewed coffee
- 1 cup cold oat milk (or preferred plant-based milk)
- 1 tbsp maple syrup or brown sugar
- 1/4 tsp ground cinnamon
- Ice cubes
- [Optional] 1/2 tsp vanilla extract
- [Optional] Whipped coconut cream or dairy-free whipped topping for garnish

## Instructions:

1. **Brew the Espresso**: Brew a shot of espresso or a small cup of strong coffee. If you don't have an espresso machine, use your preferred brewing method (e.g., French press or pour-over).
2. **Prepare the Cinnamon Syrup**: In a small bowl, combine the maple syrup or brown sugar with the ground cinnamon. Stir until well mixed.
3. **Mix the Ingredients**: In a tall glass, add the cinnamon syrup mixture, followed by the brewed espresso or coffee. Stir until the syrup is fully dissolved.
4. **Add Ice**: Fill the glass with ice cubes, leaving some space for the milk.
5. **Pour the Oat Milk**: Gently pour the cold oat milk into the glass, stirring to combine with the coffee and cinnamon mixture.
6. **Optional Garnish**: For a decadent touch, top with a dollop of whipped coconut cream or dairy-free whipped topping.
7. **Serve and Enjoy**: Stir well and enjoy your sweet, iced cinnamon roll latte!

## Tips and Recommendations:

- **Adjust Sweetness**: If you prefer a sweeter latte, add a little more maple syrup or brown sugar to taste.
- **Spiced Twist**: Try adding a pinch of ground nutmeg or a splash of almond extract for an added layer of flavor.
- **Frothy Texture**: For a frothier texture, use a milk frother to froth the oat milk before adding it to the glass.
- **Chill the Coffee**: To make this an even colder treat, refrigerate your brewed coffee before preparing the latte.

## Variations:

- **Vanilla Cinnamon Roll Latte**: Add 1/2 teaspoon of vanilla extract to enhance the sweet, warm flavor.
- **Iced Caramel Cinnamon Roll Latte**: Drizzle caramel syrup over the top for a rich, sweet finish.
- **Dairy-Free Cinnamon Roll Latte**: Stick with oat milk or try almond milk, cashew milk, or coconut milk for a different texture.

## Pairing Suggestions:

- Pair with a **vegan cinnamon roll** or a **banana bread muffin** to enhance the cinnamon flavors in the drink.
- For a light snack, serve with **vegan shortbread cookies** or **apple slices with peanut butter**.
- A **fresh fruit salad** would balance the richness of the latte with a refreshing, healthy bite.

## Interesting Fact:

Did you know that **cinnamon** is one of the oldest known spices, used for centuries for its sweet and spicy flavor as well as its health benefits? It's not just a great flavor for your latte - it also adds a warm, comforting touch.

## Cultural Connection:

The **cinnamon roll** is a classic sweet pastry that has its origins in Sweden, where it is known as "kanelbulle." It's enjoyed worldwide in various forms, and in this latte, it provides a delightful flavor profile that's both familiar and innovative. The **Iced Cinnamon Roll Latte** combines the rich tradition of cinnamon rolls with modern coffee culture, making it a perfect fusion of the old and new.

# Peanut Butter Cup Iced Coffee

*Craving something that combines the bold richness of coffee with the sweet, creamy indulgence of peanut butter and chocolate? Meet the Peanut Butter Cup Iced Coffee. This decadent iced coffee creation blends your love for coffee with the irresistible flavors of peanut butter and chocolate, creating a treat that's as satisfying as a peanut butter cup. Perfect for a hot day or when you're in the mood for a dessert-like drink, this coffee is a deliciously creamy, nutty, and chocolaty indulgence.*

## Ingredients:

- 1 shot (1 ounce) of espresso or strong brewed coffee
- 1 cup cold almond milk (or your preferred plant-based milk)
- 2 tbsps peanut butter (smooth or crunchy)
- 1 tbsp cocoa powder
- 1 tbsp maple syrup or agave syrup
- Ice cubes
- [Optional] 1/2 tsp vanilla extract
- [Optional] Whipped coconut cream for topping
- [Optional] Chocolate shavings or chips for garnish

## Instructions:

1. **Brew the Espresso**: Brew a shot of espresso or strong coffee using your preferred method. If you don't have an espresso machine, brew a small cup of strong coffee using a French press or pour-over.
2. **Mix Peanut Butter and Cocoa**: In a small bowl, combine the peanut butter and cocoa powder. Stir until smooth, creating a peanut butter and chocolate paste.
3. **Combine Ingredients**: In a tall glass, add the peanut butter-chocolate mixture, maple syrup (or agave), and brewed coffee. Stir thoroughly to combine all ingredients.
4. **Add Ice**: Fill the glass with ice cubes, leaving some space for the milk.
5. **Pour the Milk**: Pour cold almond milk into the glass and stir gently to mix everything together.
6. **Optional Garnish**: Top with whipped coconut cream and sprinkle with chocolate shavings or chips for a rich, indulgent finish.
7. **Serve and Enjoy**: Stir well to incorporate all the flavors and enjoy this indulgent iced treat!

## Tips and Recommendations:

- **Adjust Peanut Butter Flavor**: If you love a stronger peanut butter taste, add an extra tablespoon of peanut butter to the mixture.
- **Sweetness**: If you like your coffee sweeter, feel free to add more maple syrup or agave syrup to taste.
- **Vegan Whipped Cream**: To make this recipe fully vegan, use dairy-free whipped cream, or for a lighter touch, top with a bit of coconut whipped cream.
- **Alternative Milk**: While almond milk works well, feel free to use oat milk or cashew milk for a creamier texture.

## Variations:

- **Peanut Butter Banana Iced Coffee**: Blend a small frozen banana into the drink for a creamy, smoothie-like texture with an added fruity twist.
- **Chocolate Mocha Peanut Butter Iced Coffee**: Add an extra tablespoon of cocoa powder or a shot of chocolate syrup for an even richer chocolate experience.
- **Salted Peanut Butter Iced Coffee**: Sprinkle a pinch of sea salt on top to enhance the flavors and give your iced coffee that perfect sweet-and-salty balance.

## Pairing Suggestions:

- Pair with a **vegan chocolate chip cookie** or a **peanut butter granola bar** for an extra indulgence.
- A slice of **vegan banana bread** or **chocolate cake** complements the nutty, creamy flavors of the coffee.
- For a savory option, pair with **vegan roasted nuts** or a **vegan sandwich** to balance out the sweetness of the drink.

## Interesting Fact:

Did you know that **peanut butter** was originally invented as a health food in the late 19th century? It was initially marketed as a protein supplement for people with no teeth! Now, it's one of the world's most popular spreads and pairs perfectly with coffee.

## Cultural Connection:

The combination of peanut butter and chocolate is a classic pairing that has been loved for decades, especially in the form of the famous **Reese's Peanut Butter Cups**. This Peanut Butter Cup Iced Coffee takes that beloved flavor combination and gives it a refreshing, iced twist, blending the best of both worlds into a perfect coffee creation.

# Iced Toffee Nut Latte

*Indulge in the perfect balance of sweet and nutty with the Iced Toffee Nut Latte. This delightful coffee treat combines the richness of espresso with the buttery sweetness of toffee syrup and the warm, roasted flavor of toasted nuts. It's the ideal drink for those looking to enjoy a luxurious iced coffee experience, offering a velvety smooth texture and an irresistible sweet-nutty flavor. Whether you're relaxing on a sunny afternoon or treating yourself to a little pick-me-up, this iced latte is the perfect choice.*

## Ingredients:

- 1 shot (1 ounce) of espresso or strong brewed coffee
- 1 cup cold oat milk (or your preferred plant-based milk)
- 2 tbsps toffee syrup
- 1 tbsp crushed toasted almonds or hazelnuts
- Ice cubes
- [Optional] 1/2 tsp vanilla extract
- [Optional] Whipped coconut cream for topping
- [Optional] Toffee drizzle or extra toasted nuts for garnish

## Instructions:

1. **Brew the Espresso**: Brew a shot of espresso or strong coffee using your preferred method.
2. **Prepare the Nut Topping**: Toast your nuts (almonds or hazelnuts) in a dry pan over medium heat for 2-3 minutes, until golden brown and aromatic. Let them cool slightly, then crush them into small pieces.
3. **Combine Ingredients**: In a tall glass, add the toffee syrup and brewed espresso. Stir to combine until the syrup is fully dissolved.
4. **Add Ice**: Fill the glass with ice cubes, leaving some room at the top for the milk.
5. **Pour the Milk**: Pour cold oat milk (or your preferred plant-based milk) into the glass and stir gently to mix everything together.
6. **Optional Garnish**: Top with whipped coconut cream and a drizzle of toffee syrup or sprinkle extra toasted nuts on top for added texture and flavor.
7. **Serve and Enjoy**: Stir well to incorporate all the flavors, then sip and enjoy this sweet, nutty iced latte!

## Tips and Recommendations:

- **Nutty Variations**: Try experimenting with different nuts like toasted pecans or walnuts for a unique twist on the classic toffee nut flavor.
- **Sweetness**: Adjust the sweetness by adding more toffee syrup, or use a natural sweetener like agave syrup for a lighter touch.

- **Creaminess**: For a richer and creamier drink, consider using coconut milk or cashew milk instead of oat milk.
- **Ice-Free Option**: For a thicker, creamier version, blend the ingredients with ice for a frosty, blended iced latte.

## Variations:

- **Caramel Toffee Nut Latte**: Add a tablespoon of caramel syrup to the drink for an extra layer of sweetness.
- **Mocha Toffee Nut Latte**: Mix in a tablespoon of cocoa powder or chocolate syrup for a mocha-inspired twist on this iced coffee.
- **Dairy-Free Option**: Use coconut cream instead of whipped coconut cream for an extra creamy, dairy-free topping.

## Pairing Suggestions:

- Pair with **vegan cinnamon rolls** or **toasted croissants** to complement the toffee nut flavor.
- A slice of **vegan coffee cake** or **nutty granola bars** would pair wonderfully, enhancing the rich, nutty undertones of the latte.
- Serve alongside **chocolate chip cookies** for a sweet and savory coffee break.

## Interesting Fact:

Toffee syrup, often made from caramelized sugar and butter, is believed to have originated in the United Kingdom in the 19th century. It's now a beloved flavor in coffees, desserts, and candies, offering a rich and velvety sweetness.

## Cultural Connection:

Toffee is a classic British confection, often used in both candies and desserts. The rich, buttery flavor of toffee has been embraced globally, and its integration into coffee drinks like the Iced Toffee Nut Latte has become a favorite way to enjoy this delicious treat.

# Black and White Iced Coffee

*The Black and White Iced Coffee is the perfect marriage of bold, smooth espresso and the rich creaminess of milk, served over ice to create a refreshing yet indulgent drink. This unique iced coffee is a simple yet satisfying treat that balances the intensity of coffee with the velvety texture of milk, making it the ideal choice for those who enjoy both the boldness of black coffee and the luxurious touch of cream. Whether you're enjoying a sunny afternoon or treating yourself to a pick-me-up, this drink is bound to become a favorite!*

## Ingredients:

- 1 shot (1 ounce) of espresso or strong brewed coffee
- 1 cup cold oat milk (or any other plant-based milk)
- 1-2 tsps maple syrup or agave syrup (adjust to taste)
- Ice cubes
- [Optional] 1/2 tsp vanilla extract
- [Optional] Whipped coconut cream for topping
- [Optional] Cocoa powder or cinnamon for garnish

## Instructions:

1. **Brew the Espresso**: Brew a shot of espresso or a strong cup of coffee using your preferred method.
2. **Sweeten the Coffee**: In a small cup or jar, stir in the maple syrup or agave syrup into the brewed espresso. Adjust the sweetness to your preference.
3. **Prepare the Glass**: Fill a tall glass with ice cubes.
4. **Pour the Coffee**: Pour the sweetened espresso over the ice.
5. **Add the Milk**: Pour the cold oat milk (or other plant-based milk) into the glass with the espresso, allowing it to swirl and mix together.
6. **Optional Garnish**: For a touch of indulgence, top the iced coffee with a dollop of whipped coconut cream and a light dusting of cocoa powder or cinnamon.
7. **Serve and Enjoy**: Stir gently to combine and enjoy this creamy, refreshing iced coffee!

## Tips and Recommendations:

- **Adjust the Sweetness**: If you prefer a sweeter drink, feel free to add more maple syrup or a splash of vanilla extract.
- **Use Strong Coffee**: For a more robust flavor, increase the amount of coffee or espresso, especially if you're using a plant-based milk that might dilute the flavor.
- **Chill the Coffee**: For an even colder drink, brew your coffee ahead of time and let it cool or chill it in the fridge for an hour before serving.

- **Dairy-Free and Vegan**: For a truly vegan experience, make sure the whipped cream and milk are dairy-free. Use oat milk, almond milk, or coconut milk for a creamier finish.

## Variations:

- **Iced Mocha Black and White**: Add a tablespoon of cocoa powder or chocolate syrup for a rich mocha twist.
- **Iced Black and White with Hazelnut**: Add a splash of hazelnut syrup to give this coffee a warm, nutty flavor.
- **Cold Brew Version**: Use cold brew coffee instead of espresso for a smoother, less acidic flavor profile.

## Pairing Suggestions:

- Pair with **vegan chocolate chip cookies** or a **slice of vegan banana bread** to enhance the creamy sweetness of the iced coffee.
- A **buttery croissant** or **cinnamon roll** complements the richness of the milk and espresso, offering a perfect balance of flavors.
- For a savory option, pair with **avocado toast** or a **vegan breakfast burrito** for a satisfying brunch experience.

## Interesting Fact:

Did you know that **"Black and White"** is a popular coffee term used to describe drinks that combine coffee (black) with milk or cream (white)? This drink is a global favorite, especially in coffee shops and cafes around the world, offering the best of both worlds - bold and creamy.

## Cultural Connection:

The idea of combining black coffee with cream or milk has been around for centuries, evolving into various versions across different cultures. The **Black and White Iced Coffee** is inspired by the simplicity and elegance of this combination, offering a refreshing, modern twist that's especially popular in the warmer months.

# Iced Pistachio Latte

*The Iced Pistachio Latte is a deliciously creamy and nutty twist on your classic iced latte. With a rich pistachio syrup paired with strong espresso and chilled milk, this drink offers a refreshing, yet indulgent experience. The slight sweetness of pistachio perfectly complements the coffee, creating a balanced and satisfying flavor profile. This iced coffee treat is ideal for those who love a nutty kick with their daily caffeine boost, making it a perfect summer beverage or an anytime indulgence.*

## Ingredients:

- 1 shot (1 ounce) of espresso or strong brewed coffee
- 1 cup cold oat milk (or any other plant-based milk)
- 2 tbsps pistachio syrup (store-bought or home-made)
- Ice cubes
- [Optional] 1/4 tsp vanilla extract
- [Optional] Whipped coconut cream for topping
- [Optional] Chopped pistachios for garnish

## Instructions:

1. **Brew the Espresso**: Brew a shot of espresso or a strong cup of coffee using your preferred method.
2. **Prepare the Glass**: Fill a tall glass with ice cubes to chill the drink.
3. **Sweeten with Pistachio Syrup**: Add 2 tablespoons of pistachio syrup into the glass. You can adjust the sweetness by adding more or less syrup based on your preference.
4. **Pour the Coffee**: Pour the freshly brewed espresso over the ice and pistachio syrup.
5. **Add the Milk**: Gently pour in the cold oat milk (or your preferred plant-based milk) into the glass, stirring as you go to create a smooth blend.
6. **Optional Garnish**: Top the iced latte with whipped coconut cream and a sprinkle of chopped pistachios for a delicious finishing touch.
7. **Serve and Enjoy**: Stir the drink, serve immediately, and enjoy the creamy, nutty goodness!

## Tips and Recommendations:

- **Adjust the Sweetness**: If you prefer a sweeter latte, increase the amount of pistachio syrup or add a drizzle of maple syrup.
- **Cold Brew Option**: For a smoother, less acidic option, use cold brew coffee instead of espresso.
- **Nutty Variations**: Add a dash of cinnamon or cardamom to the pistachio syrup for an extra layer of warmth and flavor.
- **Non-Dairy Options**: Use oat milk, almond milk, or cashew milk for a creamier texture or a nuttier flavor profile.

- **Make It Decaf**: Swap out the espresso for decaffeinated coffee if you're looking to enjoy this drink without the caffeine.

## Variations:

- **Iced Pistachio Mocha**: Add a tablespoon of cocoa powder or chocolate syrup for a chocolatey twist on the pistachio latte.
- **Pistachio and Caramel**: For a sweeter, indulgent version, drizzle some vegan caramel syrup on top for extra richness.
- **Iced Pistachio Matcha Latte**: Replace the espresso with a shot of matcha for a vibrant and green twist on this latte.

## Pairing Suggestions:

- Pair with **vegan chocolate croissants** or **pistachio shortbread cookies** to highlight the nutty flavors of the iced latte.
- A **vegan banana bread** or **cinnamon roll** offers a sweet balance to the creamy, nutty notes in the coffee.
- For a savory snack, try **avocado toast** with a sprinkle of chili flakes to contrast the drink's richness.

## Interesting Fact:

Did you know that **pistachios** are often referred to as "the happy nut" due to their light green color and slightly sweet flavor? They are a great source of healthy fats and can add a delightful twist to coffee drinks like this one!

## Cultural Connection:

Pistachios are beloved in many Middle Eastern and Mediterranean cultures, often used in sweets and pastries. The **Iced Pistachio Latte** brings these rich, nutty flavors into a modern coffee experience, merging global flavors with the beloved iced coffee tradition.

# Oreo Iced Coffee

*Indulge in the deliciously nostalgic flavor of your favorite childhood treat with this Oreo Coffee. Creamy, crunchy, and utterly satisfying, this recipe blends strong coffee with the rich, chocolatey goodness of Oreo cookies. Whether you're looking to treat yourself on a hot day or add a sweet twist to your coffee routine, this delightful iced coffee is the perfect combination of rich coffee flavor and cookie-inspired sweetness.*

## Ingredients:

- 1 shot (1 ounce) of espresso or 1/2 cup strong brewed coffee
- 1 cup cold oat milk (or your choice of plant-based milk)
- 2 Oreos (or more if you like it extra cookie-flavored)
- 1 tbsp vanilla syrup or sweetener of choice
- Ice cubes
- [Optional] Whipped coconut cream for topping
- [Optional] Crushed Oreos for garnish

## Instructions:

1. **Brew the Coffee**: Brew a shot of espresso or prepare 1/2 cup of strong brewed coffee using your preferred method.
2. **Prepare the Glass**: Fill a tall glass with ice cubes to chill the drink.
3. **Crush the Oreos**: Place 2 Oreos into a plastic bag or between two sheets of parchment paper. Crush them with a rolling pin or your hands until they are small crumbs.
4. **Combine Ingredients**: Add the crushed Oreos to the brewed coffee or espresso. Stir well to let the cookie crumbs dissolve into the coffee, infusing it with their flavor.
5. **Sweeten the Coffee**: Stir in 1 tablespoon of vanilla syrup or your preferred sweetener. Adjust the sweetness to your taste.
6. **Add the Milk**: Pour in the cold oat milk (or your preferred plant-based milk) and stir the mixture gently to combine.
7. **Optional Garnish**: Top with a swirl of whipped coconut cream and sprinkle some crushed Oreos on top for a decadent finishing touch.
8. **Serve and Enjoy**: Stir the drink to mix the flavors and enjoy the creamy, cookie-inspired iced coffee!

## Tips and Recommendations:

- **For Extra Creaminess**: Try using coconut milk or cashew milk for a richer texture.
- **Cookie Variety**: While Oreos are the classic choice, you can experiment with other cookies, like chocolate chip cookies or graham crackers, for a unique twist.

- **Make It Decaf**: If you prefer a caffeine-free version, use decaf coffee or espresso.
- **Crunchy Texture**: For added crunch, leave a few larger cookie pieces in the drink. You can also blend the Oreos into the milk mixture for a smoother, milkshake-like texture.

## Variations:

- **Mint Oreo Iced Coffee**: Swap out the regular Oreos for Mint Oreos for a refreshing, minty twist.
- **Mocha Oreo Iced Coffee**: Add a tablespoon of cocoa powder or chocolate syrup for a rich, chocolatey flavor alongside the cookie goodness.
- **Vegan Oreo Milkshake**: Blend the coffee and cookies with a scoop of vegan vanilla ice cream for an even richer, dessert-like version.

## Pairing Suggestions:

- Pair with **vegan chocolate chip cookies** or **a slice of vegan cheesecake** for a sweet and indulgent treat.
- A **banana bread** or **scone** will also complement the creamy, cookie-flavored iced coffee.
- For a savory option, try **avocado toast** with chili flakes to balance the sweetness of the drink.

## Interesting Fact:

Did you know that **Oreos** were first introduced in 1912? They've become one of the best-selling cookies in the world, and now they're a fun way to add flavor and nostalgia to your iced coffee!

## Cultural Connection:

The **Oreo Iced Coffee** combines the popular coffee culture with the beloved Oreo cookie, creating a unique fusion of American snack culture and the global appeal of iced coffee. Whether you enjoy it as an afternoon pick-me-up or a sweet treat, this drink offers a playful and delicious twist on traditional iced coffee.

# Iced Tangerine Vanilla Latte

*Refresh your coffee routine with a burst of citrusy goodness and sweet vanilla warmth in this Iced Tangerine Vanilla Latte. The smooth, bold coffee is perfectly complemented by the bright tang of tangerine and the comforting sweetness of vanilla, creating a balanced and invigorating iced latte. This recipe is a delightful way to enjoy your coffee on a hot day while indulging in the tropical flavors of citrus and vanilla.*

## Ingredients:

- 1 shot (1 ounce) of espresso or 1/2 cup strong brewed coffee
- 1 cup cold oat milk (or your choice of plant-based milk)
- 2 tbsps fresh tangerine juice
- 1 tsp vanilla extract
- 1 tbsp maple syrup or sweetener of choice
- Ice cubes
- [Optional] Tangerine slices for garnish
- [Optional] A few mint leaves for garnish

## Instructions:

1. **Brew the Coffee**: Brew a shot of espresso or prepare 1/2 cup of strong brewed coffee using your preferred method.
2. **Prepare the Glass**: Fill a tall glass with ice cubes.
3. **Add Tangerine and Vanilla**: Pour 2 tablespoons of fresh tangerine juice and 1 teaspoon of vanilla extract into the glass.
4. **Sweeten the Coffee**: Stir in 1 tablespoon of maple syrup or your preferred sweetener, adjusting to your taste.
5. **Pour the Coffee**: Add the brewed espresso or coffee to the glass, combining it with the tangerine and vanilla mixture.
6. **Add Milk**: Pour in 1 cup of cold oat milk (or your preferred plant-based milk). Stir gently to combine the flavors.
7. **Optional Garnish**: Garnish with a slice of tangerine on the rim of the glass and a sprig of fresh mint for a refreshing touch.
8. **Serve and Enjoy**: Stir the drink to mix all the flavors together, and enjoy your bright, creamy iced coffee!

## Tips and Recommendations:

- **For Extra Citrus Kick**: If you love a stronger citrus flavor, add a little more tangerine juice or even a few drops of orange blossom water.
- **Dairy-Free Option**: For a completely vegan version, stick with oat or almond milk, which pairs wonderfully with the citrus notes.
- **Stronger Coffee Flavor**: If you prefer a stronger coffee flavor, increase the espresso-to-milk ratio or use a darker roast.
- **Cold Brew Option**: Try using cold brew coffee for a smoother, less acidic coffee base that pairs beautifully with the sweet and tangy flavors.

## Variations:

- **Ginger Tangerine Latte**: Add a small amount of freshly grated ginger to the drink for a spicy, zesty twist that complements the citrus.
- **Tangerine Vanilla Milkshake**: For a dessert-like version, blend the ingredients with a scoop of vegan vanilla ice cream for a creamy, milkshake-style treat.
- **Iced Tangerine Cinnamon Latte**: Add a pinch of cinnamon for a warm, spiced flavor that contrasts the bright citrus.

## Pairing Suggestions:

- Pair with a **vegan lemon poppy seed muffin** or a **tropical fruit salad** for a refreshing, light breakfast or snack.
- A **vegan coconut scone** or **citrus shortbread cookies** will also complement the fruity and vanilla notes of the iced latte.

## Interesting Fact:

Did you know that tangerines are a variety of mandarin oranges, prized for their easy-to-peel skin and sweet, tangy flavor? They're a great source of vitamin C and make for a vibrant addition to any drink!

## Cultural Connection:

While the classic latte is a staple of Italian coffee culture, this **Iced Tangerine Vanilla Latte** brings a fresh, fruity twist that is perfect for those warm, sun-filled days. The combination of citrus and vanilla evokes the sunny, sweet flavors of summer, making it a perfect treat for a light-hearted coffee break.

# Toasted Coconut Iced Coffee

*Transport your taste buds to a tropical paradise with the Toasted Coconut Iced Coffee. This drink blends rich, bold coffee with the irresistible sweetness of toasted coconut and creamy plant-based milk, creating a smooth, refreshing iced coffee experience. Whether you're lounging on a warm afternoon or need a burst of energy, this coconutty twist on your usual iced coffee will quickly become a new favorite.*

## Ingredients:

- 1 shot (1 ounce) of espresso or 1/2 cup strong brewed coffee
- 1 cup coconut milk (or any plant-based milk of your choice)
- 2 tbsps shredded unsweetened coconut
- 1 tbsp maple syrup or sweetener of choice
- Ice cubes
- [Optional] A few toasted coconut flakes for garnish
- [Optional] A sprinkle of cinnamon or cocoa powder for extra flavor

## Instructions:

1. **Toast the Coconut**: In a dry skillet over medium heat, toast 2 tablespoons of shredded coconut until golden brown, stirring occasionally to avoid burning. Set aside to cool.
2. **Brew the Coffee**: Brew a shot of espresso or prepare 1/2 cup of strong brewed coffee using your preferred method.
3. **Prepare the Glass**: Fill a tall glass with ice cubes.
4. **Sweeten the Coffee**: Stir in 1 tablespoon of maple syrup (or your sweetener of choice) into the hot coffee, dissolving it completely.
5. **Add Coconut Milk**: Pour 1 cup of coconut milk into the glass with ice.
6. **Combine the Coffee**: Add the sweetened coffee to the glass, stirring gently to combine.
7. **Garnish**: Top with a sprinkle of toasted coconut flakes for an extra layer of flavor and texture. Optionally, add a dash of cinnamon or cocoa powder for a subtle spice kick.
8. **Serve and Enjoy**: Stir everything together and enjoy your tropical iced coffee creation!

## Tips and Recommendations:

- **Coconut Flavor Boost**. For an even stronger coconut flavor, blend a small amount of coconut cream with the coconut milk before adding it to the coffee.
- **Dairy-Free Option**: Stick with coconut milk or use almond milk for a lighter, nutty version.

- **Sweetener Variations**: Experiment with different sweeteners like agave, date syrup, or coconut sugar for a unique twist on sweetness.
- **Chill the Coffee**: If you prefer a smoother, more refreshing experience, chill the brewed coffee in the fridge for a few minutes before adding it to the ice.

## Variations:

- **Iced Coconut Mocha**: Add 1 tablespoon of cocoa powder to the coffee for a rich, chocolatey twist that pairs beautifully with the coconut.
- **Coconut Cream Latte**: For a more indulgent version, top the iced coffee with a layer of coconut whipped cream instead of milk.
- **Coconut Vanilla Iced Coffee**: Add 1/2 teaspoon of vanilla extract to bring a warm, sweet touch that complements the coconut perfectly.

## Pairing Suggestions:

- Pair with a **coconut macaron** or **banana bread** for a delightful tropical snack.
- A **vegan chocolate chip cookie** or a **slice of coconut cake** would complement the coconut flavor in the iced coffee, creating a satisfying treat.

## Interesting Fact:

Coconut has been used for centuries in tropical cultures for its nourishing properties, from food to beauty treatments. The toasted coconut in this recipe adds a rich, smoky flavor that enhances the coffee's natural bitterness.

## Cultural Connection:

Coconut is a staple ingredient in many tropical cuisines, especially in Southeast Asia and the Caribbean, where it's used in both savory and sweet dishes. This **Toasted Coconut Iced Coffee** celebrates the versatility of coconut, combining its traditional flavors with the beloved, energizing boost of coffee.

# Iced White Chocolate Raspberry Mocha

*Indulge in the luscious blend of rich white chocolate, sweet raspberries, and smooth espresso with this Iced White Chocolate Raspberry Mocha. The creamy, decadent combination of flavors creates a cool and refreshing treat, perfect for any occasion. Whether you're craving a sweet escape on a warm day or seeking a unique twist on the classic mocha, this iced coffee creation is sure to delight your senses with every sip.*

## Ingredients:

- 1 shot (1 ounce) of espresso or 1/2 cup strong brewed coffee
- 1 cup almond milk (or any plant-based milk of your choice)
- 2 tbsps white chocolate chips or white chocolate sauce
- 2 tbsps raspberry syrup or fresh raspberry puree
- Ice cubes
- [Optional] Fresh raspberries for garnish
- [Optional] Vegan whipped cream for topping

## Instructions:

1. **Brew the Coffee**: Brew a shot of espresso or prepare 1/2 cup of strong brewed coffee using your preferred method.
2. **Melt the White Chocolate**: In a microwave-safe bowl or small pot, heat the white chocolate chips with a splash of almond milk until melted, stirring until smooth.
3. **Prepare the Glass**: Fill a tall glass with ice cubes.
4. **Mix the Flavors**: Pour the brewed coffee into the glass, followed by the melted white chocolate mixture. Stir well to combine the flavors.
5. **Add the Raspberry Flavor**: Pour in the raspberry syrup or fresh raspberry puree, stirring gently to infuse the coffee with a sweet berry essence.
6. **Add Almond Milk**: Top with 1 cup of almond milk (or your chosen plant-based milk) and stir to incorporate the layers.
7. **Garnish and Serve**: Garnish with fresh raspberries and a dollop of vegan whipped cream if desired. Serve immediately and enjoy!

## Tips and Recommendations:

- **For a stronger raspberry flavor**, add more raspberry syrup or puree to suit your taste.
- **For a creamier texture**, use coconut milk or oat milk, which provide a richer mouthfeel.
- **Customize the sweetness**: Adjust the amount of raspberry syrup or white chocolate to match your sweetness preference.
- **Chill your glass**: For an extra refreshing experience, chill your glass in the freezer for a few minutes before preparing the drink.

## Variations:

- **Iced Mocha with a Twist**: Add a tablespoon of cocoa powder to the white chocolate mix for a chocolatey version of this drink.
- **Vegan Iced White Chocolate Raspberry Latte**: Use coconut whipped cream to keep this drink entirely plant-based.
- **Raspberry White Chocolate Frappe**: Blend the ingredients with ice for a thicker, slushier version of this iced coffee.

## Pairing Suggestions:

- Pair with **almond biscotti** or **vegan shortbread cookies** for a delightful combination of flavors.
- A **fruit tart** or a slice of **vegan chocolate cake** would complement the sweetness and richness of the mocha.

## Interesting Fact:

Did you know that white chocolate is made from cocoa butter, but unlike dark chocolate, it doesn't contain cocoa solids? This gives it a creamy, sweet flavor that pairs wonderfully with fruity syrups like raspberry.

## Cultural Connection:

Mocha drinks have a long history, named after the Yemeni port city of Mocha, which was once famous for its coffee exports. The combination of coffee with sweet flavors like chocolate has become a beloved global treat. This version, with white chocolate and raspberry, adds a modern, fruity twist that's sure to charm coffee lovers everywhere.

# Iced Maple Bacon Coffee

*Prepare for a bold and unforgettable flavor combination with this Iced Maple Bacon Coffee. It blends the smoky, savory goodness of bacon with the sweet richness of maple syrup, creating a truly unique iced coffee experience. This daring drink combines the indulgence of breakfast with the sophistication of iced coffee, offering a delightful mix of flavors that coffee lovers are sure to remember. Whether you're a fan of sweet and salty pairings or just looking to experiment with new coffee creations, this iced coffee will surprise and satisfy!*

## Ingredients:

- 1 shot (1 ounce) of espresso or 1/2 cup strong brewed coffee
- 1 cup oat milk (or any plant-based milk of your choice)
- 2 tbsps maple syrup
- 2-3 slices cooked crispy vegan bacon (or regular bacon, if not vegan)
- Ice cubes
- [Optional] Extra maple syrup for drizzling
- [Optional] Crushed bacon bits for garnish

## Instructions:

1. **Brew the Coffee**: Brew a shot of espresso or prepare 1/2 cup of strong brewed coffee using your preferred method.
2. **Prepare the Bacon**: Cook your vegan bacon (or regular bacon) until crispy, then crumble or chop into small pieces.
3. **Mix the Maple Syrup**: In a small bowl, mix 2 tablespoons of maple syrup with the brewed coffee, stirring until the syrup is fully dissolved.
4. **Prepare the Glass**: Fill a tall glass with ice cubes.
5. **Combine the Flavors**: Pour the sweetened coffee mixture over the ice, followed by 1 cup of oat milk (or your choice of plant-based milk). Stir well to combine.
6. **Add the Bacon**: Gently stir in the crispy bacon pieces, letting them infuse the drink with their smoky flavor.
7. **Garnish and Serve**: If desired, drizzle extra maple syrup on top and garnish with more crushed bacon bits. Serve immediately and enjoy the sweet and savory treat!

## Tips and Recommendations:

- **For extra sweetness**, increase the amount of maple syrup according to your taste.
- **Adjust the bacon**: Use more bacon pieces for a stronger savory flavor or fewer for a more subtle touch.
- **For a smoother texture**, try using cashew milk or coconut milk, which add a creamy richness.
- **Experiment with different syrups**: If you're looking for a twist, try adding caramel or hazelnut syrup instead of maple for a different sweet profile.

## Variations:

- **Maple Bacon Frappe**: Blend the iced coffee with ice and a little extra oat milk for a thicker, slushy version of this drink.
- **Smoky Maple Iced Coffee**: Add a few dashes of smoked salt to intensify the savory bacon flavor, balancing the sweetness of the maple.
- **Cinnamon Maple Bacon Coffee**: Sprinkle a pinch of cinnamon on top for a warm spice contrast to the sweet maple and smoky bacon.

## Pairing Suggestions:

- Pair with **vegan pancakes** or **tofu scramble** for a full breakfast-inspired experience.
- A **maple pecan muffin** or **savory scones** would be a great match to complement the flavors in the coffee.

## Interesting Fact:

Did you know that bacon and coffee are a popular pairing in some parts of the world? The salty and savory bacon complements the rich, bold flavors of coffee, making it a breakfast treat that's beloved in many cultures.

## Cultural Connection:

The combination of coffee and bacon has been a long-standing tradition in many Western cultures, especially in America. Known for its satisfying balance of salty and sweet flavors, this drink takes inspiration from classic breakfast foods and elevates them into an indulgent, refreshing iced coffee experience.

# Raspberry Mint Mojito Cold Brew

*Bright, refreshing, and full of bold flavors, the Raspberry Mint Mojito Cold Brew is a cool, invigorating twist on your typical iced coffee. Inspired by the classic mojito cocktail, this iced coffee combines the freshness of mint and tangy raspberries with the smooth richness of cold brew coffee. Perfect for hot summer days or when you're craving something light yet energizing, this drink offers a unique and playful fusion that coffee and cocktail lovers alike can enjoy. The subtle fizz from sparkling water adds a final touch of refreshment, making it the ultimate cool treat.*

## Ingredients:

- 1 cup cold brew coffee
- 1/4 cup fresh raspberries
- 6-8 fresh mint leaves
- 1-2 tbsps maple syrup or agave syrup (adjust to sweetness preference)
- 1/4 lime, juiced
- Ice cubes
- Sparkling water
- [Optional] Additional mint and raspberries for garnish

## Instructions:

1. **Prepare the Cold Brew**: Brew a strong batch of cold brew coffee in advance.
2. **Muddle the Fruit and Mint**: In a glass, add fresh raspberries and mint leaves. Use a muddler or the back of a spoon to gently crush the fruit and leaves together, releasing the flavors.
3. **Add the Lime and Syrup**: Squeeze the juice of 1/4 lime into the glass and add 1-2 tablespoons of maple syrup (or agave syrup) to taste. Stir well to combine.
4. **Combine with Cold Brew**: Pour the cold brew coffee over the muddled mixture and stir until everything is evenly mixed.
5. **Add Ice**: Fill the glass with ice cubes to chill the drink.
6. **Top with Sparkling Water**: Add a splash of sparkling water for a refreshing fizz. Stir lightly to combine.
7. **Garnish and Serve**: Garnish with extra mint leaves and a few fresh raspberries for a vibrant presentation. Serve immediately and enjoy!

## Tips and Recommendations:

- **Adjust sweetness**: Feel free to add more maple syrup if you prefer a sweeter drink, or reduce it for a more tart flavor.
- **For a stronger mint flavor**, gently bruise the mint leaves before muddling, or increase the amount of mint used.
- **Chill the cold brew**: Make sure your cold brew is chilled before serving to ensure the drink stays cool and refreshing.

- **For a creamier version**, add a splash of coconut or oat milk instead of sparkling water for a more indulgent treat.

## Variations:

- **Berry Mojito Cold Brew**: Swap raspberries for blackberries, blueberries, or strawberries for a different berry twist.
- **Iced Raspberry Mint Latte**: Add a splash of oat milk or almond milk to the cold brew for a creamy, latte-style drink.
- **Mint Lemonade Cold Brew**: Add a touch of lemon juice instead of lime for a citrusy variation, keeping the minty freshness.

## Pairing Suggestions:

- Pair with **vegan chocolate chip cookies** or **lemon shortbread** to complement the fruity, minty flavors.
- Enjoy alongside a **fresh fruit salad** or **vegan coconut yogurt parfait** for a light, refreshing meal.

## Interesting Fact:

Did you know that cold brew coffee is made by steeping coarsely ground coffee beans in cold water for an extended period - usually 12-24 hours? This slow brewing process results in a smoother, less acidic coffee that pairs perfectly with fruity and herbal flavors.

## Cultural Connection:

The **mojito** originated in Cuba and is traditionally made with mint, lime, rum, sugar, and soda water. This **Raspberry Mint Mojito Cold Brew** is a fun, non-alcoholic twist on the classic cocktail, blending coffee culture with the refreshing elements of a mojito for a truly unique and global-inspired iced coffee creation.

# Iced Caramel Popcorn Latte

*Indulge in the sweet, crunchy flavor of your favorite movie-time snack with a twist - this Iced Caramel Popcorn Latte combines the rich, bold flavor of iced coffee with the irresistible taste of caramel and popcorn. The fusion of salty-sweet popcorn flavor, smooth caramel syrup, and creamy iced coffee creates a delightful treat that's perfect for those who love a snack and a drink in one. Whether you're craving a fun, comforting coffee experience or simply want something new to impress your guests, this latte delivers a playful and indulgent combination.*

## Ingredients:

- 1 cup cold brew coffee
- 2 tbsps caramel syrup
- 1/4 cup vegan popcorn, crushed
- 1/2 cup oat milk (or preferred plant-based milk)
- Ice cubes
- 1 tbsp maple syrup or agave syrup (optional, for extra sweetness)
- [Optional] Whipped coconut cream for topping
- [Optional] Additional caramel syrup for drizzling
- [Optional] Pinch of sea salt for garnish

## Instructions:

1. **Prepare the Cold Brew**: Brew your cold brew coffee in advance and let it chill in the fridge.
2. **Crush the Popcorn**: In a bowl, crush the popcorn into small pieces - this will release the salty-sweet flavor that complements the coffee.
3. **Mix the Coffee and Caramel**: In a glass, pour the cold brew coffee and stir in 2 tablespoons of caramel syrup. Adjust the sweetness with maple syrup or agave syrup if desired.
4. **Add the Milk**: Pour in the oat milk, stirring gently to combine.
5. **Crush Popcorn into the Drink**: Add the crushed popcorn to the coffee mixture, giving it a gentle stir to infuse the popcorn flavor.
6. **Ice It**: Fill the glass with ice cubes, making sure the drink is well chilled.
7. **Top and Garnish**: For a decadent touch, top with whipped coconut cream and drizzle with extra caramel syrup. If you like a hint of saltiness, sprinkle a pinch of sea salt on top.
8. **Serve and Enjoy**: Stir before sipping to enjoy the full caramel popcorn flavor!

## Tips and Recommendations:

- **Adjust sweetness**: If you prefer a sweeter drink, add more caramel syrup or maple syrup to taste.
- **For extra crunch**: Garnish with additional crushed popcorn for a more satisfying texture.
- **Customize the milk**: Experiment with different plant-based milks like almond or coconut milk for varied flavor profiles.
- **Chill the coffee**: Ensure your cold brew coffee is properly chilled before adding to the drink to keep it refreshing.
- **For a creamier texture**: Try blending the cold brew and oat milk together for a smoother consistency.

## Variations:

- **Caramel Macchiato Popcorn Latte**: For a classic macchiato twist, layer your caramel and oat milk and top with a shot of espresso.
- **Salted Caramel Popcorn Latte**: Add a pinch of sea salt or use salted caramel syrup for a more savory-sweet flavor.
- **Caramel Popcorn Frappe**: Blend the cold brew coffee, caramel syrup, and ice together to create a frosty, blended version of this treat.

## Pairing Suggestions:

- Pair with **vegan chocolate chip cookies** or **toffee brittle** to complement the caramel and popcorn flavors.
- Enjoy with a **vegan cinnamon roll** or **caramelized banana bread** for a cozy, indulgent snack.

## Interesting Fact:

Did you know that cold brew coffee is brewed slowly over a 12-24 hour period, making it less acidic and smoother than traditional iced coffee? Its mellow, rich flavor is perfect for pairing with sweet flavors like caramel and popcorn!

## Cultural Connection:

While caramel lattes are a staple in cafes worldwide, the addition of popcorn is a fun, creative twist that brings the nostalgic flavors of movie snacks into the world of coffee. Combining sweet, salty, and smooth elements, this drink reflects the growing trend of innovative and playful coffee creations.

# Iced Vanilla Mint Latte

*Refresh your senses with a burst of cool mint and smooth vanilla in this Iced Vanilla Mint Latte. Combining the refreshing flavors of mint with the sweet, comforting essence of vanilla, this latte offers a delightful balance of flavors. The crispness of mint paired with the creaminess of oat milk and the boldness of cold brew coffee makes for the perfect iced beverage to enjoy on a warm day or as a revitalizing afternoon pick-me-up.*

## Ingredients:

- 1 cup cold brew coffee
- 1/2 tsp vanilla extract
- 1/2 tsp fresh mint, finely chopped
- 1 tbsp maple syrup or agave syrup (optional, for extra sweetness)
- 1/2 cup oat milk (or preferred plant-based milk)
- Ice cubes
- [Optional] Mint sprig for garnish
- [Optional] A dash of ground cinnamon for added spice

## Instructions:

1. **Brew the Cold Brew**: Start by brewing your cold brew coffee and allowing it to chill in the refrigerator.
2. **Muddle the Mint**: In a small bowl, gently muddle the fresh mint leaves to release their oils and flavor. This will infuse the drink with a vibrant minty taste.
3. **Combine Ingredients**: In a glass, combine the cold brew coffee with the muddled mint and vanilla extract. Stir well.
4. **Sweeten**: Add maple syrup or agave syrup to taste, depending on how sweet you like your coffee. Stir to dissolve the sweetener.
5. **Add Milk**: Pour in the oat milk, stirring gently to combine.
6. **Add Ice**: Fill the glass with ice cubes to chill the drink.
7. **Garnish and Serve**: Garnish with a sprig of fresh mint or a dash of cinnamon for a touch of spice and color.
8. **Enjoy**: Stir before sipping to enjoy the full flavor experience of this refreshing latte.

## Tips and Recommendations:

- **Mint infusion**: If you want a stronger mint flavor, increase the amount of mint or let it steep for a few minutes longer.
- **For a richer texture**: Use a creamier plant-based milk, like coconut milk, for a more indulgent drink.
- **Adjust the sweetness**: You can skip the syrup or use more if you prefer a sweeter drink.
- **Extra froth**: If you like a frothy top, you can froth your oat milk before adding it to the coffee.
- **Serve chilled**: For an extra refreshing experience, chill the glass before pouring in the coffee.

## Variations:

- **Minty Mocha**: Add 1 tablespoon of cocoa powder for a chocolatey twist.
- **Cinnamon Vanilla Mint Latte**: Add a pinch of cinnamon to the drink for a warm spice note.
- **Iced Coconut Vanilla Mint Latte**: Replace oat milk with coconut milk for a tropical flavor combination.

## Pairing Suggestions:

- Pair with **vegan chocolate chip cookies** for a sweet treat that complements the minty freshness of the latte.
- Enjoy with a **light lemon cake** or **almond croissant** for a bright and refreshing combination.
- For a savory pairing, try a **vegan avocado toast** with lemon and chili flakes.

## Interesting Fact:

Did you know that mint is often used to enhance focus and concentration? Its cooling and refreshing properties make it the perfect herb to add to your afternoon coffee break!

## Cultural Connection:

The combination of vanilla and mint in coffee is a modern twist on classic flavor profiles. While vanilla has long been a favorite in coffee drinks worldwide, mint's popularity in beverages stretches across cultures - from Moroccan mint tea to the minty coffee concoctions enjoyed in the Middle East. This iced latte brings those global influences together into a simple, refreshing drink.

# Strawberry Kiwi Iced Coffee

*Brighten up your coffee routine with the refreshing and fruity flavors of Strawberry Kiwi Iced Coffee. This unique iced coffee combines the richness of cold brew coffee with the tangy sweetness of fresh strawberries and kiwis, creating a delightful fusion of flavors. The natural sweetness from the fruit complements the boldness of the coffee, making it a perfect summer treat or a revitalizing morning pick-me-up. Enjoy this one-of-a-kind iced coffee that's both refreshing and energizing!*

## Ingredients:

- 1 cup cold brew coffee
- 1/2 cup fresh strawberries, hulled and sliced
- 1 kiwi, peeled and sliced
- 1 tbsp maple syrup or agave syrup (optional, for extra sweetness)
- 1/2 cup plant-based milk (oat milk or almond milk work well)
- Ice cubes
- [Optional] Fresh mint leaves for garnish
- [Optional] A few extra slices of strawberries and kiwi for garnish

## Instructions:

1. **Brew the Cold Brew**: Begin by preparing cold brew coffee and letting it chill in the refrigerator.
2. **Prepare the Fruit**: In a blender, combine the sliced strawberries and kiwi. Blend until smooth, adding a splash of cold water if needed to create a smooth puree.
3. **Sweeten the Fruit**: If desired, add maple syrup or agave syrup to the fruit puree for a sweeter taste. Blend again to mix.
4. **Combine Ingredients**: In a glass, pour the chilled cold brew coffee. Add the fresh fruit puree and stir to combine.
5. **Add Milk**: Pour in the plant-based milk of your choice and mix gently.
6. **Add Ice**: Fill the glass with ice cubes to chill the drink.
7. **Garnish and Serve**: Garnish with a sprig of mint or extra slices of strawberry and kiwi for a vibrant, colorful presentation.
8. **Enjoy**: Stir the drink well before sipping to enjoy the full blend of fruity and coffee flavors.

## Tips and Recommendations:

- **Customize the sweetness**: Adjust the sweetness of your drink by adding more or less syrup, depending on your preference.
- **For a thicker texture**: Blend in a small banana or some ice cubes with the fruit puree to create a creamy, smoothie-like consistency.
- **Chill the fruit puree**: For an extra-refreshing treat, chill the fruit puree in the refrigerator before mixing it with the cold brew coffee.
- **Experiment with other fruits**: Try adding a splash of pineapple or mango for a tropical twist.

## Variations:

- **Tropical Iced Coffee**: Add a few chunks of pineapple to the fruit puree for a tropical flavor combination.
- **Berry Blast Iced Coffee**: Swap the kiwi for more strawberries or other berries, such as raspberries or blueberries.
- **Coconut Iced Coffee**: Use coconut milk instead of oat or almond milk for a richer, tropical flavor.

## Pairing Suggestions:

- Pair with **vegan coconut macaroons** or **light lemon scones** for a refreshing, fruity combination.
- Enjoy with a **berry salad** or **avocado toast** for a healthy, satisfying snack.
- For a sweet treat, pair with **vegan chocolate-covered almonds** or a **chocolate chip cookie**.

## Interesting Fact:

Did you know that kiwi is one of the best sources of vitamin C, even more than oranges? Adding kiwi to your iced coffee gives it a nutritional boost along with that sweet-tart flavor!

## Cultural Connection:

Fruity iced coffee beverages are becoming more popular globally as people look for refreshing and healthy ways to enjoy their caffeine. Combining coffee with fresh fruit, like in this **Strawberry Kiwi Iced Coffee**, blends the flavors of summer with the rich tradition of coffee culture, offering a unique way to experience coffee beyond the ordinary.

# Hot Chocolate and Hot Beverages:

# Classic Hot Chocolate

*Indulge in the timeless comfort of Classic Hot Chocolate, a drink that brings warmth and joy with every sip. This rich, velvety beverage is a perfect way to unwind during chilly nights or enjoy a sweet treat on a cozy afternoon. Made with smooth cocoa and a touch of sweetness, this classic version is sure to transport you to the heart of winter wonderlands. Whether you're nestled by the fireplace or sharing a special moment with loved ones, this hot chocolate recipe offers pure, nostalgic bliss.*

## Ingredients:

- 2 cups dairy-free milk (oat milk or almond milk work great)
- 2 tbsp unsweetened cocoa powder
- 2 tbsp maple syrup or agave syrup
- 1/4 tsp vanilla extract
- Pinch of salt
- [Optional] Vegan whipped cream or marshmallows for topping
- [Optional] A sprinkle of ground cinnamon or cocoa powder for garnish

## Instructions:

1. In a small saucepan, heat the dairy-free milk over medium heat, stirring occasionally until warm but not boiling.
2. Whisk in the cocoa powder, maple syrup, vanilla extract, and a pinch of salt until fully combined and smooth.
3. Continue to heat, whisking until the mixture is hot and well-blended (but not boiling).
4. Pour the hot chocolate into a mug.
5. [Optional] Top with whipped cream, marshmallows, and a sprinkle of cinnamon or cocoa powder for extra flair.
6. Serve immediately and enjoy!

## Tips and Recommendations:

- For a richer flavor, use full-fat coconut milk or a creamy oat milk blend.
- Add a pinch of chili powder for a spicy kick that pairs beautifully with the sweetness of the cocoa.
- Want a more decadent experience? Stir in a few squares of your favorite dark chocolate to elevate the richness.

## Variations:

- **Minty Hot Chocolate**: Add a few drops of peppermint extract to infuse a refreshing minty flavor.
- **Mocha Hot Chocolate**: Mix in a shot of espresso or strong brewed coffee for a coffee-chocolate fusion.
- **Hazelnut Hot Chocolate**: Stir in a spoonful of hazelnut spread for a nutty twist.

## Pairing Suggestions:

- Pair with a warm slice of vegan banana bread or a batch of cinnamon sugar cookies for the ultimate treat.
- Serve alongside a fresh fruit platter or dark chocolate truffles for a cozy dessert spread.

## Interesting Fact:

Did you know that hot chocolate was originally enjoyed as a cold beverage in ancient Mesoamerica? The Mayans and Aztecs drank a version of chocolate that was often spiced with chili and vanilla, far different from the sweet, creamy versions we enjoy today.

## Cultural Connection:

Hot chocolate has long been a beloved drink in various cultures. In Europe, particularly in France and Spain, it has been enjoyed since the 16th century, where it was often served as a thick, indulgent beverage with a rich history tied to cocoa trade and royal courts.

# Dark Chocolate Hot Cocoa

*Indulge in the deep, luxurious flavors of Dark Chocolate Hot Cocoa, where velvety cocoa blends seamlessly with rich, dark chocolate to create a perfectly decadent treat. This recipe elevates your usual hot chocolate experience with the boldness of dark chocolate and a smooth, creamy texture. Whether you're savoring it on a cold evening or serving it at your next gathering, this hot cocoa will surely become your go-to drink for ultimate comfort and indulgence.*

## Ingredients:

- 2 cups dairy-free milk (oat milk or coconut milk work beautifully)
- 2 tbsp unsweetened cocoa powder
- 2 oz dark chocolate (70% cocoa or higher), chopped
- 1-2 tbsp maple syrup (or to taste)
- 1/4 tsp vanilla extract
- Pinch of salt
- [Optional] Vegan whipped cream or shaved dark chocolate for topping
- [Optional] A dash of cinnamon or chili powder for an extra kick

## Instructions:

1. In a small saucepan, combine the dairy-free milk and cocoa powder over medium heat, whisking to dissolve the cocoa powder.
2. Add the chopped dark chocolate to the saucepan and stir until it melts completely into the milk mixture.
3. Stir in the maple syrup, vanilla extract, and a pinch of salt. Continue to heat, whisking occasionally until the mixture is hot and smooth, but not boiling.
4. Pour the hot cocoa into a mug.
5. [Optional] Top with vegan whipped cream, shaved dark chocolate, or a sprinkle of cinnamon or chili powder for a touch of spice.
6. Serve immediately and enjoy the indulgence of dark chocolate goodness!

## Tips and Recommendations:

- For an ultra-silky texture, blend the cocoa mixture using a hand blender before serving.
- Adjust the sweetness to your preference by adding more or less maple syrup.
- Add a splash of your favorite plant-based liqueur (like amaretto or hazelnut) for a grown-up twist.

## Variations:

- **Minty Dark Chocolate Hot Cocoa**: Add a few drops of peppermint extract to bring a refreshing minty flavor to your cocoa.
- **Salted Caramel Dark Chocolate Hot Cocoa**: Stir in a drizzle of vegan caramel sauce and a pinch of sea salt for a sweet and salty combination.
- **Mexican Dark Chocolate Hot Cocoa**: Incorporate a pinch of cinnamon and chili powder to create a spiced, bold version of this hot cocoa.

## Pairing Suggestions:

- Pair with a slice of vegan chocolate cake or coconut macaroons for a sweet treat.
- Serve alongside spiced nuts or a warm cinnamon roll to balance the richness of the cocoa.

## Interesting Fact:

Did you know that dark chocolate has been enjoyed for centuries, dating back to ancient Mesoamerican cultures, where it was mixed with spices and consumed as a drink during religious ceremonies? Today, dark chocolate remains a beloved treat, known for its intense flavor and potential health benefits.

## Cultural Connection:

Hot cocoa, especially in its more intense dark chocolate form, has roots in ancient cultures such as the Mayans and Aztecs, who made their own version using ground cacao beans and spices. Over time, it evolved into the sweet, creamy beverage we know today, cherished by many around the world.

# White Chocolate Hot Mocha

*Treat yourself to a creamy, indulgent experience with a White Chocolate Hot Mocha - a luxurious fusion of rich espresso, velvety white chocolate, and smooth dairy-free milk. This drink is perfect for anyone who loves the comforting warmth of a mocha with a sweeter, more decadent twist. It's an ideal cozy treat for chilly evenings or as a special pick-me-up during the day. With its harmonious balance of coffee and sweetness, this white chocolate mocha will become your new favorite way to enjoy a hot beverage.*

## Ingredients:

- 1 shot (1 ounce) of espresso
- 1 cup dairy-free milk (almond, oat, or coconut milk works well)
- 2 tbsp white chocolate chips or chopped white chocolate
- 1 tbsp cocoa powder (unsweetened)
- 1-2 tbsp maple syrup (or to taste)
- 1/4 tsp vanilla extract
- Pinch of salt
- [Optional] Vegan whipped cream for topping
- [Optional] White chocolate shavings or cocoa powder for garnish

## Instructions:

1. Brew a shot of espresso using your preferred method.
2. In a small saucepan, heat the dairy-free milk over medium heat, whisking occasionally.
3. Once the milk is warm, add the white chocolate chips or chopped white chocolate to the saucepan. Stir until the chocolate completely melts into the milk.
4. Stir in the cocoa powder, maple syrup, vanilla extract, and a pinch of salt, whisking until everything is well combined. Continue heating until the mixture is hot but not boiling.
5. Pour the freshly brewed espresso into a mug.
6. Pour the white chocolate milk mixture over the espresso and stir gently.
7. [Optional] Top with vegan whipped cream and garnish with white chocolate shavings or a light dusting of cocoa powder.
8. Serve immediately and enjoy the rich, sweet, and velvety indulgence of this hot mocha.

## Tips and Recommendations:

- For a richer flavor, you can add a splash of coconut cream to the milk mixture for extra creaminess.
- If you prefer a less sweet version, reduce the amount of maple syrup and let the white chocolate provide the main sweetness.
- Use a milk frother for an even creamier, frothy texture.
- If you enjoy a touch of spice, a dash of cinnamon or nutmeg adds a cozy layer of flavor.

## Variations:

- **Mint White Chocolate Hot Mocha**: Add a few drops of peppermint extract for a festive, minty twist.
- **Caramel White Chocolate Hot Mocha**: Drizzle in some vegan caramel sauce for an extra layer of sweetness and richness.
- **Nutty White Chocolate Hot Mocha**: Stir in a spoonful of almond or hazelnut butter for a nutty flavor that complements the white chocolate.

## Pairing Suggestions:

- Pair with a warm, buttery vegan croissant for a comforting breakfast treat.
- Enjoy with a slice of vegan white chocolate cheesecake or a crunchy biscotti to balance the creamy richness.
- Serve alongside roasted nuts or spiced almonds for a crunchy contrast.

## Interesting Fact:

Did you know that white chocolate isn't technically chocolate? It doesn't contain cocoa solids, but it's made from cocoa butter, giving it a smooth, sweet flavor that pairs beautifully with espresso.

## Cultural Connection:

Mocha drinks, blending espresso with chocolate, have been around for centuries. While the traditional mocha uses dark chocolate, the white chocolate version offers a new, sweet spin on the classic favorite. Whether enjoyed in a café or made at home, the mocha remains a comforting and indulgent treat loved worldwide.

# Peppermint Hot Chocolate

*Nothing says cozy winter evening like a warm cup of Peppermint Hot Chocolate. This refreshing, creamy drink is the perfect combination of rich cocoa, velvety dairy-free milk, and a burst of minty freshness. The peppermint flavor adds a cool, invigorating twist to the traditional hot chocolate, making it a festive treat for the holidays or a comforting pick-me-up on a chilly day. With a touch of sweetness and a hint of cool mint, this drink is sure to become your new favorite winter indulgence.*

## Ingredients:

- 1 cup dairy-free milk (oat, almond, or coconut milk works well)
- 2 tbsp unsweetened cocoa powder
- 1 tbsp maple syrup (or to taste)
- 1/4 tsp peppermint extract (or to taste)
- 1/4 tsp vanilla extract
- Pinch of salt
- [Optional] 1-2 tbsp vegan chocolate chips (for extra richness)
- [Optional] Vegan whipped cream for topping
- [Optional] Crushed candy canes or mint leaves for garnish

## Instructions:

1. In a small saucepan, heat the dairy-free milk over medium heat, whisking occasionally.
2. Once the milk is warm, add the cocoa powder, maple syrup, peppermint extract, vanilla extract, and a pinch of salt. Whisk until smooth and well combined.
3. [Optional] For a richer flavor, stir in vegan chocolate chips and allow them to melt completely into the mixture.
4. Continue heating the mixture until it's hot but not boiling. Stir occasionally to prevent the cocoa from settling at the bottom.
5. Pour the hot chocolate into a mug.
6. [Optional] Top with vegan whipped cream and garnish with crushed candy canes or fresh mint leaves for a festive touch.
7. Serve immediately and enjoy the perfect balance of sweet, minty, and chocolaty flavors.

## Tips and Recommendations:

- For a creamier version, use coconut milk or add a splash of coconut cream to the hot chocolate.
- If you prefer a stronger peppermint flavor, add a few more drops of peppermint extract. Just be careful not to overdo it!
- To make this a more decadent treat, stir in a bit of dairy-free chocolate syrup or top with a sprinkle of cocoa powder.

## Variations:

- **White Chocolate Peppermint Hot Chocolate**: Substitute the cocoa powder with white chocolate chips for a creamy, white chocolate twist.
- **Caramel Peppermint Hot Chocolate**: Drizzle some vegan caramel sauce into the hot chocolate for a sweet, caramelized touch.
- **Spiced Peppermint Hot Chocolate**: Add a pinch of cinnamon or nutmeg to the mix for a warm, spicy layer of flavor.

## Pairing Suggestions:

- Pair with vegan shortbread cookies or peppermint bark for a festive treat.
- Enjoy alongside a slice of vegan chocolate cake or brownies to complement the rich, creamy texture.
- For a light snack, serve with a handful of roasted almonds or spiced pecans.

## Interesting Fact:

Did you know that peppermint is one of the oldest herbs known to humans? It's been used for centuries, not only in food and drinks but also for medicinal purposes, such as aiding digestion.

## Cultural Connection:

Peppermint hot chocolate is a popular winter beverage, particularly in the holiday season. The combination of chocolate and peppermint is beloved worldwide, especially during Christmas time, when peppermint is a favorite flavor in festive treats. This cozy drink brings together the warmth of chocolate and the refreshing coolness of peppermint, making it the perfect beverage for holiday celebrations.

# Mexican Hot Chocolate

*Warm up with the bold and indulgent flavors of Mexican Hot Chocolate, a spicy, rich treat that blends the smoothness of chocolate with the aromatic kick of cinnamon and chili. This cozy beverage is inspired by the traditional Mexican way of preparing hot chocolate, often made with a blend of cocoa, spices, and sometimes a touch of heat. The combination of earthy cocoa, spicy cinnamon, and a hint of chili creates a comforting yet exhilarating drink, perfect for chilly evenings or as a festive holiday treat. Whether you're looking for a new way to enjoy hot chocolate or wanting to explore the rich cultural flavors of Mexico, this drink will leave you craving more.*

## Ingredients:

- 1 cup dairy-free milk (oat milk, almond milk, or coconut milk)
- 2 tbsp unsweetened cocoa powder
- 1 tbsp maple syrup (or to taste)
- 1/4 tsp ground cinnamon
- Pinch of ground chili powder or cayenne pepper (optional for spice)
- 1/4 tsp vanilla extract
- Pinch of salt
- [Optional] 2-3 squares of dark chocolate (for extra richness)
- [Optional] Vegan whipped cream for topping
- [Optional] Ground cinnamon for garnish
- [Optional] Chili flakes or a cinnamon stick for garnish

## Instructions:

1. In a small saucepan, heat the dairy-free milk over medium heat, stirring occasionally.
2. Once the milk is warm, whisk in the cocoa powder, maple syrup, ground cinnamon, chili powder (if using), vanilla extract, and a pinch of salt.
3. Continue to whisk the mixture until it's smooth and the cocoa powder is fully dissolved.
4. [Optional] For a richer flavor, add 2-3 squares of dark chocolate and stir until melted and well combined.
5. Heat the mixture until it's hot but not boiling, stirring occasionally.
6. Pour the hot chocolate into a mug and top with vegan whipped cream (if using).
7. [Optional] Garnish with a sprinkle of cinnamon or chili flakes, or add a cinnamon stick for a festive touch.
8. Serve immediately and enjoy the perfect balance of sweetness, warmth, and spice.

## Tips and Recommendations:

- For a milder version, reduce or omit the chili powder and cayenne pepper.
- For a more decadent treat, add a spoonful of peanut butter or almond butter to the hot chocolate for extra creaminess.
- If you prefer a thicker hot chocolate, use full-fat coconut milk or add a tablespoon of coconut cream.

## Variations:

- **Vegan Mexican Hot Chocolate with Coconut**: Use coconut milk and add shredded coconut for a tropical twist.
- **Spiced Orange Mexican Hot Chocolate**: Add a few strips of orange zest during heating, and remove before serving, to infuse the chocolate with a citrusy warmth.
- **Mexican Hot Chocolate Mocha**: For a caffeinated kick, stir in a shot of espresso or strong coffee.

## Pairing Suggestions:

- Pair with vegan churros or cinnamon-sugar tortilla chips for a deliciously indulgent snack.
- Enjoy with a slice of vegan chocolate cake or brownies for a rich dessert experience.
- For a lighter option, pair with roasted nuts or spiced almonds to balance the rich chocolate flavor.

## Interesting Fact:

Did you know that Mexican hot chocolate is traditionally prepared using a **molinillo**, a wooden whisk, to froth the milk and mix the ingredients? This traditional tool is said to create a creamy, velvety texture that enhances the drinking experience.

## Cultural Connection:

Mexican Hot Chocolate, or **"chocolate de metate,"** has deep cultural roots in Mexico. The Aztecs and Mayans enjoyed a form of hot chocolate made from ground cacao beans, often flavored with spices like chili, vanilla, and cinnamon. Today, Mexican hot chocolate remains a cherished drink, often enjoyed during the holidays and festive occasions, offering a rich connection to both history and flavor.

# Nutella Hot Chocolate

*Indulge in the decadent, creamy goodness of Nutella Hot Chocolate, a luxurious twist on your classic hot chocolate that combines the rich, nutty flavor of Nutella with velvety dairy-free milk. This drink is perfect for cozy nights or as a sweet treat when you're craving something extra special. The hazelnut chocolate spread adds a layer of depth, giving the drink a smooth, irresistible texture. Topped with whipped cream or a sprinkle of cocoa powder, this Nutella Hot Chocolate is sure to be your new favorite comfort drink.*

## Ingredients:

- 1 cup dairy-free milk (oat milk, almond milk, or coconut milk)
- 2 tbsp Nutella (or any chocolate-hazelnut spread)
- 1 tbsp unsweetened cocoa powder
- 1 tbsp maple syrup (or to taste)
- 1/2 tsp vanilla extract
- Pinch of salt
- [Optional] Vegan whipped cream for topping
- [Optional] Shaved chocolate or cocoa powder for garnish
- [Optional] Crushed hazelnuts for garnish

## Instructions:

1. In a small saucepan, heat the dairy-free milk over medium heat, stirring occasionally.
2. Once the milk is warm, whisk in the Nutella, cocoa powder, maple syrup, vanilla extract, and a pinch of salt.
3. Stir the mixture continuously until the Nutella is completely melted and the drink is smooth.
4. Continue heating until the hot chocolate is hot but not boiling, stirring occasionally.
5. Pour the hot chocolate into a mug, and top with a generous swirl of vegan whipped cream.
6. [Optional] Garnish with shaved chocolate, a dusting of cocoa powder, or a sprinkle of crushed hazelnuts for added texture and flavor.
7. Serve immediately and enjoy this velvety, indulgent treat.

## Tips and Recommendations:

- If you prefer a richer hot chocolate, increase the amount of Nutella or use full-fat coconut milk.
- For a dairy-free whipped topping, use coconut cream or a store-bought vegan whipped cream.
- Add a pinch of cinnamon or a dash of chili powder for a warm, spiced kick.

## Variations:

- **Nutella Mocha Hot Chocolate**: Add a shot of espresso to your Nutella Hot Chocolate for an energizing mocha twist.
- **Vegan Nutella Hot Chocolate with Coconut**: Use coconut milk for a tropical flavor and add a splash of coconut extract for an extra layer of coconut richness.
- **Nutella Mint Hot Chocolate**: Stir in a few drops of peppermint extract for a festive, minty version of this classic drink.

## Pairing Suggestions:

- Pair with soft, fluffy vegan marshmallows or biscotti for a deliciously crunchy contrast.
- Enjoy with a slice of vegan hazelnut cake or chocolate-dipped strawberries for a decadent treat.
- For a savory contrast, pair with a warm, herby flatbread or roasted nuts.

## Interesting Fact:

Did you know that Nutella, created by the Italian company Ferrero, was originally a way to make chocolate more affordable by adding hazelnuts to the recipe during times of chocolate shortages in the 1940s?

## Cultural Connection:

Nutella is a beloved treat worldwide, especially in Italy, where the chocolate-hazelnut spread has become a staple in homes, often enjoyed on toast, pastries, or even by the spoonful. This version of Nutella Hot Chocolate offers a deliciously comforting taste of Italy, with its smooth, nutty flavor bringing a sense of warmth and indulgence to any occasion.

# Salted Caramel Hot Cocoa

*Treat yourself to the ultimate indulgence with Salted Caramel Hot Cocoa, a rich and creamy drink that combines the deep flavor of chocolate with a sweet, buttery caramel twist, balanced by a touch of sea salt. This cozy beverage is perfect for chilly evenings, offering a luxurious, velvety texture and a delightful blend of salty and sweet. Whether you're unwinding after a long day or hosting a holiday gathering, this salted caramel hot cocoa is sure to satisfy your cravings for something comforting and decadent.*

## Ingredients:

- 1 cup dairy-free milk (almond milk, oat milk, or coconut milk)
- 2 tbsp cocoa powder
- 2 tbsp salted caramel sauce (store-bought or homemade)
- 1 tbsp maple syrup (or to taste)
- 1/2 tsp vanilla extract
- Pinch of sea salt
- [Optional] Vegan whipped cream for topping
- [Optional] Extra caramel sauce for drizzle
- [Optional] Crushed sea salt for garnish

## Instructions:

1. In a small saucepan, heat the dairy-free milk over medium heat, stirring occasionally.
2. Once the milk is warm, whisk in the cocoa powder, salted caramel sauce, maple syrup, vanilla extract, and a pinch of sea salt.
3. Stir continuously until the mixture is smooth and well combined.
4. Heat the cocoa until it's hot but not boiling, making sure all ingredients are dissolved and the drink is creamy.
5. Pour the hot cocoa into a mug, and top with a swirl of vegan whipped cream, if desired.
6. [Optional] Drizzle with extra caramel sauce and sprinkle with crushed sea salt for an extra burst of flavor.
7. Serve immediately and enjoy the perfect balance of sweet and salty in every sip.

## Tips and Recommendations:

- For an even richer flavor, use full-fat coconut milk or a blend of coconut milk and oat milk.
- Add a pinch of cinnamon or nutmeg for a warm, spiced twist.
- If you prefer a sweeter cocoa, increase the amount of maple syrup or caramel sauce.

## Variations:

- **Salted Caramel Mocha**: Add a shot of espresso to turn this hot cocoa into a delicious mocha drink.
- **Vegan Salted Caramel Hot Cocoa with Coconut**: Use coconut milk for a tropical flair and add a splash of coconut extract for an extra layer of flavor.
- **Peppermint Salted Caramel Hot Cocoa**: Stir in a few drops of peppermint extract for a festive minty version of this cozy treat.

## Pairing Suggestions:

- Pair with soft, vegan sugar cookies or a slice of vegan chocolate cake for a dessert-worthy experience.
- Enjoy with a warm, flaky croissant or almond biscotti to balance the sweetness of the drink.
- For a savory contrast, serve with roasted salted nuts or a savory vegan cheese platter.

## Interesting Fact:

Did you know that salted caramel became a popular flavor trend in the early 2000s, blending the classic sweet taste of caramel with a savory salt element to create an irresistible combination?

## Cultural Connection:

Caramel, with its deep, rich flavor, has been a staple in sweets and confections worldwide for centuries. The addition of salt to caramel, however, is a more recent innovation that began to gain popularity in France in the early 2000s. The salty-sweet combination has since become a beloved flavor profile in desserts and beverages globally.

# Almond Joy Hot Chocolate

*Indulge in the decadent fusion of chocolate, coconut, and almond flavors with this Almond Joy Hot Chocolate. Inspired by the beloved candy bar, this creamy, rich drink brings together all the deliciousness of almonds and coconut, complemented by a smooth, velvety cocoa base. Whether you're treating yourself on a cozy night in or looking for a unique twist on traditional hot cocoa, this recipe delivers a delightful blend of sweet and nutty flavors that will leave you craving more.*

## Ingredients:

- 1 cup dairy-free milk (almond milk, oat milk, or coconut milk)
- 2 tbsp cocoa powder
- 2 tbsp coconut cream (or coconut milk for a lighter version)
- 1 tbsp almond butter
- 1 tbsp maple syrup (or to taste)
- 1/2 tsp vanilla extract
- Pinch of salt
- [Optional] Vegan whipped cream for topping
- [Optional] Toasted almonds for garnish
- [Optional] Shredded coconut for garnish

## Instructions:

1. In a small saucepan, heat the dairy-free milk over medium heat, stirring occasionally.
2. Add the cocoa powder, coconut cream, almond butter, maple syrup, vanilla extract, and a pinch of salt. Whisk together until the mixture is smooth and well-combined.
3. Continue to heat the cocoa mixture until it is hot, but do not allow it to boil. Stir occasionally to prevent burning.
4. Once heated, pour the hot cocoa into your favorite mug.
5. [Optional] Top with a generous swirl of vegan whipped cream.
6. [Optional] Garnish with toasted almonds and shredded coconut for an extra burst of flavor and texture.
7. Serve immediately and enjoy the irresistible combination of chocolate, coconut, and almonds in every sip.

## Tips and Recommendations:

- For a creamier texture, use full-fat coconut milk instead of coconut cream.
- Adjust the sweetness by adding more or less maple syrup, depending on your taste preferences.
- If you love a stronger nut flavor, add a spoonful of almond extract for a more intense almond profile.

## Variations:

- **Almond Joy Mocha**: Add a shot of espresso to turn this hot chocolate into a mocha drink for a coffee twist.
- **Coconut-Free Almond Joy Hot Chocolate**: Omit the coconut cream and add a bit more almond butter for a nutty, smooth flavor.
- **Minted Almond Joy**: Stir in a few drops of peppermint extract for a refreshing, festive touch.

## Pairing Suggestions:

- Pair with a slice of vegan chocolate cake or almond biscotti for a perfect dessert pairing.
- Enjoy with a handful of roasted salted almonds or cashews for a savory contrast to the sweet drink.
- Serve with vegan coconut macaroons or a light coconut-flavored pastry for a deliciously tropical experience.

## Interesting Fact:

Did you know that coconut and chocolate are a classic pairing in many tropical desserts, often featured in candies and baked goods due to their complementary flavors and textures?

## Cultural Connection:

The combination of chocolate and coconut has been celebrated for centuries in tropical regions around the world. The Almond Joy candy bar, first introduced in the United States in 1946, popularized the mix of almonds, chocolate, and coconut, and it remains a beloved flavor profile in both sweets and beverages today.

# Raspberry White Hot Chocolate

*Indulge in the delicate, fruity sweetness of Raspberry White Hot Chocolate - a luxurious twist on traditional hot cocoa. With its creamy white chocolate base, infused with a vibrant raspberry flavor, this drink is the perfect combination of smooth and tart. Whether you're looking to treat yourself on a chilly evening or impress guests at a cozy gathering, this vibrant, indulgent drink will elevate any moment. Enjoy a creamy, fruity, and decadent experience with every sip!*

## Ingredients:

- 1 cup dairy-free milk (such as almond, oat, or coconut milk)
- 1/2 cup dairy-free white chocolate chips or chopped white chocolate
- 2 tbsp raspberry puree (or fresh raspberries for making your own)
- 1 tbsp maple syrup (or to taste)
- 1/2 tsp vanilla extract
- Pinch of salt
- [Optional] Vegan whipped cream for topping
- [Optional] Fresh raspberries and white chocolate shavings for garnish

## Instructions:

1. In a small saucepan, heat the dairy-free milk over medium heat, stirring occasionally.
2. Add the white chocolate chips and continue stirring until the chocolate has fully melted and the mixture is smooth.
3. Stir in the raspberry puree, maple syrup, vanilla extract, and a pinch of salt. Continue heating until the mixture is hot but not boiling.
4. Once heated through, pour the raspberry white hot chocolate into your favorite mug.
5. [Optional] Top with a dollop of vegan whipped cream for extra creaminess.
6. [Optional] Garnish with fresh raspberries and a sprinkle of white chocolate shavings for a beautiful finishing touch.
7. Serve immediately and enjoy the irresistible combination of creamy white chocolate and tangy raspberry.

## Tips and Recommendations:

- If you prefer a thicker consistency, add an extra tablespoon of white chocolate for a richer flavor.
- Use frozen raspberries if fresh ones aren't available, and blend them into a puree for a smoother texture.
- Adjust the sweetness by adding more or less maple syrup, depending on how sweet you like your drinks.

## Variations:

- **Raspberry White Mocha**: Add a shot of espresso to turn this into a delightful mocha.
- **Chocolate Raspberry Delight**: Swap the white chocolate for dark chocolate for a richer, more intense flavor.
- **Coconut Raspberry White Hot Chocolate**: Use coconut milk for a tropical twist that pairs perfectly with the raspberry.

## Pairing Suggestions:

- Pair with vegan shortbread cookies or raspberry almond scones for a perfect sweet treat.
- Enjoy with a slice of lemon pound cake for a lovely contrast to the creamy, rich hot chocolate.
- Serve with fresh fruit, like strawberries or blueberries, for a refreshing balance.

## Interesting Fact:

Raspberries are packed with antioxidants, making this indulgent treat not only delicious but also a source of health benefits! The raspberry's tart flavor complements the sweetness of white chocolate, creating a balanced and delightful drink.

## Cultural Connection:

White chocolate is often associated with luxury and indulgence, and it has been a popular choice for desserts and beverages around the world. The addition of raspberries brings a vibrant, fresh twist that evokes the flavors of summer, making this hot chocolate a year-round favorite.

# Chai Hot Chocolate

*Warm up with the perfect fusion of two beloved beverages - chai tea and rich hot chocolate. Chai Hot Chocolate is the cozy drink you never knew you needed, blending the spicy warmth of traditional chai with the creamy sweetness of chocolate. Infused with aromatic spices like cinnamon, cardamom, and ginger, this indulgent hot chocolate will transport you to a world of comfort and relaxation. Whether you're snuggled up at home or entertaining guests, this decadent treat will fill your cup and your heart with warmth.*

## Ingredients:

- 1 cup dairy-free milk (such as almond, soy, or oat milk)
- 1/2 cup dairy-free chocolate chips or chopped dark chocolate
- 1 tbsp chai tea concentrate (or 1 chai tea bag for brewing)
- 1 tbsp maple syrup (or to taste)
- 1/2 tsp ground cinnamon
- 1/4 tsp ground cardamom
- 1/4 tsp ground ginger
- 1/4 tsp ground cloves
- Pinch of black pepper
- [Optional] Vegan whipped cream for topping
- [Optional] Cinnamon stick and star anise for garnish

## Instructions:

1. In a small saucepan, heat the dairy-free milk over medium heat, stirring occasionally.
2. Add the chocolate chips or chopped dark chocolate and stir until melted and smooth.
3. Stir in the chai tea concentrate, maple syrup, ground cinnamon, cardamom, ginger, cloves, and black pepper. Continue stirring until all spices are fully incorporated, and the mixture is heated through but not boiling.
4. Pour the chai hot chocolate into your favorite mug, leaving room for toppings.
5. [Optional] Top with vegan whipped cream for extra creaminess.
6. [Optional] Garnish with a cinnamon stick or star anise for a decorative and aromatic touch.
7. Serve immediately and enjoy the spicy, creamy goodness of chai and chocolate combined.

## Tips and Recommendations:

- If you want a stronger chai flavor, add an extra teaspoon of chai tea concentrate or brew an extra chai tea bag in the milk before adding the chocolate.
- For a smoother texture, you can blend the drink once heated to ensure all spices are well combined.
- Adjust the sweetness by adding more maple syrup, depending on your taste preference.

## Variations:

- **Spicy Chai Hot Chocolate**: Add a dash of cayenne pepper or a pinch of chili powder for a fiery kick.
- **Iced Chai Hot Chocolate**: Let the chai hot chocolate cool, then serve over ice for a refreshing version of this drink.
- **Caramel Chai Hot Chocolate**: Stir in a spoonful of vegan caramel syrup for an extra layer of sweetness.

## Pairing Suggestions:

- Pair with vegan gingerbread cookies for a perfectly spiced treat.
- Enjoy with a slice of cinnamon swirl cake for an indulgent afternoon snack.
- Serve alongside fruit, like apple slices or orange segments, for a refreshing contrast to the rich, spiced drink.

## Interesting Fact:

Chai tea originated in India and has been enjoyed for centuries. The blend of spices was traditionally used for medicinal purposes, with each ingredient offering a unique health benefit. In recent years, chai has become a popular flavor in drinks and desserts worldwide.

## Cultural Connection:

Chai tea is an integral part of Indian culture, often served to guests as a gesture of hospitality. It's typically brewed with spices and milk, making it a comforting and nourishing drink. The fusion of chai with hot chocolate combines two beloved traditions - creating a unique, indulgent experience that blends the best of both worlds.

# Toasted Marshmallow Hot Cocoa

*Indulge in the ultimate winter comfort drink with Toasted Marshmallow Hot Cocoa. This rich and creamy hot chocolate is taken to the next level with the smoky flavor of toasted marshmallows, creating a nostalgic, campfire-inspired treat. Perfect for chilly nights, this cozy drink combines the sweetness of chocolate with the warmth of toasted marshmallow, making it a decadent choice for a special occasion or a simple, indulgent treat after a long day. Whether you're curling up with a good book or sharing it with friends, this drink will warm your soul.*

## Ingredients:

- 1 cup dairy-free milk (almond, soy, or oat milk work well)
- 1/2 cup dairy-free chocolate chips or chopped dark chocolate
- 1 tbsp cocoa powder
- 2 tbsp maple syrup (or to taste)
- 1/2 tsp vanilla extract
- 1/4 tsp ground cinnamon (optional)
- 1/4 cup vegan marshmallows (for toasting)
- [Optional] Vegan whipped cream for topping
- [Optional] A pinch of sea salt for garnish

## Instructions:

1. In a small saucepan, heat the dairy-free milk over medium heat, stirring occasionally.
2. Add the chocolate chips or chopped dark chocolate and cocoa powder, whisking until the chocolate has completely melted and the mixture is smooth.
3. Stir in the maple syrup and vanilla extract, then add the ground cinnamon if using. Continue to heat the mixture until it is hot but not boiling.
4. While the cocoa is heating, toast the marshmallows. You can do this by placing them on a skewer or fork and holding them over a gas flame, using a kitchen torch, or broiling them in the oven until golden and slightly charred.
5. Pour the hot cocoa into a mug, leaving some room for toppings.
6. Carefully add the toasted marshmallows on top of the cocoa.
7. [Optional] Top with vegan whipped cream and a pinch of sea salt for an extra touch of flavor and presentation.
8. Serve immediately, and enjoy the warm, smoky sweetness of toasted marshmallow goodness!

## Tips and Recommendations:

- If you prefer a thicker hot cocoa, use less milk or add a little extra chocolate to the mixture.
- For an even more indulgent treat, stir in a spoonful of peanut butter or almond butter for a nutty twist.
- If you want a spicier kick, add a pinch of cayenne pepper or a dash of chili powder to the cocoa mixture.

## Variations:

- **S'mores Style**: Add crushed graham crackers to the top of your hot cocoa for a complete s'mores experience.
- **Minty Toasted Marshmallow Hot Cocoa**: Add a few drops of peppermint extract to the cocoa for a refreshing minty twist.
- **Vegan Caramelized Marshmallows**: For a different flavor, drizzle caramel sauce over your toasted marshmallows before adding them to your cocoa.

## Pairing Suggestions:

- Pair with vegan shortbread cookies or ginger snaps for a crunchy, sweet contrast to the creamy cocoa.
- Serve with a warm slice of vegan chocolate cake for an extra indulgence.
- Enjoy with fresh fruit, such as strawberries or bananas, to balance the rich sweetness of the hot cocoa.

## Interesting Fact:

Did you know that marshmallows originated in ancient Egypt? They were originally made from the sap of the mallow plant, and were once considered a delicacy fit for royalty!

## Cultural Connection:

Toasted marshmallows are often associated with camping and outdoor fires, a tradition popular in many cultures. In the U.S., the combination of marshmallows, chocolate, and graham crackers is iconic, especially when enjoyed around a campfire. This **Toasted Marshmallow Hot Cocoa** takes that beloved experience and brings it indoors, making it a perfect wintertime treat.

# Red Velvet Hot Chocolate

*Get ready for a luxurious and decadent treat with Red Velvet Hot Chocolate. This visually stunning beverage combines the rich, velvety texture of creamy hot chocolate with the iconic deep red color and subtle cocoa flavor of red velvet cake. Topped with a dollop of vegan whipped cream and a sprinkling of cocoa powder or chocolate shavings, this indulgent drink is perfect for a special occasion or when you just want to treat yourself to something extra special. Whether it's Valentine's Day, a winter evening, or a celebration, this hot cocoa will make you feel like royalty.*

## Ingredients:

- 1 cup dairy-free milk (almond, oat, or soy milk)
- 1 tbsp cocoa powder
- 2 tbsp red velvet cake mix (make sure it's vegan-friendly)
- 1/2 cup dairy-free chocolate chips
- 2 tbsp maple syrup (or to taste)
- 1/4 tsp vanilla extract
- 1/4 tsp ground cinnamon (optional)
- Vegan whipped cream (for topping)
- Vegan chocolate shavings or cocoa powder (for garnish)

## Instructions:

1. In a small saucepan, heat the dairy-free milk over medium heat, stirring occasionally.
2. Add the cocoa powder, red velvet cake mix, and chocolate chips, whisking until the chocolate has completely melted and the mixture is smooth.
3. Stir in the maple syrup and vanilla extract, then add ground cinnamon for a warm, spicy touch, if desired.
4. Continue heating the mixture, whisking frequently, until it is hot but not boiling.
5. Pour the hot cocoa into your favorite mug, leaving room for toppings.
6. Top with a generous dollop of vegan whipped cream and sprinkle with cocoa powder or chocolate shavings for a touch of elegance.
7. Serve immediately, and enjoy the rich, smooth flavor of red velvet in every sip!

## Tips and Recommendations:

- If you prefer a stronger chocolate flavor, add more cocoa powder or chocolate chips to intensify the richness of the drink.
- For a deeper red color, add a few drops of red food coloring (ensure it's plant-based if you're keeping it vegan).
- If you want to add a hint of tartness, try a small splash of lemon juice for a red velvet cake-like effect.

## Variations:

- **Red Velvet Mocha**: Add a shot of espresso or strong coffee to the mix for a caffeinated twist on your red velvet hot chocolate.
- **Nutty Red Velvet**: Stir in a spoonful of almond butter or hazelnut butter for a creamy, nutty flavor that complements the richness of the cocoa.
- **Spiced Red Velvet**: Add a pinch of ground cloves or nutmeg to give the hot chocolate an extra warmth and spice.

## Pairing Suggestions:

- Pair with a slice of vegan red velvet cake for a true red velvet experience.
- Enjoy alongside vegan cinnamon rolls or chocolate chip cookies for a comforting, cozy treat.
- A side of fresh strawberries or raspberries can add a burst of fruitiness that complements the richness of the cocoa.

## Interesting Fact:

Did you know that red velvet cake is often associated with the American South? It became popular in the 1920s and was originally known for its unique combination of flavors, including cocoa and buttermilk.

## Cultural Connection:

Red velvet has become an iconic dessert flavor in many parts of the world, symbolizing celebration and indulgence. By turning this classic cake into a hot beverage, we're able to enjoy the comforting flavors of red velvet all year long, whether it's a holiday treat or an everyday indulgence.

# Coconut Hot Chocolate

*Warm up with the tropical, creamy delight of Coconut Hot Chocolate. This indulgent drink combines the rich, velvety texture of hot chocolate with the sweet, exotic flavor of coconut milk. Whether you're dreaming of a cozy winter escape or simply craving a rich, dairy-free hot cocoa, this recipe is the perfect blend of chocolatey goodness and coconutty charm. With a hint of vanilla and the option to top it with whipped coconut cream, every sip is like a mini vacation in a cup.*

## Ingredients:

- 1 cup canned coconut milk (full-fat for creaminess)
- 1/2 cup dairy-free milk (almond, oat, or soy milk)
- 2 tbsp cocoa powder
- 2 tbsp dairy-free chocolate chips
- 2 tbsp maple syrup (or to taste)
- 1/2 tsp vanilla extract
- 1/4 tsp ground cinnamon (optional)
- Vegan whipped coconut cream (for topping)
- Shredded coconut or chocolate shavings (for garnish)

## Instructions:

1. In a small saucepan, combine the coconut milk and dairy-free milk. Heat over medium, stirring occasionally.
2. Add the cocoa powder and chocolate chips, whisking until completely dissolved and smooth.
3. Stir in the maple syrup and vanilla extract, then add the ground cinnamon for a bit of spice, if you wish.
4. Continue heating the mixture, whisking frequently, until it is hot but not boiling.
5. Pour the hot chocolate into your favorite mug.
6. Top with a generous swirl of whipped coconut cream and garnish with shredded coconut or chocolate shavings for a delightful touch.
7. Serve immediately and enjoy the tropical, creamy goodness in every sip!

## Tips and Recommendations:

- For an extra-rich flavor, you can add a bit more chocolate, either in the form of chocolate chips or dark chocolate pieces.
- If you want your coconut hot chocolate a little sweeter, increase the maple syrup to your taste.
- Feel free to add a dash of cayenne pepper or chili powder for a spicy kick to balance the sweetness.

## Variations:

- **Coconut Mocha**: Add a shot of espresso or strong brewed coffee to the mix for a coffee-chocolate combination.
- **Iced Coconut Hot Chocolate**: For warmer weather, chill the mixture and serve over ice for a refreshing iced treat.
- **Minty Coconut Hot Chocolate**: Add a few drops of peppermint extract to bring a refreshing minty twist to the drink.

## Pairing Suggestions:

- Pair with a slice of coconut cake or coconut macaroons for a perfect coconut-filled treat.
- Enjoy alongside a piece of dark chocolate or a vegan brownie for an indulgent dessert experience.
- A light fruit salad with tropical fruits like pineapple and mango can balance the richness of the hot cocoa.

## Interesting Fact:

Did you know that coconut milk, unlike regular milk, is made by grating the flesh of mature coconuts and mixing it with water? It's naturally rich and creamy, making it an excellent alternative to dairy in vegan recipes.

## Cultural Connection:

Coconut milk has been used for centuries in Southeast Asia and the Pacific Islands, where coconuts are abundant. It's a key ingredient in many traditional dishes, both savory and sweet. By incorporating coconut milk into this hot chocolate recipe, we bring a taste of the tropics to a cozy, winter beverage.

# Maple Pecan Hot Cocoa

*Cozy up with a cup of Maple Pecan Hot Cocoa, a sweet and nutty twist on the classic hot chocolate. This delightful beverage combines the rich, velvety flavor of chocolate with the warmth of maple syrup and the satisfying crunch of roasted pecans. Perfect for chilly days, this drink brings together comforting flavors that feel like a warm hug in a cup. A hint of cinnamon adds a little spice, making it a truly indulgent experience that will have you sipping slowly and savoring every drop.*

## Ingredients:

- 1 cup dairy-free milk (almond, oat, or soy milk)
- 2 tbsp cocoa powder
- 1 tbsp maple syrup (or more to taste)
- 2 tbsp dairy-free chocolate chips
- 1/4 tsp ground cinnamon
- 1/4 tsp vanilla extract
- 2 tbsp chopped roasted pecans
- Vegan whipped cream (for topping)
- Crushed pecans or maple syrup drizzle (for garnish)

## Instructions:

1. In a small saucepan, heat the dairy-free milk over medium heat, stirring occasionally to prevent it from burning.
2. Once warm, whisk in the cocoa powder and chocolate chips until smooth and completely dissolved.
3. Stir in the maple syrup, ground cinnamon, and vanilla extract. Continue to heat, stirring until hot but not boiling.
4. Pour the hot cocoa into your favorite mug, leaving space for the toppings.
5. Top with a generous swirl of whipped cream.
6. Sprinkle the chopped roasted pecans over the whipped cream and drizzle with a little extra maple syrup.
7. Serve immediately and enjoy this nutty, sweet, and creamy hot cocoa treat!

## Tips and Recommendations:

- If you prefer a richer flavor, add more chocolate chips or a dash of dark chocolate for extra depth.
- Adjust the sweetness to your liking by adding more maple syrup if desired.
- To add a fun crunch, sprinkle some additional chopped pecans on top for texture.

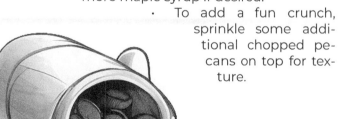

## Variations:

- **Maple Cinnamon Hot Cocoa**: Add a little extra ground cinnamon or a pinch of nutmeg for a spiced variation.
- **Salted Maple Pecan Hot Cocoa**: For a sweet-salty balance, sprinkle a pinch of sea salt on top of the whipped cream and pecans.
- **Iced Maple Pecan Cocoa**: Chill the cocoa after preparing it, and serve it over ice for a refreshing take on this rich drink.

## Pairing Suggestions:

- Pair with a warm slice of vegan pecan pie or a maple-flavored scone for a perfect treat.
- Enjoy alongside buttery shortbread cookies or a slice of banana bread to complement the nuttiness of the drink.
- A fresh fruit salad, especially with apples or pears, will balance out the richness of the hot cocoa.

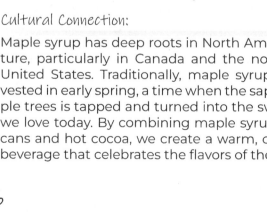

## Interesting Fact:

Did you know that pecans are native to North America and are often associated with Southern U.S. cuisine? They're not only delicious but also packed with nutrients like fiber and healthy fats.

## Cultural Connection:

Maple syrup has deep roots in North American culture, particularly in Canada and the northeastern United States. Traditionally, maple syrup was harvested in early spring, a time when the sap from maple trees is tapped and turned into the sweet syrup we love today. By combining maple syrup with pecans and hot cocoa, we create a warm, comforting beverage that celebrates the flavors of the region.

# Hazelnut Hot Mocha

*Indulge in the luxurious fusion of rich chocolate and aromatic hazelnuts with the Hazelnut Hot Mocha. This velvety drink brings together the deep, comforting flavor of mocha with a smooth nutty twist, perfect for any chocolate lover or coffee enthusiast. A sprinkle of cocoa and a dash of hazelnut syrup create an irresistible, warming beverage that's ideal for cozy afternoons or a comforting after-dinner treat. Treat yourself to this delightful mocha that combines the best of both worlds - coffee and chocolate, with an extra nutty flair!*

## Ingredients:

- 1 shot (1 ounce) of espresso
- 1 cup dairy-free milk (oat, almond, or soy milk)
- 2 tbsp cocoa powder
- 1 tbsp hazelnut syrup (or more to taste)
- 1 tbsp dairy-free chocolate chips
- 1/4 tsp ground cinnamon (optional)
- Vegan whipped cream (for topping)
- Crushed hazelnuts (for garnish)
- Cocoa powder or chocolate shavings (for garnish)

## Instructions:

1. Brew a shot of espresso using your preferred method.
2. In a small saucepan, heat the dairy-free milk over medium heat, whisking occasionally.
3. Once warm, stir in the cocoa powder and chocolate chips, mixing until smooth and fully dissolved.
4. Add the hazelnut syrup and ground cinnamon (if using), stirring to combine. Heat until just below boiling.
5. Pour the espresso into your favorite mug, then gently add the hot chocolate mixture, stirring to combine.
6. Top with a swirl of vegan whipped cream.
7. Garnish with crushed hazelnuts and a dusting of cocoa powder or chocolate shavings for a beautiful finish.
8. Serve immediately and enjoy the creamy, nutty bliss!

## Tips and Recommendations:

- For an extra creamy texture, use a milk frother to froth the dairy-free milk before combining it with the chocolate and espresso.
- If you prefer a sweeter mocha, feel free to increase the amount of hazelnut syrup or add a teaspoon of maple syrup.
- Experiment with different nut syrups, such as almond or walnut, for a unique twist.

## Variations:

- **Hazelnut Mocha Iced Drink**: For a refreshing version, let the hot mocha cool and serve it over ice.
- **Spicy Hazelnut Mocha**: Add a pinch of chili powder or cayenne pepper for a spicy kick that complements the sweetness of the mocha.
- **Dairy-Free Whipped Cream Twist**: For a richer experience, whip coconut cream and use it as a topping for an extra coconut-hazelnut flavor combo.

## Pairing Suggestions:

- Pair with a slice of vegan chocolate cake or hazelnut shortbread cookies to enhance the mocha's chocolatey richness.
- For a lighter snack, enjoy with a bowl of fresh berries or a fruit-and-nut granola bar.
- Complement the drink with a fresh croissant or a delicate almond pastry for an indulgent treat.

## Interesting Fact:

Did you know that hazelnuts are not only a delicious treat but also packed with nutrients like vitamin E, healthy fats, and fiber? They've been enjoyed for centuries, particularly in Europe, where they've been used in sweet confections like praline and chocolate spreads.

## Cultural Connection:

Mocha beverages, combining the flavors of coffee and chocolate, are believed to have originated from the Yemeni port city of Mocha, a historical center for coffee trade. Today, the combination of chocolate and coffee is a favorite worldwide, evolving into countless variations like this hazelnut-infused version that celebrates both traditional flavors and modern twists.

# Orange Hot Chocolate

*Indulge in a vibrant twist on classic hot chocolate with the Orange Hot Chocolate. The rich, creamy depth of dairy-free chocolate combines perfectly with the bright, zesty notes of fresh orange, creating a balanced and warming drink. Whether it's a cozy winter evening or a special treat to brighten your day, this drink will transport you to a blissful chocolate-orange paradise. Perfect for vegans and anyone with a sweet tooth, this beverage offers a delightful mix of citrus and chocolate that will surely become your new favorite winter drink!*

## Ingredients:

- 1 cup dairy-free milk (oat, almond, or soy milk)
- 2 tbsp cocoa powder
- 1 tbsp dairy-free chocolate chips
- 1-2 tbsp fresh orange juice (to taste)
- Zest of 1/2 orange
- 1 tbsp maple syrup (or sweetener of choice)
- 1/4 tsp ground cinnamon (optional)
- Vegan whipped cream (for topping)
- Orange slices (for garnish)
- Orange zest (for garnish)

## Instructions:

1. In a small saucepan, heat the dairy-free milk over medium heat, whisking occasionally to prevent it from boiling.
2. Stir in the cocoa powder, dairy-free chocolate chips, and maple syrup, continuing to whisk until smooth and the chocolate chips are fully melted.
3. Add the fresh orange juice and orange zest, stirring well to combine and heat through.
4. For a spiced touch, add the ground cinnamon and mix until fully incorporated.
5. Pour the hot chocolate into your favorite mug.
6. Top with a generous swirl of vegan whipped cream.
7. Garnish with fresh orange slices and a sprinkle of orange zest for a fragrant finish.
8. Serve immediately and enjoy the citrusy, chocolatey indulgence!

## Tips and Recommendations:

- **Orange Zest:** Don't skip the orange zest! It adds a fragrant burst of citrus that makes the drink extra special.
- **Sweetener:** Adjust the sweetness to your liking by adding more maple syrup or another natural sweetener, like agave or coconut sugar.
- **Extra Creaminess:** For an even creamier drink, use coconut milk or a combination of coconut milk and almond milk.

- **Chill for Iced Version:** Let the hot chocolate cool and serve it over ice for a refreshing summer version of this drink.

## Variations:

- **Spicy Orange Hot Chocolate:** Add a pinch of cayenne pepper or chili powder to the cocoa mixture for a spicy twist that complements the citrus flavor.
- **Minty Orange Hot Chocolate:** Add a drop of peppermint extract for a refreshing mint-chocolate-orange combination.
- **Dairy-Free Truffle Hot Chocolate:** Melt a dairy-free chocolate truffle into the hot cocoa for a velvety, rich experience.

## Pairing Suggestions:

- Pair with a slice of vegan orange cake or chocolate-dipped shortbread cookies to enhance the orange-chocolate flavor combo.
- Enjoy with fresh fruit salad, especially citrus fruits like grapefruit or mandarins, to highlight the bright orange notes in the drink.
- A cozy vegan scone or croissant would also be a perfect companion to your hot chocolate.

## Interesting Fact:

Did you know that chocolate and orange have been a popular flavor pairing for centuries? The combination was first introduced in the early 1900s and quickly became a classic, loved for its balance of sweet and tangy flavors.

## Cultural Connection:

Hot chocolate, in its various forms, has been enjoyed since the 16th century. Originally consumed in Mesoamerican cultures, it was often flavored with spices like cinnamon and chili. The addition of fruit flavors like orange was popularized in Europe, where citrus was a prized ingredient. Today, we celebrate this timeless pairing with a fresh, vegan twist that's just as indulgent as the original!

# Spicy Mayan Hot Chocolate

*Transport yourself to ancient Mesoamerica with the Spicy Mayan Hot Chocolate, a rich and bold drink that blends the warmth of traditional chocolate with the heat of aromatic spices. Inspired by the flavors enjoyed by the Mayans centuries ago, this velvety beverage combines dark chocolate, cinnamon, and a kick of chili, creating a fiery yet smooth drink. Perfect for chilly evenings or whenever you want to experience something truly exotic and indulgent, this hot chocolate will awaken your senses with every sip.*

## Ingredients:

- 1 cup dairy-free milk (almond, oat, or coconut milk)
- 2 tbsp cocoa powder
- 1 tbsp dairy-free dark chocolate chips (or 70% dark chocolate)
- 1/2 tsp ground cinnamon
- 1/4 tsp chili powder (or more for extra heat)
- 1/2 tsp vanilla extract
- 1-2 tbsp maple syrup (or sweetener of choice)
- Pinch of sea salt
- Vegan whipped cream (for topping)
- Chili flakes or cocoa powder (for garnish)

## Instructions:

1. In a small saucepan, heat the dairy-free milk over medium heat, whisking occasionally to prevent it from boiling.
2. Stir in the cocoa powder, dark chocolate chips, and maple syrup, whisking until the chocolate is fully melted and the mixture is smooth.
3. Add the ground cinnamon, chili powder, vanilla extract, and a pinch of sea salt. Whisk to combine and bring the mixture to a gentle simmer for 2-3 minutes, allowing the spices to infuse.
4. Pour the hot chocolate into your favorite mug.
5. Top with a generous swirl of vegan whipped cream.
6. Garnish with a sprinkle of chili flakes or a dusting of cocoa powder for an extra pop of flavor.
7. Serve immediately and enjoy the bold, spicy warmth of this indulgent drink!

## Tips and Recommendations:

- **Adjust Spice Level:** If you like your hot chocolate on the milder side, start with a small pinch of chili powder and adjust to taste. For a more intense heat, increase the amount of chili powder or add a dash of cayenne pepper.
- **Sweetener Options:** You can also experiment with other sweeteners such as agave syrup, coconut sugar, or date syrup for a more natural, caramelized sweetness.
- **Richness:** Use full-fat coconut milk for a creamier, more luxurious texture.

- **Make It Iced:** For a refreshing twist, let the hot chocolate cool down and serve over ice for a spicy summer treat.

## Variations:

- **Mayan Mocha:** Add a shot of espresso or a strong brewed coffee for a coffee-chocolate-spice combo that's sure to wake you up!
- **Coconut Mayan Hot Chocolate:** Use coconut milk and top with toasted shredded coconut for an extra tropical twist.
- **Minty Mayan Hot Chocolate:** Add a drop of peppermint extract to the chocolate mixture for a cooling contrast to the heat of the chili.

## Pairing Suggestions:

- Pair with a dark chocolate orange truffle to complement the chocolate's richness and the chili's heat.
- Enjoy with a vegan cinnamon roll or churros to highlight the warming spices in the hot chocolate.
- A slice of vegan coconut cake or a lightly spiced vegan shortbread will balance out the heat while enhancing the chocolate flavor.

## Interesting Fact:

Did you know that the Mayans were among the first to cultivate cacao, and they considered chocolate to be a divine gift from the gods? They would often drink a spicy version of chocolate, flavored with chili, as a symbol of strength and vitality.

## Cultural Connection:

The use of spices in chocolate dates back to ancient Mesoamerica, where the Mayans and Aztecs would prepare a beverage called xocolatl. Made with cacao, chili, and spices, it was both a ceremonial drink and a source of energy. The **Spicy Mayan Hot Chocolate** is a modern twist on this ancient drink, keeping the bold flavors and rich history alive in every cup.

# Lavender White Hot Chocolate

*Indulge in the delicate and soothing flavors of Lavender White Hot Chocolate, a luxurious drink that combines creamy white chocolate with the calming essence of lavender. Perfect for unwinding after a busy day, this hot beverage is both sweet and floral, creating a comforting experience for the senses. The addition of lavender adds a unique twist, elevating this classic treat into a dreamy, aromatic delight. Whether you need a peaceful evening companion or a special indulgence, this Lavender White Hot Chocolate is sure to impress.*

## Ingredients:

- 1 cup dairy-free milk (such as almond, oat, or coconut milk)
- 2 tbsp white chocolate chips (dairy-free)
- 1 tsp dried lavender buds (or 1/2 tsp lavender extract)
- 1/2 tsp vanilla extract
- 1 tbsp maple syrup (or sweetener of choice)
- Pinch of sea salt
- Vegan whipped cream (for topping)
- Lavender sprig or edible flower (for garnish)

## Instructions:

1. In a small saucepan, heat the dairy-free milk over medium heat, stirring occasionally to prevent it from boiling.
2. Add the white chocolate chips and whisk continuously until the chocolate has melted and the mixture is smooth.
3. Stir in the dried lavender buds (or lavender extract), vanilla extract, and a pinch of sea salt.
4. Lower the heat and let the mixture simmer gently for 3-4 minutes, allowing the lavender to infuse the milk.
5. Remove from heat and strain out the lavender buds (if using dried lavender) using a fine mesh strainer.
6. Pour the hot chocolate into your favorite mug.
7. Top with a dollop of vegan whipped cream.
8. Garnish with a sprig of lavender or an edible flower for a beautiful and fragrant touch.
9. Serve immediately and enjoy the floral, creamy goodness!

## Tips and Recommendations:

- **Infuse for Stronger Flavor:** If you enjoy a more intense lavender flavor, let the lavender steep in the hot milk for 5-6 minutes instead of 3-4.
- **Sweetener Options:** You can also use agave syrup, coconut sugar, or even stevia for a different sweetness profile.
- **Make It Creamier:** For a richer texture, opt for coconut milk or full-fat almond milk.
- **Add a Citrus Twist:** A small dash of lemon or orange zest can add a refreshing contrast to the sweetness and lavender.

## Variations:

- **Lavender Mocha:** Add a shot of espresso or a few tablespoons of strong brewed coffee to create a sweet and floral mocha-style drink.
- **Lavender & Honey:** Substitute maple syrup with a teaspoon of honey (or vegan honey alternative) for a more traditional sweetness that pairs well with the lavender.
- **Iced Lavender White Hot Chocolate:** Let the drink cool and serve over ice for a refreshing version of this comforting beverage.

## Pairing Suggestions:

- Pair with a light almond biscotti or a lemon shortbread cookie to complement the floral notes of the lavender.
- Enjoy alongside a slice of vegan lemon cake or a lightly spiced apple tart for a delightful treat.
- A simple coconut macaroon or a vegan scone can also add a rich, indulgent touch to the experience.

## Interesting Fact:

Did you know that lavender has been used for centuries in aromatherapy and culinary traditions? Its calming scent and soothing properties make it a favorite for relaxation and mindfulness practices.

## Cultural Connection:

Lavender is often associated with the Mediterranean, where it has been cultivated for both culinary and medicinal uses for thousands of years. In many cultures, lavender is considered a symbol of calm and purity. In this drink, it brings a touch of elegance and refinement to the otherwise simple comfort of white hot chocolate.

# Pumpkin Spice Hot Cocoa

*Embrace the cozy flavors of autumn with Pumpkin Spice Hot Cocoa, a rich and indulgent treat that combines the comforting taste of chocolate with the warm, spiced essence of pumpkin. Perfect for cool fall evenings or anytime you're craving a little seasonal magic, this hot cocoa is made with simple ingredients but packed with all the flavors you love. It's a delightful twist on traditional hot chocolate, infused with the perfect blend of pumpkin spice, vanilla, and creamy cocoa. A cup of this autumn-inspired beverage will instantly lift your spirits and satisfy your sweet cravings!*

## Ingredients:

- 1 cup dairy-free milk (such as almond, oat, or coconut milk)
- 2 tbsp unsweetened cocoa powder
- 2 tbsp pumpkin puree
- 1 tbsp maple syrup (or sweetener of choice)
- 1/2 tsp pumpkin pie spice
- 1/4 tsp ground cinnamon
- 1/4 tsp ground ginger
- 1/4 tsp ground nutmeg
- 1/2 tsp vanilla extract
- Pinch of sea salt
- Vegan whipped cream (for topping)
- Ground cinnamon or pumpkin pie spice (for garnish)

## Instructions:

1. In a small saucepan, combine the dairy-free milk, cocoa powder, pumpkin puree, and maple syrup. Heat over medium heat, whisking until smooth and well combined.
2. Add the pumpkin pie spice, cinnamon, ginger, nutmeg, vanilla extract, and a pinch of sea salt. Whisk again until the spices are evenly mixed and the mixture is hot, but not boiling.
3. Remove from heat and pour the hot cocoa into your favorite mug.
4. Top with a generous dollop of vegan whipped cream.
5. Garnish with a sprinkle of ground cinnamon or pumpkin pie spice for an extra touch of fall flavor.
6. Serve immediately and enjoy the cozy warmth of autumn in every sip!

## Tips and Recommendations:

- **Adjust the Spice Level:** If you prefer a stronger spice flavor, add more cinnamon or pumpkin pie spice to suit your taste.
- **Sweetener Options:** You can also use agave syrup, coconut sugar, or stevia for a different sweetness profile.
- **Vegan Whipped Cream:** For a lighter, dairy-free option, top with coconut whipped cream instead of traditional whipped cream.
- **For Extra Creaminess:** Use full-fat coconut milk or oat milk for a richer, creamier texture.

## Variations:

- **Pumpkin Spice Mocha:** Add a shot of espresso or a few tablespoons of brewed coffee to the hot cocoa for a pumpkin spice mocha twist.
- **Iced Pumpkin Spice Cocoa:** Let the drink cool and serve over ice for a refreshing cold version of this autumn treat.
- **Chocolate Mint Pumpkin Spice:** Add a few drops of peppermint extract to the cocoa mixture for a refreshing minty twist.

## Pairing Suggestions:

- Pair with a slice of vegan pumpkin bread or a vegan cinnamon roll for the perfect fall-inspired treat.
- Enjoy alongside a warm vegan scone or a buttery shortbread cookie for a comforting snack.
- A handful of spiced nuts or roasted pumpkin seeds also complement the sweet, spiced flavors.

## Interesting Fact:

Did you know that pumpkin spice isn't just for fall? The blend of spices - cinnamon, ginger, and nutmeg - has been used for centuries in both culinary and medicinal applications, prized for its warming, soothing qualities.

## Cultural Connection:

Pumpkin spice flavors are deeply embedded in autumn traditions in the U.S., particularly around Thanksgiving. The blend of spices used in this hot cocoa is reminiscent of the rich flavors of pumpkin pie, a staple dessert in many cultures during the harvest season.

# Gingerbread Hot Chocolate

*Step into a winter wonderland with Gingerbread Hot Chocolate, a festive and cozy drink that brings together the rich, velvety warmth of chocolate and the nostalgic flavors of gingerbread. Infused with spices like cinnamon, ginger, and molasses, this hot cocoa is a comforting treat perfect for holiday gatherings or quiet nights by the fire. With its sweet and spicy notes, it's like sipping on a gingerbread cookie in a mug! Whether you're cuddling up with loved ones or unwinding after a busy day, this drink is sure to warm both body and soul.*

## Ingredients:

- 1 cup dairy-free milk (such as almond, oat, or coconut milk)
- 2 tbsp unsweetened cocoa powder
- 2 tbsp molasses
- 1 tbsp maple syrup (or sweetener of choice)
- 1/2 tsp ground cinnamon
- 1/4 tsp ground ginger
- 1/4 tsp ground nutmeg
- 1/4 tsp ground cloves
- Pinch of sea salt
- 1/2 tsp vanilla extract
- Vegan whipped cream (for topping)
- Crushed gingerbread cookies (for garnish, optional)

## Instructions:

1. In a small saucepan, combine the dairy-free milk, cocoa powder, molasses, and maple syrup. Heat over medium heat, whisking constantly until smooth and well combined.
2. Add the cinnamon, ginger, nutmeg, cloves, and sea salt. Continue to whisk until the mixture is hot, but not boiling, and the spices are fully blended.
3. Remove from heat and stir in the vanilla extract.
4. Pour the hot cocoa into your favorite mug, filling it up to your desired level.
5. Top with a dollop of vegan whipped cream and sprinkle crushed gingerbread cookies on top for added flavor and texture.
6. Serve immediately and enjoy the comforting, spiced warmth of gingerbread in every sip!

## Tips and Recommendations:

- **Adjust the Spice Level:** If you like more of a ginger kick, increase the ginger to 1/2 teaspoon for a spicier flavor.
- **Sweetener Options:** You can swap out maple syrup for agave, brown sugar, or even coconut sugar for a deeper sweetness.
- **Gingerbread Flavor:** For a more authentic gingerbread taste, add 1/2 teaspoon of ground allspice or a bit of molasses sugar for extra richness.
- **Whipped Topping:** Try coconut whipped cream for a rich, creamy texture that complements the spices.

## Variations:

- **Gingerbread Mocha:** Add a shot of espresso or brewed coffee for a gingerbread mocha twist.
- **Iced Gingerbread Hot Chocolate:** Let the hot cocoa cool down and serve over ice for a refreshing cold version of this holiday favorite.
- **Chocolate Mint Gingerbread:** Add a few drops of peppermint extract to the hot cocoa for a festive minty gingerbread flavor.

## Pairing Suggestions:

- Pair with soft gingerbread cookies or a slice of vegan pumpkin bread to enhance the cozy, holiday vibes.
- Enjoy alongside a warm, spiced muffin or a vegan chocolate chip cookie for an indulgent treat.
- A handful of roasted almonds or spiced pecans would also complement the drink's flavors beautifully.

## Interesting Fact:

Did you know that gingerbread dates back to ancient Greece, where it was used in religious ceremonies? Over time, it became a beloved treat in many cultures, especially during the holiday season.

## Cultural Connection:

Gingerbread has long been a staple of holiday traditions in many cultures, especially in Europe. In Germany, it is often made into intricate shapes and decorated with icing, while in the U.S., gingerbread cookies are a favorite during Christmas time, evoking the warmth and comfort of the season.

# Honey Cinnamon Hot Mocha

*Indulge in the perfect blend of smooth chocolate, aromatic coffee, and the warmth of honey and cinnamon with this Honey Cinnamon Hot Mocha. This drink is the ultimate cozy pick-me-up, combining the richness of mocha with a hint of sweetness from honey and a touch of spice from cinnamon. Whether you're looking for a comforting morning brew or a relaxing evening treat, this mocha will become your go-to favorite during the cooler months. The balance of deep flavors will warm you from the inside out - it's like a hug in a cup!*

## Ingredients:

- 1 shot (1 ounce) of espresso or 1/2 cup strong brewed coffee
- 1 cup dairy-free milk (such as almond, oat, or soy milk)
- 2 tbsp unsweetened cocoa powder
- 1 tbsp honey (or maple syrup for a vegan option)
- 1/4 tsp ground cinnamon
- 1/4 tsp vanilla extract
- Pinch of sea salt
- Vegan whipped cream (for topping)
- Ground cinnamon (for garnish)

## Instructions:

1. Brew your espresso or coffee using your preferred method.
2. In a small saucepan, whisk together the dairy-free milk, cocoa powder, honey (or maple syrup), cinnamon, vanilla extract, and sea salt. Heat over medium heat, stirring constantly until hot but not boiling.
3. Pour the brewed espresso or coffee into a mug.
4. Slowly pour the hot chocolate mixture over the espresso or coffee, stirring gently to combine.
5. Top with a generous dollop of vegan whipped cream and a sprinkle of ground cinnamon for that extra cozy touch.
6. Serve immediately and enjoy the delicious harmony of mocha, honey, and spice!

## Tips and Recommendations:

- **Adjust Sweetness:** If you prefer a sweeter drink, add a little extra honey or maple syrup.
- **Spice Variations:** Experiment with a dash of ground nutmeg or cloves for an extra burst of warmth.
- **Milk Alternatives:** You can use any plant-based milk you prefer, but oat milk adds a creamy texture that's especially delightful.
- **Whipped Cream Options:** For an extra indulgence, add a drizzle of caramel or chocolate sauce on top of the whipped cream.

## Variations:

- **Iced Honey Cinnamon Mocha:** Allow the drink to cool and serve over ice for a refreshing twist on the classic.
- **Chocolate Mint Honey Mocha:** Add a drop of peppermint extract to the mixture for a minty version of this cozy drink.
- **Nutty Honey Mocha:** Stir in a tablespoon of almond butter or peanut butter for a nutty flavor and extra creaminess.

## Pairing Suggestions:

- Pair with a slice of vegan banana bread or a chocolate croissant to complement the rich mocha flavor.
- Enjoy with a bowl of spiced nuts or cinnamon-sugar almonds for a crunchy contrast to the smooth beverage.
- This drink also pairs beautifully with a soft, warm scone or a lightly toasted muffin.

## Interesting Fact:

Did you know that honey has been used as a natural sweetener for thousands of years and is believed to have healing properties? It's also packed with antioxidants, making it a perfect addition to your drink!

## Cultural Connection:

Mocha drinks originated in Yemen, where the coffee beans from the port of Mocha were highly prized. The combination of coffee and chocolate, though a modern twist, pays homage to the historic trading routes that introduced these beloved flavors to the world.

# Caramel Apple Spice

*Get cozy with a delicious twist on autumn flavors with this Caramel Apple Spice drink. Imagine the sweet, buttery richness of caramel mixed with the tartness of apples, all wrapped in a warm, spiced beverage. This drink is perfect for chilly days when you crave something comforting yet exciting. The combination of cinnamon, apple, and caramel evokes the essence of fall, making it an indulgent treat for the senses. Whether you're relaxing at home or entertaining guests, this vibrant beverage is sure to delight.*

## Ingredients:

- 1 cup unsweetened apple cider
- 1 tbsp caramel sauce (dairy-free if desired)
- 1/2 tsp ground cinnamon
- 1/4 tsp ground nutmeg
- Pinch of ground cloves
- 1/2 cup steamed almond milk (or your choice of plant-based milk)
- 1 shot (1 ounce) of espresso or strong brewed coffee
- 1 tsp vanilla extract
- [Optional] Vegan whipped cream (for topping)
- [Optional] Extra caramel sauce (for drizzle)
- [Optional] Ground cinnamon (for garnish)

## Instructions:

1. In a small pot, heat the apple cider over medium heat until it's hot but not boiling.
2. Stir in the caramel sauce, cinnamon, nutmeg, and cloves, ensuring everything is well combined.
3. Once the mixture is hot, pour in the steamed almond milk and stir gently to combine.
4. Brew your shot of espresso or coffee, then pour it into your favorite mug.
5. Pour the hot apple spice mixture into the mug over the espresso.
6. Add the vanilla extract and stir to combine the flavors.
7. Top with a dollop of vegan whipped cream, a drizzle of caramel sauce, and a sprinkle of ground cinnamon if desired.
8. Serve immediately and enjoy the warm, comforting flavors of apple and caramel with a spiced kick!

## Tips and Recommendations:

- **Spice it Up:** Adjust the spices to your liking! Add more cinnamon or a pinch of ginger for an extra kick of spice.
- **Sweetness Level:** If you prefer a sweeter drink, you can increase the amount of caramel sauce or add a touch of maple syrup.
- **Milk Alternatives:** Any plant-based milk will work, but oat milk creates a creamy texture that complements the flavors perfectly.
- **No Whipped Cream?** Try topping with a sprinkle of cinnamon or drizzle more caramel for a beautiful finish.

## Variations:

- **Iced Caramel Apple Spice:** Let the drink cool, then serve it over ice for a refreshing alternative, perfect for warmer weather.
- **Maple Caramel Apple Spice:** Swap the caramel for maple syrup for a more earthy sweetness that pairs beautifully with the apple and spice flavors.
- **Caramel Mocha Apple Spice:** Add a shot of espresso and a little cocoa powder for a mocha twist on this comforting drink.

## Pairing Suggestions:

- Pair with a warm apple cinnamon muffin or a slice of vegan pumpkin bread for a complete fall-inspired snack.
- Enjoy with a side of toasted almonds or crunchy granola bars for a balanced, cozy treat.
- This drink is also a great complement to vegan shortbread cookies or a buttery croissant.

## Interesting Fact:

Did you know that caramel is made by heating sugar until it melts and turns golden? This process creates a rich, deep flavor that complements both sweet and savory dishes. In drinks like this, it brings a touch of decadence!

## Cultural Connection:

Caramel apple flavor has long been associated with fall festivals and fairs, where the sweet and tart contrast of apples coated in caramel is a seasonal favorite. This **Caramel Apple Spice** drink draws on that nostalgic flavor combination, bringing the essence of those crisp autumn days into your cup.

# Hot Buttered Rum Coffee

*Indulge in the ultimate comfort drink with Hot Buttered Rum Coffee - a cozy, warming blend that combines the boldness of coffee with the rich, smooth taste of buttered rum. This drink is perfect for those chilly evenings when you want something both soothing and flavorful. The luxurious blend of melted butter, brown sugar, and spices creates a comforting base that's complemented by a strong coffee kick. Ideal for holiday gatherings or just a quiet evening by the fire, this drink is an irresistible way to enjoy your coffee.*

## Ingredients:

- 1 cup brewed strong coffee (or 1 shot espresso)
- 1 tbsp vegan butter (or regular butter if preferred)
- 1 tbsp brown sugar (or maple syrup for a natural sweetener)
- 1/2 tsp ground cinnamon
- 1/4 tsp ground nutmeg
- 1/4 tsp vanilla extract
- [Optional] 1 tbsp rum (for a classic touch, or leave out for a non-alcoholic version)
- [Optional] Vegan whipped cream (for topping)
- [Optional] Ground cinnamon or nutmeg (for garnish)

## Instructions:

1. Brew your coffee (or espresso) to your desired strength.
2. In a small saucepan, melt the vegan butter over low heat. Add the brown sugar, cinnamon, nutmeg, and vanilla extract. Stir until the sugar dissolves and the mixture is well combined.
3. Pour the hot coffee into a large mug.
4. Add the melted butter and spice mixture to the coffee, stirring gently to combine.
5. For an extra indulgent touch, add rum to the coffee and stir well.
6. Top with a dollop of vegan whipped cream if desired, and sprinkle ground cinnamon or nutmeg on top for an extra festive flair.
7. Serve immediately and enjoy the rich, buttery warmth of this luxurious drink!

## Tips and Recommendations:

- **For a dairy-free version:** Be sure to use vegan butter and plant-based whipped cream.
- **Adjust the sweetness:** If you prefer a sweeter drink, add more brown sugar or maple syrup.
- **Caffeine Boost:** For extra strength, replace the brewed coffee with espresso or add a shot of espresso to the mix.
- **Make it your own:** Experiment with different spices - try adding cloves or ginger for a spicier twist.

## Variations:

- **Maple Buttered Coffee:** Replace the brown sugar with maple syrup for a sweet, earthy flavor that complements the butter perfectly.
- **Iced Buttered Rum Coffee:** Let the drink cool, then pour over ice for a refreshing, cold variation on the classic recipe.
- **Hazelnut Buttered Coffee:** Add a splash of hazelnut syrup for a nutty, rich variation of this indulgent drink.

## Pairing Suggestions:

- **Pair with a slice of banana bread** or **vegan cinnamon rolls** for a comforting breakfast or brunch.
- Enjoy alongside **vegan shortbread cookies** or **dark chocolate truffles** for a sweet treat.
- This drink is a great companion to **spicy roasted nuts** or a **vegan pumpkin loaf** for a cozy snack.

## Interesting Fact:

Hot buttered rum is said to have been popularized by sailors in the 17th century who would mix rum with butter to stave off the cold and keep their energy up during long voyages. Today, it's a cozy drink often enjoyed during winter holidays.

## Cultural Connection:

This warm and soothing drink is a beloved winter tradition, especially in colder regions. Hot buttered rum itself has a rich history in America, where it was once a staple of holiday gatherings. **Hot Buttered Rum Coffee** combines this classic with the modern delight of coffee, creating a comforting, holiday-inspired beverage for coffee lovers.

# Brown Sugar Cinnamon Latte

*Indulge in the sweet and spicy warmth of a Brown Sugar Cinnamon Latte, where the comforting richness of espresso is elevated with the deep, caramel notes of brown sugar and the aromatic warmth of cinnamon. This latte is the perfect cozy treat for crisp mornings or chilly afternoons, offering a comforting balance of sweetness and spice. The combination of espresso, cinnamon, and brown sugar gives you a drink that feels both nostalgic and indulgent, making it a perfect addition to your coffee repertoire.*

## Ingredients:

- 1 shot (1 ounce) of espresso (or 1/2 cup brewed strong coffee)
- 1 cup steamed milk (or your favorite dairy-free milk)
- 1 tbsp brown sugar (or maple syrup for a different sweet twist)
- 1/4 tsp ground cinnamon
- [Optional] 1/4 tsp vanilla extract
- [Optional] Vegan whipped cream (for topping)
- [Optional] Ground cinnamon (for garnish)

## Instructions:

1. Brew a shot of espresso using your preferred method (or brew strong coffee if you prefer).
2. In a small saucepan, combine the brown sugar and cinnamon over medium heat. Add a splash of the milk (or non-dairy alternative) to help dissolve the sugar and create a smooth syrup. Stir until fully combined.
3. Steam the remaining milk (or non-dairy milk) until it's hot and frothy. You can do this using a steam wand or a milk frother.
4. Pour the brewed espresso into a mug.
5. Add the brown sugar and cinnamon syrup to the mug with the espresso and stir to combine.
6. Pour the steamed milk into the mug, holding back the foam with a spoon, and then top with the foam.
7. [Optional] Add a splash of vanilla extract for extra flavor and top with whipped cream for added indulgence.
8. Sprinkle a little extra cinnamon on top for garnish, and enjoy!

## Tips and Recommendations:

- **Dairy-Free Option:** Use almond milk, oat milk, or coconut milk for a creamy, plant-based alternative.
- **Sweetness Level:** Adjust the amount of brown sugar based on your sweetness preference. You can also substitute with maple syrup or coconut sugar for a unique twist.
- **Stronger Coffee Flavor:** If you prefer a bolder taste, increase the espresso shot or the coffee-to-milk ratio.

## Variations:

- **Vanilla Cinnamon Latte:** Add a dash of vanilla extract to the brown sugar and cinnamon syrup for an extra layer of sweetness and flavor.
- **Iced Brown Sugar Cinnamon Latte:** Let the drink cool and serve over ice for a refreshing twist on this warm beverage.
- **Caramel Cinnamon Latte:** Add a tablespoon of vegan caramel syrup to the brown sugar syrup mixture for an extra indulgent treat.

## Pairing Suggestions:

- **Pair with a slice of vegan banana bread** or **cinnamon swirl muffins** to enhance the warm, comforting flavors of the latte.
- Enjoy alongside **vegan cinnamon rolls** or **shortbread cookies** for a sweet afternoon snack.

## Interesting Fact:

Did you know that cinnamon is one of the oldest spices known to mankind, prized for its flavor and medicinal properties? It has been used for over 2,000 years in cooking, medicine, and even as currency!

## Cultural Connection:

The combination of cinnamon and brown sugar is often associated with cozy, homey flavors, making this latte a beloved drink during fall and winter months. It evokes the warmth of family gatherings and festive holidays, and the addition of espresso makes it a modern twist on the traditional spiced beverages enjoyed around the world.

# Banana Bread Latte

*Craving the warm, comforting flavors of banana bread in a cup? The Banana Bread Latte combines the sweet, nutty flavors of baked banana bread with the rich, bold base of espresso. A touch of cinnamon, a dash of vanilla, and a hint of brown sugar bring the iconic aroma and flavors of banana bread into this creamy, indulgent latte. Perfect for cozy afternoons or as a treat to start your day, this latte is like a hug in a mug.*

## Ingredients:

- 1 shot (1 ounce) of espresso (or 1/2 cup brewed strong coffee)
- 1 cup steamed milk (or your favorite dairy-free milk)
- 1/2 ripe banana, mashed
- 1 tbsp brown sugar
- 1/4 tsp ground cinnamon
- 1/4 tsp vanilla extract
- [Optional] Vegan whipped cream (for topping)
- [Optional] Ground cinnamon or chopped walnuts (for garnish)

## Instructions:

1. Brew a shot of espresso or prepare a strong cup of coffee using your preferred method.
2. In a small saucepan, heat the mashed banana, brown sugar, and cinnamon over medium heat. Stir frequently to ensure the sugar dissolves and the banana softens, creating a smooth syrup.
3. Steam the milk (or non-dairy milk) until it's hot and frothy.
4. Pour the brewed espresso into a mug.
5. Add the banana syrup mixture into the mug with the espresso and stir until well combined.
6. Gently pour the steamed milk into the mug, holding back the foam with a spoon, and top with the foam.
7. [Optional] Add a splash of vanilla extract for extra flavor and top with whipped cream if desired.
8. Garnish with a sprinkle of cinnamon or a few chopped walnuts for a crunchy finish.

## Tips and Recommendations:

- **Dairy-Free Option:** Use oat milk or almond milk for a creamy, plant-based alternative that complements the banana flavor.
- **Banana Texture:** Mash the banana until smooth to avoid any chunks in the syrup.
- **Sweetness Level:** Adjust the brown sugar to taste, especially if you prefer a sweeter drink. You can also swap it for maple syrup for a different flavor twist.
- **Stronger Coffee Flavor:** Increase the amount of espresso or coffee for a bolder taste, especially if you're using a larger cup.

## Variations:

- **Iced Banana Bread Latte:** For a cool version, let the drink cool and serve it over ice.
- **Nutty Banana Bread Latte:** Add a spoonful of almond or peanut butter to the banana syrup for a nutty twist.
- **Spiced Banana Bread Latte:** Add a pinch of nutmeg or cloves along with the cinnamon for a spicier, more festive flavor.

## Pairing Suggestions:

- **Pair with a slice of vegan banana bread** or **walnut muffins** to enhance the banana and cinnamon flavors.
- Enjoy alongside **vegan chocolate chip cookies** or **cinnamon rolls** for a sweet and cozy snack.

## Interesting Fact:

Banana bread has long been a beloved comfort food, with roots dating back to the Great Depression when people began to experiment with baking during tough economic times. Now, it's a timeless treat that pairs wonderfully with a hot cup of coffee!

## Cultural Connection:

The concept of banana bread originated in the United States during the 1930s, a time when baking with overripe bananas became a popular way to make use of food that would otherwise go to waste. This latte brings the comforting, nostalgic flavors of banana bread into the coffee world, making it an instant classic for those who love both coffee and baked goods.

# Cherry Amaretto Hot Cocoa

*Indulge in the decadent flavors of Cherry Amaretto Hot Cocoa, a drink that combines the classic richness of chocolate with the fruity tang of cherries and the nutty warmth of amaretto liqueur. The combination of creamy cocoa, sweet cherries, and the hint of almond from amaretto makes this drink a luxurious winter treat. Whether you're relaxing after a long day or celebrating a special moment, this cozy beverage is sure to delight your senses.*

## Ingredients:

- 2 tbsp cocoa powder
- 1 tbsp sugar (or sweetener of choice)
- 1/2 cup almond milk (or your preferred dairy-free milk)
- 1/2 cup water
- 1/4 cup cherry juice (or fresh cherries, blended)
- 1 tsp amaretto syrup (or amaretto liqueur for non-vegan version)
- 1/4 tsp vanilla extract
- [Optional] Vegan whipped cream (for topping)
- [Optional] Fresh cherries or a maraschino cherry (for garnish)

## Instructions:

1. In a small saucepan, combine the cocoa powder, sugar, almond milk, and water. Heat over medium heat, whisking until the cocoa is fully dissolved and the mixture is hot.
2. Once the cocoa is steaming, stir in the cherry juice and amaretto syrup. Allow the mixture to simmer for another 1-2 minutes to blend the flavors together.
3. Remove from heat and stir in the vanilla extract.
4. Pour the hot cocoa into your favorite mug.
5. [Optional] Top with vegan whipped cream for extra creaminess, and garnish with a fresh cherry or maraschino cherry for a fun, festive touch.

## Tips and Recommendations:

- **Vegan Option:** Ensure that you're using a dairy-free whipped cream or skip the topping for a lighter version.
- **Sweetness Adjustment:** If you prefer a sweeter cocoa, you can increase the amount of sugar or use maple syrup for a more natural sweetener.
- **Thicker Cocoa:** For a richer texture, you can replace some of the water with extra almond milk or add a small spoonful of coconut cream.
- **Amaretto Flavor:** If you like a stronger amaretto flavor, add an extra splash of amaretto syrup or liqueur.

## Variations:

- **Spicy Cherry Amaretto Cocoa:** Add a pinch of cayenne pepper or cinnamon for a spicy kick that balances the sweetness of the cherries and amaretto.
- **Cherry Almond Hot Cocoa:** Blend fresh cherries into a smooth puree and add it to the cocoa base for an extra layer of cherry flavor.
- **Iced Cherry Amaretto Cocoa:** For a cool version, let the cocoa cool and serve over ice with a splash of almond milk.

## Pairing Suggestions:

- **Pair with vegan shortbread cookies** or **almond biscotti** for a crunchy, nutty contrast.
- Enjoy with **dark chocolate truffles** or a **slice of cherry almond cake** to bring out the rich cherry and almond notes in the cocoa.

## Interesting Fact:

Did you know that amaretto, which means "a little bitter" in Italian, is traditionally made with almonds, apricot pits, or other stones, giving it a distinctive sweet, nutty flavor? It's the perfect complement to the richness of chocolate and cherries!

## Cultural Connection:

Amaretto has its origins in Italy, where it was traditionally made with almonds. Over time, it has become a beloved liqueur worldwide, known for its nutty, smooth flavor. When paired with the sweetness of cherries and the warmth of cocoa, it creates a drink that's both nostalgic and indulgent.

# Irish Cream Hot Chocolate

*Warm up with the indulgent Irish Cream Hot Chocolate, a luxurious treat that blends velvety cocoa with the smooth, slightly boozy flavor of Irish cream. This decadent drink is perfect for chilly evenings when you need a little extra comfort. With the richness of chocolate, the sweetness of Irish cream, and a hint of vanilla, it's a drink that will quickly become your go-to for cozy moments. Whether you're curling up with a good book or sharing it with friends, this hot chocolate brings warmth and joy in every sip.*

## Ingredients:

- 2 tbsp cocoa powder
- 1 tbsp sugar (or sweetener of choice)
- 1/2 cup almond milk (or your preferred dairy-free milk)
- 1/2 cup water
- 1/4 cup Irish cream syrup (or Irish cream liqueur for non-vegan version)
- 1/4 tsp vanilla extract
- [Optional] Vegan whipped cream (for topping)
- [Optional] Chocolate shavings or cocoa powder (for garnish)

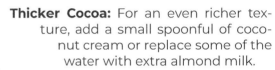

## Instructions:

1. In a small saucepan, combine the cocoa powder, sugar, almond milk, and water. Heat over medium heat, whisking until the cocoa is fully dissolved and the mixture is hot.
2. Once the cocoa is steaming, stir in the Irish cream syrup (or liqueur) and vanilla extract. Let the mixture simmer for another 1-2 minutes to combine the flavors.
3. Remove from heat and pour into your favorite mug.
4. [Optional] Top with vegan whipped cream for extra richness, and garnish with chocolate shavings or a light dusting of cocoa powder for a visually appealing finish.

## Tips and Recommendations:

- **Vegan Option:** Use a dairy-free whipped cream alternative to keep the drink vegan-friendly.
- **Sweetness Adjustment:** You can adjust the sweetness by increasing or decreasing the sugar, or opt for a more natural sweetener like maple syrup.

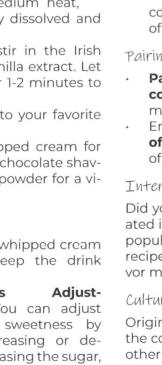

- **Thicker Cocoa:** For an even richer texture, add a small spoonful of coconut cream or replace some of the water with extra almond milk.
- **Irish Cream Flavor:** For a stronger Irish cream taste, increase the amount of Irish cream syrup or liqueur.

## Variations:

- **Mint Irish Cream Hot Chocolate:** Add a few drops of peppermint extract for a festive twist, turning your drink into a refreshing minty treat.
- **Spicy Irish Cream Cocoa:** Stir in a pinch of cinnamon or a dash of cayenne pepper for a warming spice that enhances the rich chocolate flavor.
- **Iced Irish Cream Hot Chocolate:** Let the cocoa cool and serve over ice, topped with a swirl of whipped cream for a chilled variation.

## Pairing Suggestions:

- **Pair with vegan biscotti** or **almond shortbread cookies** for a delightful crunch that complements the creamy richness of the hot cocoa.
- Enjoy with a **slice of chocolate cake** or **a bowl of fresh berries** to balance the indulgent flavors of the drink.

## Interesting Fact:

Did you know that Irish cream liqueur was first created in Ireland in the 1970s and has since become a popular addition to both coffee and hot chocolate recipes? Its creamy texture and subtle alcoholic flavor make it a favorite for cozy beverages.

## Cultural Connection:

Originally from Ireland, Irish cream liqueur combines the country's famous whiskey with fresh cream and other flavors, creating a luxurious, indulgent drink. Its unique taste has made it a beloved ingredient in both hot and cold beverages, and when paired with rich chocolate, it creates the perfect warming drink for winter.

# Pistachio White Hot Chocolate

*Indulge in the nutty, creamy perfection of Pistachio White Hot Chocolate, where velvety white chocolate meets the rich, slightly salty flavor of pistachios. This luxurious beverage is the ultimate treat for those looking to enjoy something sweet yet uniquely savory. With its beautiful green hue and the irresistible flavor of roasted pistachios, it's a comforting drink that adds a touch of elegance to any occasion. Perfect for cold winter nights or when you need a special drink to impress guests, this recipe will quickly become a new favorite.*

## Ingredients:

- 1 cup unsweetened almond milk (or your preferred dairy-free milk)
- 1/2 cup white chocolate chips or chopped white chocolate
- 1 tbsp pistachio paste (or finely ground pistachios)
- 1/2 tsp vanilla extract
- 1/4 tsp cardamom (optional, for a hint of spice)
- 1 tbsp maple syrup (or sweetener of your choice)
- [Optional] Whipped coconut cream (for topping)
- [Optional] Crushed pistachios (for garnish)

## Instructions:

1. In a small saucepan, combine the almond milk and pistachio paste (or ground pistachios). Heat over medium-low heat, whisking until the pistachios are fully incorporated into the milk.
2. Once the milk is warm, add the white chocolate chips and stir continuously until the chocolate is melted and smooth.
3. Stir in the vanilla extract, cardamom (if using), and maple syrup. Continue to heat for another 1-2 minutes, allowing the flavors to meld together.
4. Remove from heat and pour into your favorite mug.
5. [Optional] Top with a dollop of whipped coconut cream and garnish with crushed pistachios for added texture and flavor.

## Tips and Recommendations:

- **Pistachio Paste:** If you can't find pistachio paste, you can make your own by blending roasted pistachios in a food processor until smooth.
- **Sweetness Adjustment:** Feel free to adjust the sweetness by adding more or less maple syrup depending on your preference.
- **Thicker Texture:** For an extra indulgent texture, add a tablespoon of coconut cream to the mixture when heating.
- **Dairy-Free Option:** Use your favorite dairy-free white chocolate chips or chopped white chocolate to make this recipe completely vegan.

## Variations:

- **Pistachio Hazelnut Hot Chocolate:** Add a tablespoon of hazelnut syrup or a few drops of hazelnut extract for a rich, nutty twist on this recipe.
- **Spiced Pistachio White Hot Chocolate:** Add a pinch of cinnamon or nutmeg for a warming spice that complements the sweetness of the white chocolate.
- **Iced Pistachio White Hot Chocolate:** Allow the mixture to cool, then serve over ice for a refreshing twist on this indulgent treat.

## Pairing Suggestions:

- **Pair with vegan biscotti** or **pistachio shortbread cookies** to enhance the nutty flavors in your hot chocolate.
- Enjoy with **a slice of lemon cake** or **chocolate-dipped strawberries** to create a balanced dessert experience.

## Interesting Fact:

Did you know that pistachios are one of the oldest flowering nut trees, cultivated in the Middle East and Asia for thousands of years? They've long been enjoyed in both sweet and savory dishes due to their rich flavor and unique texture.

## Cultural Connection:

Pistachios have deep cultural significance in the Middle East, where they have been used in cooking and desserts for centuries. Their inclusion in sweets, from baklava to ice cream, highlights their beloved status in these regions. When paired with white chocolate, they bring a refined elegance to this hot beverage, reminiscent of the luxurious desserts served in Middle Eastern cuisine.

# Tiramisu Hot Mocha

*Indulge in the decadent fusion of rich espresso, velvety hot chocolate, and the classic flavors of tiramisu with this Tiramisu Hot Mocha. Inspired by the beloved Italian dessert, this drink combines bold coffee with a creamy, chocolatey base, topped with a hint of cocoa and a dusting of cinnamon for that authentic tiramisu experience. Perfect for a cozy night in or when you need to impress guests, this luxurious beverage delivers the perfect balance of sweetness and bitterness, making it a must-try for mocha lovers.*

## Ingredients:

- 1 shot (1 ounce) of espresso
- 1 cup steamed almond milk (or your preferred milk)
- 2 tbsp cocoa powder
- 1 tbsp maple syrup (or sweetener of your choice)
- 1/4 tsp vanilla extract
- 1/2 tsp ground cinnamon
- 1 tbsp mascarpone cheese (or vegan mascarpone for a dairy-free option)
- 1 tbsp chocolate syrup
- [Optional] Tiramisu-flavored syrup or coffee liqueur (like Kahlua)
- [Optional] Whipped coconut cream (for topping)
- [Optional] Cocoa powder or cinnamon (for garnish)

## Instructions:

1. Brew a shot of espresso using your preferred method.
2. In a small saucepan, whisk together the steamed almond milk, cocoa powder, maple syrup, vanilla extract, and ground cinnamon. Heat gently until smooth and hot, but not boiling.
3. Stir in the mascarpone cheese and chocolate syrup until the mixture becomes creamy and smooth.
4. Pour the espresso into your favorite mug, then slowly add the creamy chocolate mixture.
5. [Optional] For an extra tiramisu twist, add a splash of tiramisu-flavored syrup or a dash of coffee liqueur.
6. Top with a generous dollop of whipped coconut cream. Garnish with a light dusting of cocoa powder or cinnamon for an elegant finish.

## Tips and Recommendations:

- **For a Stronger Coffee Flavor:** If you love coffee, increase the amount of espresso for a bolder taste.
- **Sweetness Adjustment:** Feel free to adjust the maple syrup or sweetener to your taste for a more or less sweet drink.
- **Dairy-Free Option:** Use a vegan mascarpone or a rich dairy-free cream cheese for an authentic tiramisu flavor without the dairy.
- **Coffee Liqueur Twist:** Adding a splash of Kahlua or another coffee-flavored liqueur will intensify the mocha flavor, mimicking the classic tiramisu cocktail.

## Variations:

- **Iced Tiramisu Mocha:** Let the drink cool to room temperature, then serve over ice for a refreshing twist on the warm classic.
- **Spiced Tiramisu Mocha:** Add a pinch of nutmeg or cardamom to the mix for an aromatic variation.
- **Tiramisu Hazelnut Mocha:** For a nutty version, swap the maple syrup with hazelnut syrup for a deeper, richer flavor.

## Pairing Suggestions:

- **Pair with vegan biscotti** or **Tiramisu-flavored cupcakes** to complement the coffee and chocolate flavors.
- Enjoy with a slice of **chocolate lava cake** or **almond shortbread** for a luxurious dessert pairing.

## Interesting Fact:

Did you know that **tiramisu** means "pick me up" in Italian? It's named after the energizing combination of coffee and cocoa, making it the perfect match for a delicious hot mocha like this one.

## Cultural Connection:

Tiramisu is one of Italy's most famous desserts, enjoyed worldwide for its rich, layered flavors and coffee-soaked ladyfingers. The traditional dessert has inspired countless variations, including this **Tiramisu Hot Mocha**, which brings the beloved flavors of tiramisu into a warm, comforting beverage that will take you straight to Italy with every sip.

# Maple Bacon Hot Cocoa

*Craving something indulgent and unexpected? This Maple Bacon Hot Cocoa combines the richness of velvety hot chocolate with the savory crunch of crispy bacon and a hint of maple sweetness. The result is a warm, decadent beverage that delivers the perfect balance of sweet and salty flavors. Whether you're looking for a fun twist on a classic favorite or a comforting drink with a savory kick, this unique hot cocoa is sure to surprise and delight your taste buds. Get ready to experience the ultimate fusion of comfort and indulgence in every sip.*

## Ingredients:

- 1 cup almond milk (or milk of your choice)
- 2 tbsp cocoa powder
- 1 tbsp maple syrup
- 1/4 tsp vanilla extract
- Pinch of sea salt
- 1 slice crispy vegan bacon (or regular bacon for non-vegan version)
- 2 tbsp chocolate chips (optional, for extra richness)
- [Optional] Whipped coconut cream (for topping)
- [Optional] Crumbled bacon bits (for garnish)

## Instructions:

1. In a small saucepan, heat the almond milk over medium heat until hot, but not boiling.
2. Whisk in the cocoa powder, maple syrup, vanilla extract, and a pinch of sea salt until smooth and combined.
3. Stir in the chocolate chips (if using) until melted and the cocoa is rich and creamy.
4. While the cocoa is heating, cook the bacon until crispy. If using vegan bacon, cook it according to the package instructions.
5. Pour the hot cocoa into a mug and top with whipped coconut cream (optional).
6. Garnish with crumbled bacon bits for a savory crunch that complements the sweetness of the cocoa.
7. Drizzle a little extra maple syrup over the top for an added touch of sweetness.

## Tips and Recommendations:

- **For Extra Richness:** Add an extra tablespoon of cocoa powder or a handful of chocolate chips to intensify the chocolate flavor.
- **Dairy-Free Option:** Be sure to use non-dairy bacon and coconut cream for a fully plant-based experience.
- **Sweetness Adjustment:** If you prefer a sweeter hot cocoa, increase the maple syrup or drizzle in extra chocolate syrup.
- **Savory Balance:** To enhance the savory element, consider adding a dash of smoked paprika or cayenne pepper for a subtle smoky heat.

## Variations:

- **Spicy Maple Bacon Hot Cocoa:** Add a dash of chili powder or cayenne pepper to your cocoa for a spicy kick that pairs beautifully with the smoky bacon.
- **Maple Pecan Hot Cocoa:** Replace bacon with toasted pecans for a nuttier version of this sweet and salty cocoa.
- **Iced Maple Bacon Cocoa:** Let the drink cool and serve over ice for a refreshing take on this indulgent treat.

## Pairing Suggestions:

- **Pair with savory croissants** or **cheese-stuffed pretzels** for a perfect balance of sweet, salty, and buttery flavors.
- **Serve alongside a slice of rich chocolate cake** or **nutty shortbread cookies** to complement the decadent chocolate base.

## Interesting Fact:

Did you know that **bacon and chocolate** are a popular pairing in gourmet cuisine? The sweet-salty combination has been a hit in desserts and snacks, and this hot cocoa is a delicious way to enjoy the duo in a warm beverage form.

## Cultural Connection:

While bacon has traditionally been a savory breakfast item in many Western cultures, the combination of bacon with sweets is becoming a trendy fusion, offering a bold and adventurous twist on classic flavors. This **Maple Bacon Hot Cocoa** is a modern take on that sweet-savory marriage, offering comfort with a fun, exciting flair.

# NON-COFFEE HOT DRINKS:

# Masala Chai

*Warm, spicy, and full of rich flavors, Masala Chai is a beloved Indian beverage that brings together black tea and aromatic spices for an unforgettable experience. The bold, comforting taste of cinnamon, cardamom, ginger, and cloves perfectly complements the smoothness of milk, creating a drink that's both soothing and invigorating. Whether you're enjoying it to kickstart your day or winding down in the evening, Masala Chai offers a fragrant, flavorful escape that's perfect for any moment. This homemade version allows you to adjust the spices to your liking, giving you the freedom to create your own signature blend.*

## Ingredients:

- 2 cups water
- 2 tsps loose black tea leaves (or 2 tea bags)
- 1 cinnamon stick
- 4-5 green cardamom pods, crushed
- 4-5 whole cloves
- 1-2 slices fresh ginger
- 1 tbsp brown sugar (or sweetener of choice)
- 1/2 cup almond milk (or milk of your choice)
- [Optional] 1/4 tsp black pepper for extra heat
- [Optional] A dash of vanilla extract for added warmth

## Instructions:

1. In a small pot, combine the water, cinnamon stick, cardamom pods, cloves, ginger slices, and black pepper (if using). Bring to a gentle boil over medium heat.
2. Once the water begins to boil, reduce the heat and let the spices simmer for 3-4 minutes to release their flavors.
3. Add the tea leaves or tea bags to the pot and continue to simmer for an additional 2-3 minutes.
4. Stir in the sugar (or sweetener of your choice), ensuring it dissolves completely.
5. Pour in the almond milk (or milk of your choice) and bring the mixture to a simmer. Let it simmer for 2 minutes until the milk is heated through and the flavors are well combined.
6. Strain the tea into a cup, discarding the spices and tea leaves.
7. Enjoy your Masala Chai warm, garnished with a cinnamon stick or a few extra cardamom pods for visual appeal.

## Tips and Recommendations:

- **Sweetness:** Adjust the amount of sugar or sweetener based on your preference. You can also try adding a splash of maple syrup for a unique twist.
- **Spices:** If you like a more intense spice flavor, increase the amount of ginger, cardamom, or cloves.
- **Tea:** Choose a strong black tea like Assam or Darjeeling for the best flavor, or opt for an herbal tea if you prefer a caffeine-free version.
- **Milk Options:** For a richer chai, use coconut milk or oat milk, which adds a creamier texture and enhances the overall flavor.

## Variations:

- **Iced Masala Chai:** After preparing the chai, allow it to cool and serve over ice for a refreshing, chilled version of this classic drink.
- **Vegan Masala Chai:** Simply use almond, oat, or coconut milk as your base, and substitute the sugar with a plant-based sweetener like agave or maple syrup.
- **Vanilla Masala Chai:** Add a dash of vanilla extract along with the spices for a sweet, aromatic twist that complements the warm spices beautifully.

## Pairing Suggestions:

- **Pair with a buttery vegan scone** or **a cinnamon roll** to enjoy the spices of the chai alongside a light, sweet pastry.
- **Serve with a warm naan bread** or **vegetable samosas** for a savory, satisfying snack that balances the heat of the spices.

## Interesting Fact:

Did you know that **Masala Chai** is more than just a drink in India? It's a cultural staple, often enjoyed in homes, offices, and roadside stalls. The spices used in chai are said to have health benefits, from aiding digestion to boosting immunity.

## Cultural Connection:

Masala Chai has its roots in India, where it's been consumed for centuries, traditionally made with strong black tea and a variety of spices known for their medicinal properties. The drink has grown in popularity worldwide, evolving to suit different tastes and preferences, and is now enjoyed by millions of people globally.

# Earl Grey Tea Latte

*Indulge in the soothing elegance of an Earl Grey Tea Latte, where the delicate notes of bergamot-infused black tea meet the creamy richness of steamed milk. This drink combines the sophisticated flavor of traditional Earl Grey tea with the velvety smoothness of a latte, creating a warm, comforting experience with every sip. Whether you're looking for a cozy morning pick-me-up or a relaxing afternoon treat, the Earl Grey Tea Latte offers a fragrant, luxurious escape. Its aromatic tea and smooth texture make it a perfect option for anyone who loves the subtle complexity of tea but enjoys the indulgence of a latte.*

## Ingredients:

- 1 cup water
- 2 tsps loose Earl Grey tea leaves (or 1 tea bag)
- 1/2 cup almond milk (or milk of your choice)
- 1 tbsp honey or sweetener of choice (optional)
- 1/4 tsp vanilla extract (optional)
- [Optional] A dash of ground cinnamon or nutmeg for garnish

## Instructions:

1. Boil the water in a small saucepan or kettle. Once boiling, pour it over the Earl Grey tea leaves (or tea bag) in a teapot or heatproof cup. Let the tea steep for 4-5 minutes, depending on your desired strength.
2. While the tea is steeping, steam the almond milk (or milk of your choice) using a milk frother or on the stovetop until it's hot and frothy, but not boiling.
3. After steeping the tea, remove the tea bag or strain the loose leaves from the cup.
4. Add the honey or sweetener of your choice and stir until dissolved. You can also add a dash of vanilla extract for an extra touch of flavor.
5. Pour the steamed milk into the tea, gently stirring to combine.
6. For a decorative touch, sprinkle a dash of ground cinnamon or nutmeg on top, if desired.
7. Enjoy your Earl Grey Tea Latte while it's warm and comforting.

## Tips and Recommendations:

- **Sweetness:** You can adjust the level of sweetness by adding more or less honey or sweetener. For a richer flavor, try maple syrup or agave.
- **Milk Options:** For a dairy-free version, use oat milk or coconut milk, which will add a creamy texture. For a richer taste, use whole milk or half-and-half if you're not following a vegan diet.

- **Stronger Tea Flavor:** If you prefer a more robust tea flavor, steep the tea for an additional minute.
- **Garnish:** Garnish with an extra sprinkle of cinnamon or a thin slice of lemon to add a refreshing contrast to the smoothness of the milk.

## Variations:

- **Iced Earl Grey Latte:** Brew the tea and allow it to cool, then pour it over ice and top with chilled milk for a refreshing iced version.
- **London Fog:** Add a splash of lavender syrup to your Earl Grey Tea Latte for a floral twist.
- **Chai Earl Grey Latte:** For a spicier variation, blend in a pinch of cinnamon and cardamom to the tea before steaming the milk.

## Pairing Suggestions:

- **Pair with a lemon scone** or **shortbread cookies** to complement the citrusy notes of the Earl Grey.
- **Serve with a light fruit salad** or **vegan muffins** to balance the smooth creaminess of the latte.

## Interesting Fact:

Did you know that **Earl Grey Tea** is named after Charles Grey, the 2nd Earl Grey, who was a British Prime Minister in the early 19th century? The tea was created to complement the water at his estate in Northumberland, and the addition of bergamot was said to improve the flavor.

## Cultural Connection:

Earl Grey Tea has been a staple of British tea culture since the early 1800s. While its exact origins are uncertain, it has become a symbol of English tea tradition, often enjoyed in the afternoon as part of a light meal or snack.

# London Fog Tea Latte

*Embrace the elegance of a London Fog Tea Latte, where the warmth of Earl Grey tea, fragrant with bergamot, is combined with the creaminess of steamed milk and a touch of vanilla. This comforting and aromatic drink, often enjoyed as a cozy afternoon treat, is a perfect balance of delicate flavors. The London Fog Tea Latte is a delightful twist on traditional tea lattes, with a smooth, frothy texture and a hint of sweetness. Its soothing nature and refined taste make it an ideal beverage for unwinding during any time of the day.*

## Ingredients:

- 1 cup water
- 2 tsps loose Earl Grey tea leaves (or 1 tea bag)
- 1/2 cup milk (or plant-based milk such as almond, oat, or coconut)
- 1 tbsp honey or sweetener of choice (optional)
- 1/4 tsp vanilla extract
- [Optional] A dash of ground cinnamon or nutmeg for garnish

## Instructions:

1. Boil the water in a small pot or kettle. Once it comes to a boil, pour the hot water over the Earl Grey tea leaves (or tea bag) in a teapot or heat-proof cup. Let the tea steep for 4-5 minutes, or to your preferred strength.
2. While the tea is steeping, steam your milk (or plant-based milk) using a milk frother or in a small saucepan on the stovetop until it's hot and frothy. Avoid boiling the milk to preserve the smooth texture.
3. After the tea has steeped, remove the tea bag or strain out the tea leaves.
4. Add honey or sweetener of your choice and stir until it dissolves.
5. Stir in the vanilla extract for a rich, aromatic touch.
6. Pour the steamed milk into the tea, stirring gently to combine and create a smooth latte.
7. For extra flair, sprinkle a dash of cinnamon or nutmeg on top for a beautiful and flavorful finish.
8. Sip and enjoy the relaxing, luxurious flavor of your London Fog Tea Latte.

## Tips and Recommendations:

- **Sweetness:** Adjust the sweetness to your taste by adding more or less honey, maple syrup, or agave nectar.
- **Milk Options:** For a dairy-free version, use oat milk or coconut milk, which add creaminess and a touch of flavor.
- **Stronger Tea Flavor:** Steep the tea for a minute longer to intensify the bergamot flavor.

- **Garnish:** Garnish with a lemon twist or fresh lavender sprig to enhance the elegance of the drink.

## Variations:

- **Iced London Fog:** Brew the tea and let it cool before pouring it over ice. Top with chilled milk for a refreshing iced version.
- **Chai London Fog:** Add a pinch of ground cinnamon, cardamom, or cloves to your tea to create a spiced twist on the classic.
- **Lavender London Fog:** For a floral note, add a spoonful of lavender syrup to the latte for a fragrant and aromatic variation.

## Pairing Suggestions:

- **Pair with a lemon scone** or **shortbread cookies** to complement the bergamot and vanilla flavors of the latte.
- **Enjoy with a light fruit salad** or **almond biscotti** for a refreshing contrast to the smoothness of the drink.

## Interesting Fact:

Did you know that **London Fog** is a relatively new creation, gaining popularity in North America in the 1990s? Despite its name, the drink has no historical ties to the UK - it was created by a Canadian barista who wanted to combine the flavors of Earl Grey tea with a frothy milk base.

## Cultural Connection:

Though **London Fog** is not traditionally British, its components - Earl Grey tea and milk - are deeply rooted in British tea culture. Earl Grey itself has been enjoyed for centuries as a symbol of refined tea drinking, while the latte-style preparation draws inspiration from Italy's iconic espresso drinks.

# Matcha Green Tea Latte

*Indulge in the vibrant, earthy goodness of a Matcha Green Tea Latte, where the rich, antioxidant-packed matcha meets the smooth, creamy texture of steamed milk. This energizing, yet soothing drink offers a unique balance of natural sweetness and bold flavor. With its origins in Japan, matcha has been a revered drink for centuries, prized for its calming effects and health benefits. Whether you're looking to boost your energy or unwind, the Matcha Green Tea Latte provides a delicious, balanced experience that will leave you refreshed and invigorated.*

## Ingredients:

- 1 tsp matcha powder
- 1 tbsp hot water
- 1 cup milk (or plant-based milk such as almond, oat, or coconut)
- 1 tbsp honey or sweetener of choice (optional)
- [Optional] 1/4 tsp vanilla extract for added flavor
- [Optional] A pinch of cinnamon or matcha powder for garnish

## Instructions:

1. In a small bowl, sift the matcha powder to remove any clumps.
2. Add the hot water (just below boiling) to the matcha powder and whisk vigorously until the matcha is fully dissolved and a frothy layer forms on top. You can use a traditional bamboo whisk or a small handheld frother.
3. While the matcha is being prepared, steam your milk (or plant-based milk) using a milk frother or in a small saucepan on the stovetop. Heat the milk until it is hot and frothy, but not boiling.
4. Pour the steamed milk into the matcha mixture, stirring gently to combine.
5. Add honey or sweetener to taste and stir well to dissolve.
6. For a touch of elegance, garnish with a sprinkle of cinnamon or extra matcha powder on top.
7. Sip and savor the creamy, vibrant taste of your Matcha Green Tea Latte.

## Tips and Recommendations:

- **Whisking the Matcha:** Whisking the matcha properly is key to achieving a smooth, frothy texture. Use a small whisk or a milk frother for the best results.
- **Sweetness:** Adjust the sweetness by adding more or less honey, maple syrup, or agave nectar, depending on your preference.
- **Milk Options:** For a vegan version, try using oat milk for its creamy consistency or coconut milk for a tropical twist.

- **Stronger Flavor:** If you prefer a bolder matcha taste, add an extra 1/2 teaspoon of matcha powder for a more robust flavor.

## Variations:

- **Iced Matcha Latte:** Brew your matcha as usual and let it cool. Pour over ice, then top with chilled milk for a refreshing iced version.
- **Spiced Matcha Latte:** Add a pinch of ground cinnamon or cardamom to the matcha mixture for a warm, spiced twist on this classic drink.
- **Vanilla Matcha Latte:** For a sweeter, aromatic version, add 1/4 teaspoon of vanilla extract to the milk as you steam it.

## Pairing Suggestions:

- **Pair with almond biscotti** or **green tea shortbread cookies** to complement the delicate matcha flavor.
- **Enjoy with a light fruit salad** or **vegan scones** to balance the creaminess of the latte.

## Interesting Fact:

Did you know that **matcha** contains L-theanine, an amino acid that promotes a state of calm alertness? This is why matcha provides a more balanced and sustained energy boost compared to regular coffee or tea.

## Cultural Connection:

Originating from Japan, **matcha** has been part of traditional Japanese tea ceremonies for centuries. It is not only a symbol of hospitality and respect but also known for its calming, meditative properties. Over the years, the popularity of matcha has spread worldwide, becoming a staple in cafes and kitchens alike.

# Spiced Apple Cider

*Warm up your senses with the comforting, aromatic flavors of Spiced Apple Cider - a perfect drink for chilly autumn days or cozy evenings by the fire. This rich, spiced beverage is packed with the natural sweetness of apples, complemented by warming spices like cinnamon, cloves, and nutmeg. Whether you're enjoying it on a crisp fall day or as a holiday treat, this drink brings a delightful warmth to any occasion. A wonderful alternative to coffee or tea, Spiced Apple Cider is sure to become a seasonal favorite in your kitchen.*

## Ingredients:

- 4 cups apple cider (or apple juice for a lighter flavor)
- 2 cinnamon sticks
- 3-4 whole cloves
- 1 star anise
- 1/4 tsp ground nutmeg
- 1-2 tbsps maple syrup or sweetener of choice (optional)
- 1 tsp vanilla extract (optional)
- 1/2 orange, sliced (optional)
- [Optional] Garnish with a cinnamon stick or a thin orange slice

## Instructions:

1. In a medium saucepan, combine the apple cider, cinnamon sticks, cloves, star anise, and nutmeg.
2. Heat the mixture over medium heat until it begins to simmer. Stir occasionally to ensure the spices are well distributed.
3. Once it starts simmering, reduce the heat and let the cider steep for 10-15 minutes. The longer it simmers, the more flavorful it will become.
4. Taste the cider and add maple syrup or another sweetener if you desire a sweeter taste. Stir in the vanilla extract for an extra layer of warmth.
5. If you like, add orange slices to the mixture and continue to simmer for an additional 5 minutes for a citrusy twist.
6. Once the cider is hot and well-infused with spices, remove from heat.
7. Pour into mugs and garnish with a cinnamon stick or a slice of orange for a festive touch.
8. Serve hot and enjoy the cozy, spiced goodness of your homemade Apple Cider.

## Tips and Recommendations:

- **Sweetness:** Adjust the sweetness of your cider to your preference by adding more or less maple syrup or another sweetener.
- **Spice Level:** If you prefer a stronger spice flavor, feel free to add an extra cinnamon stick or a pinch of ground cloves.
- **For a stronger flavor:** Let the cider simmer longer to deepen the spiced notes.

- **Serving Tip:** For a creamy variation, you can add a splash of almond milk or oat milk to your cider before serving for a smoother texture.

## Variations:

- **Hot Spiked Apple Cider:** Add a shot of dark rum or bourbon for a warm, boozy version perfect for evening gatherings.
- **Apple Cider Fizz:** For a refreshing twist, let the cider cool and top it with sparkling water or club soda.
- **Citrus-Spiced Apple Cider:** Add a slice of fresh ginger and a few extra slices of orange or lemon for a bright, zesty flavor.

## Pairing Suggestions:

- **Pair with apple pie** or **cinnamon rolls** to complement the spiced apple flavors.
- **Enjoy with a handful of spiced nuts** or **cheese and crackers** for a balanced snack.

## Interesting Fact:

Did you know that **apple cider** has been a popular fall drink for centuries in many cultures? The combination of apples and spices has been used as both a beverage and a medicinal remedy for digestion and relaxation.

## Cultural Connection:

Apple cider has deep roots in both American and European traditions. It was a common drink in colonial times, especially during harvest festivals. Spiced apple cider, as we know it today, is a beloved seasonal drink that brings comfort and warmth during autumn and winter months. Whether enjoyed in a cozy home or at a holiday gathering, this drink has a special place in festive cultures around the world.

# Mulled Wine

*Indulge in the heartwarming charm of Mulled Wine, a festive, spiced beverage perfect for cold evenings and holiday celebrations. This traditional drink brings together rich red wine and a variety of aromatic spices like cinnamon, cloves, and star anise, creating a warm, comforting experience. Whether you're hosting a winter gathering or simply enjoying a cozy night at home, mulled wine offers a delightful way to embrace the season's flavors and aromas. Let the warmth and spice fill your home with holiday cheer.*

## Ingredients:

- 1 bottle (750 ml) red wine (such as Merlot or Cabernet Sauvignon)
- 1/4 cup brandy (optional, for a stronger kick)
- 2 cinnamon sticks
- 4-6 whole cloves
- 2 star anise
- 1/4 tsp ground nutmeg
- 1 orange, sliced
- 1/4 cup maple syrup or sweetener of choice (optional, for added sweetness)
- 1 tbsp fresh ginger, sliced (optional, for extra spice)
- [Optional] Garnish with extra orange slices or cinnamon sticks

## Instructions:

1. Pour the red wine into a large saucepan or pot.
2. Add the brandy, cinnamon sticks, cloves, star anise, nutmeg, and fresh ginger (if using) to the wine.
3. Slice the orange into thin rounds and add it to the mixture.
4. Stir in the maple syrup or your preferred sweetener to taste.
5. Heat the mixture over medium-low heat, stirring occasionally. Allow it to come to a gentle simmer, but do not let it boil.
6. Let the wine simmer for 20-30 minutes, allowing the flavors to meld together.
7. Taste and adjust the sweetness or spice levels, adding more sweetener or spices if desired.
8. Once the wine is hot and fragrant, remove from heat.
9. Strain the mulled wine into mugs or heat-resistant glasses to remove the whole spices.
10. Serve hot, garnished with an orange slice or cinnamon stick for extra flair.

## Tips and Recommendations:

- **Sweetness:** Adjust the sweetness to your taste by adding more or less maple syrup. You can also use honey or agave syrup for different flavors.
- **Spice Level:** If you prefer a stronger spice flavor, feel free to add more cinnamon, cloves, or a dash of ground ginger.
- **Serving Suggestion:** For a richer flavor, consider adding a splash of orange liqueur like Cointreau or Grand Marnier.
- **Simmering Time:** The longer the wine simmers, the more intense the flavors will be. Just be sure to avoid boiling the wine, as it can affect the taste.

## Variations:

- **Citrus-Spiced Mulled Wine:** Add a few slices of lemon or lime to enhance the citrusy notes.
- **Non-Alcoholic Mulled Wine:** Substitute the red wine with grape juice or cranberry juice for a non-alcoholic version that's just as flavorful.
- **Spiced Winter Sangria:** Use a mix of red wine and orange juice for a fruitier twist on the traditional mulled wine.

## Pairing Suggestions:

- **Pair with spiced nuts** or **cheese platters** for a savory contrast to the sweet and spiced wine.
- **Enjoy with gingerbread cookies** or **fruitcake** for a festive and comforting treat.

## Interesting Fact:

Did you know that **mulled wine** dates back to ancient Roman times, when wine was heated with spices and honey to improve its flavor and preserve it during winter? It has been a holiday tradition in many cultures for centuries.

## Cultural Connection:

Mulled wine is a beloved holiday drink in many countries, especially in Europe. Known by different names such as **Glühwein** in Germany and **Vin Chaud** in France, this spiced beverage has become a symbol of winter celebrations. Whether sipped at Christmas markets or enjoyed at cozy gatherings, mulled wine is a drink that brings people together, offering warmth and festive cheer.

# Golden Turmeric Tea

*Welcome to the world of Golden Turmeric Tea, a soothing and vibrant drink packed with health benefits. Known for its anti-inflammatory properties, turmeric brings warmth and spice to this creamy, golden elixir. Often enjoyed as a comforting, health-boosting beverage, this tea combines the earthy flavors of turmeric, black pepper, and coconut milk for a rich, aromatic experience. Whether you need a morning pick-me-up or a relaxing drink before bed, Golden Turmeric Tea offers both wellness and indulgence in a cup.*

## Ingredients:

- 1 cup unsweetened coconut milk (or any plant-based milk of your choice)
- 1 tsp ground turmeric
- 1/4 tsp ground black pepper (enhances turmeric absorption)
- 1/4 tsp ground cinnamon
- 1 tsp grated fresh ginger (optional for extra warmth)
- 1 tsp maple syrup or sweetener of your choice (optional, for sweetness)
- 1/4 tsp vanilla extract (optional, for a hint of sweetness)
- [Optional] Pinch of ground cardamom or nutmeg for extra flavor

## Instructions:

1. In a small saucepan, heat the coconut milk (or your chosen plant-based milk) over medium heat until warm but not boiling.
2. Add the ground turmeric, black pepper, cinnamon, and grated ginger (if using) to the milk. Stir well to combine.
3. Continue to heat the mixture, stirring occasionally, for 3-5 minutes to allow the spices to infuse.
4. If you prefer a sweeter tea, stir in the maple syrup or your chosen sweetener. Add vanilla extract for an extra touch of warmth and flavor.
5. Once the tea is hot and well-mixed, remove it from heat.
6. Pour the tea into a mug and enjoy! For a garnish, sprinkle a pinch of cinnamon or cardamom on top for added aroma.

## Tips and Recommendations:

- **Spice Adjustments:** Feel free to adjust the amount of turmeric, cinnamon, or ginger based on your personal taste. If you prefer a more intense flavor, increase the spices.
- **Sweetness:** Maple syrup is a natural sweetener that complements the earthiness of turmeric, but you can use agave, honey, or any sweetener you like.

- **Non-dairy Milk:** Coconut milk offers a creamy texture, but almond milk or oat milk work great if you prefer a lighter drink.
- **Temperature:** Don't let the tea boil for too long, as it may lose some of its delicate flavors. Heat it gently for the best taste.

## Variations:

- **Iced Golden Turmeric Tea:** Let the tea cool down after preparation, then serve it over ice for a refreshing summer version.
- **Golden Latte:** Blend the tea with steamed frothy milk for a smooth and velvety golden latte.
- **Citrus Infusion:** Add a squeeze of fresh lemon juice for a tangy twist that balances the warmth of turmeric.

## Pairing Suggestions:

- **Pair with light snacks** like almond biscotti or oat cakes to complement the warmth of the spices.
- **Enjoy with fruit** like fresh pineapple or berries to contrast the rich flavors of turmeric.

## Interesting Fact:

Did you know that **turmeric** has been used in traditional medicine for thousands of years? In Ayurvedic and Chinese medicine, it's known for its powerful anti-inflammatory and healing properties.

## Cultural Connection:

Golden Turmeric Tea is a drink rooted in traditional Indian culture, where turmeric has been used not only as a spice but also as a healing remedy. The drink is often enjoyed in various forms across different cultures, from "golden milk" in India to "turmeric lattes" in the West, bringing health and wellness benefits along with its soothing, comforting flavors.

# Minty Hot Cocoa

*Indulge in the ultimate comfort drink with Minty Hot Cocoa, a creamy and refreshing twist on the classic hot chocolate. With a hint of peppermint and rich cocoa, this warm beverage is perfect for cozy evenings or festive gatherings. The combination of velvety chocolate and cool mint creates a balanced, refreshing flavor that'll soothe and delight your senses. Whether you're winding down after a long day or treating yourself to a little indulgence, this Minty Hot Cocoa is sure to become a favorite.*

## Ingredients:

- 1 cup unsweetened almond milk (or any plant-based milk of your choice)
- 2 tbsps cocoa powder
- 1-2 tbsps maple syrup (or sweetener of your choice)
- 1/4 tsp peppermint extract (or 1-2 peppermint tea bags for a more intense mint flavor)
- 1/4 tsp vanilla extract (optional, for added warmth)
- 1 tbsp dairy-free chocolate chips or chopped dark chocolate (for extra richness)
- Pinch of salt (to enhance the chocolate flavor)
- [Optional] Whipped coconut cream or dairy-free whipped cream for topping
- [Optional] Crushed peppermint candies for garnish

## Instructions:

1. In a small saucepan, heat the almond milk over medium heat until warm but not boiling.
2. Add the cocoa powder and whisk until fully dissolved and smooth.
3. Stir in the maple syrup, peppermint extract, vanilla extract (if using), and a pinch of salt. Continue to whisk until well combined.
4. Add the dairy-free chocolate chips or chopped dark chocolate. Stir until the chocolate is completely melted and the cocoa is smooth and creamy.
5. Remove from heat and taste. Adjust sweetness or mint flavor if needed.
6. Pour the Minty Hot Cocoa into a mug.
7. [Optional] Top with whipped coconut cream or dairy-free whipped cream and garnish with crushed peppermint candies for a festive touch.

## Tips and Recommendations:

- **Mint Strength:** Adjust the amount of peppermint extract to suit your taste. For a stronger mint flavor, you can infuse the milk with a peppermint tea bag before adding the cocoa powder.
- **Sweetness:** Maple syrup gives a natural sweetness, but you can substitute it with agave, honey, or any other sweetener of your choice.
- **Chocolate:** For a richer flavor, use dark chocolate instead of chocolate chips. You can also experiment with different types of cocoa powder for varying intensity.
- **Dairy-Free Whip:** If you want a more indulgent treat, top your hot cocoa with whipped coconut cream or your favorite dairy-free whipped topping.

## Variations:

- **Vegan Peppermint Mocha:** For a coffee-inspired twist, add a shot of espresso or strong brewed coffee to your Minty Hot Cocoa.
- **Iced Minty Hot Cocoa:** Let the hot cocoa cool, then serve it over ice for a refreshing summertime treat.
- **Spicy Mint Cocoa:** Add a pinch of cayenne pepper or ground cinnamon for a spicy kick that complements the minty flavor.

## Pairing Suggestions:

- **Chocolate Desserts:** Pair your Minty Hot Cocoa with chocolate chip cookies, brownies, or a rich chocolate cake to enhance the indulgent chocolate flavors.
- **Savory Snacks:** Serve alongside salted pretzels or roasted nuts for a sweet-salty combo that's perfect with hot cocoa.

## Interesting Fact:

Did you know that **peppermint** has been used for centuries for its medicinal properties, especially for soothing digestion and providing a refreshing cool sensation? It's the perfect complement to the richness of hot cocoa.

## Cultural Connection:

Hot cocoa has long been a beloved treat around the world, with its roots tracing back to ancient Mesoamerican cultures where it was enjoyed as a ceremonial drink. Over time, it has evolved into the comforting beverage we know today, with variations like the **Minty Hot Cocoa** adding modern twists to this timeless classic.

# Spiced Cranberry Cider

*Warm up with a cup of Spiced Cranberry Cider, a tangy and aromatic drink that perfectly balances the tartness of cranberries with the warmth of holiday spices. This cozy beverage brings together the festive flavors of cinnamon, cloves, and orange, creating a delightful treat for any chilly day. Whether you're sipping it by the fireplace or serving it at a holiday gathering, this cider is sure to brighten up your mood and satisfy your cravings for something both refreshing and comforting.*

## Ingredients:

- 4 cups unsweetened cranberry juice
- 1/2 cup fresh orange juice
- 2 cinnamon sticks
- 4-5 whole cloves
- 1-2 tbsps maple syrup (or sweetener of your choice)
- 1/4 tsp ground ginger
- 1/4 tsp ground nutmeg
- 1/2 cup water
- [Optional] Orange slices for garnish
- [Optional] Fresh cranberries for garnish
- [Optional] A splash of brandy or rum for an adult version

## Instructions:

1. In a large saucepan, combine the cranberry juice, orange juice, water, cinnamon sticks, and cloves.
2. Bring the mixture to a simmer over medium heat, stirring occasionally.
3. Once it begins to simmer, reduce the heat to low and let it steep for about 10-15 minutes to allow the flavors to infuse.
4. Stir in the maple syrup, ground ginger, and ground nutmeg. Taste and adjust sweetness or spice levels if desired.
5. Remove the saucepan from heat. Discard the cinnamon sticks and cloves.
6. Pour the cider into mugs and garnish with fresh orange slices and cranberries if desired.
7. [Optional] Add a splash of brandy or rum to each serving for a warming adult twist.

## Tips and Recommendations:

- **Adjust the Sweetness:** If you prefer a sweeter cider, feel free to add more maple syrup or your favorite sweetener to taste.
- **Spice Levels:** You can increase the amount of ground ginger or nutmeg if you love a more intense spiced flavor.
- **Strain the Cider:** For a smoother drink, you can strain the cider before serving to remove any bits of spice or zest.
- **Non-Alcoholic Version:** Keep this cider alcohol-free for a family-friendly option. It's delicious both ways!

## Variations:

- **Apple-Cranberry Cider:** Swap half of the cranberry juice for apple cider for a sweeter, milder flavor.
- **Hot Spiked Cranberry Cider:** For a festive touch, add a splash of bourbon or spiced rum to each mug.
- **Iced Cranberry Cider:** Allow the cider to cool, then serve it over ice for a refreshing summer option.

## Pairing Suggestions:

- **Vegan Pastries:** Pair your Spiced Cranberry Cider with vegan shortbread cookies or a warm slice of gingerbread for a festive treat.
- **Savory Dishes:** This cider pairs wonderfully with savory dishes like vegan roast or stuffed squash for a holiday meal.

## Interesting Fact:

Did you know that cranberries were once used by Native Americans for food, medicine, and dye? They're a rich source of antioxidants and vitamin C, making them both delicious and beneficial for your health.

## Cultural Connection:

Cider has long been a beloved drink in many cultures, particularly in the fall and winter months. The combination of fruit juices and warming spices has made it a holiday favorite, with each region adding its own unique twist to the recipe. In this **Spiced Cranberry Cider**, the traditional flavors of cinnamon, cloves, and orange are given a modern, fruity twist with the use of cranberry juice, making it a perfect beverage for festive celebrations.

# Vanilla Rooibos Latte

*Indulge in the creamy, comforting flavors of a Vanilla Rooibos Latte, where the rich, earthy notes of rooibos tea meet the sweet warmth of vanilla and the velvety smoothness of steamed milk. This caffeine-free, aromatic drink is perfect for anyone looking to unwind with a delicious, soothing beverage. With its naturally sweet and slightly woody flavor, rooibos pairs beautifully with a hint of vanilla, creating a perfect blend of cozy and comforting. Whether you're looking for a late-night treat or a morning pick-me-up, this latte will warm both your body and spirit.*

## Ingredients:

- 1 tsp loose-leaf rooibos tea (or 1 rooibos tea bag)
- 1 cup water
- 1 cup steamed milk (dairy or plant-based)
- 1 tbsp vanilla syrup (or to taste)
- [Optional] 1/4 tsp ground cinnamon or nutmeg
- [Optional] A splash of maple syrup or sweetener of your choice

## Instructions:

1. **Brew the Rooibos Tea:** Bring 1 cup of water to a boil and pour it over the rooibos tea in a teapot or mug. Let the tea steep for 5-7 minutes, depending on how strong you like your tea.
2. **Steam the Milk:** While the tea is brewing, steam your milk until it's hot and frothy. You can use a milk frother or heat the milk on the stove and whisk it to create foam.
3. **Combine the Tea and Milk:** Strain the rooibos tea if using loose-leaf tea, and pour it into a large mug. Add the steamed milk to the tea, gently stirring to combine.
4. **Add Vanilla:** Stir in 1 tablespoon of vanilla syrup (or to taste) for a deliciously sweet touch.
5. **Optional Touches:** For extra warmth and flavor, sprinkle a little cinnamon or nutmeg on top. If you prefer a sweeter drink, add a splash of maple syrup or sweetener of your choice.

## Tips and Recommendations:

- **Adjust Sweetness:** Feel free to adjust the amount of vanilla syrup or maple syrup based on your preferred sweetness level.
- **Milk Variations:** This recipe works well with a variety of plant-based milks such as almond, oat, or coconut. Choose the one that best suits your taste and dietary needs.
- **Spice It Up:** Add a pinch of ground cinnamon or nutmeg for extra spice. You can also try a dash of ginger or cardamom for a different twist.

## Variations:

- **Iced Vanilla Rooibos Latte:** Let the brewed rooibos tea cool down and pour it over ice, then top with chilled steamed milk for a refreshing iced version.
- **Coconut Vanilla Rooibos Latte:** For a tropical twist, use coconut milk instead of regular milk, and add a splash of coconut syrup for extra flavor.
- **Sweetened Vanilla Rooibos Latte:** If you love a sweeter drink, try adding a drizzle of caramel syrup along with the vanilla syrup for a rich, indulgent treat.

## Pairing Suggestions:

- **Vegan Biscuits or Scones:** Pair with freshly baked vegan scones or biscuits for a delightful afternoon tea.
- **Cinnamon Rolls:** The warm, comforting flavors of cinnamon rolls make the perfect complement to the rich vanilla rooibos latte.
- **Fruit Tart:** A light, fruity dessert like a vegan lemon or berry tart will pair beautifully with the smooth, sweet flavors of the latte.

## Interesting Fact:

Did you know that rooibos tea comes from the leaves of a South African plant, Aspalathus linearis? It's been enjoyed for centuries by the indigenous people of the region, and it's known for its health benefits, including its ability to help with digestion and reduce inflammation.

## Cultural Connection:

Rooibos tea, often referred to as "Red Tea" due to its reddish-brown color, has been a staple in South African culture for generations. It was originally used by the indigenous Khoisan people and has since become a popular beverage around the world, known for its naturally sweet and caffeine-free qualities. The **Vanilla Rooibos Latte** is a modern twist on this traditional drink, blending the comforting flavors of vanilla with the earthy notes of rooibos for a unique and soothing experience.

# Honey Chamomile Tea Latte

*Indulge in the soothing, floral goodness of a Honey Chamomile Tea Latte, a delightful combination of calming chamomile tea, silky steamed milk, and a touch of natural honey sweetness. This warm, comforting drink is perfect for unwinding after a long day or enjoying as a relaxing morning treat. The chamomile's gentle, earthy flavor pairs harmoniously with the rich sweetness of honey, creating a serene, cozy experience. Whether you're winding down before bedtime or simply craving a peaceful moment, this latte is your perfect companion.*

## Ingredients:

- 1 tbsp loose-leaf chamomile tea (or 1 chamomile tea bag)
- 1 cup water
- 1 cup steamed milk (dairy or plant-based)
- 1 tbsp honey (or to taste)
- [Optional] 1/4 tsp ground cinnamon or nutmeg for garnish
- [Optional] A splash of vanilla syrup for extra sweetness

## Instructions:

1. **Brew the Chamomile Tea:** Bring 1 cup of water to a boil, then pour it over the chamomile tea in a teapot or mug. Allow it to steep for 5-7 minutes, depending on how strong you like your tea.
2. **Steam the Milk:** While the tea is brewing, steam your milk until it's hot and frothy. You can use a milk frother or heat the milk on the stove and whisk it to create foam.
3. **Combine the Tea and Milk:** Strain the brewed chamomile tea to remove the leaves (if using loose-leaf tea) and pour it into a mug. Add the steamed milk to the tea and stir gently to combine.
4. **Add Honey:** Stir in 1 tablespoon of honey (or to taste) for a natural sweetness. If you'd like a little extra sweetness, add a splash of vanilla syrup.
5. **Optional Garnish:** Sprinkle a little cinnamon or nutmeg on top for a warming spice finish.

## Tips and Recommendations:

- **Sweetness Variations:** Adjust the sweetness by adding more or less honey, or experiment with maple syrup or agave for a different twist.
- **Milk Alternatives:** This recipe works beautifully with a variety of plant-based milks such as almond, oat, or coconut. Choose your favorite based on taste or dietary preferences.
- **Additional Spice:** Add a pinch of ground ginger or cardamom for an extra layer of warmth and flavor.

## Variations:

- **Iced Honey Chamomile Latte:** Let the chamomile tea cool down, then pour it over ice and top with chilled steamed milk for a refreshing iced version.
- **Lavender Honey Chamomile Latte:** For a floral twist, add a few drops of lavender extract along with the chamomile for a soothing and aromatic drink.
- **Spiced Honey Chamomile Latte:** For a cozy fall flavor, try adding a dash of cinnamon or nutmeg directly into the milk before steaming.

## Pairing Suggestions:

- **Vegan Biscotti or Shortbread Cookies:** Pair with crispy vegan biscotti or buttery shortbread cookies for a sweet, light snack that complements the floral notes of the chamomile.
- **Apple Cinnamon Muffins:** A warm, apple cinnamon muffin would be the perfect accompaniment to this cozy, floral latte.
- **Fresh Fruit Tart:** Pair with a light, fruity dessert like a citrus or berry tart for a refreshing contrast to the rich, smooth tea latte.

## Interesting Fact:

Chamomile is one of the oldest and most widely used herbs in the world. It's known for its calming effects, often used to help with sleep, reduce stress, and promote digestive health. Its delicate flowers have been cherished for centuries, both in herbal remedies and culinary creations.

## Cultural Connection:

Chamomile has a rich history, used for its medicinal and soothing properties by many cultures, including ancient Egypt, Greece, and Rome. Known as a symbol of relaxation, chamomile tea has long been a staple in evening rituals. The **Honey Chamomile Tea Latte** brings together this age-old beverage with the sweetness of honey and the comforting texture of steamed milk, making it a modern, cozy twist on a timeless classic.

# Coconut Ginger Chai

*Step into a world of bold flavors and warming spices with a Coconut Ginger Chai. This vibrant, dairy-free chai latte combines the aromatic blend of traditional chai spices with the creamy richness of coconut milk and a zing of fresh ginger. Perfect for chilly mornings or cozy afternoons, this spiced drink brings both warmth and refreshment, elevating your chai experience to a whole new level. The coconut milk adds a velvety texture while ginger provides a spicy kick, creating the ultimate balance of heat and sweetness.*

## Ingredients:

- 1 chai tea bag or 1 tbsp loose-leaf chai tea
- 1 cup water
- 1 tbsp fresh ginger, grated
- 1 cup coconut milk (or other plant-based milk of your choice)
- 1-2 tbsps maple syrup (or to taste)
- [Optional] 1/4 tsp ground cinnamon or nutmeg
- [Optional] A pinch of black pepper (for extra spice)

## Instructions:

1. **Brew the Chai Tea:** Boil 1 cup of water in a small pot. Add the chai tea bag or loose-leaf tea and let it steep for 4-5 minutes.
2. **Add Ginger:** Grate the fresh ginger and add it to the brewing tea. Let it simmer for an additional 2-3 minutes to infuse the flavors.
3. **Prepare the Coconut Milk:** While the tea is brewing, heat the coconut milk in a separate small pot over medium heat. Stir occasionally to prevent it from boiling over.
4. **Combine the Tea and Coconut Milk:** Once the chai is steeped and the ginger is infused, strain out the tea leaves and ginger. Pour the brewed chai into a mug and slowly add the heated coconut milk. Stir well to combine.
5. **Sweeten:** Add 1-2 tablespoons of maple syrup (or to taste) for sweetness. Stir until fully dissolved.
6. **Optional Garnish:** Sprinkle ground cinnamon or nutmeg on top for an aromatic finish. For an extra kick, add a pinch of black pepper.

## Tips and Recommendations:

- **Adjust Spice Levels:** If you love a spicier chai, increase the amount of grated ginger or add a pinch of cayenne pepper for a warm heat.
- **Sweetness Variations:** For a more natural sweetener, try using agave syrup or coconut sugar.
- **Milk Alternatives:** While coconut milk is the star of this recipe, feel free to experiment with almond milk, oat milk, or cashew milk for a slightly different texture and flavor.
- **Make It Frothy:** Use a milk frother to create a frothy texture for your coconut milk before adding it to the tea for a creamier latte experience.

## Variations:

- **Iced Coconut Ginger Chai:** Allow the chai to cool, then pour it over ice for a refreshing iced version.
- **Vanilla Coconut Ginger Chai:** Add a splash of vanilla extract or a teaspoon of vanilla syrup for a smooth, sweet undertone that complements the spices.
- **Coconut Ginger Chai with Cardamom:** Boost the flavor profile with a pinch of ground cardamom for a more complex chai experience.

## Pairing Suggestions:

- **Vegan Scones or Cinnamon Rolls:** Enjoy with warm vegan scones or cinnamon rolls to complement the spicy chai. The richness of coconut and the warmth of ginger pair beautifully with these baked goods.
- **Almond or Coconut Biscotti:** Pair with a crispy almond or coconut biscotti for a crunchy treat that balances the creamy, spiced drink.
- **Apple Crumble:** The spiced flavors of this chai go wonderfully with a warm, comforting apple crumble dessert.

## Interesting Fact:

Did you know that chai is an ancient drink with origins in India, where it has been brewed for centuries? The word "chai" simply means "tea" in Hindi, but it's the blend of spices and tea leaves that makes this drink so unique. The combination of spices like cinnamon, cardamom, and ginger was traditionally believed to have medicinal properties.

## Cultural Connection:

The traditional Indian chai is known for its complex flavor profile, typically made by brewing tea leaves with milk, sugar, and a variety of spices. **Coconut Ginger Chai** takes inspiration from this beloved beverage, adding the creamy richness of coconut milk and a zesty ginger twist for a refreshing modern take on an age-old recipe. This spiced latte is perfect for those who appreciate the depth of chai and the added flavor of tropical coconut.

# Cardamom Rose Tea

*Step into a world of floral elegance and warm spices with Cardamom Rose Tea. This delicate yet flavorful blend combines the exotic fragrance of rose petals with the rich, aromatic notes of cardamom, creating a tea that's both soothing and uplifting. Perfect for a moment of calm or an afternoon indulgence, this tea is an aromatic escape from the ordinary. The gentle sweetness of rose and the warm spiciness of cardamom make this a unique and comforting brew, perfect for any time of the day.*

## Ingredients:

- 1 tsp loose-leaf black tea (or 1 tea bag)
- 1/2 tsp ground cardamom
- 1 tbsp dried rose petals
- 1 1/2 cups water
- 1/4 cup coconut milk (or any plant-based milk)
- 1-2 tsps maple syrup or honey (optional)
- [Optional] 1/4 tsp ground cinnamon or ginger (for extra spice)
- [Optional] Rose petals for garnish

## Instructions:

1. **Brew the Tea Base:** Bring 1 1/2 cups of water to a boil in a small pot. Add the loose-leaf black tea or tea bag, ground cardamom, and dried rose petals to the pot. Allow the tea to steep for 4-5 minutes.
2. **Heat the Milk:** While the tea is steeping, gently heat the coconut milk (or your preferred plant-based milk) in a separate small pot over low heat. Stir occasionally to prevent it from boiling.
3. **Combine and Strain:** Once the tea has steeped, strain out the tea leaves and rose petals.
4. **Sweeten (Optional):** Add maple syrup or honey to taste. Stir to combine.
5. **Add the Milk:** Pour the heated coconut milk into the brewed tea, stirring gently until well-mixed.
6. **Optional Garnish:** Garnish with a few fresh rose petals or a light dusting of cinnamon for an extra touch of elegance.

## Tips and Recommendations:

- **Adjust Sweetness:** If you prefer a sweeter tea, adjust the amount of maple syrup or honey to your taste. You can also try stevia or agave for a different sweetener option.
- **Cardamom Intensity:** For a stronger cardamom flavor, increase the amount of ground cardamom.
- **Milk Alternatives:** Coconut milk provides a rich, creamy texture, but you can substitute with almond milk, oat milk, or any other plant-based milk you prefer.
- **For Extra Spice:** If you enjoy a spicier chai-like flavor, add a pinch of ground cinnamon or ginger for a warming twist.

## Variations:

- **Iced Cardamom Rose Tea:** Allow the tea to cool completely, then pour over ice for a refreshing twist.
- **Lavender Rose Tea:** Add a teaspoon of dried lavender to the brew for a calming, fragrant alternative to the rose flavor.
- **Rose Cardamom Latte:** For a creamier drink, add more milk and froth it before adding to the tea, creating a cozy latte-style version of this drink.

## Pairing Suggestions:

- **Vegan Scones or Shortbread:** Pair with warm vegan scones or delicate shortbread for a light, elegant snack that complements the floral notes of the tea.
- **Almond Cake or Rose-flavored Treats:** Enjoy with a slice of almond cake or a light rose-flavored pastry for a perfect afternoon tea experience.
- **Fruit Tart:** A fresh fruit tart, especially one with berries, pairs wonderfully with the floral complexity of this tea.

## Interesting Fact:

Did you know that cardamom is often called the "Queen of Spices" due to its unique flavor and versatility in both sweet and savory dishes? It's also known for its digestive benefits and ability to promote relaxation, making it the perfect addition to a soothing tea.

## Cultural Connection:

Cardamom and rose are commonly found in Middle Eastern and South Asian teas, where they are used not only for flavor but also for their believed therapeutic properties. **Cardamom Rose Tea** draws inspiration from these traditions, offering a beautiful blend of flavor and wellness. This tea invites you to slow down, sip, and enjoy a moment of peace, much like the rich cultural heritage from which it originates.

# Raspberry Hibiscus Tea Latte

*Get ready for a vibrant and refreshing twist on the traditional latte with Raspberry Hibiscus Tea Latte. The tart and fruity notes of raspberry blend beautifully with the floral, slightly tangy hibiscus tea, creating a colorful and uplifting drink. Paired with creamy plant-based milk, this latte is perfect for those who crave a caffeine-free, antioxidant-packed treat. It's a delightful way to unwind and refresh your senses while enjoying the natural goodness of hibiscus and raspberry.*

## Ingredients:

- 1 tbsp dried hibiscus petals
- 1/4 cup fresh raspberries (or 2 tbsps raspberry puree)
- 1 1/2 cups water
- 1 tsp maple syrup or honey (optional)
- 1/2 cup plant-based milk (such as oat milk, almond milk, or coconut milk)
- [Optional] 1/4 tsp vanilla extract
- [Optional] Fresh raspberries or dried hibiscus petals for garnish

## Instructions:

1. **Prepare the Hibiscus Tea:** Bring 1 1/2 cups of water to a boil in a small pot. Add the dried hibiscus petals and let them steep for 5-7 minutes until the water turns a rich red color.
2. **Make Raspberry Puree:** In a small saucepan, heat the fresh raspberries over low heat for 3-4 minutes until softened. Mash them with a fork or blend them to make a puree.
3. **Combine Tea and Raspberry Puree:** Strain the hibiscus tea to remove the petals, then stir in the raspberry puree. If you prefer a sweeter taste, add 1 teaspoon of maple syrup or honey to the mix.
4. **Heat the Milk:** In a separate small pot, heat your plant-based milk over low heat, stirring occasionally. If desired, add vanilla extract to enhance the flavor.
5. **Assemble the Latte:** Pour the hibiscus-raspberry mixture into your favorite mug. Gently add the warm milk to the tea, creating a beautiful swirl of color.
6. **Optional Garnish:** Garnish with a few fresh raspberries or a sprinkle of dried hibiscus petals for an added touch of elegance.

## Tips and Recommendations:

- **Adjust Sweetness:** The raspberry puree may be naturally sweet, but feel free to add more maple syrup or honey if you prefer a sweeter latte.
- **Milk Alternatives:** For a richer, creamier texture, use coconut milk. Oat milk is also a great choice for a naturally sweet and smooth finish.
- **Extra Flavor:** For a warm, comforting touch, add a pinch of cinnamon or a dash of ginger to the milk as it heats.

## Variations:

- **Iced Raspberry Hibiscus Tea Latte:** Allow the tea to cool and serve over ice for a refreshing summer drink.
- **Raspberry Hibiscus Iced Tea:** Skip the milk entirely for a light, fruity iced tea version that's perfect for warm days.
- **Berry Hibiscus Latte:** Add a handful of mixed berries (such as blueberries or strawberries) to the raspberry puree for a more complex berry flavor.

## Pairing Suggestions:

- **Vegan Scones or Biscuits:** Pair with a warm, flaky vegan scone or a buttery biscuit for a classic afternoon tea experience.
- **Fruit Salad:** A light, citrusy fruit salad with melon, berries, and mint perfectly complements the tartness of the raspberry hibiscus latte.
- **Vegan Chocolate Cake:** For a sweet indulgence, enjoy with a slice of rich vegan chocolate cake or brownies for a comforting treat.

## Interesting Fact:

Did you know that hibiscus is often used in herbal teas for its potential health benefits, including its ability to lower blood pressure and improve digestion? Paired with the antioxidant-rich raspberries, this latte is as beneficial as it is tasty!

## Cultural Connection:

Hibiscus tea has deep roots in cultures around the world, particularly in the Caribbean, Africa, and the Middle East, where it's enjoyed both hot and cold. This **Raspberry Hibiscus Tea Latte** draws inspiration from these global traditions, offering a modern twist on a timeless herbal drink.

# Ginger Lemongrass Tea

*Feel refreshed and invigorated with Ginger Lemongrass Tea, a soothing, aromatic blend that's perfect for calming your senses. The spicy warmth of ginger combined with the fresh, citrusy zing of lemongrass creates a comforting yet uplifting drink that's ideal for cozy evenings or when you need a little boost. With its natural anti-inflammatory and digestive benefits, this herbal tea offers a healthy, caffeine-free alternative that packs both flavor and wellness in every sip.*

## Ingredients:

- 1 tbsp fresh ginger, thinly sliced
- 2 stalks lemongrass, bruised and chopped
- 3 cups water
- 1 tbsp honey or maple syrup (optional)
- [Optional] 1/4 tsp ground turmeric for extra warmth
- [Optional] A few fresh mint leaves for garnish

## Instructions:

1. **Prepare the Ginger and Lemongrass:** Slice the fresh ginger and bruise the lemongrass by gently smashing it with the back of a knife to release the oils. Chop the lemongrass into smaller pieces to infuse the flavor better.
2. **Boil the Ingredients:** In a medium-sized pot, bring 3 cups of water to a boil. Add the ginger and lemongrass, and let it simmer on low heat for 10-12 minutes to allow the flavors to infuse.
3. **Sweeten the Tea:** If desired, add 1 tablespoon of honey or maple syrup to the tea for a touch of sweetness. Stir well.
4. **Optional Turmeric:** For an extra layer of flavor, add a pinch of ground turmeric for warmth and depth. Stir until fully combined.
5. **Serve the Tea:** Pour the tea into a mug, straining out the ginger and lemongrass.
6. **Garnish:** Optionally, garnish with a few fresh mint leaves for a burst of color and freshness.

## Tips and Recommendations:

- **Adjust the Spice Level:** If you prefer a spicier tea, increase the amount of ginger or let it simmer longer for a more intense flavor.
- **Cool Down:** For a refreshing iced version, allow the tea to cool down, then pour over ice and garnish with mint leaves.
- **Aromatic Enhancements:** Add a few cardamom pods or a cinnamon stick during the simmering process for additional aromatic depth.

## Variations:

- **Ginger Lemongrass Limeade:** After brewing the tea, mix it with fresh lime juice and a splash of sparkling water for a zesty, refreshing iced drink.
- **Coconut Ginger Lemongrass Tea:** Add a splash of coconut milk or coconut cream to the finished tea for a creamy twist.
- **Spiced Ginger Lemongrass Latte:** Froth some plant-based milk (like oat or almond milk) and add it to the tea for a creamy, comforting version.

## Pairing Suggestions:

- **Vegan Coconut Scones:** Serve with light, fluffy vegan coconut scones that complement the aromatic flavors of the tea.
- **Rice Paper Rolls:** Enjoy with fresh vegan rice paper rolls filled with veggies and herbs for a light, refreshing meal.
- **Spiced Nuts:** Pair with a bowl of lightly spiced nuts to balance the spicy and citrusy notes of the tea.

## Interesting Fact:

Did you know that ginger has been used for thousands of years in traditional medicine across the world? It's known for its ability to soothe the digestive system and reduce inflammation.

## Cultural Connection:

Ginger and lemongrass are staples in Southeast Asian cuisine and herbal medicine, often used in teas and soups for their invigorating qualities. This **Ginger Lemongrass Tea** brings together these two iconic ingredients, offering a taste of tropical wellness from the comfort of your own home.

# Almond Vanilla Rooibos Latte

*Indulge in the warm, comforting flavors of this Almond Vanilla Rooibos Latte, where the rich, earthy taste of rooibos meets the sweet, aromatic essence of vanilla and the nutty depth of almond. Naturally caffeine-free, this vegan-friendly latte is perfect for unwinding after a long day or enjoying as a relaxing treat any time of the day. The combination of creamy almond milk and the subtle sweetness of vanilla transforms this herbal tea into a rich, indulgent experience.*

## Ingredients:

- 1 tbsp rooibos tea leaves (or 1 rooibos tea bag)
- 2 cups water
- 1/2 tsp vanilla extract
- 1 tbsp almond butter or almond paste
- 1 cup unsweetened almond milk (or any plant-based milk of choice)
- [Optional] 1 tbsp maple syrup or sweetener of choice (to taste)
- [Optional] A pinch of ground cinnamon for garnish

## Instructions:

1. **Brew the Rooibos Tea:** Bring 2 cups of water to a boil in a small pot. Once boiling, add the rooibos tea leaves (or tea bag) and reduce the heat. Let it steep for about 5-7 minutes to extract a rich, full flavor.
2. **Prepare the Almond Milk:** While the tea is brewing, in a separate pot, heat the almond milk over medium heat, stirring frequently. Add the almond butter or almond paste, and whisk until smooth and creamy.
3. **Combine the Flavors:** Once the rooibos tea has finished steeping, strain out the tea leaves or remove the tea bag. Pour the brewed tea into a mug and add the vanilla extract, stirring gently.
4. **Froth the Almond Milk:** Froth the almond milk mixture using a milk frother or by whisking vigorously until it's smooth and frothy.
5. **Assemble the Latte:** Pour the frothed almond milk over the brewed rooibos tea, creating a layered effect. Add sweetener, if desired, and stir gently to combine.
6. **Garnish:** Optionally, sprinkle a pinch of cinnamon on top for a hint of warmth and spice.

## Tips and Recommendations:

- **For a creamier texture:** Use almond milk with a higher fat content or add a little extra almond butter for richness.
- **Sweetness:** Adjust the level of sweetness by adding more or less maple syrup, or try adding a drop of stevia for a sugar-free option.
- **Variation with spices:** Try adding a pinch of ground cardamom or nutmeg for an aromatic twist.
- **Serve cold:** For a refreshing iced version, cool the tea and almond milk mixture, then pour over ice for a chilled treat.

## Variations:

- **Coconut Vanilla Rooibos Latte:** Swap almond milk for coconut milk for a tropical, creamy twist.
- **Spiced Almond Vanilla Rooibos Latte:** Add a pinch of ground ginger or cloves for a spiced variation that's perfect for the colder months.
- **Caramelized Almond Rooibos Latte:** Add a drizzle of homemade caramel sauce to the tea for a rich, caramelized flavor.

## Pairing Suggestions:

- **Vegan Croissants:** Enjoy this latte alongside flaky vegan croissants for a luxurious, brunch-worthy pairing.
- **Almond Biscotti:** Pair with crunchy almond biscotti for a delightful contrast to the smooth and creamy latte.
- **Vegan Chocolate Cake:** Complement the natural sweetness of the latte with a slice of vegan chocolate cake for a decadent dessert option.

## Interesting Fact:

Did you know that rooibos tea is grown exclusively in South Africa? It's known for its naturally sweet flavor and health benefits, including supporting digestion and reducing inflammation.

## Cultural Connection:

Rooibos tea has deep cultural roots in South Africa, where it has been enjoyed for centuries. Traditionally consumed for its soothing and restorative properties, it has become popular worldwide as a caffeine-free alternative to black and green teas.

# Caramel Apple Chai Latte

*Warm up with the Caramel Apple Chai Latte, a perfect fall-inspired drink that combines the spiced richness of chai with the sweet, comforting flavors of caramel and apple. This drink is a cozy hug in a cup, balancing the heat of cinnamon, ginger, and cardamom with the fruity freshness of apple and the decadent sweetness of caramel. It's a vegan-friendly, caffeine-free alternative to traditional lattes that is sure to delight your senses and evoke the cozy vibes of autumn.*

## Ingredients:

- 2 chai tea bags (or 2 tbsps loose-leaf chai tea)
- 2 cups water
- 1/2 cup unsweetened apple juice
- 1/2 cup unsweetened almond milk (or any plant-based milk of choice)
- 1 tbsp caramel syrup (vegan option)
- 1/4 tsp ground cinnamon
- 1/4 tsp ground ginger
- [Optional] 1 tbsp maple syrup (for extra sweetness)
- [Optional] Whipped coconut cream (for topping)

## Instructions:

1. **Brew the Chai Tea:** In a small pot, bring 2 cups of water to a boil. Add the chai tea bags (or loose-leaf tea in a strainer) and steep for 5-7 minutes, depending on how strong you like your chai.
2. **Prepare the Apple Milk Mixture:** While the tea is brewing, in another pot, combine the apple juice and almond milk. Heat gently over medium heat, stirring occasionally until hot but not boiling.
3. **Mix the Spices and Caramel:** Once the tea is brewed, remove the tea bags or strain the loose-leaf tea. Add the ground cinnamon and ginger to the tea, stirring to incorporate.
4. **Combine Tea and Milk:** Pour the hot apple milk mixture into the brewed chai, mixing well to combine all the flavors. Add the caramel syrup and stir until fully dissolved.
5. **Sweeten to Taste:** If you like your drink sweeter, add maple syrup or your favorite sweetener to taste.
6. **Serve:** Pour the chai apple caramel mixture into a mug and top with whipped coconut cream for a creamy finish, if desired.
7. **Garnish:** Optionally, sprinkle a pinch of cinnamon or drizzle extra caramel syrup over the top for a beautiful finishing touch.

## Tips and Recommendations:

- **For extra creaminess:** Use full-fat coconut milk or oat milk for a richer texture.
- **Spice adjustment:** Add a pinch of cardamom or cloves for extra spice complexity.
- **Sweetness balance:** Adjust the sweetness by experimenting with different sweeteners like agave, coconut sugar, or brown sugar for a deeper, molasses-like flavor.
- **Caramel drizzle:** For a decorative touch, drizzle a bit of caramel syrup along the sides of the mug before pouring in the drink for a beautiful effect.

## Variations:

- **Iced Caramel Apple Chai Latte:** Let the chai tea cool, then pour it over ice and top with chilled apple milk for a refreshing twist.
- **Coconut Caramel Apple Chai Latte:** Use coconut milk for a tropical, creamy version of this drink that pairs perfectly with the chai spices.
- **Spicy Caramel Apple Chai Latte:** Increase the cinnamon, ginger, and add a pinch of cayenne pepper for a spicy kick.

## Pairing Suggestions:

- **Vegan Cinnamon Rolls:** Enjoy the warmth of this chai latte with a flaky, cinnamon-infused vegan roll to bring out the spice flavors.
- **Apple Scones:** Pair with a light, crumbly scone to enhance the apple flavor and provide a perfect contrast to the drink's creamy richness.
- **Vegan Pecan Pie:** Complement the caramel sweetness with a slice of vegan pecan pie for a comforting dessert experience.

## Interesting Fact:

Did you know that chai is a traditional Indian drink, made by blending strong black tea with a variety of spices, which are thought to promote digestion and overall health? It's a centuries-old beverage that's still beloved around the world.

## Cultural Connection:

Chai has long been a staple of Indian culture, where it's often served during social gatherings or as a comforting beverage during the day. The addition of caramel and apple brings a modern twist to this classic drink, while still honoring its rich cultural roots.

# Rosewater White Hot Chocolate

*Indulge in the delicate sweetness of Rosewater White Hot Chocolate, a luxurious and aromatic twist on the classic hot chocolate. This creamy, velvety drink combines smooth white chocolate with the subtle, floral essence of rosewater, creating a heavenly beverage that's both comforting and sophisticated. Perfect for a cozy night in or as a special treat for guests, this vegan-friendly hot chocolate is an elegant way to enjoy a sweet, aromatic escape.*

## Ingredients:

- 1 cup unsweetened almond milk (or any plant-based milk of choice)
- 1/2 cup vegan white chocolate chips or chopped white chocolate
- 1 tbsp rosewater
- 1 tsp vanilla extract
- 1 tbsp maple syrup (or preferred sweetener)
- Pinch of sea salt
- [Optional] Vegan whipped cream (for topping)
- [Optional] Dried rose petals or crushed pistachios (for garnish)

## Instructions:

1. **Heat the Milk:** In a small pot, heat the almond milk over medium heat until it is hot but not boiling. Stir occasionally to prevent it from scalding.
2. **Melt the White Chocolate:** Add the vegan white chocolate chips to the warm milk. Stir gently until the chocolate is fully melted and the mixture becomes smooth and creamy.
3. **Flavor the Drink:** Add the rosewater, vanilla extract, maple syrup, and a pinch of sea salt to the milk and chocolate mixture. Stir to combine and dissolve the sweetener completely.
4. **Serve:** Pour the hot chocolate into a mug, and top with a dollop of vegan whipped cream, if desired.
5. **Garnish:** For an extra touch of elegance, sprinkle dried rose petals or crushed pistachios on top to enhance the floral and nutty notes.

## Tips and Recommendations:

- **Adjust the Rosewater:** Rosewater has a potent flavor, so adjust the amount to your preference. Start with a small amount and taste to make sure it doesn't overpower the drink.
- **Vegan White Chocolate:** Not all white chocolate is vegan-friendly, so be sure to use a variety that contains no dairy. You can also substitute with a vegan white chocolate bar and chop it into small pieces.
- **Creamier Texture:** For a richer drink, use full-fat coconut milk or cashew milk, which will provide an even creamier texture and a subtle flavor that complements the rosewater.

## Variations:

- **Rose and Lavender Hot Chocolate:** Add a drop of culinary lavender extract or a small amount of dried lavender buds to the milk along with the rosewater for a fragrant and floral combination.
- **Iced Rosewater White Chocolate:** Chill the drink after making it and serve over ice for a refreshing twist on the classic.
- **Raspberry Rose Hot Chocolate:** For a fruity twist, add a splash of raspberry syrup or muddle fresh raspberries into the drink before serving.

## Pairing Suggestions:

- **Vegan Shortbread Cookies:** A buttery, crumbly shortbread cookie complements the smooth, creamy texture of this rosewater-infused drink.
- **Vegan Scones:** Serve with a fresh batch of scones, perhaps with a drizzle of raspberry or lemon glaze, for a perfect balance of sweetness and floral notes.
- **Dark Chocolate Truffles:** The richness of dark chocolate truffles pairs beautifully with the delicate flavors of the white chocolate and rosewater, making for an indulgent treat.

## Interesting Fact:

Did you know that **rosewater** has been used for centuries in culinary and medicinal practices? Its delicate flavor and soothing properties have made it a beloved ingredient in Middle Eastern cuisine and traditional desserts.

## Cultural Connection:

Rosewater has deep roots in Middle Eastern and South Asian cultures, where it's frequently used in sweets like Turkish Delight and Persian baklava. By incorporating rosewater into this white hot chocolate, we blend a classic Western drink with a dash of Eastern elegance, creating a truly unique fusion.

# Honey Lavender Chamomile Tea

*Unwind with the calming and soothing flavors of Honey Lavender Chamomile Tea, a perfect drink to enjoy before bed or any time you need to relax. This gentle infusion combines the floral notes of chamomile and lavender with the natural sweetness of honey, creating a peaceful and aromatic tea experience. Whether you're winding down after a busy day or simply seeking a quiet moment of comfort, this tea offers a serene escape in every sip.*

## Ingredients:

- 1 cup boiling water
- 1 tbsp dried chamomile flowers
- 1 tsp dried lavender buds
- 1 tsp honey (or more, to taste)
- 1/2 tsp lemon juice (optional)
- [Optional] Fresh lavender sprig (for garnish)
- [Optional] Lemon slice (for garnish)

## Instructions:

1. **Boil the Water:** Bring 1 cup of water to a boil.
2. **Steep the Herbs:** Place the dried chamomile flowers and lavender buds in a tea infuser or directly into the boiling water. Let it steep for 5-7 minutes, depending on your desired strength.
3. **Add Honey and Lemon:** Remove the infuser or strain the tea to remove the flowers. Stir in honey and lemon juice (if using), adjusting the sweetness and tartness to your preference.
4. **Serve:** Pour the tea into a mug and garnish with a fresh lavender sprig or a lemon slice, if desired.
5. **Enjoy:** Sip and relax as the soothing floral notes ease you into tranquility.

## Tips and Recommendations:

- **Steeping Time:** If you prefer a stronger herbal flavor, allow the tea to steep for a few extra minutes. For a lighter flavor, steep for less time.
- **Honey Alternatives:** You can substitute honey with maple syrup, agave syrup, or stevia for a vegan or sugar-free option.
- **Cold Version:** If you want to enjoy this as a refreshing cold drink, let the tea cool and serve over ice. Add a few fresh mint leaves for an extra burst of flavor.

## Variations:

- **Lavender Chamomile Mint Tea:** Add a few fresh mint leaves during the steeping process for a refreshing twist.
- **Lemon Ginger Honey Lavender Tea:** Add a few thin slices of fresh ginger to the boiling water along with the herbs for a warm, spicy kick that complements the floral flavors.
- **Citrus Twist:** For a zesty variation, add orange or lime slices to the tea instead of lemon for a fresh, citrusy flavor.

## Pairing Suggestions:

- **Vegan Shortbread Biscuits:** Enjoy this tea alongside a delicate shortbread biscuit for a satisfying and light pairing.
- **Almond Croissants:** The buttery, nutty flavor of almond croissants balances beautifully with the floral notes of the tea.
- **Fruit Tart:** Pair with a light, fruity tart for a touch of sweetness that complements the tea's soothing flavors.

## Interesting Fact:

Did you know that **lavender** is often used in aromatherapy for its calming effects? It's believed to help reduce anxiety and improve sleep quality, making it the perfect addition to this relaxing tea.

## Cultural Connection:

Chamomile and lavender have been used for centuries in various cultures for their medicinal and soothing properties. Chamomile tea is especially popular in Europe, while lavender is a staple in Mediterranean herbal traditions. Together, these two herbs form a powerful and peaceful combination that transcends borders and cultures.

# Cinnamon Almond Milk Steamer

*Indulge in the velvety smoothness of a Cinnamon Almond Milk Steamer, a warm and cozy drink that's perfect for chilly evenings or any time you need a comforting, caffeine-free treat. The creamy almond milk is frothed to perfection, infused with the sweet and spicy warmth of cinnamon, making this a delightful alternative to traditional hot chocolate or lattes. Whether you're unwinding after a busy day or treating yourself to something special, this steamer will wrap you in a soothing embrace.*

## Ingredients:

- 1 cup unsweetened almond milk
- 1/2 tsp ground cinnamon
- 1 tbsp maple syrup or agave syrup (adjust to taste)
- 1/4 tsp vanilla extract
- [Optional] Pinch of ground nutmeg
- [Optional] Almond slices or cinnamon stick for garnish

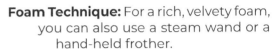

## Instructions:

1. **Heat the Almond Milk:** In a small pot, heat the almond milk over medium heat until hot but not boiling, stirring occasionally.
2. **Add Spices:** Once the milk is warm, whisk in the cinnamon and vanilla extract. Add a pinch of nutmeg if desired, and continue stirring until the milk is well combined and frothy.
3. **Sweeten:** Stir in the maple syrup or agave syrup, adjusting the sweetness to your taste.
4. **Froth the Milk:** For extra frothiness, use a milk frother or whisk vigorously by hand until the milk forms a creamy foam.
5. **Serve:** Pour the steamer into your favorite mug and garnish with a sprinkle of cinnamon, a few almond slices, or a cinnamon stick for a festive touch.
6. **Enjoy:** Sip and savor the warm, comforting flavors of this creamy drink.

## Tips and Recommendations:

- **Milk Alternatives:** Feel free to use other plant-based milks like oat, coconut, or cashew milk for different textures and flavors.
- **Extra Spice:** For an extra kick, add a pinch of ground ginger or cloves to the mix.
- **Foam Technique:** For a rich, velvety foam, you can also use a steam wand or a hand-held frother.
- **Cold Version:** If you'd prefer an iced version, simply let the steamer cool down and pour over ice for a refreshing treat.

## Variations:

- **Vanilla Cinnamon Steamer:** Add a splash of vanilla almond milk in place of regular almond milk for an extra hit of vanilla flavor.
- **Chocolate Cinnamon Steamer:** Stir in a tablespoon of cocoa powder or dairy-free chocolate chips for a chocolatey twist on this warming drink.
- **Caramel Cinnamon Steamer:** For a sweeter treat, drizzle some dairy-free caramel syrup into your steamer before serving.

## Pairing Suggestions:

- **Vegan Scones:** Serve with warm, flaky vegan scones for a delightful afternoon treat.
- **Almond Biscotti:** The crisp texture and nutty flavor of almond biscotti complement the creamy cinnamon steamer perfectly.
- **Oatmeal Cookies:** Pair with soft oatmeal cookies for a wholesome, comforting combination.

## Interesting Fact:

Did you know that **cinnamon** has been used for thousands of years as both a spice and a medicinal herb? It is believed to have numerous health benefits, including helping to regulate blood sugar levels and reducing inflammation.

## Cultural Connection:

Cinnamon has a long history in many cultures, from its use in ancient Egyptian embalming practices to its prominence in European and Middle Eastern cuisines. This steamer, with its warm spice and comforting qualities, evokes the cozy flavors of traditional winter drinks enjoyed around the world.

# Orange Blossom Herbal Tea Latte

*Delight in the delicate floral notes of Orange Blossom Herbal Tea Latte, a soothing and aromatic drink that brings together the elegance of orange blossom with the warmth of herbal tea. Perfect for those looking to unwind or enjoy a caffeine-free indulgence, this latte combines fragrant floral flavors with creamy almond milk for a unique and refreshing experience. Whether enjoyed as a peaceful morning ritual or an evening treat, this herbal tea latte will calm your senses and brighten your day.*

## Ingredients:

- 1 cup herbal tea (orange blossom or chamomile)
- 1 cup unsweetened almond milk (or any plant-based milk of choice)
- 1 tbsp honey or maple syrup (adjust to taste)
- 1/2 tsp vanilla extract
- 1-2 drops orange blossom water
- [Optional] Orange zest or a thin slice of orange for garnish
- [Optional] Ground cinnamon for a light dusting

## Instructions:

1. **Brew the Tea:** Brew 1 cup of orange blossom or chamomile herbal tea using hot water. Steep for about 5 minutes, or until the tea is fragrant and flavorful.
2. **Heat the Milk:** In a small pot, gently heat the almond milk over medium heat, stirring occasionally until warm but not boiling.
3. **Sweeten and Flavor:** Stir in the honey or maple syrup and vanilla extract. Add 1-2 drops of orange blossom water to enhance the floral aroma.
4. **Froth the Milk:** Use a milk frother or whisk vigorously to froth the almond milk until it becomes creamy and smooth.
5. **Combine the Tea and Milk:** Pour the brewed tea into a mug, then gently pour the frothed milk over the tea, creating a beautiful, layered effect.
6. **Garnish and Serve:** For extra flair, garnish with a sprinkle of ground cinnamon or a slice of fresh orange. Serve immediately and enjoy the calming floral flavors.

## Tips and Recommendations:

- **Milk Alternatives:** You can use any plant-based milk such as oat milk, coconut milk, or cashew milk for a creamier or richer texture.
- **Orange Blossom Water:** Be cautious with the amount of orange blossom water, as it is quite potent. Start with a few drops and adjust to taste.
- **Extra Floral Touch:** If you enjoy floral flavors, try adding a few lavender buds or a touch of rosewater for a unique twist.
- **Cold Version:** For a refreshing iced version, allow the tea to cool and serve over ice, topped with cold frothed milk.

## Variations:

- **Citrus Twist:** Add a splash of freshly squeezed orange juice to the tea for an extra citrusy burst.
- **Spiced Orange Blossom Latte:** Add a pinch of ground ginger or cardamom for a hint of warmth and spice.
- **Lavender Orange Blossom Latte:** Blend a few lavender buds with the orange blossom water for a more complex floral flavor profile.

## Pairing Suggestions:

- **Vegan Lemon Scones:** Pair this fragrant latte with vegan lemon scones to complement the citrus and floral notes.
- **Almond Biscotti:** The nutty crunch of almond biscotti makes a perfect match for the smooth, floral sweetness of the latte.
- **Fresh Fruit Salad:** A refreshing fruit salad with a citrus base would be a light, flavorful accompaniment to this delicate tea latte.

## Interesting Fact:

Did you know that **orange blossom** is often used in perfumes due to its sweet and fragrant aroma? It is also considered a symbol of purity and fertility in many cultures.

## Cultural Connection:

Orange blossom is cherished in many cultures, especially in Mediterranean regions, where it is used in culinary creations and as a symbol of prosperity and good fortune. The practice of incorporating orange blossoms into drinks has ancient roots, with its calming, soothing qualities celebrated for centuries.

# Toasted Coconut Chai

*Warm up with the rich, aromatic flavor of Toasted Coconut Chai, a vegan twist on the classic chai latte that combines fragrant spices with the sweet, nutty flavor of toasted coconut. This drink is a perfect fusion of creamy, spiced chai and tropical coconut, creating a comforting, flavorful experience that feels like a cozy escape to the beach. Whether you need a calming afternoon treat or a warming evening beverage, this unique chai latte will bring warmth to your soul and delight to your taste buds.*

## Ingredients:

- 1 cup coconut milk (or any plant-based milk)
- 1 tbsp shredded coconut (toasted)
- 1 chai tea bag or 1 tbsp loose-leaf chai tea
- 1/2 tsp ground cinnamon
- 1/4 tsp ground ginger
- 1/4 tsp ground cardamom
- 1-2 tsps maple syrup or agave nectar (to taste)
- [Optional] Pinch of ground cloves or nutmeg for added spice
- [Optional] Extra toasted coconut flakes for garnish

## Instructions:

1. **Toast the Coconut:** In a dry skillet, toast the shredded coconut over medium heat for 2-3 minutes, stirring frequently, until golden brown and fragrant. Set aside.
2. **Brew the Chai Tea:** Brew the chai tea by steeping the tea bag or loose-leaf tea in 1 cup of hot water for about 5 minutes, or until strong and flavorful.
3. **Heat the Milk:** In a small pot, heat the coconut milk over medium heat until warm but not boiling.
4. **Add Spices:** Stir in the cinnamon, ginger, cardamom, and maple syrup (or agave nectar). Taste and adjust sweetness if desired.
5. **Combine the Tea and Milk:** Pour the brewed chai tea into a mug, then slowly pour in the spiced coconut milk. Stir gently to combine.
6. **Garnish and Serve:** Top with a sprinkle of toasted coconut and, if desired, a pinch of ground cloves or nutmeg. Serve immediately and enjoy the warmth and comfort of your toasted coconut chai.

## Tips and Recommendations:

- **For a Creamier Texture:** Use full-fat coconut milk for a richer, creamier latte.
- **Adjusting Spice Levels:** If you prefer a spicier chai, increase the amount of cinnamon, ginger, or cardamom according to your taste.
- **Sweeteners:** Feel free to use other sweeteners such as coconut sugar, brown sugar, or stevia if preferred.
- **Chilled Version:** To enjoy this drink cold, brew the tea and let it cool, then serve over ice with cold coconut milk.
- **Extra Toasted Coconut:** For an added coconut boost, sprinkle extra toasted coconut on top of your latte for texture and flavor.

## Variations:

- **Coconut Vanilla Chai:** Add a few drops of vanilla extract to the milk mixture for a sweet, comforting twist.
- **Iced Toasted Coconut Chai:** Brew the chai tea and let it cool. Then serve over ice with cold coconut milk and toasted coconut on top.
- **Chocolate Toasted Coconut Chai:** Add a teaspoon of cocoa powder to the milk mixture for a rich, chocolatey flavor paired with the tropical coconut.

## Pairing Suggestions:

- **Vegan Cinnamon Rolls:** The warmth of cinnamon rolls pairs beautifully with the spicy sweetness of this chai latte.
- **Almond Biscotti:** The crunchy texture of almond biscotti complements the smooth, creamy drink.
- **Tropical Fruit Salad:** A refreshing fruit salad with pineapple, mango, and coconut will enhance the coconut flavor in this drink.

## Interesting Fact:

Did you know that **chai** is a Hindi word meaning "tea," and it's traditionally brewed with a blend of spices, such as cinnamon, cardamom, and ginger? It's a staple in Indian culture, often enjoyed with family and friends.

## Cultural Connection:

Chai has a long-standing tradition in India, where it's often brewed fresh in homes and street stalls, creating a sense of community. The drink has traveled the world and has become beloved in many cultures, especially for its bold, spicy flavor and warming qualities. Toasting coconut adds a modern twist to this timeless favorite.

# Chocolate Mint Rooibos Latte

*Indulge in the perfect balance of sweet chocolate and refreshing mint with a Chocolate Mint Rooibos Latte, an innovative non-coffee drink that combines the smooth, earthy flavor of rooibos tea with the rich decadence of cocoa and a hint of mint. This delightful, caffeine-free treat is perfect for cozy evenings or as a soothing afternoon pick-me-up. Its creamy texture and fragrant minty notes will transport you to a peaceful, relaxing moment, no matter the season. It's the perfect drink for those who crave a dessert-like experience without the coffee!*

## Ingredients:

- 1 rooibos tea bag (or 1 tbsp loose-leaf rooibos tea)
- 1 cup almond milk (or any plant-based milk)
- 1 tbsp cocoa powder (unsweetened)
- 1/2 tsp peppermint extract
- 1-2 tsps maple syrup or agave nectar (to taste)
- 2 tbsps dark chocolate (chopped, for melting)
- [Optional] Whipped coconut cream (for topping)
- [Optional] Fresh mint leaves (for garnish)

## Instructions:

1. **Brew the Rooibos Tea:** Brew the rooibos tea by steeping the tea bag or loose-leaf tea in 1 cup of hot water for 5-7 minutes, or until the tea is strong and flavorful.
2. **Heat the Milk:** In a small pot, heat the almond milk over medium heat until warm but not boiling.
3. **Mix in the Cocoa and Sweetener:** Stir in the cocoa powder and maple syrup (or agave nectar) to the warmed milk. Whisk until the cocoa powder dissolves completely and the mixture is smooth.
4. **Melt the Chocolate:** In a separate bowl or small pot, melt the dark chocolate over low heat, stirring until smooth.
5. **Combine the Tea and Chocolate Mixture:** Add the brewed rooibos tea to the chocolate milk mixture and stir to combine. Add the peppermint extract and mix well.
6. **Serve and Garnish:** Pour the chocolate mint rooibos latte into a mug. Top with whipped coconut cream and garnish with fresh mint leaves for an extra touch of indulgence.
7. **Enjoy:** Sip slowly, savoring the creamy, minty, chocolatey goodness.

## Tips and Recommendations:

- **Dairy-Free Option:** For a richer flavor, try using coconut milk or oat milk instead of almond milk.
- **Extra Minty:** Increase the amount of peppermint extract to make the mint flavor more pronounced, or garnish with extra fresh mint.
- **Vegan Whipped Cream:** If you're looking for a vegan-friendly topping, whipped coconut cream is a delicious alternative to traditional cream.
- **Adjust Sweetness:** Taste the latte before serving and adjust the sweetness with more maple syrup or agave nectar, depending on your preference.

## Variations:

- **Chocolate Mocha Mint:** Add a shot of espresso or decaf espresso for a slight coffee flavor that enhances the chocolate and mint.
- **Iced Chocolate Mint Rooibos:** Allow the brewed rooibos tea to cool and serve the chocolate mint latte over ice for a refreshing, cold version.
- **Spicy Chocolate Mint:** Add a pinch of ground cinnamon or cayenne pepper for a spicy kick that complements the chocolate and mint flavors.

## Pairing Suggestions:

- **Vegan Chocolate Chip Cookies:** The rich flavor of chocolate chips pairs perfectly with the smooth, minty chocolate latte.
- **Almond Biscotti:** A crunchy biscotti complements the creamy, decadent texture of the latte.
- **Coconut Macaroons:** The chewy texture and coconut flavor of macaroons will enhance the tropical notes in the drink.

## Interesting Fact:

Did you know that **rooibos** is a plant native to South Africa and is known for its naturally sweet flavor and numerous health benefits, including being rich in antioxidants?

## Cultural Connection:

Rooibos tea has been enjoyed in South Africa for centuries, where it is often sipped as a traditional beverage. Its calming, caffeine-free properties have made it a popular choice around the world, especially in modern tea lattes, like this creative chocolate mint version.

# Apricot Vanilla Oolong Latte

*Delight in the subtle elegance of the Apricot Vanilla Oolong Latte, a beautifully balanced drink that combines the floral complexity of oolong tea with the delicate sweetness of apricot and the warm, aromatic touch of vanilla. This non-coffee latte is the perfect choice for anyone seeking a sophisticated, caffeine-free indulgence. The smooth, fruity notes of apricot blend seamlessly with the earthy undertones of oolong tea, while the vanilla adds a comforting, aromatic sweetness. It's a lovely, refreshing drink to enjoy on its own or paired with your favorite snacks.*

## Ingredients:

- 1 oolong tea bag (or 1 tbsp loose-leaf oolong tea)
- 1 cup oat milk (or any plant-based milk of your choice)
- 1 tbsp apricot jam or apricot puree
- 1/2 tsp vanilla extract
- 1-2 tsps maple syrup or agave nectar (to taste)
- [Optional] 1/4 tsp ground cinnamon (for a warm spice touch)
- [Optional] Whipped coconut cream (for topping)
- [Optional] Dried apricot slices (for garnish)

## Instructions:

1. **Brew the Oolong Tea:** Steep the oolong tea bag or loose-leaf tea in 1 cup of hot water for 3-5 minutes, depending on how strong you like your tea.
2. **Heat the Milk:** In a small pot, heat the oat milk over medium heat until warm but not boiling.
3. **Mix in the Apricot Jam and Vanilla:** Stir in the apricot jam (or apricot puree), vanilla extract, and maple syrup (or agave nectar) to the warm milk. Whisk until smooth and the jam is fully dissolved.
4. **Combine the Tea and Milk:** Pour the brewed oolong tea into a mug, then slowly add the apricot vanilla milk mixture, stirring gently.
5. **Serve and Garnish:** Top with whipped coconut cream for added richness, and garnish with dried apricot slices for an extra touch of flavor and elegance.
6. **Enjoy:** Sip slowly and savor the perfect harmony of fruity apricot, aromatic vanilla, and floral oolong.

## Tips and Recommendations:

- **Dairy-Free Option:** For a richer, creamier texture, try using coconut milk or cashew milk instead of oat milk.
- **Extra Sweetness:** Adjust the sweetness by adding more maple syrup or agave nectar if you prefer a sweeter drink.
- **Spiced Option:** For a cozy twist, add a pinch of ground cinnamon or cardamom to the milk mixture for a hint of spice.
- **Frothy Texture:** For a frothy texture, use a milk frother or whisk the milk vigorously as it heats.

## Variations:

- **Iced Apricot Vanilla Oolong Latte:** Allow the tea and milk mixture to cool, then serve over ice for a refreshing summer version.
- **Apricot Ginger Latte:** Add a small piece of fresh ginger to the milk mixture for a spicy kick that pairs wonderfully with the apricot.
- **Vanilla Almond Oolong Latte:** Replace vanilla extract with almond extract for a nutty, fragrant twist.

## Pairing Suggestions:

- **Almond Biscotti:** The crisp, almond-flavored biscotti complements the smooth, creamy texture of the latte.
- **Vegan Scones:** Serve with a warm, flaky scone for a traditional tea-time experience.
- **Fruit Salad:** The lightness of a fresh fruit salad pairs well with the fruity apricot flavor in the latte.

## Interesting Fact:

Did you know that **oolong tea** is often referred to as "the champagne of teas"? It's prized for its delicate, floral aroma and smooth, complex flavor.

## Cultural Connection:

Oolong tea has a rich history in China and Taiwan, where it is celebrated for its traditional role in tea ceremonies. It's a drink often enjoyed slowly, as its flavor changes and develops with each sip, making it the perfect base for creative tea lattes like this one.

# Peppermint Stick Tea Latte

*Indulge in the soothing, refreshing flavors of the Peppermint Stick Tea Latte, a delightful combination of cool, crisp peppermint and creamy, frothy milk that is perfect for cozy winter evenings or anytime you crave a comforting treat. The natural minty taste, paired with the velvety texture of steamed milk, makes this a wonderfully festive drink. Whether you're sipping by the fireplace or relaxing with a good book, this non-coffee latte will warm both your body and soul.*

## Ingredients:

- 1 peppermint tea bag (or 1 tbsp loose-leaf peppermint tea)
- 1 cup oat milk (or any plant-based milk of your choice)
- 1 tbsp maple syrup or agave nectar (to taste)
- 1/2 tsp vanilla extract
- 1/2 tsp crushed peppermint candy or peppermint extract
- [Optional] 1/4 tsp ground cinnamon (for an extra warmth)
- [Optional] Whipped coconut cream (for topping)
- [Optional] Crushed candy canes or peppermint sticks (for garnish)

## Instructions:

1. **Brew the Peppermint Tea:** Steep the peppermint tea bag (or loose-leaf tea) in 1 cup of hot water for 4-5 minutes, depending on how strong you like the mint flavor.
2. **Heat the Milk:** In a small pot, heat the oat milk over medium heat until it's warm but not boiling.
3. **Flavor the Milk:** Stir in the maple syrup (or agave nectar), vanilla extract, and crushed peppermint candy (or a few drops of peppermint extract). Mix until the candy is dissolved and the milk is fully infused with the minty flavor.
4. **Combine Tea and Milk:** Pour the brewed peppermint tea into a mug, then gently add the flavored milk mixture. Stir to combine.
5. **Serve and Garnish:** Top with a dollop of whipped coconut cream, and sprinkle with crushed candy canes or garnish with a peppermint stick for an extra festive touch.
6. **Enjoy:** Sip slowly and let the minty goodness relax your senses!

## Tips and Recommendations:

- **Extra Minty:** For an added mint flavor, increase the amount of crushed peppermint or peppermint extract.
- **Sweetness Adjustments:** Customize the sweetness by adding more maple syrup or agave nectar to suit your taste.
- **Frothy Texture:** For a frothy latte, use a milk frother or whisk the milk vigorously as it heats.
- **Spice Variation:** If you like a little spice, try adding a dash of ground cinnamon or nutmeg to the milk for added warmth and flavor.

## Variations:

- **Iced Peppermint Stick Latte:** Let the tea and milk mixture cool, then serve over ice for a refreshing, cool version of this latte.
- **Chocolate Peppermint Latte:** Stir in a tablespoon of cocoa powder or melted dark chocolate to create a rich, chocolatey twist.
- **Sugar-Free Version:** Use stevia or monk fruit sweetener in place of maple syrup for a low-sugar version of this festive treat.

## Pairing Suggestions:

- **Vegan Shortbread Cookies:** Pair your peppermint stick latte with buttery vegan shortbread cookies for a lovely balance of flavors.
- **Vegan Chocolate Cake:** A slice of rich vegan chocolate cake pairs beautifully with the minty notes of this latte.
- **Crispy Almond Biscotti:** The crisp texture of almond biscotti complements the smooth, creamy texture of the latte.

## Interesting Fact:

Did you know that peppermint has been used for centuries for its calming and medicinal properties? It is known to help relieve headaches, ease digestive issues, and promote relaxation - perfect for a cozy beverage!

## Cultural Connection:

Peppermint is a popular flavor in many cultures, especially during the winter months. It's often associated with holiday traditions, and in some cultures, it's believed to have soothing properties for both the body and the mind. This **Peppermint Stick Tea Latte** draws from those traditions, offering a modern, dairy-free twist on a classic flavor combination.

# Maple Cinnamon Spice Tea

*Warm up with a cup of Maple Cinnamon Spice Tea, a cozy and aromatic beverage that combines the sweetness of pure maple syrup with the comforting warmth of cinnamon and spice. This tea is the perfect antidote to chilly weather, providing a rich, heartwarming experience. With a balance of spicy and sweet flavors, it's a delightful drink to sip on during the fall and winter months or whenever you need a little extra comfort in your day.*

## Ingredients:

- 1 black tea bag (or 1 tbsp loose-leaf black tea)
- 1/2 tsp ground cinnamon
- 1/4 tsp ground ginger
- 1 tbsp pure maple syrup
- 1 cup hot water
- 1/2 cup almond milk (or any plant-based milk of your choice)
- [Optional] 1/4 tsp ground nutmeg (for extra spice)
- [Optional] Cinnamon stick (for garnish)
- [Optional] Vegan whipped cream (for topping)

## Instructions:

1. **Brew the Tea:** Steep the black tea bag (or loose-leaf tea) in 1 cup of hot water for 3-5 minutes, depending on your preferred strength.
2. **Prepare the Spices:** While the tea is brewing, in a small bowl, combine the ground cinnamon and ginger (and nutmeg, if using).
3. **Infuse the Tea:** After brewing the tea, add the cinnamon and ginger blend to the tea and stir to combine. Let it steep for an additional 2-3 minutes to allow the spices to infuse.
4. **Sweeten the Tea:** Stir in the pure maple syrup for a natural sweetness that balances the spices.
5. **Heat the Milk:** In a small pot, warm the almond milk over medium heat, but don't let it boil.
6. **Combine and Serve:** Pour the spiced tea into a mug and add the warm almond milk. Stir gently to mix everything together.
7. **Garnish and Enjoy:** Optionally, top with a dollop of vegan whipped cream and a cinnamon stick for an elegant finish. Sip and enjoy the cozy, spiced goodness!

## Tips and Recommendations:

- **Adjust Sweetness:** If you prefer a sweeter drink, feel free to add more maple syrup or even a splash of agave nectar.
- **Stronger Spice Flavor:** For an extra kick, add more ground ginger or even a pinch of cloves.
- **Milk Variations:** For a creamier texture, use coconut milk or cashew milk, both of which complement the spices beautifully.
- **Tea Strength:** If you prefer a stronger tea base, steep the tea bag for a bit longer or add an extra bag.

## Variations:

- **Iced Maple Cinnamon Spice Tea:** Let the tea and milk mixture cool, then serve over ice for a refreshing twist on this spiced beverage.
- **Maple Chai Spice Tea:** Swap out the black tea for a chai tea bag, and add an extra pinch of cardamom for a bold, flavorful twist.
- **Vanilla Maple Cinnamon Tea:** Add a dash of vanilla extract to the tea for a sweet, creamy layer of flavor.

## Pairing Suggestions:

- **Vegan Scones:** Enjoy this comforting tea with flaky, plant-based scones for a delicious afternoon treat.
- **Vegan Oatmeal Cookies:** The cinnamon and maple flavors will pair wonderfully with warm, chewy oatmeal cookies.
- **Toasty Vegan Bread:** Pair with a slice of warm vegan cinnamon raisin bread to complement the spiced flavors.

## Interesting Fact:

Did you know that cinnamon has been used for thousands of years, not just for flavor, but also for its health benefits? It's known to help regulate blood sugar levels and has anti-inflammatory properties!

## Cultural Connection:

Maple syrup has deep roots in North American culture, especially in regions like Canada and the northeastern United States, where it's harvested each spring. This **Maple Cinnamon Spice Tea** combines the classic flavors of maple syrup with the beloved spices of cinnamon and ginger, making it a perfect seasonal drink that's both comforting and rich in tradition.

# Lavender Mint White Hot Cocoa

*Indulge in the soothing, aromatic blend of Lavender Mint White Hot Cocoa, a refreshing twist on classic hot chocolate. This velvety cocoa is infused with calming lavender and refreshing mint, creating a delicate and luxurious flavor profile. The creamy sweetness of white chocolate combines beautifully with these floral and herbal notes, offering a relaxing drink perfect for unwinding after a long day or enjoying as a cozy treat on chilly evenings. A true comfort drink with a touch of elegance.*

## Ingredients:

- 1 cup almond milk (or any plant-based milk)
- 1/2 cup white chocolate chips (vegan, if desired)
- 1 tbsp dried lavender buds
- 1/2 tsp peppermint extract
- 1/4 tsp vanilla extract
- 1/2 tsp maple syrup (or to taste)
- [Optional] Vegan whipped cream for topping
- [Optional] Fresh mint sprig for garnish
- [Optional] Dried lavender buds for garnish

## Instructions:

1. **Prepare the Lavender Infusion:** In a small saucepan, combine the almond milk and dried lavender buds. Heat over medium heat, stirring occasionally, until the milk is hot but not boiling (about 4-5 minutes).
2. **Strain the Lavender Milk:** Once the milk is infused with the lavender, strain the milk through a fine mesh strainer to remove the lavender buds, then return the infused milk to the saucepan.
3. **Melt the White Chocolate:** Add the white chocolate chips to the strained lavender milk. Stir gently until the chocolate has completely melted, and the milk is smooth and creamy.
4. **Add the Mint and Sweetener:** Stir in the peppermint extract and vanilla extract. Adjust sweetness by adding maple syrup to taste.
5. **Serve and Garnish:** Pour the lavender mint white hot cocoa into your favorite mug. If desired, top with a dollop of vegan whipped cream, a sprig of fresh mint, and a sprinkle of dried lavender buds for a fragrant finish.
6. **Enjoy:** Sip slowly and enjoy the calming, luxurious flavors of your homemade cocoa.

## Tips and Recommendations:

- **Stronger Lavender Flavor:** If you prefer a more pronounced lavender taste, you can steep the lavender in the milk for a little longer (up to 7 minutes).
- **Mint Adjustments:** If you want a more intense mint flavor, increase the peppermint extract to 1 teaspoon or add a couple of crushed fresh mint leaves during the infusion step for extra freshness.

- **Sweetness:** Adjust the maple syrup to suit your taste, or substitute with agave nectar or coconut sugar for a different sweetness profile.
- **Vegan White Chocolate:** Look for high-quality vegan white chocolate that's creamy and smooth for the best results.

## Variations:

- **Iced Lavender Mint Hot Cocoa:** Let the cocoa cool and serve it over ice for a refreshing iced version of this indulgent drink.
- **Lavender Mint Mocha Cocoa:** For a richer flavor, add 1 tablespoon of cocoa powder or a shot of espresso (if you want a mild coffee flavor) to your white hot cocoa for a mocha twist.
- **Lavender Mint Cocoa with Coconut Milk:** For a tropical twist, substitute almond milk with creamy coconut milk. This variation adds a richer texture and a subtle coconut flavor.

## Pairing Suggestions:

- **Vegan Shortbread Cookies:** The buttery sweetness of shortbread will complement the floral and minty flavors of the hot cocoa.
- **Cranberry Scones:** A tangy, fruity scone pairs beautifully with the soothing notes of lavender and mint.
- **Vegan Chocolate Truffles:** Rich, decadent truffles make for the perfect sweet treat alongside this creamy drink.

## Interesting Fact:

Lavender has been used for centuries not only for its delightful fragrance but also for its calming effects. It's known to reduce anxiety and promote relaxation - perfect for an evening of unwinding.

## Cultural Connection:

Lavender is often associated with Provence, France, where fields of the fragrant herb bloom every summer. Combining this timeless ingredient with the refreshing qualities of mint creates a blend that's both sophisticated and soothing, making **Lavender Mint White Hot Cocoa** a luxurious treat inspired by European herbal traditions.

# Pineapple Ginger Green Tea Latte

*Escape to a tropical paradise with the Pineapple Ginger Green Tea Latte, where the bright, citrusy notes of pineapple meet the warming spice of fresh ginger, all balanced by the earthy richness of green tea. This refreshing and health-boosting drink is perfect for anyone seeking a flavorful, vibrant alternative to traditional hot beverages. The combination of ginger's zing, pineapple's sweetness, and the gentle smoothness of green tea will transport your senses, leaving you feeling invigorated and relaxed at the same time.*

## Ingredients:

- 1 cup brewed green tea (preferably loose leaf or high-quality tea bags)
- 1/2 cup unsweetened pineapple juice (fresh or from a carton)
- 1/2 tsp fresh ginger, grated
- 1 tbsp maple syrup (or sweetener of choice)
- 1/2 cup coconut milk (or other plant-based milk)
- 1/4 tsp vanilla extract
- [Optional] Pineapple slices for garnish
- [Optional] Ground ginger for a finishing touch

## Instructions:

1. **Brew the Green Tea:** Brew your green tea using your preferred method, either from loose leaf or tea bags. Allow it to steep for 3-4 minutes, then remove the tea bags or strain out the leaves.
2. **Prepare the Ginger Pineapple Mixture:** In a small saucepan, combine the pineapple juice and grated ginger. Heat over medium heat, stirring occasionally, until it's warm but not boiling (about 2-3 minutes).
3. **Sweeten the Mixture:** Add the maple syrup (or your preferred sweetener) to the pineapple and ginger mixture. Stir to dissolve, then remove from heat.
4. **Combine the Tea and Pineapple Ginger Mix:** Pour the brewed green tea into a large mug or glass. Add the warm pineapple-ginger mixture and stir to combine.
5. **Add Coconut Milk and Vanilla:** In the same saucepan or a separate small pot, heat the coconut milk over low heat until it's warm but not boiling. Stir in the vanilla extract.
6. **Froth the Coconut Milk:** Use a milk frother or whisk to froth the warm coconut milk until it's creamy and slightly foamy.
7. **Assemble the Latte:** Pour the frothed coconut milk on top of the green tea and pineapple-ginger mixture, creating a creamy, frothy layer.
8. **Serve and Garnish:** For an extra tropical touch, garnish with a slice of fresh pineapple or a sprinkle of ground ginger. Serve immediately and enjoy the vibrant, soothing flavors.

## Tips and Recommendations:

- **Adjusting Sweetness:** Depending on your preference, you can adjust the sweetness of this drink by adding more maple syrup or using a natural sweetener like agave nectar or stevia.
- **Fresh Ginger:** Freshly grated ginger provides the best flavor and potency, but if you prefer a milder taste, you can reduce the amount or substitute with ginger powder (1/4 teaspoon).
- **Coconut Milk Alternatives:** For a lighter version, you can use almond milk or oat milk. If you prefer a richer taste, try using full-fat coconut milk.
- **Serving Tip:** For a more tropical presentation, serve in a clear glass mug to showcase the beautiful layers of tea, pineapple, and frothy coconut milk.

## Variations:

- **Iced Pineapple Ginger Green Tea Latte:** Let the drink cool down and serve it over ice for a refreshing iced version. This is perfect for warmer weather or a chilled pick-me-up.
- **Pineapple Ginger Chai Latte:** Add 1/4 teaspoon of ground cinnamon and 1/4 teaspoon of ground cloves to give the drink a spiced chai twist.
- **Pineapple Ginger Lemonade Latte:** For a tangier flavor, replace some of the pineapple juice with fresh lemon juice. This gives a citrusy, zingy contrast to the creamy coconut milk.

## Pairing Suggestions:

- **Coconut Macaroons:** These sweet, chewy treats pair beautifully with the tropical flavors of pineapple and coconut.
- **Avocado Toast:** A savory snack like avocado toast will balance the drink's sweetness and add a nice contrast of textures.
- **Vegan Banana Bread:** The sweetness and warmth of banana bread complement the tropical and spicy flavors of this latte.

## Interesting Fact:

Did you know that **ginger** has been used for thousands of years in traditional medicine for its ability to reduce nausea, improve digestion, and reduce inflammation? It's a perfect addition to this refreshing, healing drink.

# Blueberry Basil White Tea

*Introducing the Blueberry Basil White Tea, a sophisticated and refreshing drink that combines the delicate flavors of white tea with the sweet, fruity notes of blueberries and the aromatic, herbal zing of fresh basil. This unique infusion is a perfect balance of sweet, savory, and floral elements, creating a cup that is both calming and invigorating. Whether you're winding down after a long day or looking for a creative twist on your daily tea routine, this tea offers a rejuvenating experience with every sip.*

## Ingredients:

- 1 tsp high-quality white tea leaves (or 1 white tea bag)
- 1/2 cup fresh blueberries (or frozen)
- 2-3 fresh basil leaves, torn or chopped
- 1 tbsp honey or maple syrup (optional, adjust to taste)
- 1 cup hot water (not boiling, around 170°F/77°C)
- [Optional] Lemon slice for garnish
- [Optional] Additional blueberries for garnish

## Instructions:

1. **Prepare the White Tea:** Heat water to about 170°F (77°C) or just below boiling. Place the white tea leaves or tea bag in your teapot or cup.
2. **Infuse the Blueberries and Basil:** Add the fresh or frozen blueberries and torn basil leaves to the hot water with the tea. Stir gently to help release the flavors.
3. **Steep the Tea:** Allow the tea to steep for 4-5 minutes, ensuring the flavors from the blueberries and basil are fully infused into the tea. If you prefer a stronger tea, you can let it steep a bit longer, but be mindful not to over-steep the delicate white tea.
4. **Sweeten the Tea:** Remove the tea bag or strain out the tea leaves. Stir in honey or maple syrup if desired, adjusting the sweetness to your taste.
5. **Serve and Garnish:** Pour the tea into your favorite cup. Garnish with a fresh lemon slice and extra blueberries for a refreshing and visually appealing touch. Serve hot and enjoy the light, aromatic infusion.

## Tips and Recommendations:

- **Experiment with Herbs:** Try adding a small sprig of mint alongside the basil for an added layer of freshness.
- **Cold Brew Option:** For a chilled version, brew the tea as directed, let it cool, then refrigerate it for 1-2 hours. Serve over ice for a refreshing summer drink.
- **Adjusting Sweetness:** For a more naturally sweet taste, try using agave syrup or stevia, or simply let the natural sweetness of the blueberries shine through without any added sugar.
- **Enhanced Flavor:** Add a pinch of dried lavender for a floral twist or a slice of ginger for a slight zing.

## Variations:

- **Blueberry Lavender Basil White Tea:** Add a small spoonful of dried lavender buds for a calming floral note that complements the basil and blueberry flavors.
- **Blueberry Lemon Basil White Tea:** Swap out the lemon garnish for a bit of lemon zest during the steeping process to enhance the citrusy brightness.
- **Blueberry Green Tea:** For a more robust tea, substitute the white tea with green tea leaves, which pair wonderfully with the blueberries and basil.

## Pairing Suggestions:

- **Vegan Scones:** A buttery, vegan-friendly scone with a hint of lemon or vanilla will complement the herbal and fruity flavors of this tea.
- **Light Salads:** Pair this tea with a simple mixed greens salad topped with balsamic vinaigrette for a refreshing, light meal.
- **Almond Biscotti:** A crunchy almond biscotti is a perfect snack to dip in the warmth of this delicate tea.

## Interesting Fact:

Did you know that **white tea** is made from the youngest buds of the tea plant, giving it a delicate flavor and a higher concentration of antioxidants than other types of tea? It's often praised for its health benefits, including boosting skin health and improving cardiovascular health.

## Cultural Connection:

White tea is often associated with Chinese tea culture, where it's traditionally consumed for its pure, unadulterated taste. This **Blueberry Basil White Tea** puts a modern, creative twist on the classic by incorporating fresh fruit and herbs, merging East and West in one delightful cup.

# Cranberry Orange Rooibos Latte

*Warm up with a comforting Cranberry Orange Rooibos Latte, where the naturally sweet, earthy notes of rooibos tea meet the tangy brightness of cranberries and the refreshing zest of orange. This festive, vegan-friendly latte is the perfect way to cozy up on chilly days, offering a caffeine-free alternative that's both soothing and packed with flavor. With the deep, rich flavor of rooibos as the base, the cranberry and orange combination adds a vibrant burst that will uplift your spirits with each sip.*

## Ingredients:

- 1 tbsp rooibos tea leaves (or 1 rooibos tea bag)
- 1/4 cup fresh cranberries (or frozen)
- 1 tbsp orange zest (about 1 small orange)
- 1 cup water
- 1/2 cup unsweetened almond milk (or any plant-based milk of choice)
- 1 tbsp maple syrup (or sweetener of choice, adjust to taste)
- [Optional] Cinnamon stick or a pinch of ground cinnamon for garnish
- [Optional] Orange slice for garnish

## Instructions:

1. **Brew the Rooibos Tea:** In a small saucepan, bring 1 cup of water to a boil. Add the rooibos tea leaves or tea bag and let steep for 5-7 minutes, depending on your preferred strength.
2. **Prepare the Cranberries and Orange:** While the tea is steeping, add the fresh or frozen cranberries and orange zest to a separate saucepan. Cook over medium heat, mashing the cranberries gently to release their juices. Stir occasionally and cook for about 3-5 minutes until the cranberries have softened and the mixture becomes slightly syrupy.
3. **Combine the Tea and Cranberry Mixture:** Once the rooibos tea has steeped, strain out the tea leaves or remove the tea bag. Pour the brewed rooibos into the saucepan with the cranberry mixture, stirring well to combine. Add maple syrup to taste and let simmer on low for 2-3 minutes, allowing the flavors to meld.
4. **Froth the Milk:** In a separate pan or using a milk frother, heat the almond milk (or your chosen plant-based milk) until hot but not boiling. Froth it until it becomes silky and creamy.
5. **Assemble the Latte:** Pour the cranberry-orange rooibos mixture into your cup, then gently pour the steamed, frothed milk on top.
6. **Garnish and Serve:** For an extra festive touch, garnish with a cinnamon stick or a sprinkle of ground cinnamon. Add a slice of orange on the rim of your cup for a pop of color and a hint of citrus fragrance.

## Tips and Recommendations:

- **Sweetness Adjustment:** If you prefer a sweeter latte, adjust the amount of maple syrup or use your favorite sweetener to taste. You can also experiment with agave syrup or coconut sugar for a different flavor profile.
- **Milk Alternatives:** The creaminess of coconut milk works wonderfully in this recipe, adding a subtle sweetness. For a lighter option, try oat milk or rice milk.
- **Cold Brew Option:** For a refreshing summer twist, make a cold brew version of this latte by cooling the cranberry-rooibos mixture and serving it over ice, topped with chilled frothed milk.
- **Add a Spice Kick:** For a bit of extra warmth, try adding a pinch of ground ginger or cloves to the cranberry mixture while it simmers.

## Variations:

- **Spiced Cranberry Orange Rooibos Latte:** Add a pinch of ground cinnamon, cloves, or nutmeg to the cranberry mixture for a spiced version that's perfect for the colder months.
- **Vanilla Cranberry Orange Rooibos Latte:** Stir in a few drops of vanilla extract into the brewed tea for a warm, comforting flavor that pairs perfectly with the cranberry and orange.
- **Cranberry Lemon Rooibos Latte:** Swap the orange zest for lemon zest for a more tart, citrusy twist.

## Pairing Suggestions:

- **Vegan Shortbread Cookies:** The rich, buttery flavor of vegan shortbread pairs beautifully with the fruity and warm flavors of the cranberry orange rooibos latte.
- **Vegan Chocolate Cake:** The deep flavors of a rich, dairy-free chocolate cake contrast nicely with the fruity and floral rooibos base of the latte.
- **Toasted Almonds:** A light, salty snack like toasted almonds or cashews can enhance the sweetness of the drink and add a satisfying crunch.

# MOCKTAILS AND CREATIVE CONCOCTIONS:

# Virgin Espresso Martini

*Who says you need alcohol to enjoy the smooth, luxurious vibes of an espresso martini? This Virgin Espresso Martini gives you all the rich, coffee-forward flavor of the classic cocktail without the booze, making it a perfect choice for anyone seeking a sophisticated, caffeine-packed mocktail. With a blend of fresh espresso, coffee liqueur-flavored syrup, and a touch of sweetness, this drink is ideal for elevating any occasion - whether it's a cozy evening in or a chic gathering with friends. Get ready to indulge in a delightful, energizing treat!*

## Ingredients:

- 1 shot (1 ounce) of freshly brewed espresso
- 1 tbsp coffee-flavored syrup (or substitute with simple syrup and a drop of vanilla extract)
- 1/2 cup ice cubes
- 1/4 cup chilled almond milk (or your preferred plant-based milk)
- 1/4 tsp vanilla extract (optional, for extra depth of flavor)
- [Optional] Coffee beans for garnish
- [Optional] Cocoa powder or cinnamon for garnish

## Instructions:

1. **Brew the Espresso:** Begin by brewing a fresh shot of espresso. Make sure it's hot and rich to form the base of your mocktail.
2. **Prepare the Shaker:** Fill a cocktail shaker with the ice cubes.
3. **Mix the Ingredients:** Add the brewed espresso, coffee-flavored syrup, and almond milk (or chosen plant-based milk) into the shaker. If you're using vanilla extract, add it now.
4. **Shake Well:** Seal the shaker and shake vigorously for 10-15 seconds. The goal is to create a frothy, creamy texture and cool down the drink.
5. **Serve:** Strain the mixture into a chilled martini glass, ensuring the foam settles nicely on top.
6. **Garnish and Enjoy:** Garnish with a few coffee beans or a sprinkle of cocoa powder or cinnamon for added elegance and flavor. Serve immediately.

## Tips and Recommendations:

- **Sweetness Level:** Adjust the sweetness by adding more or less coffee-flavored syrup, or even using flavored syrups like caramel or hazelnut for a twist.
- **For a Frothy Texture:** If you prefer extra foam, froth your milk using a milk frother before adding it to the shaker.
- **Caffeine Kick:** If you're craving a stronger coffee flavor, simply add a second shot of espresso or use a stronger coffee syrup.
- **Chill the Glass:** For an extra cool presentation, chill your martini glass by filling it with ice and water before serving the mocktail.

## Variations:

- **Minty Virgin Espresso Martini:** Add a few fresh mint leaves to the shaker for a refreshing twist. Shake well and strain the mixture into your glass for a cool, herbal touch.
- **Chocolate Espresso Martini:** Drizzle some chocolate syrup into the glass before pouring in the mocktail for a delicious, chocolatey finish.
- **Nutty Espresso Martini:** Add a tablespoon of almond syrup or hazelnut syrup to the mix for a nutty, rich flavor.
- **Spicy Espresso Martini:** Add a pinch of ground cinnamon or a dash of cayenne pepper for a little spice and warmth.

## Pairing Suggestions:

- **Vegan Chocolate Mousse:** The rich, creamy texture of a vegan chocolate mousse pairs perfectly with the bold flavors of this mocktail.
- **Vegan Dark Chocolate Truffles:** The deep, slightly bitter taste of dark chocolate complements the smoothness of the espresso and coffee notes in the drink.
- **Vegan Caramel Popcorn:** Sweet and salty caramel popcorn adds a fun, crunchy contrast to the smoothness of the mocktail.

## Interesting Fact:

Did you know that **espresso martinis** were invented by bartender Dick Bradsell in the 1980s? The story goes that a customer asked for a drink that would "wake me up and then f*** me up" - and the espresso martini was born! This virgin version keeps the same bold flavors, minus the alcohol.

## Cultural Connection:

The **Espresso Martini** became popular in the 1980s, particularly in London, as an after-dinner drink that combined the richness of coffee with the elegance of a martini. Though originally an alcoholic beverage, the "virgin" version makes the espresso martini accessible to anyone, allowing you to indulge in its sophisticated flavors without the alcohol.

# Berry Mojito Mocktail

*Get ready for a refreshing burst of flavor with this Berry Mojito Mocktail - a vibrant, non-alcoholic twist on the classic Cuban cocktail. Infused with the zesty freshness of lime, the coolness of mint, and a blend of juicy berries, this mocktail is perfect for sipping on a warm afternoon or serving at a lively get-together. The sweet-tart berries and fragrant mint provide a lively balance, while the sparkling water gives it a crisp finish. Whether you're hosting friends or just treating yourself, this berry-packed mojito mocktail will be a hit!*

## Ingredients:

- 1/4 cup mixed berries (strawberries, raspberries, blueberries, or blackberries)
- 6-8 fresh mint leaves
- 1 tbsp fresh lime juice (about half a lime)
- 1 tbsp agave syrup or maple syrup (adjust to taste)
- 1/2 cup sparkling water (or club soda)
- 1/4 cup ice cubes
- [Optional] 1-2 slices of lime for garnish
- [Optional] Fresh mint sprigs for garnish
- [Optional] Additional berries for garnish

## Instructions:

1. **Muddle the Berries and Mint:** In a cocktail shaker or sturdy glass, add the mixed berries and mint leaves. Use a muddler or the back of a spoon to gently press the ingredients, releasing the juices and essential oils from the berries and mint.
2. **Add Lime and Sweetener:** Pour in the fresh lime juice and agave syrup (or maple syrup) to the muddled mix. Stir to combine, ensuring the syrup dissolves evenly.
3. **Add Ice and Mix:** Fill the shaker or glass with ice cubes and pour in the sparkling water or club soda. Secure the lid (if using a shaker) and shake gently for a few seconds, or stir well if mixing by hand.
4. **Serve:** Strain the mocktail into a tall glass filled with ice.
5. **Garnish and Enjoy:** Garnish with fresh mint sprigs, lime slices, and a few whole berries for a festive and colorful touch. Serve immediately and enjoy the refreshing, fruity flavors.

## Tips and Recommendations:

- **Adjust Sweetness:** You can adjust the sweetness by adding more or less agave syrup or maple syrup, depending on your taste preference. If you prefer a sugar-free option, you can use a stevia-based sweetener.
- **Berry Selection:** Feel free to experiment with different berry combinations. You could even add a few slices of cucumber for a more refreshing twist.
- **Chill Your Glass:** For an extra-cool presentation, chill your serving glass by filling it with ice water before making the mocktail.
- **Mint:** If you're a fan of mint, try muddling a few extra leaves to intensify the minty flavor.

## Variations:

- **Tropical Berry Mojito:** Add chunks of pineapple or mango to the muddled fruit mixture for a tropical flair.
- **Citrus Berry Mojito:** Add a splash of orange juice for a citrusy twist that pairs perfectly with the berries and mint.
- **Sparkling Berry Lemonade Mojito:** Replace the lime juice with fresh lemon juice for a more tangy, lemonade-inspired mocktail.

## Pairing Suggestions:

- **Vegan Tacos:** The fresh, citrusy flavors of the mojito pair beautifully with light, flavorful vegan tacos, such as grilled vegetable tacos or avocado and black bean tacos.
- **Vegan Summer Rolls:** These fresh, light summer rolls with peanut dipping sauce complement the refreshing and tangy notes of the berry mojito.
- **Vegan Coconut Macaroons:** The delicate sweetness of coconut macaroons balances the fresh and minty mojito mocktail, offering a light yet indulgent treat.

## Interesting Fact:

Did you know that **mojitos** originated in Cuba in the 16th century? The drink was originally made with a primitive form of rum, lime, and indigenous herbs to treat various ailments, making it a drink with a rich cultural history. The **Berry Mojito Mocktail** brings this classic into the modern day, offering all the refreshing flavors without the alcohol!

## Cultural Connection:

The classic **Mojito** was popularized by Cuban culture and later became a global favorite, especially in the summer months. The drink is known for its light, refreshing qualities and is often associated with tropical climates and relaxing beachside moments. This **Berry Mojito Mocktail** retains all of the moji-

# Non-Alcoholic Irish Coffee

*Indulge in the smooth, rich flavors of a Non-Alcoholic Irish Coffee - a cozy, comforting mocktail that captures the essence of the classic Irish coffee, minus the whiskey. With a robust, full-bodied coffee base, topped with velvety whipped cream, this non-alcoholic version delivers all the warmth and richness without the alcohol. Whether you're enjoying a quiet evening or treating yourself to a luxurious coffee moment, this drink offers the perfect blend of sweet, creamy, and bold flavors. Ready to experience this delightful twist on a beloved classic?*

## Ingredients:

- 1 cup freshly brewed strong coffee (preferably dark roast or Irish-style coffee)
- 2 tbsps maple syrup or agave syrup (adjust to taste)
- 1/4 cup vegan heavy cream or coconut whipped cream (for topping)
- 1/2 tsp ground cinnamon (optional)
- 1/2 tsp vanilla extract (optional, for added flavor)
- [Optional] Whipped coconut cream for garnish
- [Optional] Ground nutmeg or cinnamon for garnish

## Instructions:

1. **Brew the Coffee:** Brew a strong cup of coffee using your preferred method - whether that's a French press, drip coffee maker, or pour-over. For an authentic Irish-style coffee flavor, opt for a dark roast or rich coffee blend.
2. **Sweeten the Coffee:** Pour the hot coffee into your favorite mug and stir in the maple syrup or agave syrup to taste. Adjust the sweetness to your preference.
3. **Prepare the Cream:** In a separate small bowl or mixing cup, whisk the vegan heavy cream (or coconut whipped cream) until it thickens slightly. You want it to be soft and fluffy but not too stiff.
4. **Assemble the Drink:** Carefully float the whipped cream on top of the sweetened coffee. This will create a beautiful, creamy layer atop the dark coffee base.
5. **Optional Garnish:** Sprinkle a pinch of ground cinnamon or nutmeg on top of the whipped cream for a touch of spice and extra flair.
6. **Serve and Enjoy:** Sip and savor this rich, creamy non-alcoholic treat, perfect for any time you crave the comforting warmth of Irish coffee without the alcohol.

## Tips and Recommendations:

- **Adjust the Sweetness:** Maple syrup adds a rich, caramel-like sweetness, but you can adjust the sweetness by using agave syrup or another natural sweetener if you prefer a lighter taste.
- **Vegan Whipped Cream:** If you don't have vegan whipped cream on hand, you can use coconut cream whipped to the same consistency or make your own whipped coconut cream at home.
- **Flavored Variations:** For a hint of vanilla or a subtle aromatic flavor, add a 1/2 teaspoon of vanilla extract to the coffee mix before adding the whipped cream.
- **Temperature:** If you prefer a colder version, chill the coffee in the fridge for an iced Irish coffee mocktail, adding ice and cold whipped cream on top.

## Variations:

- **Caramel Non-Alcoholic Irish Coffee:** Add a tablespoon of caramel syrup to the sweetened coffee before topping with whipped cream.
- **Spiced Non-Alcoholic Irish Coffee:** For extra warmth, add a pinch of cinnamon or nutmeg directly into the coffee before stirring in the sweetener.
- **Minted Non-Alcoholic Irish Coffee:** Add a few fresh mint leaves into the coffee mixture for a refreshing twist that complements the richness of the whipped cream.
- **Decaf Version:** If you're sensitive to caffeine, use a decaffeinated coffee blend to enjoy this cozy drink without the buzz.

## Pairing Suggestions:

- **Vegan Shortbread Cookies:** The rich, buttery flavor of shortbread is the perfect match for the creamy, sweet notes of the non-alcoholic Irish coffee.
- **Vegan Scones:** Pair your Irish coffee with freshly baked scones, especially with a dollop of vegan clotted cream or jam for a comforting afternoon treat.
- **Vegan Chocolate Truffles:** Indulge in the rich combination of dark chocolate truffles and the creamy coffee mocktail for an extra touch of luxury.

## Interesting Fact:

Did you know that Irish coffee was originally created in the 1940s by Joe Sheridan, a chef at an airport in Ireland? The drink was served to warm up weary travelers, combining rich coffee with whiskey and a layer of cream. Today, **Non-Alcoholic Irish Coffee** al-

# Sparkling Blackcurrant Lemonade

*Looking for a refreshing, vibrant drink to brighten up your day? Sparkling Blackcurrant Lemonade is the perfect combination of tart, fruity blackcurrant and the zesty punch of lemon, topped off with a delightful fizz. This sparkling mocktail is a perfect thirst-quencher for hot summer days, or anytime you want a drink that's both refreshing and fun to sip. The sweetness of blackcurrant, balanced by the citrusy kick of lemon, creates a harmonious blend, while the sparkle from soda water adds a lively, effervescent touch. Ready to add some sparkle to your routine?*

## Ingredients:

- 1/2 cup blackcurrant syrup (or blackcurrant juice)
- 1/2 cup fresh lemon juice (about 2 lemons)
- 1 tbsp maple syrup (optional, adjust to taste)
- 1 cup sparkling water or club soda
- Ice cubes
- Fresh mint leaves for garnish
- 2-3 thin lemon slices for garnish
- [Optional] Blackcurrant berries for garnish

## Instructions:

1. **Prepare the Lemon and Blackcurrant Mix:** In a small jug or mixing bowl, combine the blackcurrant syrup (or juice) and fresh lemon juice. Stir well to mix.
2. **Sweeten the Drink:** Add the maple syrup to the mix and stir until it's fully dissolved. Taste and adjust the sweetness as desired.
3. **Fill with Ice:** Add ice cubes to a tall glass, about halfway full.
4. **Pour the Mix:** Pour the blackcurrant and lemon mixture over the ice.
5. **Add the Sparkle:** Top with sparkling water or club soda, gently stirring to combine and create a fizzy effect.
6. **Garnish and Serve:** Garnish with a few fresh mint leaves, lemon slices, and optional blackcurrant berries for an extra burst of color and flavor.
7. **Enjoy:** Sip and enjoy the refreshing sparkle and fruity flavors of this mocktail. Perfect for hot days or as a delightful drink to share with friends!

## Tips and Recommendations:

- **Adjusting Sweetness:** If you prefer a less sweet drink, reduce the amount of maple syrup or opt for a sugar-free sweetener.
- **Herbal Twist:** For an aromatic twist, infuse the drink with a few sprigs of rosemary or basil alongside the mint.
- **Chilled Version:** For an even colder drink, chill your sparkling water and blackcurrant syrup in advance.
- **Double Up:** Make a larger batch by multiplying the ingredients and serving in a pitcher for a crowd.

## Variations:

- **Ginger Sparkle:** Add a few slices of fresh ginger to the mix for a spicy kick that complements the sweetness of the blackcurrant.
- **Berry Fusion:** Combine blackcurrant syrup with other berry syrups (like raspberry or strawberry) to create a mixed berry version of this lemonade.
- **Herbal Infusion:** For a more sophisticated flavor, infuse the sparkling lemonade with a hint of lavender or chamomile. Simply steep the flowers in hot water for a few minutes, then add them to the drink once cooled.

## Pairing Suggestions:

- **Vegan Lemon Bars:** The tangy, sweet flavor of lemon bars pairs beautifully with the refreshing and tart notes of the sparkling blackcurrant lemonade.
- **Vegan Scones with Clotted Cream:** These light, fluffy scones are a perfect match, balancing out the drink's fruity zing with a rich, creamy bite.
- **Fresh Fruit Salad:** A refreshing, light fruit salad with berries, melons, and citrus will enhance the vibrant fruitiness of this sparkling mocktail.

## Interesting Fact:

Did you know that blackcurrants are native to Europe and have been used for centuries in cooking and beverages? They're not only delicious but also packed with vitamin C - up to four times more than oranges! In the UK, blackcurrants are often used to make cordial, jams, and even health supplements.

## Cultural Connection:

Blackcurrants have a long history in European cuisine, especially in the UK, where they're used to make a popular syrup known as "blackcurrant cordial." In some regions, blackcurrants are also associated with traditional remedies for cold and flu due to their high vitamin C content. This **Sparkling Blackcurrant Lemonade** takes inspiration from these European traditions, offering a modern twist on a classic fruit drink with a fizzy flair.

# Virgin Piña Colada Coffee

*Imagine the tropical sweetness of a piña colada combined with the rich depth of coffee. Virgin Piña Colada Coffee brings you the best of both worlds: a creamy, coconut-infused coffee mocktail with a refreshing pineapple twist. This delightful creation offers a non-alcoholic escape to a tropical paradise, perfect for those who crave the flavors of the Caribbean without the rum. Indulge in this sweet, smooth, and frothy coffee treat that will transport you to a sunny beach - no passport required.*

## Ingredients:

- 1 shot (1 ounce) of strong brewed coffee (or 1 shot espresso for a bolder flavor)
- 1/2 cup coconut milk (or coconut cream for extra richness)
- 1/4 cup pineapple juice
- 1 tbsp maple syrup (or agave syrup for a vegan alternative)
- 1/2 tsp vanilla extract
- Ice cubes
- Shredded coconut (for garnish)
- Pineapple wedges (for garnish)
- [Optional] A pinch of ground cinnamon or nutmeg

## Instructions:

1. **Brew Your Coffee:** Start by brewing a strong shot of coffee or espresso. Let it cool slightly.
2. **Mix the Coconut Base:** In a blender, combine the coconut milk, pineapple juice, maple syrup, and vanilla extract. Blend on high until smooth and frothy.
3. **Assemble the Drink:** Fill a tall glass with ice cubes, then pour in the brewed coffee (or espresso).
4. **Add the Piña Colada Mix:** Pour the coconut and pineapple mixture into the glass, gently stirring to combine with the coffee.
5. **Garnish and Serve:** Garnish with a sprinkle of shredded coconut and a pineapple wedge on the rim of the glass. Optionally, sprinkle a pinch of cinnamon or nutmeg for added flavor.
6. **Enjoy:** Sip and enjoy the smooth, tropical coffee experience with every refreshing gulp!

## Tips and Recommendations:

- **Coffee Strength:** If you prefer a stronger coffee flavor, opt for a double shot of espresso or a more concentrated brew.
- **Creaminess:** For an even richer taste, you can use coconut cream instead of coconut milk.
- **Make it Iced:** For an iced version, blend the ingredients with ice or serve over crushed ice for an extra chill factor.
- **Sweetness Adjustment:** Taste the mixture before serving and adjust the sweetness to your liking by adding more maple syrup or using a sugar-free alternative.

## Variations:

- **Caramel Twist:** Add a tablespoon of caramel syrup to the mix for a sweet, buttery flavor that pairs beautifully with the coconut and pineapple.
- **Mocha Piña Colada:** For a chocolatey twist, stir in a tablespoon of cocoa powder or chocolate syrup with the coconut and pineapple mixture.
- **Dairy-Free Option:** For a fully dairy-free version, use almond milk, oat milk, or a blend of coconut and almond milk for a nutty, smooth texture.

## Pairing Suggestions:

- **Vegan Coconut Muffins:** The tropical coconut flavor in the muffins complements the drink's coconut base and adds a sweet, soft contrast.
- **Vegan Banana Bread:** The warm spices and soft texture of banana bread make a perfect pairing for the fruity sweetness of the Virgin Piña Colada Coffee.
- **Tropical Fruit Salad:** A vibrant fruit salad with pineapple, mango, and papaya will enhance the fresh, fruity notes of this coffee mocktail.

## Interesting Fact:

Did you know that the piña colada was originally created in Puerto Rico in the 1950s? The combination of rum, coconut cream, and pineapple juice became an instant hit, and now you can enjoy a non-alcoholic version with a coffee twist. This Virgin Piña Colada Coffee is a nod to the classic, with the added depth of coffee making it a perfect mocktail for any time of the day.

## Cultural Connection:

The Piña Colada, Puerto Rico's national drink, is celebrated worldwide for its tropical flavors. By blending this iconic drink with coffee, the **Virgin Piña Colada Coffee** introduces a new twist to a beloved classic. The fusion of tropical fruits and rich coffee has become a refreshing trend in the mocktail world, bringing together the best of both indulgent cocktails and the comfort of coffee culture.

# Cucumber Mint Lime Refresher

*Cool, crisp, and utterly refreshing, the Cucumber Mint Lime Refresher is the ultimate thirst-quencher for hot days. This vibrant mocktail blends the subtle, soothing flavor of cucumber with the zesty kick of lime and the coolness of fresh mint. Perfect for sipping on a sunny afternoon or serving at your next gathering, this invigorating drink will awaken your senses and leave you feeling refreshed. It's a light, hydrating beverage with a burst of natural flavors that makes it an ideal alternative to sugary sodas.*

## Ingredients:

- 1/2 cucumber, peeled and sliced
- 1/4 cup fresh mint leaves
- 1 tbsp fresh lime juice (about half a lime)
- 1 tbsp agave syrup (or honey for a non-vegan option)
- 1 cup cold sparkling water
- Ice cubes
- [Optional] 1-2 slices of lime for garnish
- [Optional] Fresh mint sprigs for garnish

## Instructions:

1. **Prepare the Cucumber and Mint:** In a blender, combine the cucumber slices and fresh mint leaves. Blend until smooth, adding a little water if necessary to help it blend properly.
2. **Strain the Mixture:** Pour the cucumber-mint mixture through a fine mesh strainer or cheesecloth into a pitcher to remove any pulp, leaving you with a smooth, refreshing cucumber-mint juice.
3. **Mix the Drink:** Add the fresh lime juice and agave syrup to the cucumber-mint juice. Stir well to combine.
4. **Serve Over Ice:** Fill a tall glass with ice cubes and pour the cucumber-mint-lime mixture over the ice.
5. **Add Sparkle:** Top with cold sparkling water, stirring gently to combine.
6. **Garnish and Serve:** Garnish with a slice of lime and a sprig of mint for an extra pop of color and flavor. Serve immediately for the freshest taste.
7. **Enjoy:** Sip and enjoy the cooling, zesty, and refreshing flavors of your Cucumber Mint Lime Refresher!

## Tips and Recommendations:

- **Adjust Sweetness:** If you prefer a sweeter drink, feel free to add more agave syrup or adjust to taste. You can also use stevia or a different sweetener of your choice.
- **Herb Variations:** Experiment by adding basil or thyme to the drink for a unique herbal twist.
- **Chill the Ingredients:** For an even cooler experience, chill the cucumber, mint, and lime juice beforehand. This will keep your refresher nice and cold without diluting it too quickly.
- **Cucumber Prep:** If you don't mind the extra texture, you can leave the skin on the cucumber for a more rustic drink.

## Variations:

- **Berry Twist:** Add a handful of fresh berries like strawberries or blueberries to the cucumber-mint blend before straining for a fruity variation of this drink.
- **Spicy Kick:** For a spicy twist, add a few slices of jalapeño pepper to the cucumber and mint before blending. The heat pairs wonderfully with the coolness of the cucumber and mint.
- **Sparkling Lemonade:** Swap out the lime juice for fresh lemon juice to create a zesty sparkling lemonade version of this refresher.

## Pairing Suggestions:

- **Vegan Wraps:** Pair this refreshing mocktail with a light vegan wrap filled with fresh vegetables and hummus for a light lunch or snack.
- **Crispy Veggie Chips:** Enjoy with a side of homemade crispy vegetable chips to balance the freshness of the drink with a crunchy, savory snack.
- **Fruit Skewers:** Serve with tropical fruit skewers for a perfect sunny afternoon snack, complementing the citrusy and minty flavors of the drink.

## Interesting Fact:

Did you know that cucumbers are 95% water, making them one of the most hydrating foods you can eat? This drink makes the most of that hydration, making it not only refreshing but also nourishing!

## Cultural Connection:

The use of mint and cucumber in beverages is a popular tradition in many Mediterranean cultures, known for their cooling properties in hot climates. This Cucumber Mint Lime Refresher is a modern, vibrant twist on those classic drinks, bringing together fresh ingredients for a rejuvenating experience. Whether you're sipping it poolside or at a brunch gathering, this drink captures the essence of summer and relaxation in every sip.

# Coconut Water Berry Splash

*Refresh your senses with the Coconut Water Berry Splash, a tropical burst of hydration and flavor! Combining the subtle sweetness of coconut water with a medley of fresh berries, this mocktail is the ultimate in vibrant, health-boosting refreshments. Whether you're lounging by the pool or hosting a summer soirée, this drink is a refreshing, low-calorie option that doesn't sacrifice taste. With a touch of lime and a splash of sparkling water, it's an irresistible way to stay hydrated while enjoying the fruity goodness of nature.*

## Ingredients:

- 1 cup coconut water (preferably unsweetened)
- 1/2 cup mixed fresh berries (strawberries, blueberries, raspberries, etc.)
- 1 tbsp fresh lime juice (about 1/2 lime)
- 1 tsp agave syrup (optional, for extra sweetness)
- 1/2 cup sparkling water (or more to taste)
- Ice cubes
- [Optional] A few whole berries and a lime slice for garnish

## Instructions:

1. **Prepare the Berries:** In a blender, combine the mixed berries and coconut water. Blend until smooth. If you prefer a smoother drink, you can strain the mixture through a fine mesh sieve to remove the seeds and pulp.
2. **Add Lime and Sweetener:** Add fresh lime juice and agave syrup (if using) to the berry-coconut water mixture. Stir well to combine.
3. **Serve Over Ice:** Fill a glass with ice cubes and pour the berry-coconut mixture over the ice.
4. **Add Sparkle:** Top with sparkling water, stirring gently to mix. Adjust the amount of sparkling water based on your preference for fizz.
5. **Garnish and Serve:** Garnish with a few whole berries and a slice of lime for a colorful and festive touch.
6. **Enjoy:** Sip and savor the refreshing taste of this tropical berry splash!

## Tips and Recommendations:

- **Adjust Sweetness:** The natural sweetness of coconut water and berries should be enough for most, but if you like it sweeter, feel free to add a bit more agave syrup or a sweetener of your choice.
- **Berry Varieties:** Experiment with different berry combinations depending on what's in season. Blackberries, strawberries, and even pomegranate seeds work well for added flavor.
- **Coconut Water Substitute:** If coconut water isn't available, you can substitute with regular water or fruit juice, but coconut water adds a unique tropical flavor and electrolytes that are hard to replicate.
- **Chill Your Ingredients:** For an extra refreshing experience, chill the coconut water and berries in advance before blending.

## Variations:

- **Tropical Twist:** For an even more tropical flavor, add a few chunks of fresh pineapple to the blender.
- **Mint Infusion:** Add a few fresh mint leaves to the berry-coconut mixture for a cool, refreshing flavor that pairs beautifully with the berries.
- **Citrus Boost:** Use a mix of lime and orange juice for an extra citrusy zing. The combination of coconut water, lime, and orange is a crowd-pleaser!

## Pairing Suggestions:

- **Vegan Tacos:** Pair this refreshing mocktail with some crispy, vegan tacos for a perfect fusion of tropical flavors and savory goodness.
- **Light Salads:** Serve alongside a light salad, such as a quinoa or arugula salad with citrus dressing, to complement the fresh, fruity notes of the drink.
- **Tropical Fruit Platter:** Enjoy with a platter of fresh tropical fruits like pineapple, mango, and watermelon for a truly refreshing experience.

## Interesting Fact:

Did you know that coconut water is often referred to as "nature's sports drink"? Its high potassium content makes it a natural hydrator, which is why it's such a great base for a refreshing mocktail!

## Cultural Connection:

Coconut water has been a staple in tropical regions for centuries. It's often enjoyed straight from the coconut in many countries in Southeast Asia and the Caribbean. By blending coconut water with berries, this mocktail brings a new twist to an ancient tradition, offering a modern and refreshing way to hydrate with a taste of the tropics.

# Iced Mango Passionfruit Sparkler

*Chill out with the ultimate tropical refreshment - Iced Mango Passionfruit Sparkler! This vibrant, fruity mocktail is a celebration of sunny flavors, combining the sweet, luscious mango with the tangy brightness of passionfruit. Topped off with a sparkling fizz, it's the perfect drink to enjoy on a hot day, whether you're lounging by the pool or hosting a summer gathering. The combination of tropical fruits and a splash of soda water offers an irresistible, refreshing experience, making it a must-try for fans of sweet and sparkling beverages.*

## Ingredients:

- 1/2 cup mango puree (fresh or frozen)
- 1/4 cup passionfruit juice (or 1-2 fresh passionfruits, pulp scraped)
- 1 tbsp fresh lime juice (about 1/2 lime)
- 1 tsp agave syrup or maple syrup (optional, for sweetness)
- 1/2 cup sparkling water (or club soda)
- Ice cubes
- [Optional] Lime slices and mint leaves for garnish

## Instructions:

1. **Prepare the Mango-Passionfruit Base:** In a blender, combine the mango puree, passionfruit juice (or pulp), and fresh lime juice. Blend until smooth. Taste and add sweetener if desired, then blend again to incorporate.
2. **Fill the Glass:** Add a generous handful of ice cubes to a tall glass.
3. **Pour the Mango-Passionfruit Mixture:** Pour the blended mango-passionfruit mixture over the ice.
4. **Add the Sparkle:** Top with sparkling water or club soda, and gently stir to combine. Adjust the amount of sparkling water based on your preference for fizz.
5. **Garnish and Serve:** Garnish with lime slices and a sprig of mint for a fresh, vibrant presentation.
6. **Enjoy:** Sip and savor the refreshing tropical flavors of your sparkling mocktail!

## Tips and Recommendations:

- **Sweetness Level:** If you prefer a sweeter drink, increase the amount of agave syrup or maple syrup, or choose a sweeter sparkling water.
- **Fruits:** Fresh passionfruit adds a more intense, natural flavor, but passionfruit juice works well for a quicker and easier option.
- **Fruit Variations:** Experiment with adding other tropical fruits like pineapple or papaya to the blend for an even more exotic flavor profile.
- **Chill Your Glass:** For an extra refreshing experience, chill your glass in the freezer for a few minutes before serving.

## Variations:

- **Tropical Fusion:** Blend in a few chunks of fresh pineapple or coconut water for an even more tropical twist.
- **Minty Fresh:** Add a handful of fresh mint leaves to the blender for a cool, minty flavor that complements the tropical fruit base.
- **Spicy Kick:** Add a pinch of chili powder or a slice of jalapeño to the blend for a touch of heat that balances the sweetness of the mango and passionfruit.

## Pairing Suggestions:

- **Vegan Tacos:** Pair with vibrant vegan tacos filled with fresh avocado, mango salsa, and cilantro for a delicious, summery meal.
- **Crispy Plantain Chips:** The slight sweetness of mango and passionfruit will complement the salty, crispy texture of plantain chips for a perfect snack.
- **Tropical Fruit Platter:** Serve with a platter of fresh tropical fruits like pineapple, guava, and dragon fruit for a colorful and healthful spread.

## Interesting Fact:

Did you know that passionfruit is also known as "lilikoi" in Hawaii? It's famous for its intensely aromatic flavor and is often used in tropical drinks, desserts, and even savory dishes!

## Cultural Connection:

Mangoes and passionfruit are beloved tropical fruits that have been enjoyed in cultures around the world. Mangoes are native to South Asia but are now cultivated in many tropical and subtropical regions, while passionfruit hails from South America. Together, these fruits bring the essence of the tropics into a refreshing drink that's perfect for warm weather, celebrations, or simply a moment of relaxation.

# Watermelon Basil Iced Tea

*Cool off and refresh with this delightful Watermelon Basil Iced Tea - a perfectly balanced drink that combines the hydrating sweetness of watermelon with the herbaceous, aromatic punch of fresh basil. This mocktail is light, invigorating, and just the right mix of fruity and herbal, making it an ideal choice for hot summer days. The natural sweetness of watermelon paired with the herbal zing of basil makes this iced tea a sophisticated yet simple treat. Enjoy it as a standalone refreshment or serve it alongside your favorite summer meal for a truly refreshing experience.*

## Ingredients:

- 2 cups watermelon, cubed
- 1 tbsp fresh basil leaves, chopped (plus extra for garnish)
- 1 bag black tea or green tea
- 2 cups boiling water
- 1 tbsp agave syrup or maple syrup (optional, for sweetness)
- 1 tbsp fresh lime juice (about 1/2 lime)
- Ice cubes
- [Optional] Basil sprig for garnish

## Instructions:

1. **Brew the Tea:** In a heatproof container, pour 2 cups of boiling water over the tea bag. Steep for about 5 minutes, then remove the tea bag and let the tea cool to room temperature.
2. **Prepare the Watermelon Puree:** In a blender, combine the cubed watermelon and lime juice. Blend until smooth.
3. **Infuse with Basil:** Add the chopped basil to the watermelon puree and pulse a few times to release the basil's flavor.
4. **Sweeten (Optional):** Taste the watermelon-basil mixture. If you prefer a sweeter drink, stir in agave syrup or maple syrup to taste.
5. **Combine Tea and Watermelon Puree:** Pour the cooled tea into a large pitcher, followed by the watermelon-basil mixture. Stir well to combine.
6. **Serve Over Ice:** Fill glasses with ice cubes and pour the watermelon basil iced tea over.
7. **Garnish and Enjoy:** Garnish each glass with a sprig of fresh basil and a slice of lime for a pop of color and extra freshness.

## Tips and Recommendations:

- **Chill the Tea:** For an extra-refreshing experience, chill the brewed tea before combining it with the watermelon puree.
- **Sweetness Level:** If your watermelon is naturally sweet, you may not need any added sweetener. Taste and adjust accordingly.
- **Herb Variations:** For a twist, try substituting the basil with mint or adding a small sprig of rosemary for an added layer of flavor.

- **Frozen Watermelon Cubes:** For an extra-chilly treat, freeze some of the watermelon cubes and use them as ice cubes in your drink.

## Variations:

- **Watermelon Mint Iced Tea:** Replace basil with fresh mint leaves for a minty, cooling variation that's just as refreshing.
- **Citrus Infusion:** Add a splash of orange or lemon juice to the mix for a zesty citrus kick that complements the sweetness of the watermelon.
- **Sparkling Water:** For a fizzy twist, top the iced tea with sparkling water or club soda just before serving.

## Pairing Suggestions:

- **Vegan Wraps:** Pair with a fresh vegetable wrap or hummus and veggie platter for a light, summery lunch.
- **Vegan Tacos:** The herbaceous and fruity flavors of the iced tea pair beautifully with the bold, savory taste of vegan tacos, especially those filled with avocado and roasted vegetables.
- **Fruit Salad:** A refreshing fruit salad with seasonal fruits like strawberries, kiwi, and oranges makes for a perfect side dish alongside this iced tea.

## Interesting Fact:

Did you know that watermelon is made up of over 90% water? It's one of the most hydrating fruits, making it the ideal base for a refreshing drink like this!

## Cultural Connection:

Watermelon and basil both have rich histories in various cuisines. Watermelon, a native of Africa, has been enjoyed for centuries in hot climates for its hydrating properties, while basil is a revered herb in Mediterranean cooking, often used to add freshness to dishes and drinks. The combination of these two in this iced tea is a nod to the vibrant, health-conscious culture of summer refreshment.

# Virgin Strawberry Daiquiri Latte

*The Virgin Strawberry Daiquiri Latte is a tropical twist on your usual latte, combining the sweet, fruity punch of strawberries with the zesty kick of lime and a touch of smooth creaminess. Inspired by the iconic strawberry daiquiri, this alcohol-free version captures all the refreshing flavors of summer in a cozy, frothy latte. Whether you're relaxing at home or entertaining friends, this creamy, berry-infused mocktail will transport you to a beachy paradise with every sip.*

## Ingredients:

- 1/2 cup fresh strawberries, hulled
- 1 tbsp lime juice (freshly squeezed)
- 1 tbsp maple syrup or agave syrup (optional, for sweetness)
- 1 shot (1 ounce) of espresso or strong brewed coffee
- 1 cup steamed oat milk (or your preferred plant-based milk)
- Ice cubes
- [Optional] 1/4 tsp vanilla extract
- [Optional] Lime slice or fresh strawberry for garnish

## Instructions:

1. **Prepare the Strawberry Puree:** In a blender, combine the fresh strawberries and lime juice. Blend until smooth. If you prefer a sweeter drink, add maple syrup or agave syrup to taste and blend again.
2. **Brew the Coffee:** Brew one shot of espresso or prepare a small cup of strong brewed coffee using your preferred method.
3. **Steam the Milk:** Steam the oat milk (or your chosen plant-based milk) until it's hot but not boiling. Use a milk frother or steam wand to create a smooth, velvety texture.
4. **Assemble the Drink:** In a tall glass, add a handful of ice cubes. Pour the strawberry-lime puree over the ice, followed by the shot of espresso or brewed coffee.
5. **Add the Steamed Milk:** Gently pour the steamed oat milk over the mixture, creating a layered effect. Stir gently if you prefer the flavors to mix.
6. **Garnish and Serve:** Garnish with a slice of lime or a fresh strawberry on the rim of the glass for an extra touch of color and flavor. Enjoy immediately!

## Tips and Recommendations:

- **Blender Tip:** If you prefer a smoother texture, strain the strawberry puree to remove any seeds before adding it to your drink.
- **Caffeine-Free Option:** For a completely caffeine-free version, use decaffeinated coffee or simply replace the espresso with a strong brewed herbal tea like rooibos or hibiscus.
- **Sweetness Level:** Depending on the ripeness of your strawberries, you may need to adjust the sweetness. Taste and add more syrup if desired.
- **Texture Boost:** For a creamier texture, try adding a splash of coconut cream to the steamed oat milk.

## Variations:

- **Tropical Twist:** For an exotic twist, add a small amount of coconut milk to the steamed oat milk for a rich, tropical flavor.
- **Frozen Version:** Blend the strawberry puree and milk with ice for a frozen slushie version of the Virgin Strawberry Daiquiri Latte.
- **Minty Fresh:** Add a few fresh mint leaves to the strawberry puree for a refreshing minty accent.

## Pairing Suggestions:

- **Vegan Scones:** Pair with freshly baked vegan scones, either plain or with fruit preserves, for a delightful afternoon treat.
- **Berry Salad:** Enjoy with a vibrant berry salad, complete with a drizzle of maple syrup and a few mint leaves to complement the fruity flavors in the latte.
- **Coconut Macaroons:** For a bit of sweetness and crunch, try pairing with coconut macaroons, which harmonize beautifully with the tropical flavors.

## Interesting Fact:

Did you know that the traditional strawberry daiquiri is a Cuban invention? While this version is alcohol-free, it still carries the essence of the daiquiri with its refreshing fruitiness and lime kick.

## Cultural Connection:

The **Strawberry Daiquiri** is a classic cocktail that originated in Cuba, made famous by Ernest Hemingway. Over time, the drink has evolved into numerous variations, with the "virgin" version being a popular choice for those who want the fruity, refreshing taste without the alcohol. This Virgin Strawberry Daiquiri Latte blends that classic tropical flavor into a cozy, comforting latte - perfect for those who enjoy the taste of summer in every season.

# Pineapple Mint Iced Coffee Cooler

*The Pineapple Mint Iced Coffee Cooler is a refreshing, tropical twist on your classic iced coffee. With the vibrant sweetness of fresh pineapple, the cooling sensation of mint, and a bold shot of espresso, this drink is a perfect balance of energizing coffee and fruity flavors. It's ideal for hot summer days, offering a unique blend of flavors that will leave you feeling rejuvenated and re-freshed - without the need for alcohol. A delightful way to enjoy your coffee in a whole new light!*

## Ingredients:

- 1 shot (1 ounce) of espresso or cold brew coffee
- 1/2 cup fresh pineapple, chopped
- 1/4 cup fresh mint leaves, packed
- 1 tbsp agave syrup or maple syrup (optional, for sweetness)
- 1 cup ice cubes
- 1/2 cup cold water or coconut water
- [Optional] 1/4 tsp lime zest for an added zing
- [Optional] Pineapple slice and mint sprig for garnish

## Instructions:

1. **Prepare the Pineapple Mint Puree:** In a blender, combine the fresh pineapple and mint leaves. Blend until smooth. Add a little cold water or coconut water to help with blending if needed.
2. **Brew the Coffee:** Brew one shot of espresso or prepare a small cup of cold brew coffee using your preferred method. Let it cool slightly.
3. **Mix the Drink:** In a tall glass, add the ice cubes. Pour the pineapple-mint puree over the ice, followed by the brewed coffee. Stir well to combine the flavors.
4. **Sweeten to Taste:** If you like your drink sweeter, add agave syrup or maple syrup to taste and stir until dissolved.
5. **Finish and Garnish:** For an extra touch, zest a little lime over the top or garnish with a slice of pineapple and a sprig of mint. Serve chilled and enjoy immediately!

## Tips and Recommendations:

- **Fresh Pineapple:** For the best flavor, use fresh pineapple rather than canned. It adds a vibrant, natural sweetness that pairs wonderfully with the mint and coffee.
- **Cold Brew Option:** If you prefer a smoother, less acidic coffee flavor, substitute the espresso with cold brew coffee for a milder taste.
- **Minty Freshness:** To intensify the mint flavor, slap the mint leaves gently between your hands before adding them to the blender. This releases more of the mint's essential oils.
- **Coconut Water:** For a more tropical flavor, use coconut water instead of regular water to blend the pineapple-mint puree. It complements the tropical fruitiness of the drink.

## Variations:

- **Caramel Twist:** Add a drizzle of vegan caramel sauce to the bottom of the glass before pouring in the drink for a caramelized twist that adds extra depth to the flavor.
- **Dairy-Free Creaminess:** If you prefer a creamier texture, top your Pineapple Mint Iced Coffee Cooler with a splash of coconut milk or oat milk.
- **Citrus Kick:** For a tangy, refreshing twist, add a splash of fresh orange juice along with the pineapple for a citrusy burst.

## Pairing Suggestions:

- **Tropical Smoothie Bowl:** Pair with a tropical smoothie bowl topped with coconut flakes, chia seeds, and sliced fruits for a fully refreshing summer breakfast.
- **Vegan Tacos:** Enjoy with a light vegan taco, such as a jackfruit taco or grilled vegetable taco, to balance the flavors of the cooler with savory bites.
- **Almond Croissants:** For a touch of sweetness, pair with vegan almond croissants, which offer a delicate, nutty flavor that complements the coffee's boldness.

## Interesting Fact:

Did you know that mint is one of the oldest herbs used for its medicinal properties? It has been valued for centuries not only for its refreshing taste but also for its ability to ease digestive discomfort.

## Cultural Connection:

Iced coffee has been a beloved beverage worldwide, particularly in hot climates, where it offers both a refreshing and energizing experience. The combination of coffee and tropical fruits, like pineapple, draws inspiration from the many fusion drinks that blend different cultural flavors for a truly unique beverage experience. This Pineapple Mint Iced Coffee Cooler is a modern take on the traditional iced coffee, bringing a refreshing tropical vibe that is perfect for a summer day.

# Raspberry Lemon Sparkling Coffee

*The Raspberry Lemon Sparkling Coffee is a zesty, refreshing blend of bold coffee, bright citrus, and fizzy bubbles - an invigorating combination that will awaken your senses! The natural sweetness of fresh raspberries and the tartness of lemon pair beautifully with the smooth depth of cold brew coffee, creating a sparkling beverage that's as fun as it is delicious. Perfect for warm days or a unique brunch drink, this mocktail is a deliciously unexpected way to enjoy your coffee.*

## Ingredients:

- 1 shot (1 ounce) of cold brew coffee or chilled brewed espresso
- 1/4 cup fresh raspberries
- 1 tbsp freshly squeezed lemon juice
- 1/2 tsp maple syrup or agave syrup (optional, for sweetness)
- 1/2 cup sparkling water or club soda
- Ice cubes
- [Optional] Lemon slice and fresh mint leaves for garnish
- [Optional] 1/2 tsp lemon zest for added citrus intensity

## Instructions:

1. **Prepare the Raspberry Puree:** In a small blender or food processor, combine the fresh raspberries with the maple syrup (if using) and a splash of water. Blend until smooth. Strain the mixture through a fine mesh sieve to remove the seeds.
2. **Mix the Coffee and Lemon:** In a tall glass, pour the cold brew coffee or chilled espresso and freshly squeezed lemon juice. Stir well to combine.
3. **Add the Raspberry Puree:** Pour the raspberry puree into the glass with the coffee mixture and stir gently.
4. **Top with Sparkles:** Add the ice cubes to the glass, then pour sparkling water or club soda over the mixture to create a fizzy, bubbly effect. Stir once more to combine everything.
5. **Garnish and Serve:** Garnish with a slice of lemon and a sprig of fresh mint. Optionally, sprinkle some lemon zest on top for extra citrus brightness. Serve immediately and enjoy the refreshing bubbles!

## Tips and Recommendations:

- **Cold Brew Coffee:** Cold brew is ideal for this recipe as it has a smoother, less acidic taste than regular brewed coffee, which balances well with the tart raspberries and lemon.
- **Sweetness Level:** Adjust the sweetness to your taste. If you prefer a sweeter drink, you can increase the maple syrup or add a little more agave syrup.
- **Fruit Variations:** Try swapping raspberries for other berries, like blackberries or blueberries, for a different twist on this sparkling coffee mocktail.
- **Serve it Chilled:** Make sure your coffee is chilled before mixing, so the drink stays refreshingly cool without diluting the bubbles from the sparkling water.

## Variations:

- **Berry Citrus Sparkle:** Add a mix of fresh berries, like blueberries, blackberries, or strawberries, for a colorful and flavorful twist.
- **Herbal Touch:** Infuse your sparkling coffee with a sprig of rosemary or basil for a herbal note that complements the citrusy flavor.
- **Coconut Infusion:** For a tropical spin, add a splash of coconut water instead of sparkling water for a smooth, hydrating drink.

## Pairing Suggestions:

- **Lemon Scones:** Pair with a light, crumbly lemon scone to complement the citrus notes in the drink.
- **Vegan Bagels with Cashew Cream Cheese:** A savory-sweet pairing that balances the tartness and brightness of the drink with creamy cashew cheese and fresh veggies.
- **Coconut Macaroons:** The sweet, chewy coconut treats make a perfect match with the tangy raspberry lemon coffee, adding a bit of indulgence to the refreshing drink.

## Interesting Fact:

Did you know that cold brew coffee has about twice the caffeine concentration of regular brewed coffee? It's the perfect choice when you need an energy boost with a smoother taste!

## Cultural Connection:

The tradition of mixing coffee with sparkling water can be traced back to Italy, where "Caffè Shakerato" is a popular iced coffee drink. The idea of combining the deep, rich flavors of coffee with refreshing, fizzy elements is a modern twist that's gaining popularity worldwide. This Raspberry Lemon Sparkling Coffee is a delightful evolution of that tradition, bringing together vibrant fruits and sparkling refreshment in a unique and energizing mocktail.

# Non-Alcoholic Ginger Mojito Coffee

*The Non-Alcoholic Ginger Mojito Coffee is a vibrant and invigorating blend that combines the freshness of mint, the zing of ginger, and the bold richness of coffee - without any alcohol! Perfect for a refreshing afternoon pick-me-up or a fun twist on your regular coffee routine, this drink is packed with flavor and has the perfect balance of sweetness, spice, and coolness. Inspired by the classic mojito cocktail but with a bold coffee twist, it's an exciting, non-alcoholic concoction that will keep you refreshed and energized.*

## Ingredients:

- 1 shot (1 ounce) of espresso or strong brewed coffee
- 1 tbsp freshly squeezed lime juice
- 1/2 tsp fresh grated ginger
- 6-8 fresh mint leaves (plus extra for garnish)
- 1/2 tbsp maple syrup or agave syrup (optional, adjust sweetness to taste)
- 1/2 cup chilled sparkling water or club soda
- Ice cubes
- [Optional] 1 lime wedge for garnish

## Instructions:

1. **Prepare the Ginger:** In a small bowl or cup, grate fresh ginger until you have about 1/2 teaspoon of ginger.
2. **Muddle the Mint and Lime:** In a tall glass, add the mint leaves and lime juice. Using a muddler or the back of a spoon, gently press the mint leaves to release their oils and flavor, then mix with the lime juice.
3. **Add the Ginger and Coffee:** Add the freshly grated ginger and pour in your shot of espresso (or brewed coffee). Stir gently to combine the flavors.
4. **Sweeten to Taste:** Add maple syrup or agave syrup to the coffee mixture, adjusting to your desired level of sweetness.
5. **Add Ice and Sparkle:** Fill the glass with ice cubes, then pour sparkling water or club soda over the top to create a fizzy effect.
6. **Garnish and Serve:** Stir gently to mix everything together. Garnish with extra mint leaves and a lime wedge. Serve immediately and enjoy the refreshing zing!

## Tips and Recommendations:

- **Fresh Ginger:** Freshly grated ginger brings a sharp, spicy kick to the drink. You can also use ginger syrup for a milder, sweeter option.
- **Cold Brew Coffee Option:** If you prefer a smoother, less acidic base, try using cold brew coffee instead of hot espresso.
- **Adjust the Sweetness:** Feel free to adjust the sweetness according to your preference. You can also try adding a little coconut sugar or stevia if you prefer a lower glycemic option.

- **Mint Flavor:** If you love mint, feel free to add more mint leaves. Just remember to muddle them gently to release the flavor without overpowering the drink.

## Variations:

- **Citrus Burst:** Add a splash of orange juice or a few slices of cucumber for an extra refreshing citrusy twist.
- **Spiced Ginger:** For an extra kick, add a pinch of ground cinnamon or cayenne pepper to the ginger mixture.
- **Iced Coffee Version:** For a chilled, summer version, use cold brew coffee and serve over crushed ice for a slushy texture.

## Pairing Suggestions:

- **Vegan Chocolate Mint Cookies:** The refreshing mint in this drink pairs wonderfully with rich, chocolatey treats. Vegan mint chocolate cookies or brownies would be an excellent choice.
- **Avocado Toast with Lime:** Pair with a savory, creamy avocado toast topped with fresh lime and herbs to balance the drink's sweetness and spice.
- **Tropical Fruit Salad:** A light, vibrant fruit salad with citrus, pineapple, and mango complements the freshness and zest of the coffee mocktail.

## Interesting Fact:

Did you know that ginger has been used for centuries for its medicinal properties, including its ability to aid digestion and reduce inflammation? It's a fantastic addition to any drink for both flavor and wellness benefits!

## Cultural Connection:

The **Mojito** originates from Cuba, where it was traditionally made with rum, mint, lime, and sugar - an incredibly refreshing combination. This Non-Alcoholic Ginger Mojito Coffee is a modern twist on that classic, replacing the rum with coffee and adding ginger for extra zing. The result is a drink that blends the best of both worlds: the freshness of a mojito with the deep, energizing flavor of coffee.

# Minty Pineapple Basil Cooler

*Get ready for a tropical burst of refreshment with the Minty Pineapple Basil Cooler! This non-alcoholic coffee mocktail combines the bright, sweet tang of pineapple with the herbal, aromatic kick of fresh basil, all balanced by a hint of mint. Topped off with sparkling water for that fizzy finish, it's the perfect way to cool down and invigorate your senses. Whether you're lounging by the pool or need a mid-afternoon boost, this unique drink brings the flavors of summer right to your glass - without the alcohol. It's light, refreshing, and oh-so-delicious!*

## Ingredients:

- 1 shot (1 ounce) of espresso or strong brewed coffee
- 1/4 cup fresh pineapple juice
- 1 tbsp fresh lime juice
- 6-8 fresh basil leaves (plus extra for garnish)
- 6-8 fresh mint leaves (plus extra for garnish)
- 1/2 tbsp maple syrup or agave syrup (optional, adjust sweetness to taste)
- 1/2 cup chilled sparkling water or club soda
- Ice cubes

## Instructions:

1. **Prepare the Basil and Mint:** In a tall glass, add the fresh basil leaves and mint leaves. Using a muddler or the back of a spoon, gently muddle the herbs to release their oils and flavors.
2. **Add the Juices and Coffee:** Pour in the fresh pineapple juice and lime juice. Follow with your shot of espresso or brewed coffee. Stir the mixture well to combine all the ingredients.
3. **Sweeten to Taste:** If desired, add maple syrup or agave syrup for a touch of sweetness. Stir again to ensure the sweetness is evenly distributed.
4. **Ice and Sparkle:** Fill the glass with ice cubes, then top off with chilled sparkling water or club soda to add a fizzy and refreshing finish.
5. **Garnish and Serve:** Garnish with extra basil and mint leaves for an added visual touch. Serve immediately and enjoy the tropical refreshment!

## Tips and Recommendations:

- **Fresh Pineapple:** Fresh pineapple juice works best for this drink, as it adds a natural sweetness and depth of flavor. If using canned juice, make sure it's 100% pineapple juice with no added sugar.
- **Adjust the Sweetness:** You can adjust the sweetness to your liking by adding more or less maple syrup or agave syrup. If you prefer a tangier flavor, skip the sweetener altogether.
- **Frozen Pineapple:** For a thicker, colder drink, you can freeze pineapple chunks and blend them into the drink instead of using ice.

- **Coffee Strength:** For a smoother, less intense coffee flavor, opt for cold brew coffee, which has a mellower profile compared to hot espresso.

## Variations:

- **Tropical Twist:** Add a splash of coconut water or coconut milk for a creamy, coconut-flavored version of this drink.
- **Minty Lime Cooler:** If you're more of a lime lover, increase the lime juice to 2 tablespoons for an extra citrusy punch.
- **Citrus Infusion:** Add a few slices of orange or grapefruit to the mix for a burst of citrus that complements the pineapple and lime.

## Pairing Suggestions:

- **Vegan Coconut Cookies:** The sweet, coconut flavor of a vegan coconut cookie pairs beautifully with the tropical flavors of this drink.
- **Avocado Toast with Tomato and Basil:** The rich, creamy texture of avocado toast with fresh tomatoes and basil makes for a perfect savory counterpart to this fruity cooler.
- **Tropical Fruit Salad:** A light and refreshing tropical fruit salad, featuring pineapple, mango, and kiwi, would perfectly complement the vibrant flavors of the cooler.

## Interesting Fact:

Did you know that basil is considered a symbol of good luck in some cultures? So not only is it delicious, but it might just bring some positive vibes to your day!

## Cultural Connection:

This drink is inspired by tropical flavors from the Caribbean and Southeast Asia, where pineapple, basil, and mint are common ingredients in refreshing beverages and dishes. Adding coffee into the mix gives it an exciting modern twist, combining the vibrant flavors of the tropics with the bold depth of espresso, making it the perfect global fusion.

# Sparkling Blueberry Lavender Lemonade

*Step into a world of refreshing elegance with the Sparkling Blueberry Lavender Lemonade! This non-alcoholic mocktail combines the floral aroma of lavender, the tart brightness of fresh lemons, and the sweet, juicy burst of blueberries - all balanced with a fizzy, sparkling finish. The result is a beautifully layered, aromatic drink that's as delightful to the senses as it is to the tastebuds. Whether you're celebrating a summer afternoon or simply craving a refreshing and unique beverage, this drink is sure to become a new favorite. Enjoy the sophisticated, bubbly flavors that transport you to a garden in full bloom!*

## Ingredients:

- 1/2 cup fresh blueberries (or frozen)
- 1 tbsp dried lavender buds
- 1/2 cup freshly squeezed lemon juice
- 1 tbsp maple syrup or agave syrup (adjust to taste)
- 1 cup chilled sparkling water or club soda
- Ice cubes
- 1/2 cup water (for making the lavender infusion)
- Lemon slices (for garnish)
- Fresh lavender sprigs (for garnish)

## Instructions:

1. **Infuse the Lavender:** In a small saucepan, bring 1/2 cup of water to a boil. Once boiling, add the dried lavender buds and reduce the heat to low. Let it simmer for 5 minutes to infuse the water with the lavender flavor. Remove from heat and strain the lavender infusion to discard the buds. Set aside to cool.
2. **Make the Blueberry Syrup:** In a blender, blend the fresh blueberries until smooth. If you prefer a smoother texture, strain the mixture through a fine mesh sieve to remove the skins. Pour the blueberry puree into a small saucepan and heat it over medium heat for 5-7 minutes, stirring occasionally until it thickens slightly. Stir in the maple syrup or agave syrup, adjusting the sweetness to your taste. Remove from heat and allow it to cool.
3. **Mix the Drink:** In a tall glass, add a handful of ice cubes. Pour in the freshly squeezed lemon juice, cooled lavender infusion, and blueberry syrup. Stir well to combine.
4. **Add the Sparkle:** Top the drink with chilled sparkling water or club soda, filling the glass to the top. Stir gently to combine, keeping the bubbles intact.
5. **Garnish and Serve:** Garnish with a slice of lemon and a sprig of fresh lavender. Serve immediately and enjoy the refreshing, floral burst!

## Tips and Recommendations:

- **Blueberry Sweetness:** If you prefer a sweeter drink, feel free to add more maple syrup or agave syrup to taste, especially if the blueberries are tart.
- **Lavender Infusion:** If you don't have dried lavender, you can use a few drops of lavender extract as an alternative. However, use it sparingly, as it can be quite potent.
- **Chill the Glass:** For an extra refreshing touch, chill your glass in the freezer for 10 minutes before preparing the drink.
- **Herbal Variations:** If you want to experiment, try swapping the lavender for other herbs like mint or basil to create different flavor profiles.

## Variations:

- **Citrus Twist:** Add a splash of orange juice along with the lemon juice for a citrusy blend that brightens the drink even more.
- **Berry Fusion:** For a mixed berry version, add raspberries or strawberries to the blueberry syrup for a richer berry flavor.
- **Non-Sparkling Option:** If you prefer a still drink, simply omit the sparkling water and top with plain water or iced tea for a soothing version.
- **Lavender Lemonade:** Skip the blueberry syrup and create a simple lavender lemonade by combining lavender infusion, lemon juice, and sweetener, topped with still or sparkling water.

## Pairing Suggestions:

- **Vegan Lemon Shortbread Cookies:** The light, buttery texture of lemon shortbread cookies complements the floral and citrus notes in the drink.
- **Chilled Cucumber Salad:** A crisp, refreshing cucumber salad with a lemon vinaigrette is a perfect savory side to balance the sweet, aromatic lemonade.
- **Avocado Toast:** A simple, creamy avocado toast with a sprinkle of chili flakes and lemon zest pairs beautifully with the bright and floral flavors of this drink.

# Virgin Raspberry Bellini Latte

*Celebrate a blend of elegance and creativity with the Virgin Raspberry Bellini Latte, a sparkling twist on the classic Italian Bellini. This non-alcoholic mocktail combines the bright, tangy flavor of fresh raspberries with the creamy richness of steamed oat milk, topped off with a gentle fizz. It's the perfect drink for any occasion, whether you're hosting a brunch, treating yourself to a luxurious pick-me-up, or simply enjoying a refreshing, caffeine-free indulgence. The combination of fruity sweetness and creamy texture, with a dash of sparkle, will transport you to a sun-kissed terrace overlooking the Italian countryside!*

## Ingredients:

- 1/2 cup fresh raspberries (or frozen, thawed)
- 1 tbsp maple syrup or agave syrup (optional, to taste)
- 1/2 cup chilled sparkling water or club soda
- 1 cup oat milk (or your preferred plant-based milk)
- 1/2 tsp vanilla extract
- 1/4 tsp ground cinnamon (optional, for extra flavor)
- Ice cubes
- Fresh raspberries and mint sprigs (for garnish)

## Instructions:

1. **Prepare the Raspberry Puree:** In a blender, blend the fresh (or thawed) raspberries until smooth. If you prefer a smoother texture, strain the puree through a fine mesh sieve to remove the seeds.
2. **Sweeten the Puree:** Pour the raspberry puree into a small saucepan and heat over medium heat for 3-5 minutes, stirring occasionally. Add maple syrup or agave syrup to sweeten the mixture to your taste. Once heated, remove from heat and set aside to cool.
3. **Steam the Oat Milk:** In a small pot or milk frother, steam the oat milk until it's hot and frothy. If you don't have a milk frother, you can use a whisk or a hand-held frother to create froth.
4. **Assemble the Drink:** Fill a tall glass with ice cubes. Pour the raspberry puree over the ice, followed by the steamed oat milk. Stir gently to combine.
5. **Add the Sparkle:** Top the drink with chilled sparkling water or club soda. Stir gently to combine, leaving the bubbles intact.
6. **Garnish and Serve:** Garnish the drink with fresh raspberries and a sprig of mint. Serve immediately and enjoy the refreshing, bubbly goodness!

## Tips and Recommendations:

- **Sweetness:** Adjust the sweetness by adding more maple syrup or agave syrup to the raspberry puree if you prefer a sweeter drink.
- **Flavor Variations:** For an extra flavor boost, try adding a dash of ground cinnamon or nutmeg to the oat milk before steaming for a warm, spiced undertone.
- **Chill the Glass:** For an extra refreshing touch, chill your glass in the freezer for a few minutes before assembling the drink.
- **Texture:** If you prefer a creamier texture, you can use coconut milk or almond milk instead of oat milk, but oat milk pairs beautifully for a smooth and rich mouthfeel.

## Variations:

- **Peach Bellini Twist:** Substitute the raspberries with fresh peaches or a peach puree for a more traditional Bellini flavor.
- **Minty Raspberry Bellini:** Add a few fresh mint leaves to the raspberry puree and muddle them for an extra burst of minty freshness.
- **Berry Medley:** Create a mixed berry version by adding strawberries and blueberries to the raspberry puree for a deeper berry flavor.

## Pairing Suggestions:

- **Vegan Croissants:** Flaky, buttery vegan croissants are perfect for pairing with this light and refreshing drink, offering a lovely balance of flavors.
- **Citrus Salad:** A zesty citrus salad with grapefruit, orange, and a drizzle of olive oil provides a light, tangy complement to the richness of the raspberry latte.
- **Vegan Scones:** Pair with vegan scones or shortbread cookies for a delightful afternoon tea experience.

## Interesting Fact:

Did you know that Bellinis were originally created in Venice, Italy, and named after the 15th-century Venetian artist Giovanni Bellini? This non-alcoholic version brings the refreshing, sparkling essence of the original without the alcohol, making it perfect for all occasions!

# Kiwi Coconut Mint Refresher

*Looking for a revitalizing and refreshing drink that combines tropical flavors with a cool, minty kick? The Kiwi Coconut Mint Refresher is your perfect summer companion. This invigorating drink blends the tangy, vibrant sweetness of kiwi with the creamy richness of coconut milk and the freshness of mint leaves. It's a tropical mocktail that's both hydrating and energizing, offering the perfect balance of fruity, creamy, and cool. Ideal for a hot day or when you need a burst of freshness, this drink is like a vacation in a glass!*

## Ingredients:

- 2 ripe kiwis, peeled and chopped
- 1/2 cup coconut milk (or coconut water for a lighter option)
- 1 tbsp maple syrup or agave syrup (optional, to taste)
- 1/4 cup fresh mint leaves, plus extra for garnish
- 1/2 cup cold water or coconut water
- 1/2 cup ice cubes
- Juice of 1/2 lime
- [Optional] 1/2 tsp spirulina powder for added nutrition
- Fresh kiwi slices, mint sprigs, or lime wedges (for garnish)

## Instructions:

1. **Prepare the Kiwi Puree:** In a blender, combine the chopped kiwis, coconut milk (or water), maple syrup (if using), and lime juice. Blend until smooth and creamy.
2. **Add Fresh Mint:** Add the fresh mint leaves to the blender and pulse a few times to incorporate the mint into the puree.
3. **Adjust Sweetness:** Taste the mixture and adjust the sweetness if desired by adding more maple syrup or agave syrup.
4. **Mix with Water:** Pour in the cold water (or coconut water) and blend again until the mixture is fully combined.
5. **Serve Over Ice:** Fill a tall glass with ice cubes and pour the kiwi coconut mixture over the ice.
6. **Garnish and Serve:** Garnish with fresh kiwi slices, a sprig of mint, or a lime wedge. Serve immediately for a refreshing and revitalizing drink!

## Tips and Recommendations:

- **Sweetness:** Adjust the sweetness according to your taste. If you like a less sweet drink, use coconut water instead of coconut milk and skip the added sweetener.
- **Mint Freshness:** For an even more intense mint flavor, muddle a few mint leaves at the bottom of the glass before pouring in the drink.
- **Nutrition Boost:** Add a teaspoon of spirulina powder or a handful of spinach to the mixture for a green boost without compromising the flavor.
- **Texture:** If you prefer a thicker, smoothie-like consistency, reduce the amount of water or coconut water and add more coconut milk.

## Variations:

- **Pineapple Coconut Mint Refresher:** Swap out the kiwi for fresh pineapple for a sweeter, tropical twist.
- **Citrus Kiwi Refresher:** Add a squeeze of orange or lemon juice to the mix for an extra citrus zing.
- **Green Kiwi Refresher:** Add a handful of spinach or kale to the blend for an added green boost, making this a refreshing green smoothie mocktail.

## Pairing Suggestions:

- **Vegan Wraps or Tacos:** Pair with light and flavorful vegan wraps or soft tacos filled with fresh veggies, guacamole, or hummus. The coolness of the drink complements the savory flavors beautifully.
- **Coconut Rice:** A side of coconut rice or quinoa salad will enhance the tropical vibe of the Kiwi Coconut Mint Refresher, creating a delightful meal pairing.
- **Fruit Salad:** Complement with a light fruit salad featuring tropical fruits like mango, pineapple, and papaya for a full-on tropical experience.

## Interesting Fact:

Did you know that kiwis are actually a type of berry? Despite their fuzzy exterior, kiwis are technically classified as a berry, packed with more vitamin C than an orange, making them a great addition to your diet for immunity support!

## Cultural Connection:

The **Kiwi Coconut Mint Refresher** draws inspiration from tropical flavors found in many parts of the world, particularly the Pacific Islands and Southeast Asia, where coconut, mint, and tropical fruits like kiwi thrive. Combining these ingredients creates a drink that is both refreshing and deeply rooted in tropical culinary traditions, offering a mini-escape to a paradise of flavors with every sip.

# Apple Cinnamon Spritz Coffee

*Get cozy with this autumn-inspired drink that blends the warmth of cinnamon, the crispness of apple, and the smoothness of coffee. The Apple Cinnamon Spritz Coffee is a delightful, non-alcoholic mocktail that perfectly captures the flavors of fall in a cup. The effervescence of sparkling water adds a refreshing twist to the usual spiced apple beverage, making it an ideal pick-me-up or a fun alternative to your usual coffee. Whether you're sipping it by the fire or serving it at a gathering, this festive drink brings comfort and cheer with every bubbly sip.*

## Ingredients:

- 1 shot (1 ounce) of espresso
- 1/2 cup fresh apple juice (preferably cold-pressed)
- 1/2 tsp ground cinnamon
- 1 tbsp maple syrup or agave syrup (optional, for sweetness)
- 1/4 cup sparkling water (or soda water for extra fizz)
- 1/4 cup steamed oat milk (or any preferred milk)
- Ice cubes
- [Optional] 1-2 slices of fresh apple, for garnish
- [Optional] Cinnamon stick, for garnish

## Instructions:

1. **Brew the Espresso:** Start by brewing a shot of espresso using your preferred method. Set aside.
2. **Prepare the Apple-Cinnamon Base:** In a small pot, heat the apple juice and ground cinnamon over low heat. Stir constantly until the mixture is warm, about 1-2 minutes.
3. **Sweeten (Optional):** Add maple syrup or agave syrup to the apple-cinnamon mixture and stir to combine. Taste and adjust sweetness as needed.
4. **Assemble the Drink:** In a tall glass, fill with ice cubes. Pour the warm apple-cinnamon mixture over the ice, leaving some room at the top.
5. **Add the Espresso:** Gently pour the freshly brewed espresso over the apple mixture. Let it settle slightly for a layered effect.
6. **Top with Fizz:** Add the sparkling water on top of the espresso mixture, giving it a light stir to combine.
7. **Finish with Milk:** Steam your oat milk (or your preferred milk) until frothy, then pour it over the drink, allowing it to blend smoothly with the other ingredients.
8. **Garnish and Serve:** Garnish with fresh apple slices and a cinnamon stick for an extra festive touch. Serve immediately and enjoy!

## Tips and Recommendations:

- **Adjusting Sweetness:** Depending on your preference for sweetness, you can add more or less maple syrup. Alternatively, a drizzle of honey also works beautifully in this drink.
- **Cinnamon Flavor:** If you prefer a stronger cinnamon taste, feel free to add a pinch of ground cinnamon to the top of the drink for a little extra warmth.
- **Espresso Strength:** For a bolder flavor, use a double shot of espresso. If you prefer a milder flavor, you can opt for a shot of decaf espresso or reduce the amount of coffee.
- **Milk Options:** If you're not a fan of oat milk, feel free to substitute with almond milk, coconut milk, or your preferred dairy-free option. The key is to use a milk that froths well for the creamy finish.

## Variations:

- **Caramel Apple Cinnamon Spritz Coffee:** Add a drizzle of vegan caramel sauce to the apple-cinnamon base for an extra indulgent touch.
- **Iced Version:** For a refreshing cold version, simply blend the apple-cinnamon mixture with ice and skip the steaming milk. Top with cold espresso and sparkling water.
- **Spicy Kick:** For a little extra heat, add a pinch of cayenne pepper or ground ginger to the apple-cinnamon mixture. It will complement the sweetness of the apple juice and the boldness of the coffee.

## Pairing Suggestions:

- **Vegan Apple Pie:** The perfect pairing to this spiced drink is a slice of warm, vegan apple pie. The cinnamon and apple flavors in the drink will enhance the dessert's richness.
- **Crispy Vegan Tacos:** Pair this spritz coffee with a side of crispy vegan tacos or loaded nachos for a satisfying, cozy meal.
- **Cinnamon Rolls:** A cinnamon roll or sticky bun is an ideal breakfast or snack to go with your **Apple Cinnamon Spritz Coffee**, making the morning even more special.

## Interesting Fact:

Did you know that **apple cinnamon** is one of the most popular flavor combinations for fall? It's so beloved that it's used in everything from baked goods to beverages, evoking feelings of warmth and comfort. Apple and cinnamon are also a classic pairing in many cultures, with the spices being known for their antioxidant and digestive benefits.

# Tropical Punch Iced Coffee

*Escape to a tropical paradise with the Tropical Punch Iced Coffee, a refreshing blend of rich coffee, vibrant fruit juices, and a splash of citrus. Perfect for sunny afternoons or when you're craving a little island getaway, this drink combines the boldness of coffee with the sweetness of pineapple, orange, and coconut. The effervescent fizz from sparkling water adds an extra kick, while a touch of mint gives it a refreshing finish. With every sip, you'll be transported to a tropical beach, making this the ultimate summer coffee mocktail!*

## Ingredients:

- 1 shot (1 ounce) of espresso
- 1/2 cup pineapple juice (preferably fresh or 100% juice)
- 1/4 cup orange juice
- 1 tbsp coconut cream (for richness)
- 1/2 tsp lime juice
- 1/4 cup sparkling water
- Ice cubes
- Fresh mint leaves (for garnish)
- [Optional] 1 tbsp agave syrup or maple syrup (for sweetness)
- [Optional] Pineapple slices or orange wedges (for garnish)

## Instructions:

1. **Brew the Espresso:** Start by brewing a shot of espresso using your preferred method. Set aside to cool.
2. **Prepare the Tropical Juice Mix:** In a shaker or small pitcher, combine the pineapple juice, orange juice, coconut cream, and lime juice. If you'd like a sweeter drink, add a tablespoon of agave syrup or maple syrup to taste. Stir or shake well until the coconut cream is fully incorporated.
3. **Assemble the Drink:** Fill a tall glass with ice cubes. Pour the tropical juice mixture over the ice, filling the glass halfway.
4. **Add the Espresso:** Slowly pour the cooled espresso over the juice mixture, allowing it to settle slightly to create a layered effect.
5. **Top with Fizz:** Add the sparkling water on top of the drink for a fizzy, refreshing finish.
6. **Garnish and Serve:** Garnish with fresh mint leaves, and if desired, add a slice of pineapple or a wedge of orange for a tropical touch. Serve immediately and enjoy the tropical vibes!

## Tips and Recommendations:

- **Adjusting Sweetness:** If you prefer a sweeter drink, feel free to add more agave syrup or maple syrup. You can also use a sweetened coconut cream for an even creamier texture.
- **Stronger Coffee Flavor:** For a bolder coffee taste, consider using a double shot of espresso or cold brew coffee.

- **Coconut Variations:** If you're not a fan of coconut, you can substitute the coconut cream with a splash of coconut milk for a lighter flavor.
- **Juice Options:** You can experiment with other tropical juices like mango or guava for a unique twist on this drink.

## Variations:

- **Tropical Iced Coffee Float:** Add a scoop of vegan coconut or pineapple sorbet on top of your iced coffee for a fun, float-style treat.
- **Tropical Iced Coffee with Ginger:** For a spiced kick, add a few slices of fresh ginger to the tropical juice mixture. It pairs wonderfully with the citrus flavors.
- **Iced Coffee Mocktail with Berry Twist:** Add a handful of fresh berries, such as strawberries or blueberries, to the tropical juice mix for an extra burst of flavor and color.

## Pairing Suggestions:

- **Vegan Coconut Macaroons:** These chewy, coconut-flavored cookies perfectly complement the coconut notes in the drink.
- **Tropical Fruit Salad:** A light and refreshing fruit salad with mango, papaya, and kiwi would balance the richness of the iced coffee.
- **Vegan Banana Bread:** Pair your **Tropical Punch Iced Coffee** with a slice of soft, moist banana bread for a satisfying, tropical-inspired snack.

## Interesting Fact:

Did you know that **pineapple** was once considered a symbol of wealth and hospitality in Europe? During the 17th century, the fruit was so rare and expensive that it was often used as a decorative centerpiece at dinner parties, signaling the host's status. Pineapple is now a popular tropical fruit used in many drinks for its sweetness and tang.

# Virgin Blue Lagoon Latte

*Dive into the deep blue with the Virgin Blue Lagoon Latte, a vibrant, refreshing mocktail that combines the best of tropical flavors with the richness of coffee. Inspired by the sparkling blue lagoons of the tropics, this latte features a striking blue hue from butterfly pea flower extract, creating an eye-catching drink that is as beautiful as it is delicious. Topped with a frothy coconut cream layer, it offers a sweet, creamy finish with a burst of citrus to balance the richness. Whether you're hosting a gathering or simply treating yourself to something extraordinary, this mocktail will add a splash of fun to your day.*

## Ingredients:

- 1 shot (1 ounce) of espresso
- 1/2 tsp butterfly pea flower extract (for the blue color)
- 1/2 cup coconut milk (or any plant-based milk)
- 1 tbsp agave syrup (or maple syrup)
- 1/2 tsp fresh lime juice
- 1/4 cup ice cubes
- 2 tbsps coconut cream (for topping)
- [Optional] A few drops of vanilla extract (for a sweet twist)
- [Optional] Fresh mint leaves (for garnish)

## Instructions:

1. **Brew the Espresso:** Start by brewing a shot of espresso using your preferred method. Set aside to cool slightly.
2. **Prepare the Blue Lagoon Layer:** In a small glass or bowl, dissolve the butterfly pea flower extract in a tiny splash of hot water (about 1-2 teaspoons). Stir well until the blue color fully dissolves.
3. **Make the Coconut Milk Base:** In a small saucepan or microwave, heat the coconut milk gently until warm but not boiling. Add the agave syrup and lime juice, stirring until combined.
4. **Assemble the Drink:** Fill a tall glass with ice cubes. Pour the blue butterfly pea flower mixture into the glass, followed by the warm coconut milk mixture.
5. **Add the Espresso:** Slowly pour the espresso over the back of a spoon into the glass to create a layered effect.
6. **Top with Coconut Cream:** Gently spoon coconut cream on top of the drink to create a frothy, creamy layer.
7. **Garnish and Serve:** Garnish with fresh mint leaves for a pop of color and a refreshing touch. Serve immediately and enjoy the tropical vibes!

## Tips and Recommendations:

- **Color Intensity:** The blue color intensity of the butterfly pea flower can vary based on the amount used. For a more vibrant hue, add a little extra extract, but be mindful not to overpower the flavor.
- **Sweetness Adjustment:** If you prefer a sweeter drink, feel free to add more agave syrup or try a flavored syrup like vanilla or coconut for an added layer of flavor.
- **Dairy-Free Option:** The recipe is already vegan, but if you prefer a different milk, you can substitute coconut milk with almond milk or oat milk.
- **Coconut Cream Texture:** For a fluffier coconut cream topping, refrigerate the can of coconut cream overnight and use the solidified top part for a whipped consistency.

## Variations:

- **Blue Lagoon Latte with a Twist:** Add a few drops of vanilla extract or a splash of coconut syrup for a richer, more aromatic flavor.
- **Frozen Blue Lagoon Latte:** Blend all the ingredients (except the espresso) with ice to create a smoothie-like texture for a cool, frozen treat on hot days.
- **Citrus Blue Lagoon Latte:** Experiment with a different citrus flavor by swapping lime juice for lemon or orange juice for a new twist on the classic.

## Pairing Suggestions:

- **Vegan Coconut Macaroons:** The tropical coconut flavor of these chewy macaroons pairs beautifully with the rich, creamy notes of the Blue Lagoon Latte.
- **Fruit Tartlets:** A light fruit tart, especially with citrus or tropical fruits, complements the drink's refreshing and vibrant flavors.
- **Light Vegan Scones:** These subtly sweet scones would balance the boldness of the espresso and enhance the tropical sweetness of the latte.

## Interesting Fact:

Did you know that **butterfly pea flower** is often used in traditional Thai and Malaysian drinks, known for its natural color-changing properties? When combined with an acid like lime juice, it shifts from blue to purple, adding an element of surprise and fun to any drink.

# Cranberry Limeade Iced Coffee

*Refresh your senses with the tangy-sweet delight of a Cranberry Limeade Iced Coffee. This vibrant mocktail combines the rich, bold flavors of freshly brewed coffee with the tartness of cranberry and the zesty kick of lime, creating an unforgettable iced beverage. The addition of a touch of sweetness and a splash of soda makes it the perfect summer cooler or a fun pick-me-up for any time of day. It's the ideal blend of coffee and fruit, offering a balance of boldness and brightness in every sip.*

## Ingredients:

- 1 shot (1 ounce) of brewed espresso
- 1/4 cup cranberry juice (preferably unsweetened)
- 1 tbsp lime juice (freshly squeezed)
- 1 tbsp agave syrup or maple syrup (optional, adjust for sweetness)
- 1/4 cup sparkling water or club soda
- 1/2 cup ice cubes
- [Optional] 1-2 lime slices (for garnish)
- [Optional] Fresh mint leaves (for garnish)

## Instructions:

1. **Brew the Espresso:** Brew a shot of espresso using your preferred method. Set aside to cool for a few minutes.
2. **Prepare the Cranberry-Lime Base:** In a shaker or mixing glass, combine the cranberry juice, lime juice, and agave syrup (if using). Stir well until the syrup dissolves completely.
3. **Assemble the Iced Coffee:** Fill a tall glass with ice cubes. Pour the cooled espresso over the ice, followed by the cranberry-lime mixture.
4. **Add Sparkling Water:** Gently pour the sparkling water or club soda into the glass, allowing the fizzy bubbles to create a light, refreshing effervescence.
5. **Garnish and Serve:** Garnish with a slice of lime and a sprig of fresh mint for an extra touch of color and fragrance. Stir gently before sipping.

## Tips and Recommendations:

- **Adjusting Sweetness:** If you prefer a sweeter drink, feel free to add more syrup or switch to a flavored syrup like raspberry or elderflower for a unique twist.
- **Citrus Boost:** For an extra citrusy punch, you can add a splash of lemon juice along with the lime juice to deepen the tangy profile.
- **Cold Brew Alternative:** If you prefer a smoother coffee flavor, substitute the espresso with cold brew coffee for a less intense but still bold taste.
- **Chill the Cranberry Juice:** For an even more refreshing experience, chill the cranberry juice ahead of time or use frozen cranberry ice cubes.

## Variations:

- **Cranberry Mint Iced Coffee:** Add a handful of fresh mint leaves to the cranberry-lime mixture before shaking to infuse the drink with a fragrant minty note.
- **Spiced Cranberry Limeade:** For a spicy kick, add a pinch of ground cinnamon or ginger to the cranberry-lime base, creating a warming contrast to the cold drink.
- **Non-Coffee Version:** For a non-caffeinated option, replace the espresso with a shot of chilled herbal tea, such as hibiscus or rooibos, to maintain the tartness and vibrancy without the coffee.

## Pairing Suggestions:

- **Vegan Lemon Bars:** The tangy and sweet flavors of vegan lemon bars will complement the cranberry-lime combo and provide a zesty contrast to the iced coffee.
- **Crispy Plant-Based Spring Rolls:** Serve with a side of light, crispy spring rolls filled with veggies for a perfect balance of fresh and savory alongside the fruity iced coffee.
- **Vegan Scones:** A fresh, crumbly scone with berries or citrus will pair nicely with the coffee's fruity notes, adding a comforting touch to the drink.

## Interesting Fact:

Did you know that **cranberries** are one of the only fruits native to North America? They've been used for centuries in traditional medicine and were even carried by sailors to prevent scurvy, thanks to their high vitamin C content.

## Cultural Connection:

The **Cranberry Limeade Iced Coffee** draws inspiration from the vibrant, refreshing flavors of summer beverages often enjoyed in coastal regions. Cranberry and lime are both commonly used in North American beverages, offering a tangy and thirst-quenching combination that has become a staple in refreshing mocktails. This recipe reimagines those classic flavors with the rich depth of espresso, offering a perfect fusion of coffee culture and fruity refreshment.

# Honeydew Basil Sparkling Coffee

*Indulge in the refreshing and fragrant allure of Honeydew Basil Sparkling Coffee, a perfect fusion of smooth coffee, sweet melon, and aromatic basil. The subtle sweetness of honeydew pairs effortlessly with the herbal freshness of basil, while the effervescence of sparkling water gives this drink a light, invigorating twist. This vibrant mocktail brings a unique and sophisticated flair to your coffee experience, making it an exciting and refreshing treat for any time of day. Whether you're hosting a brunch or looking for a creative new coffee experience, this sparkling coffee is sure to delight!*

## Ingredients:

- 1 shot (1 ounce) of brewed espresso
- 1/2 cup honeydew melon, cubed
- 2-3 fresh basil leaves (plus more for garnish)
- 1 tbsp agave syrup or maple syrup (optional, for sweetness)
- 1/4 cup sparkling water or club soda
- 1/2 cup ice cubes
- [Optional] 1-2 basil leaves (for garnish)
- [Optional] Honeydew slices or melon balls (for garnish)

## Instructions:

1. **Prepare the Honeydew Basil Puree:** In a blender, combine the honeydew melon cubes with basil leaves. Blend until smooth.
2. **Sweeten to Taste:** Taste the honeydew basil puree and add the agave or maple syrup if you'd like it sweeter. Blend again to combine.
3. **Brew the Espresso:** Brew a shot of espresso using your preferred method and set aside to cool slightly.
4. **Assemble the Drink:** In a tall glass, add the ice cubes. Pour the cooled espresso over the ice, followed by the honeydew basil puree.
5. **Add Sparkling Water:** Top with sparkling water or club soda, gently stirring to combine.
6. **Garnish and Serve:** Garnish with a few fresh basil leaves and a slice of honeydew or melon balls for a touch of elegance. Enjoy!

## Tips and Recommendations:

- **Sweetness Adjustments:** If you prefer a sweeter drink, feel free to increase the amount of agave syrup or opt for a flavored syrup, like vanilla or elderflower.
- **Citrus Twist:** Add a splash of fresh lime or lemon juice to brighten the flavors even more. The citrus pairs beautifully with both the basil and honeydew.
- **Chilled Espresso:** If you prefer a smoother texture and cooler temperature, chill the espresso before adding it to the drink to prevent it from melting the ice too quickly.
- **Frozen Melon Option:** For an even colder drink, blend the honeydew with ice to create a slushier texture, perfect for hot days.

## Variations:

- **Melon Mix:** Swap the honeydew for cantaloupe or watermelon for a different take on this refreshing mocktail. Each melon brings its own sweetness and flavor.
- **Basil-Infused Sparkling Water:** If you want to enhance the basil flavor, try infusing the sparkling water with fresh basil leaves for 10-15 minutes before adding it to your drink.
- **Dairy-Free Version:** For a creamy texture, substitute the sparkling water with a splash of coconut milk or oat milk for a smoother, indulgent twist.

## Pairing Suggestions:

- **Vegan Summer Rolls:** Fresh and light, these rolls filled with veggies and herbs make a perfect side to balance the refreshing qualities of the Honeydew Basil Sparkling Coffee.
- **Crispy Chickpea Salad:** Pair this drink with a crunchy, light salad featuring roasted chickpeas for a satisfying, healthy meal.
- **Lemon Poppy Seed Muffins:** The citrusy and slightly sweet flavors of these muffins will enhance the herbal and melon notes of the coffee, making for a balanced and enjoyable treat.

## Interesting Fact:

Did you know that **honeydew melon** is not only a hydrating fruit but also a rich source of vitamins C and B6, which can help boost your immune system and improve mood? It's no wonder it makes for such a refreshing addition to any beverage!

## Cultural Connection:

Melon-based drinks are popular in many cultures, especially during hot summer months. In Southeast Asia, for example, you might find refreshing melon drinks served with herbs and spices. The combination of melon and basil in this recipe brings together both the coolness of summer and the aromatic elements often used in Mediterranean and Asian cuisine. This **Honeydew Basil Sparkling Coffee** takes inspiration from these global influences, creating a unique and revitalizing drink.

# Cherry Lemonade Iced Latte

*Brighten your day with a Cherry Lemonade Iced Latte, a refreshing blend of rich coffee, tart cherry, and zesty lemon, all served over ice for the ultimate summer sip. This creative mocktail combines the boldness of iced coffee with the sweet-tart tang of homemade cherry lemonade, creating a drink that's both invigorating and indulgent. Whether you're lounging on a warm afternoon or seeking a new iced coffee experience, this beverage is the perfect balance of fruity sweetness and coffee richness!*

## Ingredients:

- 1 shot (1 ounce) of brewed espresso
- 1/4 cup cherry juice or homemade cherry syrup*
- 1/4 cup fresh lemon juice
- 1 tbsp maple syrup or agave syrup (optional, for added sweetness)
- 1/2 cup ice cubes
- 1/2 cup chilled almond milk or oat milk (for a dairy-free option)
- [Optional] Fresh cherries and lemon slices for garnish*For homemade cherry syrup: Blend fresh cherries with a little sugar and water, then strain to create a syrup.

## Instructions:

1. **Brew the Espresso:** Start by brewing your espresso shot using your preferred method. Set it aside to cool.
2. **Prepare the Cherry Lemonade Mix:** In a small mixing glass, combine the cherry juice or syrup with the fresh lemon juice. Add the maple or agave syrup if you'd like a sweeter drink. Stir to mix well.
3. **Assemble the Drink:** Fill a tall glass with ice cubes. Pour the cooled espresso over the ice.
4. **Add Cherry Lemonade Mix:** Pour the cherry-lemon mixture into the glass with espresso and ice.
5. **Top with Milk:** Gently pour the chilled almond milk (or your milk of choice) into the glass, stirring slightly to combine.
6. **Garnish and Serve:** Garnish with fresh cherries and a slice of lemon on the rim of the glass for a decorative touch. Serve immediately and enjoy!

## Tips and Recommendations:

- **Balance the Tartness:** If the cherry lemonade mix is too tart for your taste, feel free to add more sweetener, or use a sweeter variety of cherry juice.
- **For Extra Flavor:** Add a splash of vanilla extract or a pinch of cinnamon to the milk for an additional layer of flavor.
- **Chilled Espresso:** For a smoother texture, make the espresso ahead of time and refrigerate it to prevent melting the ice too quickly.

- **Vegan Whipped Cream:** Top your Cherry Lemonade Iced Latte with a dollop of dairy-free whipped cream for an indulgent finishing touch.

## Variations:

- **Tropical Twist:** Add a splash of pineapple juice to the cherry lemonade mix for a tropical vibe that complements the coffee.
- **Berry Blast:** For an extra burst of berry flavor, mix in a little raspberry or strawberry puree with the cherry and lemon juice.
- **Frozen Cherry Latte:** Blend the espresso, cherry lemonade mixture, and ice together to create a frozen version of this refreshing drink.

## Pairing Suggestions:

- **Vegan Scones:** Pair your Cherry Lemonade Iced Latte with freshly baked vegan scones. Their crumbly texture and mild sweetness balance the tangy and bold flavors of the coffee.
- **Grilled Veggie Wraps:** The slight bitterness of the coffee and tartness of the lemonade makes this drink a perfect companion for savory dishes like grilled vegetable wraps or a light Mediterranean salad.
- **Lemon Poppy Seed Muffins:** A light, lemony muffin complements the citrus notes in the drink and adds a touch of sweetness.

## Interesting Fact:

Did you know that **cherries** are one of the few fruits that contain melatonin, a natural sleep aid? Drinking this vibrant mocktail could help you relax as you enjoy a refreshing afternoon treat!

## Cultural Connection:

Iced coffee is a beloved drink around the world, often enjoyed as a cool refreshment on hot days. The combination of coffee with fruit flavors like cherry and lemon has its roots in many cultures that blend coffee with fresh, local fruits. This **Cherry Lemonade Iced Latte** is a modern twist on that tradition, bringing a fruity zing to your coffee experience with a light and playful flair.

# Virgin Mojito Iced Coffee

*Looking for a refreshing twist on your regular iced coffee? Try the Virgin Mojito Iced Coffee, where the classic flavors of mint, lime, and a touch of sweetness meet the deep, rich taste of coffee. This invigorating mocktail is perfect for hot afternoons when you crave something cool and energizing. With a burst of fresh mint, a squeeze of tangy lime, and a smooth iced coffee base, it's like enjoying a mojito with a coffee kick. Light, zesty, and utterly refreshing, this drink is sure to become your new summer favorite!*

## Ingredients:

- 1 shot (1 ounce) of brewed espresso (or cold brew for a smoother option)
- 1/4 cup fresh lime juice (about 2 limes)
- 6-8 fresh mint leaves, plus extra for garnish
- 1 tbsp maple syrup or agave syrup (optional, for sweetness)
- 1/2 cup ice cubes
- 1/2 cup chilled coconut water or almond milk (for a tropical twist, use coconut water)
- [Optional] Lime slices and a sprig of mint for garnish

## Instructions:

1. **Brew the Espresso:** Brew your espresso shot using your preferred method, or use cold brew coffee for a smoother, less acidic flavor. Set it aside to cool.
2. **Muddle the Mint:** In a glass, gently muddle the fresh mint leaves with the lime juice and maple syrup (if using) to release the mint oils and infuse the lime.
3. **Add Ice and Coffee:** Fill a tall glass with ice cubes. Pour the cooled espresso (or cold brew) over the ice.
4. **Mix the Drink:** Add the muddled mint and lime mixture to the glass with coffee and ice. Stir gently to combine the flavors.
5. **Top with Coconut Water or Milk:** Pour in the chilled coconut water or almond milk, stirring again for an even blend of flavors.
6. **Garnish and Serve:** Garnish with a sprig of fresh mint and a slice of lime on the rim of the glass. Serve immediately and enjoy!

## Tips and Recommendations:

- **Balance the Sweetness:** Adjust the amount of sweetener to your taste. If you prefer a less sweet version, skip the syrup or use a natural sweetener like stevia.
- **For Extra Flavor:** Add a pinch of ground ginger or a splash of vanilla extract to the lime-mint mix for added depth.
- **Frozen Version:** To make this drink even more refreshing, freeze the mint-lime syrup in ice cube trays and use these cubes instead of regular ice.

- **Cold Brew Coffee:** If you're looking for a smoother, less acidic flavor, cold brew coffee is a great option, especially in combination with the minty lime.

## Variations:

- **Tropical Mojito Iced Coffee:** Swap the lime juice for fresh pineapple juice to create a tropical, pineapple-mint coffee mocktail.
- **Coconut Mojito Iced Coffee:** For an even more tropical twist, increase the amount of coconut water and top with coconut whipped cream for a creamy finish.
- **Berry Mojito Iced Coffee:** Add a handful of muddled berries (like raspberries or strawberries) to the mint and lime mix for a fruity variation.

## Pairing Suggestions:

- **Vegan Tacos:** Pair this **Virgin Mojito Iced Coffee** with zesty vegan tacos. The refreshing mint-lime flavor complements the spices of a Mexican-inspired meal.
- **Avocado Toast:** The light, refreshing nature of this iced coffee pairs beautifully with creamy avocado toast for a light breakfast or brunch.
- **Vegan Chocolate Chip Cookies:** For a sweet treat, pair this drink with vegan chocolate chip cookies. The minty coffee flavor contrasts nicely with the chocolatey goodness.

## Interesting Fact:

Did you know that **mint** has been used for centuries not just in cooking, but for medicinal purposes too? It's known to help with digestion and soothe headaches, making this mocktail as therapeutic as it is delicious!

## Cultural Connection:

The **Mojito** is a classic Cuban cocktail, often associated with refreshing summer nights and vibrant Caribbean flavors. This **Virgin Mojito Iced Coffee** brings a non-alcoholic twist to the classic drink by incorporating coffee for an extra burst of energy, making it a global fusion of two beloved refreshers: coffee and mojito.

# Pineapple Sage Iced Tea

*Escape to a tropical paradise with a glass of Pineapple Sage Iced Tea - an invigorating blend of sweet pineapple and aromatic sage. This refreshing iced tea is a vibrant fusion of earthy, herbal flavors and juicy fruitiness, making it the perfect drink to cool down on a hot day. With a hint of sweetness and a dash of sophistication from the sage, it's a mocktail that's as unique as it is delicious. Whether you're lounging by the pool or enjoying a sunny afternoon, this iced tea will transport you to a serene garden oasis with every sip.*

## Ingredients:

- 2 cups water
- 2-3 pineapple sage sprigs (or regular sage if unavailable)
- 1 cup fresh pineapple chunks (or pineapple juice if fresh isn't available)
- 1-2 tsps honey or maple syrup (optional, for sweetness)
- 2 black tea bags or 2 tbsps loose-leaf black tea
- 1 tbsp fresh lime juice (optional, for a citrusy kick)
- Ice cubes
- [Optional] Pineapple slices and a sprig of sage for garnish

## Instructions:

1. **Boil the Water:** In a small saucepan, bring the water to a boil. Once boiling, remove it from the heat and add the tea bags or loose-leaf tea. Let it steep for about 5 minutes to create a strong tea.
2. **Infuse with Sage:** While the tea is steeping, add the fresh pineapple sage sprigs to the hot tea. Allow the herbs to infuse for an additional 5-10 minutes to impart a rich, earthy flavor.
3. **Prepare Pineapple Juice:** If you're using fresh pineapple, blend the pineapple chunks until smooth. If using pineapple juice, skip this step.
4. **Sweeten the Tea:** After the tea has steeped and cooled slightly, remove the tea bags and strain out the sage leaves. Stir in honey or maple syrup to taste for a gentle sweetness.
5. **Chill the Tea:** Let the tea cool to room temperature, then refrigerate it until cold (about 30 minutes to an hour).
6. **Assemble the Drink:** Fill a tall glass with ice cubes. Pour the chilled pineapple sage tea over the ice. Add fresh pineapple juice or blend a small amount of pineapple with lime juice for an extra burst of flavor.
7. **Garnish and Serve:** Garnish with a fresh sprig of sage and a slice of pineapple for an attractive presentation. Serve immediately and enjoy!

## Tips and Recommendations:

- **Adjust Sweetness:** If you prefer a less sweet drink, reduce the amount of honey or syrup, or skip it entirely for a more herbal, refreshing flavor.
- **Fresh vs. Juice:** Fresh pineapple will create a more vibrant, natural flavor, but pineapple juice is a convenient and equally delicious alternative.
- **Herbal Infusion:** If you enjoy strong herbal flavors, feel free to leave the sage sprigs in the tea for a longer time. Just be careful not to overdo it, as sage can become overpowering if steeped for too long.
- **Iced Version:** To keep your iced tea extra cool without diluting the flavor, freeze small pineapple cubes in ice trays and use them as ice cubes.

## Variations:

- **Tropical Twist:** Add a splash of coconut water or coconut milk for a tropical, creamy variation.
- **Citrus Burst:** For a zesty flavor, squeeze in extra lime or lemon juice.
- **Minty Fresh:** Add a few fresh mint leaves to the infusion process for a refreshing minty twist.

## Pairing Suggestions:

- **Vegan Tacos:** The fresh, vibrant flavor of this iced tea complements the spiciness of vegan tacos, especially those with smoky flavors like chipotle or paprika.
- **Fresh Fruit Salad:** Serve alongside a light fruit salad with tropical fruits like mango, papaya, and kiwi for a refreshing, wholesome snack.
- **Vegan Cheese Platter:** The earthy herbal notes of sage in this tea pair wonderfully with a vegan cheese platter featuring soft cheeses like cashew-based brie or tangy vegan cheddar.

## Interesting Fact:

Did you know that **pineapple sage** has been used for centuries in herbal medicine? It's known for its calming effects and is said to help with digestion and reduce stress. It's no wonder this soothing iced tea is the perfect summer refresher!

## Cultural Connection:

Sage has a long history of use in various cultures, particularly in Mediterranean and Native American traditions, where it's believed to have cleansing and healing properties. Paired with tropical pineapple, this modern take on iced tea combines the benefits of ancient herbal wisdom with the fresh, bright flavors of the tropics.

# Grapefruit Rosemary Sparkler

*Bursting with tangy citrus and the aromatic depth of fresh rosemary, the Grapefruit Rosemary Sparkler is the perfect balance of refreshing, bold, and herbaceous flavors. This fizzy mocktail is a delightful way to cool off on a hot day or add a bit of elegance to any gathering. The sparkling water elevates the drink with a lively effervescence, while the combination of grapefruit and rosemary offers a sophisticated twist on traditional citrus beverages. Whether you're entertaining or simply unwinding, this drink promises a sparkling escape in every sip.*

## Ingredients:

- 1 cup fresh grapefruit juice (about 2 medium grapefruits)
- 1-2 tsps fresh rosemary leaves, finely chopped
- 1 tbsp agave syrup or honey (optional, for sweetness)
- 1/2 tsp fresh lime juice (optional, for extra zest)
- 1 cup chilled sparkling water or club soda
- Ice cubes
- [Optional] Grapefruit slices and rosemary sprigs for garnish

## Instructions:

1. **Prepare the Grapefruit Juice:** Squeeze the fresh grapefruits until you have 1 cup of juice. Strain the juice to remove pulp and seeds for a smoother drink.
2. **Infuse the Rosemary:** In a small saucepan, add the rosemary leaves and 2 tablespoons of water. Heat gently on medium-low heat for about 2 minutes until the rosemary is fragrant and infused into the water. Allow it to cool.
3. **Sweeten the Juice:** Combine the fresh grapefruit juice, cooled rosemary infusion, and agave syrup or honey (if using) in a shaker or mixing glass. Add lime juice for extra brightness if desired. Shake well to blend.
4. **Serve with Ice:** Fill a tall glass with ice cubes. Pour the grapefruit-rosemary mixture over the ice, filling the glass about three-quarters full.
5. **Top with Sparkling Water:** Slowly pour the chilled sparkling water or club soda into the glass, topping off the drink and allowing it to fizz and sparkle.
6. **Garnish and Serve:** Garnish with a sprig of rosemary and a slice of grapefruit for an elegant, refreshing presentation. Serve immediately and enjoy the bubbly goodness!

## Tips and Recommendations:

- **Adjust Sweetness:** If you prefer a sweeter drink, you can increase the amount of agave syrup or honey to taste. You can also try using a splash of orange juice for added sweetness and depth.
- **Herbal Twist:** Feel free to experiment with other herbs, such as thyme or basil, for a unique variation.
- **Sparkling Water Alternatives:** For a more complex flavor, try using flavored sparkling waters, such as lemon or cucumber, to complement the grapefruit and rosemary.
- **Chill the Glasses:** For an extra touch of elegance, chill your serving glasses in the freezer before serving to keep the drink colder longer.

## Variations:

- **Citrus Medley:** Combine grapefruit with other citrus juices, such as orange or lemon, for a layered citrus flavor.
- **Ginger Sparkler:** Add a splash of ginger ale or ginger beer for a spicy kick.
- **Berry Infusion:** Muddle a few fresh berries (like raspberries or blackberries) at the bottom of the glass for a fruity twist before adding the grapefruit mixture.

## Pairing Suggestions:

- **Vegan Crostini:** Pair with crispy vegan crostini topped with avocado and roasted tomato for a light, savory snack.
- **Vegan Cheese Platter:** The bright, herby flavors of this mocktail work well with a variety of vegan cheeses, especially soft, creamy varieties like cashew-based cheese or vegan goat cheese.
- **Grilled Veggies:** Serve with grilled vegetables or a light vegetable salad to complement the citrusy, herbal notes.

## Interesting Fact:

Did you know that **rosemary** has been used for thousands of years in both cooking and medicine? Ancient Greeks and Romans considered it a symbol of remembrance and used it to enhance memory and focus. It's also believed to have anti-inflammatory and antioxidant properties.

## Cultural Connection:

The **rosemary sprig** has long been associated with Mediterranean cuisine and culture. Its strong, aromatic flavor has made it a staple in both savory and sweet dishes throughout history. When paired with grapefruit in this mocktail, it creates a refreshing yet deeply herbal experience that reflects the Mediterranean love for fresh, bold ingredients.

# Virgin Margarita Coffee

*Imagine the vibrant, zesty flavor of a margarita, but with the bold, comforting depth of coffee. Welcome to the Virgin Margarita Coffee, a refreshing twist on both the classic margarita and your favorite morning brew. This drink combines the tangy brightness of lime with the warmth of coffee and a dash of salt, mimicking the perfect margarita, but without the alcohol. It's a fun, energizing mocktail that's perfect for brunch or as a creative way to enjoy your coffee - especially if you're craving something bold and different. Serve it iced or chilled for a refreshing treat that's sure to spark your taste buds!*

## Ingredients:

- 1 shot (1 ounce) of brewed espresso (or strong coffee)
- 1 tbsp fresh lime juice (about 1 lime)
- 1 tsp agave syrup or simple syrup (adjust to taste)
- 1/4 tsp salt (or more to taste)
- 1/4 cup chilled sparkling water or club soda
- Ice cubes
- [Optional] Lime wedge or twist for garnish
- [Optional] Salt for rimming the glass

## Instructions:

1. **Brew the Coffee:** Brew a shot of espresso or a strong cup of coffee using your preferred method. If you want an extra bold flavor, use a darker roast.
2. **Prepare the Glass:** Optionally, rim your glass with lime juice and salt for that margarita feel. To do this, rub a lime wedge around the rim of your glass, then dip it into a small plate of salt.
3. **Mix the Ingredients:** In a cocktail shaker, combine the freshly brewed espresso, lime juice, and agave syrup (or simple syrup). Add the salt and shake gently to combine.
4. **Serve Over Ice:** Fill a glass with ice cubes, then pour the coffee-lime mixture over the ice.
5. **Add Sparkling Water:** Top off the drink with chilled sparkling water or club soda, giving it a fizzy lift. Stir gently to combine.
6. **Garnish and Serve:** Garnish with a lime wedge or twist on the rim for a touch of elegance and a hint of extra lime flavor. Serve immediately and enjoy your refreshing Virgin Margarita Coffee!

## Tips and Recommendations:

- **Adjust the Salt:** If you prefer a stronger margarita-like flavor, add a bit more salt, but be cautious - it can quickly overpower the drink.
- **Sweeten to Taste:** The sweetness can be adjusted based on your preference. Add more agave syrup if you like a sweeter coffee flavor.
- **Chill Your Coffee:** For a cooler, more refreshing drink, allow the brewed coffee to cool completely before mixing it with the other ingredients, or use ice cubes to chill the coffee before serving.
- **Use a Milk Frother:** If you want a creamier twist on this mocktail, froth some oat milk or coconut milk and top it with a foam layer to add smooth texture.

## Variations:

- **Iced Coffee Version:** If you prefer a classic iced coffee version, simply pour over more ice and skip the sparkling water.
- **Minty Twist:** Add a few crushed mint leaves to the shaker to introduce a fresh, minty layer that pairs beautifully with the lime and salt.
- **Spicy Kick:** Spice it up with a pinch of cayenne pepper or a few dashes of hot sauce for a margarita-style heat.

## Pairing Suggestions:

- **Guacamole and Chips:** The zesty lime and salt notes in the coffee pair wonderfully with creamy guacamole and crispy tortilla chips, making this the perfect drink for a casual snack or appetizer.
- **Vegan Tacos:** Pair this mocktail with vegan tacos, especially those with a citrusy or spicy filling like a black bean or jackfruit taco.
- **Coconut Cake:** The refreshing, slightly salty profile of this coffee complements the sweetness of coconut-based desserts like vegan coconut cake or coconut macaroons.

## Interesting Fact:

Did you know that the **margarita** is one of the most popular cocktails worldwide, and its origins are somewhat mysterious? While it's debated whether it was invented in Mexico or the United States, it's widely loved for its combination of tequila, lime, and salt - a flavor profile we've cleverly recreated in this non-alcoholic version!

## Cultural Connection:

The **margarita** has deep roots in Mexican culture, often associated with festive occasions, beachside relaxation, and celebrations. This Virgin Margarita Coffee is a playful homage to that tradition, offering the refreshing qualities of the margarita with the cozy, energizing flavors of coffee - a fusion that reflects the spirit of creativity and fun.

# Raspberry Mint Lemonade Iced Coffee

*Refresh yourself with a delightful twist on the classic iced coffee with this Raspberry Mint Lemonade Iced Coffee! This creative concoction is a burst of vibrant flavors that balances the rich, bold notes of coffee with the refreshing tang of lemonade, the sweetness of raspberries, and the coolness of mint. Perfect for a summer afternoon or a revitalizing morning treat, this mocktail offers the best of both worlds: a pick-me-up from coffee and a refreshing zing from fruity lemonade. Whether you're lounging by the pool or simply in need of a flavorful escape, this drink will surely brighten your day.*

## Ingredients:

- 1 shot (1 ounce) of brewed espresso (or strong cold brew coffee)
- 1/4 cup fresh lemon juice (about 2 lemons)
- 1/4 cup fresh raspberries (plus more for garnish)
- 1 tbsp maple syrup or agave syrup (adjust to taste)
- 4-5 fresh mint leaves (plus more for garnish)
- 1/2 cup cold water or sparkling water
- Ice cubes
- [Optional] Lemon slice or twist for garnish

## Instructions:

1. **Brew the Coffee:** Brew a shot of espresso or strong cold brew coffee. Let it cool slightly or chill it in the fridge to speed up the process.
2. **Prepare the Raspberry-Lemonade Mixture:** In a small blender or food processor, combine the fresh raspberries, lemon juice, and maple syrup. Blend until smooth.
3. **Muddle the Mint:** In a tall glass, lightly muddle the mint leaves using a muddler or the back of a spoon to release their oils and aroma.
4. **Combine the Ingredients:** Pour the cooled espresso (or cold brew) into the glass with the muddled mint, followed by the raspberry-lemonade mixture. Add cold water or sparkling water to create a refreshing fizz.
5. **Add Ice:** Fill the glass with ice cubes to chill the drink further and to create a refreshing iced experience.
6. **Garnish and Serve:** Garnish with fresh mint leaves, a few whole raspberries, and a lemon slice or twist for a touch of elegance. Serve immediately and enjoy!

## Tips and Recommendations:

- **Make It Extra Fizzy:** Use sparkling water instead of still water to add an extra level of effervescence and a lively twist.
- **Adjust the Sweetness:** The raspberry lemonade mix can be made as sweet as you like. If you prefer a more tart flavor, reduce the amount of syrup.
- **Chill the Coffee:** To avoid diluting the drink with melting ice, chill your coffee or cold brew in advance. Alternatively, you can freeze coffee ice cubes and use them for an extra coffee boost.
- **Minty Variation:** If you're a fan of mint, feel free to add a few more mint leaves for a stronger mint flavor. You can also blend the mint with the raspberry mixture for a smoother texture.

## Variations:

- **Berry Blend:** Add other berries like blackberries or strawberries to the raspberry lemonade mixture for a mixed berry twist.
- **Dairy-Free Option:** For a richer flavor, top the drink with coconut milk foam or a splash of almond milk for a creamy finish.
- **Iced Latte Version:** If you prefer a creamier iced coffee, swap out the cold water or sparkling water with chilled oat milk or almond milk for a smooth, dairy-free latte base.

## Pairing Suggestions:

- **Vegan Pastries:** Pair this iced coffee with a sweet vegan pastry like a raspberry almond croissant or a lemon poppy seed muffin to complement the drink's fruity and tangy flavors.
- **Fresh Fruit Salad:** Enjoy with a refreshing fruit salad to highlight the drink's citrusy and berry notes.
- **Veggie Wraps:** The light and zesty qualities of this iced coffee go wonderfully with fresh veggie wraps, especially those with avocado, cucumber, and a tangy dressing.

## Interesting Fact:

Did you know that **cold brew coffee** is made by steeping coarsely ground coffee beans in cold water for an extended period of time (usually 12-24 hours)? This method produces a smoother, less acidic coffee that's perfect for iced coffee drinks like this one!

## Cultural Connection:

Lemonade is a beloved drink worldwide, with variations found in many cultures - from the classic American version to Middle Eastern lemonade made with rose water. This **Raspberry Mint Lemonade Iced Coffee** combines cultural influences from both lemonade traditions and the coffee culture, making it a modern, refreshing twist on classic beverages.

# Orange Basil Iced Latte

*Take your iced latte to a whole new level with this Orange Basil Iced Latte! This refreshing twist blends the citrusy brightness of orange with the aromatic freshness of basil, creating a perfectly balanced drink that's both invigorating and indulgent. The smooth, bold flavor of espresso pairs beautifully with the zesty orange and the herbaceous undertones of basil, giving you a unique and revitalizing coffee experience. Ideal for warm days or when you're craving something both refreshing and energizing, this iced latte will surprise and delight your taste buds.*

## Ingredients:

- 1 shot (1 ounce) of brewed espresso (or cold brew coffee)
- 1/4 cup freshly squeezed orange juice (about 1 medium orange)
- 1 tbsp maple syrup or agave syrup (adjust to taste)
- 4-5 fresh basil leaves (plus more for garnish)
- 1/2 cup cold almond milk or oat milk (or your preferred milk)
- Ice cubes
- [Optional] Orange slice or zest for garnish

## Instructions:

1. **Brew the Coffee:** Brew a shot of espresso or prepare your cold brew coffee. If you're in a hurry, cold brew coffee can be made ahead of time and stored in the fridge for a smooth, less acidic taste.
2. **Prepare the Orange-Basil Syrup:** In a small saucepan, combine the freshly squeezed orange juice, maple syrup (or agave), and 4-5 basil leaves. Heat over low-medium heat for 2-3 minutes, stirring occasionally until the syrup is well combined and fragrant. Let it cool.
3. **Muddle the Basil:** In a tall glass, gently muddle a few extra basil leaves using a muddler or the back of a spoon. This will release the herb's natural oils, giving your drink a fragrant, basil-forward note.
4. **Combine the Ingredients:** Pour the brewed espresso (or cold brew) into the glass with the muddled basil. Add the cooled orange-basil syrup mixture and stir well to combine.
5. **Add Milk and Ice:** Fill the glass with ice cubes and pour in the almond milk or oat milk, adjusting the amount for your preferred level of creaminess. Stir again to combine.
6. **Garnish and Serve:** Garnish with fresh basil leaves, a slice of orange, or a zest of orange peel for an extra burst of citrus. Serve immediately and enjoy the refreshing flavors!

## Tips and Recommendations:

- **Basil Intensity:** If you love basil, feel free to muddle a few more leaves for a stronger basil flavor.
- **Sweetness Level:** The sweetness of the orange and maple syrup can be adjusted depending on your taste. If you like it sweeter, add more syrup. If you prefer a tangier drink, reduce the sweetness and let the orange shine through.
- **Chilled Coffee Option:** Make your iced latte even smoother by using cold brew coffee, which has a naturally sweeter and smoother profile than regular espresso.
- **Frozen Basil Ice Cubes:** Freeze a few basil leaves in ice cube trays with water and use them to cool your iced latte without diluting the flavors.

## Variations:

- **Citrus Twist:** For a more complex citrus flavor, add a dash of lemon or lime juice to the orange-basil syrup.
- **Dairy-Free Option:** Use any plant-based milk like coconut milk for a richer, creamier texture, or almond milk for a lighter finish.
- **Spicy Kick:** Add a pinch of cayenne pepper or ginger to the orange-basil syrup for a subtle spicy kick that complements the citrus and basil notes.

## Pairing Suggestions:

- **Citrusy Muffins:** Pair with a lemon poppy seed muffin or a citrus-infused scone to complement the fresh, zesty flavors of the drink.
- **Vegan Croissants:** The light, flaky texture of a vegan croissant pairs wonderfully with the creamy and aromatic flavors of the iced latte.
- **Avocado Toast:** For a savory pairing, enjoy this iced latte with avocado toast topped with fresh herbs, garlic, and a squeeze of lemon.

## Interesting Fact:

Did you know that basil, a key ingredient in this iced latte, is not only a culinary herb but also a symbol of love and protection in many cultures? In ancient Rome, basil was believed to have protective qualities and was even used as an offering to gods.

# Cinnamon Pear Sparkling Coffee

*Looking for something sweet, refreshing, and uniquely satisfying? The Cinnamon Pear Sparkling Coffee is the perfect balance of crisp fruitiness, warm spices, and effervescent fizz. This mocktail blends the rich flavor of coffee with the sweet, subtle tartness of pear, all finished with a sparkling twist. Infused with cinnamon for a hint of warmth and complexity, it's a drink that's both cozy and invigorating, ideal for any time of day when you're craving something special. This creative concoction combines the best of both worlds - a soothing coffee base with the lively pop of bubbles and the fresh, seasonal flavors of pear and spice.*

## Ingredients:

- 1 shot (1 ounce) of brewed espresso (or strong brewed coffee)
- 1/4 cup fresh pear juice (about half a ripe pear, juiced)
- 1/4 tsp ground cinnamon (or a cinnamon stick for infusing)
- 1 tsp maple syrup or agave syrup (adjust to taste)
- 1/2 cup sparkling water (chilled)
- Ice cubes
- [Optional] Thin pear slices and a cinnamon stick for garnish

## Instructions:

1. **Brew the Coffee:** Start by brewing a shot of espresso or prepare a strong cup of coffee. The bold, robust flavor of the coffee will serve as a perfect base for the fruity pear and the effervescent soda.
2. **Prepare the Pear Juice:** Juice a ripe pear to yield about 1/4 cup of fresh pear juice. If you don't have a juicer, you can blend the pear and strain it through a fine mesh sieve.
3. **Combine Cinnamon and Maple Syrup:** In a small saucepan, gently heat the pear juice with the ground cinnamon and maple syrup (or agave) over low heat for 2-3 minutes, stirring until well combined and fragrant. If you're using a cinnamon stick, allow it to infuse in the juice as it heats. Remove from heat and let it cool.
4. **Assemble the Drink:** In a tall glass, fill about half with ice cubes. Pour in the cooled cinnamon-pear mixture, followed by the freshly brewed espresso.
5. **Add the Sparkling Water:** Top the drink with chilled sparkling water, giving it a gentle stir to mix the flavors without losing the bubbles.
6. **Garnish and Serve:** Garnish with thin pear slices or a cinnamon stick for an extra touch of elegance. Serve immediately, and enjoy the refreshing, spiced burst of flavor!

## Tips and Recommendations:

- **Pear Juice:** If pear juice isn't available, you can blend fresh pears and strain the juice yourself, or substitute with store-bought pear nectar.
- **Sweetness Adjustments:** The sweetness of this drink can be adjusted by adding more maple syrup or agave syrup, depending on how sweet you like your drinks.
- **Spice Level:** For a stronger cinnamon flavor, add a pinch more ground cinnamon or steep a cinnamon stick in the pear juice while it heats.
- **Ice or No Ice?** If you prefer a less diluted drink, you can freeze some pear juice in ice cube trays and use those cubes instead of regular ice. This way, the pear flavor intensifies as the drink cools.

## Variations:

- **Apple Spice:** Swap the pear juice for apple juice for a slightly different flavor profile. Add a slice of apple as garnish to emphasize the fruity theme.
- **Ginger Twist:** For a little extra zing, add a few drops of ginger syrup or a small piece of fresh ginger to the pear juice before heating.
- **Caffeine-Free Option:** If you prefer a caffeine-free version, simply replace the espresso with a strong brewed herbal coffee or decaffeinated coffee.

## Pairing Suggestions:

- **Spiced Muffins:** Pair with warm cinnamon rolls or pear muffins to complement the spiced notes in the coffee.
- **Vegan Shortbread:** A simple shortbread cookie or a crispy vegan biscotti would be a perfect complement to the drink's effervescence and spice.
- **Light Vegan Salad:** Enjoy this drink with a fresh pear and walnut salad with a citrus vinaigrette for a light, balanced meal.

## Interesting Fact:

Did you know that pears were considered a symbol of longevity in ancient China? The fruit was believed to bring good health and was often given as a gift in traditional Chinese culture.

# BONUSES:

Use this QR code to claim your bonuses!

# EXPLORE MORE GREAT READS:

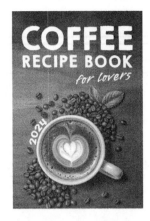

**Coffee Lovers' Recipe Book:**
**Over 200 Ways to Brew Your Perfect**
**Cup + Barista Secrets for Beginners**

ASIN: B0CVVJ6Q8B
ASIN: B0CVSQTG8B
ASIN: B0CVXSQL15

**The Coffee Book:**
How to Make the Best Cafe-Style Drinks
at Home. Recipes for Your Coffee
Machine and More

ASIN: B0D41ZX6H9
ASIN: B0D3SCPVW1
ASIN: B0D4619NSJ

**Make It Easy Japanese Home**
**Cooking Cookbook for Beginners:**
A Journey Through Japanese Cuisine

ASIN: B0D37NXXYW
ASIN: B0D7671V62

**Easy Chinese Cookbook for**
**Beginners**
Simple Recipes for Authentic Flavors
and Asian Cuisine in English with
Pictures

ASIN: B0DCNJLNRR
ASIN: B0DCL5LWVV
ASIN: B0DCPB1QX6

# EXPLORE MORE GREAT READS:

**Healthy Smoothie Recipe Book for Weight Loss:** 65 Blender Recipes Under 300 Calories for Good Health

ASIN: B0CZ11DR3H
ASIN: B0CYQM3T3L

**Kids Smoothie Recipe Book:** A-Z Guide to Healthy, Yummy, Nutritious Blends They'll Love Making. Illustrated for Kids

ASIN: B0D2JC8J4H
ASIN: B0D2391MWV

**Healthy Diabetic Smoothies Cookbook for Beginners:** 70 Diabetic-Friendly Colorful Recipe Photos with Glycemic Index (GL), Calorie, and Nutritional Information

ASIN: B0CS3N9C6K
ASIN: B0CR9GMVXT

**Healthy Diabetic Juicing Cookbooks for Beginners:** Master Low GI Recipes for Stable Blood Sugar, Diabetes Management, Weight Control, Enhanced Vitality, and Delicious Nutrient-Packed Drinks

ASIN: B0D795PCJ4
ASIN: B0D786FKD8

## EXPLORE MORE GREAT READS:

### Daily Inspirational and Motivational Quotes:
A Book with Reflection Space

Daily Inspirational and Motivational Quotes
by Alexander Mindset

ASIN: B0DBGL6ZQV
ASIN: B0DBGBC3SP
ASIN: B0DCZXN29G

### Inspirational Quotes for Kids, Preteens, and Teens:
A Motivational Book for Young Minds

Quotes for Kids and Teens B0DJ6MCWHV

ASIN: B0DJ6MCWHV
ASIN: B0DJ5G93NB
ASIN: B0DJ726BNR

### Healthy Air Fryer Cookbook for Beginners:
Simple, Easy Recipes with Colorful Photos + Meal Plan

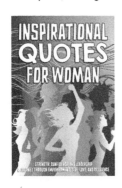

Inspirational Quotes for Women B0DJZ8Y4G7

ASIN: B0DJZ8Y4G7
ASIN: B0DJY5H4KM
ASIN: B0DJZZGBNM

### Meow-Therapy:
Your Cat, Your Purr-sonal Therapist

Meow-Therapy

ASIN: B0DDGYNHZF
ASIN: B0DCWYFMNQ
ASIN: B0DHJP5K6H

Made in the USA
Las Vegas, NV
29 December 2024